# Autobiography of An Indian Indentured Labourer

# Autobiography of An Indian Indentured Labourer

## MUNSHI RAHMAN KHAN
(1874-1972)

*Jeevan Prakash*

*Translated by*

**Kathinka Sinha-Kerkhoff**

**Ellen Bal**

**Alok Deo Singh**

SHIPRA

This publication was initiated by Amrit Consultancy, The Hague (The Netherlands). The work is published under the auspices of the Indian Association of Labour Historians, New Delhi. It was financially supported by the International Institute of Social History, Amsterdam, The Netherlands.

Rs. 995; US$ 39.80

ISBN: 978-93-91978-11-2

2023
(First Soft Cover Impression of
Hard-bound Edition Published in India in 2005)

*Autobiography of An Indian Indentured Labourer*
*Munshi Rahman Khan*



*Published by:*
**SHIPRA PUBLICATIONS**
LG 18-19, Pankaj Central Market,
I.P. Ext., Patparganj, Delhi 110092, India
+91 11 22235152/6152; 9650028065
info@shiprapublication.com
www.shiprapublication.com

# Contents

# Acknowledgements

This English translation of Munshi Rahman Khan's autobiography is really and truly the outcome of a collaborative effort involving all kind of people based in India, Surinam and the Netherlands. To be precise, the project started more than fifteen years ago when late Prof. J.D. Speckman of the University of Leiden (the Netherlands) motivated Mohan Gautam to read the handwritten manuscript. Dr. Mohan K. Gautam of the University of Leiden became therefore the first scholar to have read the full original manuscript. He also made an English summary of it and mentioned this in several unpublished papers during conferences. A few years ago, Albert Rahman in the Netherlands and grandson of Munshi Rahman Khan, requested the International Institute of Social History (IISH) in Amsterdam to publish a Dutch as well as English annotated translation of the autobiography. Accordingly, the manuscript was given to Sandew Hira (the Netherlands) and Maurits Hassankhan (Surinam) who sent the handwritten text to India where Harjeet Singh and Kenneth Soymurum entered the devanagari version in the computer and also made a preliminary English translation. The Dutch and annotated translation by Sandew Hira Hira was published in 2003 and is, among others, based on this English translation by Singh and Soymurum. Subsequently, Prof. Marcel van der Linden and Prof. Willem van Schendel of the IISH asked us to provide an introduction as well as revised annotated English translation of the work. Subsequently, Prof. Sabyasachi Bhattacharya supported the publication under the auspices of the Association of Indian Labour Historians (AILH) in New Delhi. Finally, it was Mr. D. Kumar of Shipra publications who agreed to publish the book.

A project that has started so long ago and involved so many people thus owes many debts. We therefore have to thank an enormous number of people who cannot all be mentioned separately here. However, in addition to all the people mentioned above, we specially want to thank Md. Masoom Reza who visited the Hamirpur region in Uttar Pradesh where Rahman Khan was born, made photographs and interviewed people in the region. We also express our special thanks to all relatives of Munshi Rahman Khan in Surinam, the Netherlands and in India, who primarily enabled the publication of this book and who provided us with photographs and other additional information about and written material of Rahman Khan. The final responsibility of the book is ours of course.

Kathinka Sinha-Kerkhoff
Ellen Bal
Alok Deo Singh

# Introduction *

At present, an estimated 20,000,000 people of Indian origin live outside the borders of India.[1] They, or their ancestors, left the subcontinent for numerous reasons, from different parts, as individuals or in organised groups, at different moments in time. Comparatively large-scale emigration took place during the 19th century when many unskilled labourers and small-scale entrepreneurs left British India to work elsewhere (Jain 1993: 4-10). Surpluses earned by European traders in the wake of geographical discoveries were invested in mines and plantations in South America, Asia, Africa and the Caribbean. This created an enormous demand for a cheap and regular labour force. By the second quarter of the 19th century, British India had become one of the alternative reservoirs of labour replacing the freed slaves in British colonies. This process continued into the early decades of the 20th century (Jayaram 2004: 18). Besides, the development of colonial economies elsewhere also created several commercial and petty industrial opportunities and again many entrepreneurs as well as unskilled labourers from British India settled in other colonial economies such as those of the Dutch and the French.

Between 1838 and 1924 about 500,000 British Indians left for the Caribbean and started working in countries such as Trinidad and Tobago, British Guyana, Jamaica and Dutch Guyana or Surinam (Jayawardena 1968: 428-429).[2] This so-called indentured labour migration, named after the contract signed by the individual labourer to work on plantations (Jayaram 2004: 21), was closely connected with the growing opposition to African slavery and its eventual prohibition. England abolished slavery in 1833, France in 1848 and the Netherlands in 1863. The migration from Indian labourers to Surinam, a Dutch colony, was likewise related to this abolition of slave trade. A convention on emigration to Surinam was signed between the governments of England and the Netherlands on 8

---

* Kathinka Sinha-Kerkhoff, Ellen Bal

September 1870 in The Hague that allowed the Dutch to employ Indian labour. Following this convention the first ship named *Lalla Rukha* left from the port of Calcutta [now Kolkata] and arrived on 5 June 1873 in Paramaribo, the capital of Surinam (Gautam 2003: 206). Between 1873 and 1916, sixty-four boats carried approximately 34,000 British-Indian indentured labourers to the Dutch colony Surinam, bordering British Guyana in the west and French Guyana in the east. Large numbers of these labour migrants considered themselves transient and they returned to British India after completing their contracts. A much larger number, however, decided to establish a life in the new countries, on a permanent basis. While one-third of the migrants returned to British India after completing their contract, two-third settled in Surinam. Munshi Rahman Khan was one of them.

Here we present the translation of a unique document in the history of these indentured labourers in the Caribbean: the autobiography of the contract labourer Munshi Rahman Khan.[3] After finishing his 5-year contract, he settled as an independent agriculturalist in Surinam, where he stayed until he died in 1972, at the ripe age of 98. This Rahman Khan had kept a diary on a day to day basis (Gautam 1995), which he later on developed into his autobiography entitled *Jeevan Prakash*, Life's Light, thereby bringing forth the only written autobiography of a first generation indentured labourer in the Caribbean.[4]

Munshi Rahman Khan was born in British India on 11 August 1874 in the village Bharkhari (Hamirpur, United Provinces). As the only son of the *pathan* Mohammed Khan, who held a good position as a *zamindar's* assistant, he received education and even passed middle school, which enabled him to become a schoolteacher, *a munshi,* himself. Notwithstanding his background and fine position, Rahman Khan felt restless and at the back of mind was the prediction of one healer Hakim Nawab Ali that he would leave his country one day and never return. A visit to Kanpur, to see the *Ramlila*, became the turning point in his life. Here, on the very last day of his stay, when he was about to take the train back home, he met two men who offered him the job of *sardar*, supervisor, of labourers in the sugar business in one of the overseas colonies. This job would allow him to earn more than he ever could in 'Hind', or 'Hindustan', as he refers to his motherland. Many years later he wrote that 'their sugary talk swept me off my feet and I forgot everything: my family, my country, and myself'. He accompanied them to the depot in Kanpur and from there, left to the depot in Calcutta, and never saw his family again. In 1898, Munshi Rahman Khan, at the age of 24, set off for the Dutch colony Surinam in South America.[5] Mohan Gautam[6] who also translated parts of the manuscript provides the following description of this life episode:

> The clock of the *bazar* (Parade grounds vicinity in Kanpur) indicated that it was 7 o'clock. While I was standing on the bridge of the canal and looking at the water, two Muslims, who later proved to be money-minded devils, came to me. Thinking them to be sympathetic gentlemen, I greeted them. Because they were wearing clean and fine dresses, they were looking nice. They replied my greetings and asked me from where I was coming. I said, 'I am coming from an inn (*sarai*) of the Parade grounds'. Then they asked me where I was going. I told them by the train of 8 o'clock I am going to Chandpur.They asked again, 'We would like you to have a job?' I said, 'What kind of job?' They said it is a government job. Then they asked, 'Are you educated?' I said, 'Yes. I have passed the middle school'.
>
> They happily told me, 'Then you could become a *saradara* (headman) and receive a salary of 12 *Annas* per day. The work has to do with sugar. There you will have to supervise the labourers and you will have to travel on the government's boat on the expenses of the government. And at every third or fourth month on the same boat you will have to bring the load of sugar and return to your plantation. The ship from Calcutta takes three months to reach there (*Sriram tapu*). If you are doubtful about your salary, then come with us and we get you registered in the government office. Come now, we will show you those labourers whom you will have to supervise. From today on the government will pay for all expenses such as your food, etc. You will not have any sort of problem. Enjoy your drink and food happily, live comfortably and carry on the government work honestly, this is the only way of getting your own promotion'.
>
> Hearing such tempting words I became very happy. I just forgot my own self, got separated from my own family and fell into the trap of my luck. I thought that these people were rightly

> telling all these things for my welfare, as a salary of 12 Annas per day becomes 24 Rupees a month in India. To get such a high salary at that time [in India] was very difficult. Come on. Let me take this job and experience it. Further let me see what will happen. If the registration in the government is realised then every thing will be alright. There will not be any risk in getting the salary. Having thought so shortsightedly I told them, 'Alright, let us move, let me first see it'. As soon as I had said so they both accompanied me while keeping my mind busy with big attractive plans. They took me across the canal to the depot of Babu Ram Narain Singh. At that time Babu Sahib was in the house (Depot). First all those three persons talked very seriously, then they called me inside. And having taken me into the courtyard they showed me the collected recruited men and women and said, 'Please, see all these people, they will be going with you. And this Babu who is a government employee will get you registered at the court sitting of Magistrate Sahib Bahadur'
>
> Having told this those people with their devilish appearances left me there and disappeared. Then Babu Ram Narain Singh told me, 'You stay in this courtyard and in my absence keep a watch on all these people'. All these talks I accepted and I began to live in the Depot. The bird was now trapped. Now nothing could be altered. Well, it could have been if I would have said, 'no' to the Magistrate. Then I would have escaped. But this way was not known to me. If it had been known to me, then what could I have done? Because the Great Allah had removed my subsistence from India and transported it into Surinam. And he had banished me forever from Hindustan. It was sad and very sad (Munshi R. Khan's Jivan Prakash, Part I, Chapter 17, pp 128-130)[7].

During the first 5 years of his life in Surinam, Rahman Khan worked as an indentured labourer on one of the many plantations in the Dutch colony. He stayed in touch with his relatives in India who regularly beged him to return, and though he continued writing and occasionally sent them money, he never set foot in India again. Instead he settled as an independent agriculturalist, and also worked for some time as a *sardar*, in railroad construction and as a lockkeeper. He started a family of his own; married and got five sons and two daughters. In 1920, he bought a piece of land in Dijkveld, now a suburb of the capital Paramaribo, where he continued to live until a few months before he died, in 1972, 3 years before Surinam became an independent nation.

Rahman Khan had completed his autobiography already in 1943. He, however, did not stop writing then and later added some more writings to the autobiography. What we have here is basically the life of a man who came from 'Hind' and who had spent 24 years of his life in the Bundelkhand area of British India and another 45 years in Surinam, before he assembled and ordered his writings and developed them in his autobiography. Usually he wrote in Hindi [or Hindustani], with a 'flavor of Braj' [also known as bhaka] and Urdu[8], and used the devanagari script.[9] He was a prolific writer and his contemporaries in Surinam were well aware of his knowledge as well as of his writings. Although much of his work remained unpublished[10], it was not unknown. In 1951, Queen Juliana of the Netherlands knighted him Companion of the Order of Orange-Nassau for his literary qualities. After his death he was remembered in Surinam as a great (Hindi) poet and a forerunner of the so-called Sarnami movement (Damsteegt 1990)[11].

Several scholars knew of the existence of Rahman's autobiography, but it was Mohan Gautam[12] who made the first public presentation based on the autobiography (1995), thereby making the existence of the document known to a much larger audience. The autobiography itself, however, was published only in 2003 by Sandew Hira, who brought out a Dutch translation of the manuscript during the commemoration of 130-years migration history of the British Indians to Surinam. Since most of the other existing studies on Surinam are also written in Dutch, and have therefore remained inaccessible to an audience outside the Netherlands and Surinam, we believe that this full English translation of *Jeevan Prakash* has much to offer to the non-Dutch speaking population in India and to non-Hindi speaking academics and others.[13]

Quite a number of excellent studies have discussed the migration and settlement process of Hindostanis in Surinam (e.g., De Klerk 1998 [1953]; Bhagwanbali 1996; Hoefte 1998; Gobardhan 2001). These studies, however, ignore the developments that took place in the homeland simultaneously and do not take into account the possibility that developments in the homeland may have also affected the situation in the diaspora, or vice versa. Little attention has been paid to the linkages between the country of origin and the country of settlement, not in terms of ideology and imaginings about the homeland, but in terms of factual relations between the two. Rahman Khan integrates the two settings in such a way that it becomes easy to understand if and how transnational relations influenced local developments and identities in British India and Surinam at that time. He was indeed aware of the tremendous changes that took place in 'his' Hindustan, which he had left and to which he never returned. He stayed in touch with his relatives back home, and received several books from his Indian family members, as well as a newspaper published by the *Shri Venkateshwar Steam Press* of Bombay [now Mumbai].[14] Besides, new migrants brought news from the homeland and different religious leaders from India visited Surinam. Rahman Khan not only comments on the changing scenario in India but also compares it with local developments in Surinam. He has thereby produced a unique historical document that not only illustrates historical facts about India and Surinam that were already known, but also shows the relationship between the two settings.

His life story, as described in the four volumes comprising his autobiography, casts light on a number of issues that have hitherto remained underexposed, and highlights issues that have been discussed by scholars without the rich illustrations provided by Rahman Khan. Moreover, it also stimulates new thinking about old issues. In this introduction, we discuss two of them. Firstly, the book asks us to reflect on the relation between the first generation of Muslim migrants, their homeland and the new place in which they settled. Secondly, it invites us to a more in-depth look into the seemingly equal problems that existed in India and Surinam at the same time. Such comparison allows us to further examine connections, similarities and disparities in the context of migration, transnationalism, 'home', longing and belonging. We conclude our introduction with a short outline of the autobiography.

## British-Indian indentured labour migration to Surinam

Historical sources (e.g., Grierson 1883) show that the migrants, who left for Surinam, mostly came from the Bhojpuri area of British

India, now covering the western part of Bihar and eastern Uttar Pradesh.[15] On arrival in Surinam, they started working as indentured labourers on 5-year contracts. After 5 years of very demanding work on the plantations, they could make use of a 'free passage' and return to Calcutta.[16] By 1915, an estimated one third had made use of this opportunity (Ramdin 2000: 152). Whereas in the English colonies these migrants were known as 'East Indians', in Surinam they came to be known as well as identified as *Hindostanis*.[17] At the advent of Surinam's independence in 1975, a great proportion of the inhabitants of the colony migrated to the Netherlands.[18] These days, approximately half of all Hindostanis, some 160,000 people, are living in the Netherlands. The others have stayed back in Surinam.

Though the first generation of migrants shared some traditions and at times a language,[19] their cultural traditions varied, they came with dissimilar ambitions and personal histories, and they were variously equipped physically as well as mentally, to face the long journey and the new circumstances in which they had to live and work. Besides, men and women had themselves enlisted as singles; family migration was rare. During their stay in the depots[20] or during the long journey to Surinam, which could last for months,[21] some 'singles' became 'couples' and those friendships or even marriages were long lasting. These migrants gave various reasons for their migration. Often it was a combination of poverty, personal and localised difficulties, coupled with a spirit of enterprise that brought people to one of the depots. The area where most of them came from, Bihar and the U.P, was part of a region that the Muslim rulers had designed as *Hindustan*. The immigration registers preserved in Paramaribo show that almost 80 percent of the migrants that arrived by ships from British India came from the U.P. (encompassing Agra and Oudh). They mostly headed from the districts of Gorakhpur, Basti, Gonda, Fyzabad, Jaunpur, Benares, Azamgarh, Ghazipur and Ballia (De Klerk 1998 [1953]: 48-49). The U.P. was one of the most populated regions of British India and most people were involved in agriculture. The pressure on the soil was high and the region was known for its internal migration.[22]

Most migrants had stated they were Hindu, often from the so-called depressed classes. Brahmins made up only 5 per cent, though according to the census of India of 1931, they constituted 11 per cent of the Hindu population in U.P. (De Klerk 1998 [1953]: 104).

Besides the fact that many Brahmins might have had less motivation to migrate, the emigration agents in India did not favour the recruitment of high caste Hindus for work on the overseas plantations. They generally preferred contract labourers from lower castes (De Klerk 1998 [1953]: 105). For this reason, some Brahmins desperate to migrate might have provided false names that prevented migration officers of recognizing them as upper-castes. The percentage of Muslims among the British Indian migrants was around 17.5 percent while the percentage of Muslims in the U.P. was around 12 per cent at the time of migration (De Klerk 1998 [1953]: 112). Thus the percentage of Muslims among the emigrants was relatively large. Reasons could have been that many recruitment agents were Muslims and that Muslims, unlike Hindus, faced no religious sanctions when travelling overseas. Besides, Muslims were not only over-represented in urban areas from where recruitment was easier (De Klerk 1998 [1953]: 112-113), they also faced severe hardships and low status as Rahman Khan himself describes.[23] Among them were *saiyads, sheikhs, pathans, mughals, julahas, fakirs, ghosis* and *hajams*.

By and large, the Hindostani migrants underwent dissimilar migratory experiences and encountered different problems while settling in the Dutch colony. While some may have identified as 'transients' rather than 'settlers', subsequent generations seem to have realized that they were in a 'position of no return' and abandoned the idea of going back to India. Surinam became their country of 'permanent abode'. Despite all their differences, having experienced a unique migration history and having been subjected to different economic and political situations, descendants from Indian indentured labourers in Surinam evolved as a distinct community with its own and varied dynamics. Today, both in Surinam and in the Netherlands, Hindostanis form clearly distinct ethnic communities. In Surinam, they constitute a relatively large group (possibly the largest), and are surrounded by other powerful ethnic groups of African, Chinese and Indonesian[24] descent. The formation of political parties is along ethnic rather than religious lines, and many Hindostanis (Muslims and Hindus) have been united in the United Hindustani Party (in Dutch: VHP) since 1949 (Ramsoedh and Bloemberg 2001:139). In the Netherlands, however, Hindostanis form approximately 1 percent of the Dutch population (Choenni 2003:

55), a rather small and invisible community (as some among them complain).

Munshi Rahman Khan was one of the Muslim migrants. He narrates his birth in a *pathan* family and starts his autobiography with a history of 'Hind' in which he describes how the *pathans* migrated from the region now known as Afghanistan. Some of them settled down in the Bundelkhand region of U.P., and Rahman Khan combines this general history with the personal history of Muslims in the latter area. He describes, for example, how and why his father Mohammad Khan finally settled in the village Bharkhari, where Rahman Khan was born. But he also writes about his childhood, his years in school, his relation with his father and friends, his restless feelings and his eagerness to travel. Rahman Khan's presentation of his youth is one in which upper-caste Muslims like himself were on a par with upper-caste Hindus. In particular, Rajput Hindus and *pathan* Muslims seem to have enjoyed similar status, and harmonious relations existed between educated Brahmins and Muslims[25]. Urdu was not associated with Muslims only, and Muslims also used Hindi. Differences between the two languages were not well marked and 'Hindustani' seemed to have been the lingua franca. Rahman Khan was very proud of his education, which made him feel equal to educated Hindus. He was in particular close to upper-caste Hindus and held their religious thinking in high esteem. Not only that, he had made special efforts to master their philosophy, which in his view matched the behaviour codes of *pathans*. While remaining a staunch *pathan* with Allah at the top, he had integrated the Hindu pantheon within this hierarchy and respected the whole.

Interestingly, his history of Hind stops with his migration to Surinam in 1898. After that year, Surinam becomes the location of (hi)story-telling. With his emigration to Surinam, Rahman Khan takes the Hindustan of his youth, which remains his homeland, to Surinam. Though after 1898 he for at least 20 years lives among other migrants who arrive from that same Hindustan, Rahman Khan increasingly disassociates himself from the Hindustan that develops in British India after that year. After 5 years of contract work, Rahman Khan enjoys not only a privileged position as supervisor of labourers (*sardar*) but is also held in high esteem as a *guru* (*munshi*) with many a *pandit* as his student. Though there is not much interaction between Hindostanis and people from other ethnic backgrounds, there seems to be no animosity either. Inter-ethnic harmony appears optimal and Rahman Khan seems quite happy in this world in which he is recognized and respected. He enjoys the company of educated Hindus as well as Muslims and abandons the idea of 'return to his homeland'.

## II. Communal tensions in India and Surinam: Parallels and Differences

Increasingly however, things start changing in Surinam[26] in such a way that Rahman Khan begins feeling alienated from his Hindu Hindostani 'brothers'. He is in particular disturbed by the arrival of Arya Samajis from British India in Surinam in 1929[27], who according to him not only create a schism among the Hindus in Surinam but who he also holds responsible for his own status deterioration. Rahman Khan, a Muslim who hitherto had been treated as a *pandit*, now complains that Hindus who are ignorant of Hindu philosophy and have always by-passed its rules of conduct, now exclude him from the Hindu community because he is a Muslim. This is not the Hindustan that Rahman Khan envisioned as his ideal home, but he also realises that return to the Hindustan he left behind is no longer possible. His parents have died, the rest of his family is scattered[28], correspondence[29] has stopped and in Surinam he has started a family of his own. Moreover, post-1898 U.P (*Bharat* for Rahman Khan), or so tell the newspapers that Rahman Khan receives, is now a place where Muslims feel the need of a separate country and where Hindus are involved in purification and cow protection movements. This is not the kind of Hindustan that Rahman Khan recognises from his youth or envisions in Surinam, where he has his family, his friends among different communities and where he enjoys a certain status.

Clearly, by the late 1920s, Rahman Khan has become part of a Muslim diaspora in Surinam for whom Hindustan is the place of their forefathers, the region of their religious-cultural inheritance. He and other Muslims realise that they have lost their 'safe haven'. Moreover, they start fearing that the place in which they now live might change into the *Bharat* they hear of. With this knowledge that the Hindustan from his youth is lost and replaced by a *Bharat* that he does not like, Rahman Khan embarks on a mission to revert this trend of alienation among Hindostanis, and to build up a pre-migration Hindustan in Surinam.

## Communalism in India

The Indian indentured labourers left British India at a time when there was not much of a national identity or a 'common bond of unity and fellow feeling'. People generally felt themselves as Bengali, Sikh, Rajput, Maratha or Hindustani, but not Indian (Cf. Nag 2001: 47-54). Neither nationalist nor communal identities had crystallised. The Muslims who migrated to Surinam thus left long before communal outbursts struck the homeland and long before the famous Lahore resolution of 1940, by which the Muslim League stated that 'India should be grouped to constitute independent states [...] because Hindus and Musalmans belong to two different religious philosophies, social customs, and literature' (Nag 2001: 47-55).

Rahman Khan describes the advent of a new thinking among certain groups of Hindus in British India, which according to him disturbs the communal peace that had hitherto existed between Hindus and Muslims in Hindustan. Actually, between the time that he had left in 1898 and the time that British India became an independent India, tremendous developments took place in 'Hindustan'. Not only did organisations such as the *Hindu Mahasabha* (founded in 1909) and the *Rashtriya Swayamsevak Sangh* (RSS) (established in 1925) start advocating homogenising notions of 'Hinduism' and 'the Hindu community', they also made a sharp division between these, and 'the Islam' and 'the Muslim community' (Puniyani 2003). Besides, so-called reform organisations such as the Arya Samaj began doubting the existing hierarchical notions within Hinduism.[30] Between 1900 and 1945, various developments took place that finally caused the partition of British India in 1947 (Hassan 1993).

At that time, an English barrister, Cyril Radcliffe, who had never previously visited South Asia, designed borders between areas dominated by Muslims and by non-Muslims, as determined by statistical census data (Chatterji 1999). This looked like the logical outcome of a British tradition of 'divide and rule' during their long rule over the Indian subcontinent. By that time religion had become a primary criterion for the categorisation of time and of society (Gottschalk 2000: 27). When the first census of the whole of British India was taken in 1871, society was mainly divided on the basis of caste and religion (Bijlert 2002: 38-9). Though neither Muslims nor Hindus had constituted homogenous communities, these means of categorisation for census purposes, along with a similar kind of history writing, presented Hindus and Muslims as fixed categories and divided history into a Hindu and a Muslim period. Later, when representational politics were introduced, the size of the population of these groups, described and enumerated in the census data, became very important, and religion became the basis on which the majority Hindus started campaigning against the minority Muslims. In the long run, this led to a bifurcation of space that is Partition, which was supported by the so-called 'two nation theory' according to which Muslims were imagined as one homogeneous group, indeed as a separate nation, and Hindus as another.[31]

In short, imagined communities became somewhat real communities and during the struggle for independence from British rule, several nationalists now had great difficulties to unite these communities under a common banner. Serious differences developed between a section of Hindus and Muslims, centred on the power-sharing formula. When a last attempt to build a political alliance between the Indian National Congress Party and the Muslim League failed in July 1946, the President of the latter political party, Muhammad Ali Jinnah as well as Jawaharlal Nehru of the Indian National Congress, felt that they had no other choice than to subscribe to the partitioning of British India, to support the establishment of two independent nations, and to resort to direct action to achieve Pakistan (Cf. Jalal 1985). The spatial division of British India according to religious identification culminated in its actual partition according to Radcliffe's outlines. In this way, 'a truncated and moth-eaten Pakistan' was created for the Muslims, with one wing in East and one in the West, and in between those wings, the Hindus got their 'Hindustan' (Pandey 2001: 21).

This trend was also clearly observable in the U.P., where it was in particular through so-called purification and cow protection movements that communal differences were displayed. Though cows had been, for centuries, cultural symbols of non-violence, the tradition of using the alleged literal sanctity of the cow to disenfranchise Muslims, some of whom eat beef and/or slaughter the cows that many Hindus eat, can be traced to the end of the nineteenth century when in various places in British India, as scholars have convincingly shown, people often used 'holy cows' to protect their (political) interests. These scholars demonstrate that it was in particular during 1888 and 1917, and in the Bhojpuri-speaking districts of eastern Uttar Pradesh (U.P.)[32] and western Bihar[33] that powerful Cow-Protection Societies or *Gaurakshini Sabhas* were launched (e.g., Pandey 1992; Singh 2002). Developments in these districts culminated in serious rioting between Hindus and Muslims in particular during the *Bakr-id* festivals. During the 1880s and 1890s, the Gaurakshini Sabhas circulated numerous pamphlets, leaflets and pictures of the cow to drive home the sanctity of this particular symbol. This literature sought to emphasise that since all men drank the cow's milk, the cow was the universal mother and the killing of a cow matricide; and since all the gods dwelt in the cow (as several pictures suggested), cow-slaughter was the gravest insult to 'every Hindu'.

Several scholars have shown the politics behind the 'Myth of the Holy Cow' and have for instance demonstrated why particular Hindus who felt economically and socially threatened rallied round the cow. They have shown why these Hindus became active in the fight for a ban on cow-slaughter or the right to practise *kurbani* and explain why sectarian symbols became symbols of authority and focal points of strife, and also how this finally led to communalism in British India (Krishna 1982; Bandhyopadhyay 2003). They also show how several Hindu Samaj and reform movements, in order to 'purify' their respective religions and combat the powerful propaganda of the Christian missionaries in 19th century colonial India, agitated over sectarian symbols with particular concern for cow-protection. These movements of revivalism and reform, these scholars argued, played no small part in deepening the consciousness of different classes of Indians as members of particular religious denominations.

These scholars also explain why increasingly Muslims in the United Provinces supported the demand for Pakistan (Brennan 1993: 322-360). Among others they describe how the Urdu-speaking elites of U.P. increasingly started to define themselves as religious communities and how amidst *shuddhi* and Gauraksha Sabhas of the Hindus, Muslims established Anjuman-I-Islamias, *tabligh* [preaching and proselytising of Islam] and *tanzim* outfits (Cf. Metcalf 2004: 174-176). The 'pan-Indian ideology of revitalization movements was thus shattered, which involved 'the separation from and rejection of joint Hindu-Muslim culture' and 'the definition and affirmation of newer communal symbols' (Hasan 2002: 308).[34]

## Communal Tensions in Surinam

Rahman Khan in his autobiography does not show a complete awareness of the exact nature of the communal problems in the U.P, but he knows about their existence and their consequences. In Volume IV of his autobiography he describes, for instance, the communal problems in Ayodhya in 1934 in a *chaupai* and how this 'communal fire' has finally destroyed his Hindustan. He warns for the same to happen in Surinam, if no steps are undertaken, and explains how this new way of life and thinking has also started to influence certain Hindus in Surinam; a regrettable trend he feels. Rahman Khan feels that because of this 'new thinking' (i.e., ideas supported by Arya Samaj leaders in India as well as in Surinam), he and other Muslims are separated from Hindu Hindostanis in Surinam and are also denied their homeland Hindustan. Parallels with simultaneous happenings in British India are obvious.[35]

The cordial relation between Hindus and Muslims is one of the most unique features in the Caribbean. Though right from the days of indenture differences exist[36], a harmonious 'take and give' relation prevails. The *Tazia* festival[37] for instance, basically a Shia Muslim religious festival commemorating the martyrdom of Prophet Mohammad's grandson Hussein at Karbala, is celebrated all over the Caribbean by Muslims as well as Hindus. Nevertheless, communal relations in the Caribbean have at times turned sour. We argue however that though these communal tensions bore resemblance to communalism as existed in India they were in fact greatly influenced by individual and localised circumstances[38], as Rahman Khan shows in his autobiography.

Though in Surinam Hindu-Muslim relations never developed along the same communal lines as in India, irritation arose occasionally and various sources indicate that in the late 1920s and early 1930s, tensions between Hindus and Muslims did give rise to communal antagonism, generally known as the Boycott (Biswamitre 1978: 223-24; De Klerk 1998 [1953]: 197). Surinam was spared the bitter clashes between Hindus and Muslims that were witnessed in India, but many elderly Muslims we interviewed still remember how after 1929 till at least 1943, many Hindus started boycotting Muslims by cutting all socio-cultural and economic links that had previously existed between the two communities. Though the movement was not very widespread, did not encompass all members of the two religious groups and the altercations were mainly verbal, many Hindostanis nevertheless recollect this period as a dark page in the history of the ethnic group. In their memories, like in India, cow slaughtering became a focal point of strife and allegedly antagonised Hindus and Muslims in parts of Surinam.

In the last part of his book, Rahman Khan provides a very detailed, and the most extensive written description of this period, in which the Hindu-Muslim tensions arose in Surinam and again subsided. According to him, there had been major frictions amongst the Hindus, in particular between a small minority who had become members of the Arya Diwaker and those who remained part of the Sanatan Dharm. Furthermore, discord arose between upper- and lower-caste Hindus and even amongst (self-appointed) *brahmins*. To the mind of Rahman Khan, the seeds of discord in Surinam were however planted in British India. He describes how these problems had first started there, where before 'people of either religion' had 'lived together in peace' and where there had been 'no sign of the Arya Samaj'. He seems convinced that it was 'the formation of the Arya Samaj that had led to social unrest in the country'. After all, its basic philosophy was, according to Rahman Khan, to 'criticize other religions and present itself as the true way of life.' Swami Dayanand Saraswati, the founding father of the reform movement, had taught his disciples to be strict in his teachings, thereby causing a rift between themselves and others, and especially between Hindus and Muslims. 'A negative impact on the society resulted and riots broke out in India leading to bloodshed and death of several innocents. It was through the newspapers that we learnt about it', Rahman Khan writes'.

Though Surinam received its first representative from the Arya Samaj already in 1912 (Vertovec 2000: 54), Rahman Khan feels that with the arrival of the Arya Samaji Mehta Jaimani in Surinam in 1929, 60 years of brotherly relations between Hindus and Muslims became disturbed. 'In a few days, the seed of discontent and ill will amongst the communities' was planted. After his return to India, conflicts between Arya Samajis and followers of the Sanatan religion arose. Soon, however, it became clear that the first could not overcome the latter and they resolved their differences, at the cost however, of the relations between Hindus and Muslims.[39] Rahman Khan explains that the internal differences amongst Hindus caused a 'wave of hatred that began in 1933 and spread all over and engulfed the whole of Surinam by 1934 turning the two communities into bitter enemies'. He believes that the situation reveals that the Hindus had thought of boycotting the Muslims for quite some time.

In the end, Hindus were united by rallying around the cow, which completely antagonised them from the Muslim community. As discontent increased, feelings of hatred increased, and as the day of *Bakr-id* neared, Muslims started loosing their cool and began considering *kurbani* on the appointed day, according to Rahman Khan, for the very first time in Surinam. We quote:

> When the unethical Hindus came to know about this plan they went berserk. The upper caste Hindus collected donations among themselves and bought a pig to be slaughtered close to the *Masjid* on the festival of *Bakr-Id*. They went through with this uncalled-for act of killing that day and God knows what they did with the swine's body. While the Muslims sacrificed the animal according to their rituals, the Hindus of Livorno acted sinfully.

The very last part of Volume IV includes a correspondence between Rahman Khan and his Hindu opponents in the form of letters, full of verses. The content of the writings reveals worked up emotions on both sides. The letter writers argue about intelligence, true faith and believers, the knowledge of holy scriptures, and they call each other names. In one *chaupai* Rahman Khan tells his opponent he has two eyes but still is blind, and writes that 'a useless son like you is born for nothing'. It therefore comes all the more as a surprise that only a few pages later, Rahman Khan refers to the end of the Boycott. At the time that British India is on the verge of breaking up due to communal problems, in Surinam, in 1943, after 10 years of discord, the Boycott is finally put to an end in a meeting between Hindus, Muslims and representatives of the colonial government, although the unrest continued in some scattered places[40], 'just as salt in *daal* does not spread evenly'. Right before ending the story of the light of his life, Rahman Khan expresses the wish that 'soon a day will arrive when there shall be no remnants of an unhappy past anymore and when everyone would hoist a flag of peace and love'.[41]

## III. Munshi Rahman Khan's Legacy

Rahman Khan's life history is of extreme value as it sheds light on various aspects of diaspora studies and studies of communalism. Firstly, in most diaspora studies the relation between the homeland and the diaspora community, whether imagined or real, plays a key role. Indeed, important criteria for calling a particular group of migrants a diaspora are that the members of that group retain a collective memory of the original homeland and that they are committed to the maintenance or restoration of that homeland.[42] Yet, though diaspora studies frequently focus on the relationship of diasporas with their 'roots', they generally discuss migrant discourses without taking into account the historical changes 'back home', their bearing on diaspora policies, on homeland perceptions of the diaspora and on views of the homeland by the diaspora.[43] From Munshi Rahman Khan's autobiography we learn that and how developments in the 'homeland' and those in the diaspora community are related.

Secondly, Rahman Khan's book is of great importance as it shows that although communal problems are universal, they do not necessarily lead to communalism. As stated before, the more than 300,000 Hindostanis are now living in two countries: Surinam and the Netherlands. Since the 1960s, and particularly in 1973 and 1974, about 80,000 to 100,000 Hindostanis have settled in the Netherlands (Baumann 2001: 62), thereby becoming 'twice migrants'. Their decision to leave the country had to do with Surinam's nearing independence and Hindostani fear of Afro-Surinamese dominance. Although it generally has been assumed that religious divisions among Dutch Hindostanis play a greater role than they do in Surinam, political implications of religious differences have remained insignificant. In Surinam, where the Hindostanis now form a relatively large (possibly the largest) ethnic community in Surinam, surrounded by other powerful ethnic groups, the formation of political parties is along ethnic rather than religious lines and many Hindostanis (Muslims and Hindus) have been united in the United East Indian Party (in Dutch VHP) since 1949.[44]

Munshi Rahman Khan was one of the persons who supported the alliance on ethnic rather than on religious basis. In India by 1915, the issue of cow protection, unlike the Gaurakshini Sabha movements of the 1890s, received active support from all classes of Hindus, in particularly in U.P. and Bihar. As a result, Hindu-Muslim conflicts over the controversial question of cow-sacrifice on the occasion of Bakr-id took place in many parts of the two provinces. Here, these clashes, which resulted in the desecration of mosques and temples and human casualties on both Hindu and Muslim sides, definitely catalysed the process of Hindu-Muslim bitterness in British India. Scholars have argued, however, that initially this divide between Hindu and Muslims in many parts of British India was neither of stable nor permanent nature and that this kind of strife did not inevitably or automatically lead to 'communalism'. As Gyan Pandey argued: 'The contradictions in the locality remained many-sided, and it would be difficult to argue that the confrontation between Hindus and Muslims was the primary one among them' (Pandey 1983, p. 125). With this in mind, we have to read Munshi Rahman Khan's account on the communal tensions in Surinam where the contradictions in the locality did indeed not lead to communalism.[45]

## Understanding Munshi Rahman Khan

Apart from the aforementioned reasons, Rahman Khan's autobiography is invaluable, as it is one of the very few personal accounts of an indentured labourer that have been unearthed. Though official and personal correspondence have provided some understanding of the people behind the 'historical facts', it remains difficult to understand how the first generation of migrants experienced their migration process. Whereas oral history can supplement the information gathered from other sources, it throws light on the lives of second and third generations of migrants more than on the actual migrants, whose memories and experiences often disappeared with their deaths.[46] Available archival sources provide a 'top down', *etic*, picture of the process of migration and settlement. They reveal colonial perspectives rather than indentured experiences. Moreover, as every personal history is unique, we cannot understand the experience of migration by describing the general trends only. Autobiographies like this rare one of Munshi Rahman Khan provide us exactly with that kind of information that we did not get through these other methods. Lastly, available studies show that migration from British India to Dutch Surinam was unique. These studies are, however, generally written in Dutch. We now have a translation in

English that allows us to compare Rahman Khan's life with the lives of indentured labourers in other settings.

Before reading his autobiography, Munshi Rahman Khan was not unknown to us. Other scholars had described him as an important person not only for his history writing on indentured labourers in Surinam, both Hindus ánd Muslims, but also for his unique way of thinking that integrates religions and cultures. We had also gone through some of his other writings in devanagari. Inspired by the Ramayana of Tulsidas, which was used in Surinam and which was compiled by Pandit Jwala Prasad Misra and published in Bombay in 1896, Rahman Khan translated the biography of Prophet Mohammad from Urdu into devanagari script, and in similar verses as used by Tulsidas in his Ramayana. He also believed that the Koran should be made available to those who could not read or understand Arabic or Urdu – Hindus and Muslims alike.

The first Muslim organisation in Surinam, the Surinamese Islamic Association (SIV), was established in 1929. By that time Muslims in Surinam felt the need for more institutionalisation. They also required more information about their religion and turned to Lahore, which at that time was part of British-India. From there they came to know about Mirza Ghulam Ahmad of Qadian, a reformer whose followers are known as *Ahmadis* and *Quadianis*. Lahore encouraged Muslims in Surinam to contact Ameer Ali in Trinidad. Ameer Ali, who had received his schooling in Lahore indeed visited Surinam and preached the ideology of Ahmadiyyaism.[47] As a result, the so-called traditionalist Muslims also started organising themselves in organisations such as the Kalifaat Anjuman, the Hidayat ul-Islam and the Sunnat wal Djamaat (Prins 1961/1962: 22-23). In Surinam, like in Trinidad, the introduction of the new ideology therefore eventually caused a schism between the Muslims. The SIV came to be dominated by the *Ahmadiyya* doctrine causing many *Sunni* Muslims to leave and to form other, more orthodox, groups (Kassim 1999: 176-77). At present, Hindostani Muslims in both the Netherlands and Surinam are divided into several denominations. Still, the most significant division is between *Sunnis* and *Ahmadis*.

Rahman Khan does neither explicitly mention these internal differences among the Muslims in Surinam nor his personal affinities. From personal interviews with family members, we now know that he did not like that one of his sons, and his family, became

*Ahmadis*.[48] Yet, from his autobiography we gather that he greatly valued Ameer Ali's visit to Surinam. During the period of the so-called Boycott when relations between Hindu and Muslim Hindostanis deteriorated, Rahman Khan was concerned about the spiritual future of his fellow Muslim Hindostanis. Like other contemporaries, he believed that the Muslims in Surinam were in great need of some spiritual advice. In one of his verses included in his autobiography, he therefore welcomes Moulvi Ameer Ali of Trinidad, who came to teach the Muslims about their religion.

Though Rahman Khan does not write about the fragmentation of Muslims in Surinam, it appears, however, that this schism did cause some agony within him. Nevertheless, while some of his own family members became *Ahmadis*, he does not refer to this in his autobiography. This could possibly partly be explained by the fact that the real rupture between *Sunnis* and *Ahmadis* was only brought about after the World War II, when *moulvis* and *maulanas* from Pakistan started to arrive in Surinam. According to many of our informants, they were primarily responsible for stirring up the differences between local *Sunnis* and *Ahmadis*. The process of fragmentation resembled the alienation between *Aryas* and *Sanatans* among the Hindus three decades earlier and was possibly also caused by the continuing involvement from men from Pakistan where in 1974 *Ahmadis* were officially declared non-Muslims. These conflicts have remained unresolved until today.

Although Rahman Khan was a religious person and very devoted to Allah, his God, the autobiography demonstrates that he derived his sense of respectability and erudition first and foremost from his knowledge of Hindi and the religious Hindu scriptures. He appears very caste conscious and clearly identified with the high caste Hindus – much more with them than with low caste Muslims – yet who first shocked him when they denounced their caste in the Calcutta depot, and thereafter when they many years later tried to use their upper-caste status to articulate their superior positions, and to cut off ties with the Muslims. Being considered a knowledgeable man of Hinduism and Indian languages, Rahman Khan's prestige started to crumble and he was cast off for being a Muslim, by those he had always considered his equals. This, so it appears, hurt him more than anything else.

We interviewed various people in Surinam and the Netherlands who knew Munshi Rahman Khan as a scholar, a teacher, a friend, or a relative. Their stories brought to light the vastness of his knowledge, his amiability and his will power.[49] His relatives in Surinam[50] as well as in the Netherlands[51] not only initiated this translation in English and provided all possible help to get it realised, they also provided added information in the form of letters, other writings by Rahman Khan, photos and of course memories. Through all these memories, certain aspects were empathized that remained underexposed in his writings.

His relationship with Mahatma Gandhi, for instance, was believed to have been very good, right from his childhood[52]. Some relatives even alleged there had been letters between the two of them. Although we know from his writings that Rahman Khan indeed admired Gandhi, who he saw as an important mediator between Hindus and Muslims, no such correspondence has ever been found. Besides, his autobiography provides no evidence of such a close and personal relation.

Another aspect that was commented upon by some of his family members was his relation with his mother, both his wives, his daughters or with women in general. Rahman Khan's life story gives hardly any inside information on the lives of female contemporaries. His world was clearly a men's world. He gives no clue as to the kind of marriage he had with his first wife in India, whether they got any children, how she felt about his departure for Surinam, and what happened to her after he left. We only know that she died 4 years after his going away. As for his second wife with whom he got five sons and two daughters, we come to know very little about her, other than that she got very ill during the pregnancy of her fourth son Chotekhan. Chotekhan's wife, Hadja Hafidjan Rahman-Bakridi told us that her mother-in-law, a daughter of immigrants, had been a kind, caring, and strong woman. She felt that Rahman Khan had been happy with her. Another (male) family member wondered however about the relationship between Rahman Khan and his wife. Rahman Khan himself provides no further details neither about his relation with his wife nor about that with his daughters. Our informants told us that among his students, there were no girls. In many ways the autobiography reflects the unequal gender relations at the time (Hoefte 1998: 106-113 and Sewradj-Debipersad 2001: 14-39) and it teaches us less to nothing about how Hindostani women experienced life on the plantations at the time.[53]

There are a few notable exceptions however where Rahman Khan does refer to the women in his life. While narrating his experiences at arrival in Paramaribo, Rahman Khan details how one migrant Hindostani woman 'misuses' him and tries to pose as his wife in order to be allotted a room with him. He has no good words for such behaviour. Furthermore, Rahman Khan details his relation with Mr. and Mrs Horst[54], the owners of the plantation on which he worked. Though critical too, Rahman Khan admires not only the man but also his wife who he describes as 'typical Dutch'. He almost seems to identify with the Horst family, shares their problems, and trusts one of his daughters to the care of Mrs. Horst. He remains in a caring relationship with Mrs. Horst even after the death of her husband. Besides, the plight of another woman is described with some empathy, though not without irony. In this case, Rahman Khan condemns the deeds and attitudes of one of the Horst brothers who migrates to 'America'. In America he marries a much younger girl who had nursed him during an illness. He takes her to Surinam and promises her a life in paradise. In Surinam however, she is unable, Rahman Khan details, to adjust to the rough life there and does not do much more than crying. Rahman Khan feels sorry for the girl and condemns the way in which her husband has misled her and the lack of support she receives from him. The last woman described by Munshi Rahman Khan, a '*mulattin*', does not receive his empathy however, which instead goes to her husband, an American who is the manager of the plantation and who, Rahman Khan feels, is exploited by 'this extremely wicked woman' who ruins her husband and the plantation 'by her selfishness and spendthrift'.

As for his sons, Rahman Khan does not hide his personal affection towards his sons, the 'five loving stars'. He is in particular fond of his eldest son Suleman Khan, yet here again not much information is given. Apart from the fact that he says that the birth of this son is the main reason for not having returned to India and the fact that Suleman Khan and his family depart for British Guyana 'due to some family problems', his autobiography does not provide more details. We come to know however that he had a few very close friends and for one of them he even wrote a poetic obituary.[55] From his other writings we can also substantiate Rahman Khan's great admiration for the Dutch royal family and his satisfaction of serving under Dutch rule. Munshi Rahman Khan even attached a poem in honour of the Queen of the Netherlands and another welcoming a Dutch Commissioner in Surinam in 1945 after having completed his opus magna in 1943.

Lastly, Munshi Rahman Khan received prizes for his literary qualities as well as for his social activities (Chickrie 2002: 391). Yet, it was only after going through the autobiography itself, that we really discovered the light in his life. The present generation of 'Hindostanis' in the Netherlands, Surinam, and India can read his autobiography as a long lesson in 'inclusive nationalism' (i.e., without expulsion of particular religious groups) taught by their *aja* (forefather). Munshi Rahman Khan, who used to write 'Ohm' with the same ease as '786'[56] above his letters, is a unique historical person and also a personification of lower-middle class colonial subjects who migrated from one colony to another. In Surinam, these migrants faced a new colonial power and new rules and regulations, languages and cultures. Munshi Rahman Khan did not know English and never learnt much of Dutch. Instead he cultivated Hindi and Urdu and could converse in the local language (*Sranang Tongo*). He was proud of his ethnic and class background and whenever his knowledge was questioned or his status undermined he would defend his position by trying to prove his superiority. Besides Allah, it was the Dutch Queen who he served[57] and he restored his Hindostan within Dutch-Surinam. There he died in 1972 having preserved not only Islam and his 'Puktunwali way of life'[58], but also ethnic unity. His autobiography will keep his personal experiences, philosophies and dreams alive. We shall conclude this introduction with a short outline of his *Jeevan Prakash*, Life's Light.

## IV. A short outline of Jeevan Prakash

Rahman Khan was both a novelist and a poet. He produced four volumes of flowery prose, full of life details, alternated with verses (*dohas* and *chaupais*), in the following way:

जगदीश्वर पद वन्द कर, गुरू को करूँ प्रणाम।
होय ज्ञान मम हृदय महँ, बल बुद्धि दें अभिराम।।
लिखौ हिन्द इतिहास यहँ, कर संक्षेप बखान।
निषि दिन दुनियाँ बदलती, जानै सकल जहान।।

(I bow to God and pay respect to Him in the hope that He provides me with the knowledge and strength needed to write this book. I am first writing a brief history of Hind as everybody should know that the world changes day by day).

Rahman Khan starts his autobiography with *Tavarikh Hind*, a short history of Hindustan. He is a *pathan* and clearly identifies with its history. He describes how the Mughal rulers of India always respected *pathans* who acted as buffers to keep invaders out of Mughal India. He also depicts how some of them settled down in the North-Western Provinces and Oudh, known as the United Provinces of Agra and Oudh (the present Uttar Pradesh) of British India. Rahman Khan's short history of Hindustan ends at the end of the 19th century, at the time when he departs for Surinam. Clearly, the moment he boards the ship to cross the *kala pani*[59], Rahman Khan dissociates himself from a history of people who were so near and dear to him and from a country of which he was so proud to be part of.

In Volume I, he describes his life in the Bundelkhand region, where he had his schooling in a government middle school at Maudaha, a *tehsil* headquarter (revenue sub-division) of the Hamirpur District and where he ultimately became a teacher (*munshi)*. He combines the local history of the place with anecdotes and real life happenings. He, for example, also describes the life of some close and dear family members and friends, his own (mis-) deeds, his marriage to a *pathan* girl, and the continuation of his studies. He provides us with a picture of the U.P., in which the happy times have become past and in which Muslims start loosing status as well as face a severe deterioration in their economic position. A very important event is the prediction by one *Hakim* that Rahman Khan would leave his land of birth and go to a foreign country.

This part is of particular interest for two reasons. Firstly, it shows that in the Hindustan that Rahman Khan knew he and his family were respected. There was still no sign of the communal tensions, which later on rocked the Province. Rahman Khan himself knows Hindi as well as Urdu and shows keen interest in the Ramayana while remaining a staunch Muslim. Secondly, it shows how Rahman Khan landed up in Surinam. Rahman Khan depicts himself as a young, impatient and proud man, who wants something more out of life. Searching for the light in his life, he goes as far as to give up his job as a teacher and decides to travel within the Province. Remembering the Hakim's prediction, he seems to go in search of its fulfilment. In Kanpur, where he attends the *Ramlila*, two men convince him that his future lies in *Sri Ram Tapu,* the 'island' of Sri Ram [Surinam]. Being 'swept of his feet' by such 'sugary talk' and the promise of a salary he could never earn in his homeland, he forgets about his family, his country, and himself, and accompanies the two men to the local depot in Kanpur.

From there he travels to Calcutta, where he spends another 3 months in a depot, and where he is particularly flabbergasted by the behaviour of upper-caste Hindus, who not only give up certain caste symbols but also change their names. Rahman Khan, who has a great respect for *pandits* as well as the *vedas*, cannot understand why, in his opinion, these upper-castes degrade themselves to the level of *sudhras*, lower castes. He, in turn, remains a strong believer in the Islam and maintains his identity.

Rahman Khan finally boards the Avon, which takes him away from his country forever. After a troublesome 3-month sea journey, he leaves his history behind and starts a new life when he arrives at the Fort of New Amsterdam near Paramaribo, the capital of Surinam, on 13 April 1898. He concludes the first volume with the following *doha*:

करि मंजिल बहु दूर की। देख्यों जलधि तूफान।
कुदरत से अल्लाह ने। पहुँचायो जलयान।।
शुक्र खुदा का मान कर। सबने नायो माथ।
खुषी भयो नर नारि सब। पहुँचे डीपू साथ।
तीन महीने हम पानी पर। बसि ऐवुन अस गाँव।
आज खुदा के हुक्म से। धरा जमीं पर पाँव।।
जो बीती इस देह पर। सो लिख दीन्ह बनाय।
भूल होय जो कांड में। माफ करै सब भाय।।
हुआ करम अल्लाह का। हो गई उनकी षान।।
पहिल कांड जीवन चरित्र खतम कीन्ह रहमान।।

(We travelled a great deal and saw sea and storms. With Allah's blessings we reached safely by ship. Everyone thanked God (*Khuda*) and felt happy when we reached the depot [in Paramaribo]. Having been 3 months on sea had made a village out of the ship called Avon. Today we put our feet on earth with God's blessings. I have written down my life experiences and apologise for any mistakes or omissions.).[60]

Volume II starts with a *doha* that summarises its content:

जगपति रहमान है। हैं करतार जगदीष।
उनसे मैं विनती करूँ। और नवावहुँ षीष।।
पहिल काण्ड उन करम से। पूरण भयो मम काम।।
अब आगे करिहैं कृपा । दे हैं बुधि बसु याम।।
युगुल काण्ड जीवन चरित। सेवक लिखै सिर नाय।
होय अज्ञाता मम हृदय। सो तुम देहु नसाय।।
मम बहती जो हिन्द में। सो लिखि पहले काण्ड।
जब बीती सूरीनाम में। लिखूँ दूसरे काण्ड।।

(God is the creator. His blessings helped me complete the first part of this autobiography in which I narrated what happened in Hind. I now proceed to the second part with details about what happened in Surinam. I seek God's blessings and hope He provides me the wisdom needed to write this second part).

In this volume, Rahman Khan describes how he was assigned to plantation 'Skerpi' [Lust en Rust, 'Energy and Rest'] where he remains as a contract labourer (No. 452 Aa) for 5 years. He describes the kind of work he was allotted and his relation with his *dipua bhai* whom he had met in the depot in Calcutta and with whom he started sharing a room in Skerpi. Rahman Khan also describes how he soon became very popular as a Ramayana specialist in his plantation and among the Hindostanis from surrounding plantations. He also started teaching Hindi. Clearly, Rahman Khan has broken with his past and enjoys his new status and life. His marriage with a *sheikh* girl, daughter of migrants, in Surinam, with whom he gets five sons and two daughters, makes this fissure even more dramatic. In the meantime his first wife dies and Rahman Khan decides not to return to his parents after his contract expires but instead becomes a *sardar* in 1903 and starts living in Livorno where he buys a piece of land. He however remits money to his parents and maintains communicating with them through letters. Here Rahman Khan finishes the second volume and starts the third:

जो बीती कन्तराक में। लिखी दूसर काण्ड।
जब बीती फिरीमान में। लिखूँ तीसरे काण्ड।।1।।
गुरू की कृपा कटाक्ष से। भयो हृदय महँ ज्ञान।

(What happened during the contract period has been written in the second part. In the third part you will read, with *Guru's* [God's] blessings, what happened to me when I had become a *freeman* [i.e., when not working any longer on a 5-year contract like the indentured labourers].).

In Volume III Rahman Khan describes his life as a *freeman*. He announces in a *chaupai*:

जस चरित्र हिन्द तक भयऊ। पहिल काण्ड में सो लिखि दयऊ।।
नहिं विस्तार कीन्ह अस जानी। बढ़ै ग्रन्थ संक्षेप बखानी।।
पाँच वर्श परवषहिं बिताओ। काण्ड दूसरे में लिखि गायो।।
स्ववष काल जहाँ कीन्ह निवासा। करब तीसरे काण्ड प्रकाश।।
लिखिहौं तीसरे में जस बीती। पढ़ि हैं सज्जन सहित सप्रीती।।
नहिं कछु दोश हृदय महँ धीर हैं। सेवक जानि अनुग्रह करि हैं।।

(In the first part I have narrated the happenings in Hind. The second part describes 5 years as an indentured labourer. The period of 'freemanship' is detailed in the third part. I do not keep any ill-feelings and therefore request people to read what I have written).

After the death of his good friend, Rahman Khan faces many other calamities. Not only he himself, but also his sons and wife suffer from health problems. Interestingly, Rahman Khan believes in black magic and has no difficulty to integrate different belief systems with his own faith in Allah. Whereas Rahman Khan does not deny the existence of other deities and spirits, he does not doubt Allah who is placed above all the others.[61] Many verses in praise of Allah, which demonstrate human smallness, are intermingled with at times very technical treatises about his work as a supervisor of labourers. Besides the fact that this part is a mine of information about plantation life and inter-human relations of different people with various backgrounds, we also start understanding Rahman Khan as a very honest, strict and able plantation supervisor and lock-keeper, who is also involved in several social-cultural activities.

Rahman Khan is proud and aware of his status as an educated *pathan,* which, he feels, puts him on a level quite similar to that of *brahmins*. He gets somewhat used to being admired, loved and respected, not only by Muslim Hindostanis but by Hindu Hindostanis as well, in particular by the *pandits* of the Sanatan Dharma. Rahman Khan, a knower of Hindi and the Ramayana, has become the guru of many a *brahmin*. Besides, he also has good relations with the Muslims on the plantation. He seems particularly close with the plantation owner Mr. Rudolf Horst and his wife, who do actually share in the upbringing of one of Rahman Khan's daughters.

In 1912, Rahman Khan moves to 'Hansu' [Meerzorg plantation] and buys land there. He again moves in 1916, and in 1921, when the last ship brings British Indian labour migrants back to India[62], Rahman Khan settles down in Dijkveld No. 4, where he constructs a house. Most of his work is written in this place.

While Volume I revealed that Rahman Khan was highly perturbed by the behaviour of upper-caste Hindus in the Calcutta depot, Volume II and III relate very good relations with these same caste Hindus, who highly respected him. In Volume IV however, the last volume, the bomb explodes. Times have changed and new developments take place among the Hindus in Surinam, who now can be categorised either as so-called orthodox Sanatanis or progressive Aryas. Simultaneous developments influence Muslims in Surinam, many of whom feel attracted to the Ahmadiyya ideology. Though initially the divisions seem to cause intra- rather than inter-communal tensions, in Volume IV Rahman Khan describes how Hindus and Muslims gradually grew apart. Rahman Khan announces in a *doha*:

ईश्वर दीनदयाल है, करै दीन पर छोह।
चूक दीन की धरत नहिं, कबहुँ करत नहिं कोह।।
अन्तर्यामी प्रभु अहैं जानत जन की परि।
उनके सुमिरन से कटैं, कठिन जाल जंजीर।।

अलख नाम सुमिरन करूँ, धरूँ चरण निज माथ।
करि है मनसा पूर्ण मम, हैं वे करूणा नाथ।।
काण्ड तीसरे में व्यथा, जस बीती लिखि दीन्ह।
अब चौथे महँ लिखत हाँ, जस हिन्दुन ने कीन्ह।।

(God is very generous and kind to His people. Those who remember Him never face any difficulty in life. The recitation of His name itself fulfils man's wish. I have written part three as experienced by me and now, in part four I am going to write, about the deeds of the Hindus).

At a time when 'back home', the U.P. burst of communal strife and cow protection movements, purification and mutual conversion rituals are great sources of conflict, Rahman Khan describes similar developments in Surinam. This part shows that by the 1930s, Rahman Khan's privileged position is undermined. The dark years of the Hindu boycott against Muslims have started. By that time, others try to surpass Rahman Khan, as they have received some education and aspire for better jobs. Besides, many among them are born and brought up in Surinam, are Dutch nationals (*ingezetenen*) and no longer consider return to Hindustan. Rahman Khan is in particular upset when the same *brahmins*, who had given up caste before while crossing the *kala pani*, now reclaim their status and privileges. He feels an outcast, as Muslims are no longer desired in Hindu circles, he no longer is requested to recite the *vedas*, and Hindus rather offend him by asking him to convert.

Nevertheless, as we have shown elsewhere (Bal and Sinha-Kerkhoff 2004), whereas in India communal problems only increase and finally lead to the partition of British India and the formation of Pakistan and India, Surinam cools down, and by the time Rahman Khan finishes his autobiography (1943), ethnic unity proves stronger than religious divisions. Light returns in Rahman Khan's life.

# Endnotes

1. Figures differ however and range from 12- to 26, 000,000. Besides, the so-called Non-resident Indians (NRIs) are generally separated from 'overseas Indians' who do not hold Indian passports. Typically, these figures do not include people of Indian origin who now reside in Pakistan and Bangladesh. Besides, these figures do usually also exclude those now settled in Sri Lanka, Myanmar and Nepal. The Global Organization of People of Indian Origin (GOPIO) holds that there are, 'about 22 million' People of Indian Origin (PIOs), 'spread in more than 125 countries with more than 20 languages' (Report 2003: 5). One wonders whether people with 'mixed' parentage are included in these figures. Note also that these figures are based on the origin of (the ancestors of) people and not on the self-identification of people as PIOs.
2. In Dutch the name of the country is spelled and pronounced as 'Suriname'.
3. Munshi Rahman Khan wrote his autobiography in Hindi and used the devanagari script. The full handwritten text is with one of his grandsons, Albert Rahman, who resides in the Netherlands (albertrahman@wanadoo.nl). Sandew Hira sent this text to India where Harjeet Singh and Kenneth Soymurum entered the devanagari version in the computer and also made a preliminary English translation. The Dutch and published annotated translation by Hira (2003) is, among others, based on this English translation. Subsequently, the International Institute of Social History (IISH) in Amsterdam was approached. The latter assigned the task to us to provide a revised and annotated translation in English of the digital devanagari version of the original manuscript. Though some (typing) errors have slipped in the computerised version of the manuscript, we believe that these are minor and do not affect the content and meaning of the original text. Maurits Hassankhan, who resides in Surinam and who along with Sandew Hira in the Netherlands has published a historical database of Surinam, now plans to publish the original (devanagari) manuscript. The database is already available in English on the internet: http://www.archief.nl/suriname_english/engels/efrm_database.html?hdr_searching.

4. Mrs. Alice Bhagwandy Sital Persaud (later Alice Bahadur Singh) (1892-1965) also wrote an autobiography between April 1958 and April 1962. Unlike Rahman Khan she was born in Paramaribo, Surinam. Her father was born in Jyrabad in Uttar Pradesh. This *brahmin*, Sital Persad Doobay, had left India along with his mother when still a child. On arrival, his mother started working as an assistant nurse in a hospital on the Jagtlust plantation. Sital Persad later on became an interpreter of Hindi and Urdu. Alice Bhagwandy wrote her autobiography in English and the full handwritten text is available to the public at the University of Guyana, Special Collections Room. Sushila Patil and Moses Seenarine edited part of this text in 1996, which is now accessible through: http://www.icouk.org/Articles/art19.htm.
5. Dutch Guyana, or Surinam, is situated on the north coast of South America, to the east of British Guyana, from which it is separated by the river Corantijn. The colony had an area of 54,291 square miles. At the peace of Breda, in 1667, between England and the United Netherlands, Surinam was assured to the Netherlands in exchange for the colony of New Netherlands in North America. Since then the colony was twice in the possession of England, from 1799 to 1802 and from 1804 to 1816. During Dutch colonial time, the administration and executive authority were in the hands of a governor assisted by an advisory council consisting of the governor as president, a vice-president and three members, all nominated by the Queen of the Netherlands. The population of Surinam at the end of 1932 numbered 158, 194, including so-called Negroes and Red Indians living in the forests. The Indian population at the end of 1931 was 36, 150 among whom 19, 635 were males and 16, 515 females. The capital of Surinam is Paramaribo and the country's principal products were sugar, cacao, bananas, coffee, rum, rice, gold, rubber and bauxite (See File No. 169-13/34-L & O, 1934).
6. Mohan K. Gautam of the University of Leiden in the Netherlands was the first scholar to have read the full original manuscript. He also made an English summary of it (Gautam 1995). We were greatly inspired by this effort.
7. This translation by Mohan Gautam appeared in 'The construction of the Indian Image in Surinam' and is available on the web (www.caribbeanhindu.com/surinam.htm). See also Mohan Gautam (2002).
8. Though some people we interviewed in Surinam and the

Netherlands, among whom were some of his relatives, are not sure about the extent to which Rahman Khan was fluent in Urdu, we know from his own autobiography that he learnt the Persian writing system (*nastaliq*) at school in India. Besides, he translated a biography of the Prophet Mohammed from Urdu into Hindi (in verses using the devanagari script) (n.d). We have made a summary of this translation, which Rahman Khan had undertaken 'for the benefit of my Hindu and Muslim brothers who do not know the Urdu language'. Rahman Khan did not declare himself, however, 'an Islamic or even Urdu scholar'. In fact, in his autobiography he puts much more emphasis on his knowledge of Hinduism and Hindi. Though even here, he often relates his humbleness. He ends his introduction to his translation of Mohammed's life, for instance, with the following lines: 'To conclude, I request the Hindi scholar that if he sees any mistakes in this book he please should communicate this to me. I will be grateful to him and will correct my mistakes in the next version of this work'. In fact the Urdu and Hindi grammar are quite identical and some consider them as one single language (see, for instance, Taj 1997).

9. Rahman Khan's autobiography (at least the digital version of it that we used) is more or less legible for those who are acquainted with standard Hindi as taught in schools in India. The Hindi used by Rahman Khan contains also some words, which now could be recognised as being Braj, Awadhi, Bundeli, Khari Boli and Urdu words and seem to be part of the Bazari Hindi, Hindustani or Urdu used by the migrants to communicate with each other. Actually, Mohan Gautam shows that in Surinam during 1891-1961, the time during which Rahman Khan wrote, a new kind of spoken language developed that was called Surinami Hindi which, during the 1970s, became known as Sarnami. Besides, another variety of Hindi was used during cultural, religious and social gatherings (Gautam 2003: 200-216). Yet, the beautiful *dohas* (two line poems) and *chaupais* (verses), which Rahman Khan included in his autobiography are in the *masnavi* or sufi (*bhakti*) style and are, despite their apparent simplicity, hard to translate. Though we have made an effort to convey the meaning of the lines, in the translated form these verses have lost their elegance. The style Rahman Khan uses for his verses is quite similar to the writings of the mystic Indian poet Kabir (1398-1518) of eastern Uttar Pradesh and the style of his *chaupais* is that, which is commonly found in the Ramayana epic.

10. Two of his booklets with verses were published (Khan 1953 and Khan 1954).
11. Some writers also count Munshi Rahman Khan among those 'prominent persons and scholars in Urdu born in India, who did their best to educate their fellow-Muslims here' [in Surinam] (Ghafoerkhan 2003).
12. J.D. Speckman of the University of Leiden (the Netherlands) seems to have been able to motivate Mohan Gautam to read the autobiography.
13. As translation is not only a linguistic or hermeneutic matter but also a cultural one we have added footnotes in the main text where thought necessary and wrote this introduction to help readers understand the historical contexts of this ego-document. Actually, the imbalance of historical learning means that citizens in India or the Caribbean nations know much more about Europe than they know about each other (Cf. Brennan 2001: 51-52). We therefore also hope that this translation will somewhat reduce this imbalance.
14. Rahman Khan was in touch with its proprietor, Khemraj Shrikrishnadass; this press was established in 1871. It still exists and claims to be the 'oldest publisher of Indological (Religious) books in India' (http:/www.khe-shri.com). The newspaper published by this press also provided Rahman Khan with knowledge about contemporary developments in India. Rahman Khan failed however to publish his own works through this publisher, whereas the works of Nathuram a Hindu, had been accepted for publication. Rahman Khan was furious about this and thereafter, the relationship between him and the successor of Khemraj Shrikrishnadass (i.e., Seth Babu Murlidhar jee Saheb) turned sour (see also, Hira 2003: 24-29). We have tried to trace some of the newspaper articles to which Rahman Khan refers in his autobiography but have, until now, not succeeded.
15. Indentured labour was also recruited from other regions such as Maharashtra, Tamil Nadu and Andra Pradesh. Yet, most of the migrants who landed up in Surinam were from the North Western Provinces, Oudh and Bihar (McNeill 1915).
16. Kathinka Sinha-Kerkhoff and Ellen Bal are involved in a WOTRO (the Netherlands) supported project '*A Diaspora coming Home? Overseas Indians re-establishing links with India*', in which the issue of 'return migration' after expiry of contract or indeed after the abolition of the system of indenture, is an important one. Here we can sustain with what Ramdin (2000: 152) wrote: 'There was

little doubt that apart from the introduction in 1895 of the payment of a premium linked to commutation of the claim of a free passage, immigrants who were either born in the Colony or who had arrived in childhood, seldom wished to return'. Yet, some among the first generation of indentured labourers thought their tenure was a 'temporary sojourn' and that after completion 'they would go back to their mother country'. Accordingly, they tried to save money as much as possible and remitted savings regularly. At times there was regular communication between India and Surinam (Gautam 1995). See also Mohapatra (1995) on those who returned to Calcutta. For a long time, Rahman Khan identified as one who eventually would return to Hindustan. Yet, when his children had families of their own in Surinam and were in fact Dutch colonial citizens, he knew there was no question of return any longer and that he would die 'in an alien country'.

17. Immigrants, who were born in British India and settled in Surinam, as well as their offspring, identified and are labelled as Hindostanis and not as Indians or East Indians like those who settled in other colonies. We here prefer the spelling Hind*o*stanis as we feel it allows inclusion of both Hindus as well as Muslims. Rahman Khan wrote Hind*u*stanis however while accounting for both groups.
18. Mass emigration started in 1973 and in the years 1974 and 1975 more than 36,000 Hindostanis migrated to the Netherlands. Emigration continued due to a military coup in 1980 and the murder of a number of civilians known as the 'December murders' in 1982 (Choenni 2003: 54-55).
19. Among Hindostanis, different regional languages were used such as Bhojpuri, Hindi or Hindustani (Urdu), Avadhi, Braj, Pahari, Magahi, Maithili, etc. Once in Surinam they also learned Sranan Tongo, Dutch and some English and gradually a new language developed, which J.H. Adhin in 1964 coined as Sarnami-Hindustani, which later on just became Sarnami (Marhé 2003: 196).
20. Known as 'depot brotherhood' (*dipua bhai*) (Gautam 1995: 3).
21. Known as 'ship brotherhood' (*jahazia bhai*) (Gautam 1995: 3).
22. For further reading see Zachariah (1965), Reeves (1991) and Whitcombe (1971).
23. See, for instance Robinson (1993) for further reading on the effects of the socio-economic status decline among Muslims in the United Provinces.
24. The descendants of contract migrants from the Dutch East Indies, now known as Indonesia, are commonly referred to as 'Javanese'.

This stream of migration began in 1890 and the last contingent arrived on the eve of the Second World War, in 1939. Though Javanese migration exceeded that of the Hindostanis, the Javanese experienced a far lower growth rate than the Hindostanis (Dew 1996: 27-28).

25. This did not exclude occasional communal conflicts however and Sunthar and Elizabeth Visuvalingam in their article on Hindu-Muslim relations in colonial Benares during the beginning of the 19th century reason that in pre-colonial days, 'Hindu-Muslim interaction had been primarily a socio-cultural process characterized by syncretism-cum-conflict that took within its stride alternating politico-religious domination: it permitted constant re-negotiation and readjustment' (http://www. svabhinava.org/1809riot/).
26. For instance, whereas 'for over forty years Hindi and Urdu were taught in the schools' in Surinam, the Dutch colonial Government sought to discontinue this since 1934 and as a result, 'a number of Indian teachers (were) thrown out of employment' (Memorandum on Indians in Surinam File No. 169-13/34-L & O 1934). This caused increased competition among Hindostani teachers.
27. Though some studies on the impact of the Arya Samaj in colonial India connect it to the birth of the national movement, others feel it spurred communalism (see also Chandra 1984: 249n22). Rahman Khan would have agreed with the latter opinion and did neither recognize nor comment on the anti-British character of the Arya Samaj.
28. We have carried out extensive fieldwork in U.P. among others with the aim to trace some of Rahman Khan's directly related kin. Our findings are described in the notes that supplement the main translated text constituting the autobiography.
29. Relatives of Rahman Khan in the Netherlands preserve some of the letters he received from India. These letters contain among others messages from his ageing parents and other relatives asking him to return or visit them at least once, details about his property in India and about money sent by Rahman Khan to them and about books and letters sent to him. In the last preserved letter, dated 7 January 1910, Rahman Khan is warned that he would suffer the loss of his property in India, as there was nobody left to look after. We have gone through these letters and used them for a better understanding of his autobiography. See also Hira (2003: 29-42) who published some of these letters in Dutch and Gautam

(1995: 18) who made an English translation of one of the verses Rahman Khan received from his father.

30. Social reform movements of 19th century colonial India such as the Arya Samaj were, on the one hand, an attempt by the educated elite to reform Hinduism and, on the other, an attempt to defend itself from ideological onslaught by the colonial rulers. Swami Dayanand Saraswati acted as the intellectual mentor of the Arya Samaj, which 'sought to reform only those features which they thought acted as obstacles in the way of economic and social advancement of the educated elite' (Kishwar 1989: 79). This was very evident in its programme concerning caste discrimination and the low status of women. Interestingly, Rahman Khan rejects Dayanand's call to purge Hinduism of distortions by restoring its Vedic purity and defend it from attack by colonial Christianising forces, a call which received a ready response from the educated (Hindu) elite in India (in particular in Punjab). Actually, Rahman Khan does neither take into account the colonial context nor the position of women. Identifying somewhat as *pandit* and fearing his own position, he exclusively refers to the attack on the caste hierarchy by the Arya Samaj and rejects this on the basis that Hinduism in no way allows such a breakdown of the caste hierarchy (see also pages .... in this book).
31. M.A. Jinnah, the founder of Pakistan, said in one of his speeches in 1940: 'The Hindus and Muslims belong to two different religious philosophies, social customs, and literatures. They neither intermarry nor interdine together and, indeed, they belong to two different civilizations, which are based mainly on conflicting ideas and conceptions' (Pandey 1965: 86).
32. UP refers to present-day Uttar Pradesh, previously known as the United Provinces of Agra and Awadh. See for instance Pandey (1983).
33. The present-day Jharkhand was part of Bihar during this period. This Bhojpuri area comprises therefore exactly the region from which the Hindostanis had migrated to Surinam.
34. Suthar and Elizabeth Visuvalingam feel that that in colonial Benares (U.P.), 'British justice–which claimed, and largely tried, to be neutral–treated both religions on an 'equal' footing, thereby winning the respect of both Hindus and Muslims, but at the same time tending to legislate their differences into frozen barriers, and to arrest the process of mutual fecundation. Even where the colonial state did not consciously or actively embark on a policy of divide-

and-rule, riots were made possible precisely by the absence of clear Hindu or Muslim domination, and by the relative impartiality of British rule. Indeed, it could be argued that the logic of divide-and-rule was as much imposed on the imperial state by its Hindu and Muslim subjects, even before it was overtly or tacitly exploited by the former to its own advantage' (http://www. svabhinava.org/1809riot).

35. Related to this the scholar Mushirul Hasan writes, 'It is common to connect the two-nation theory with the Aligarh reformer, Saiyid Ahmad Khan, and not his contemporary Dayanand Saraswati, the high priest of the Arya Samaj. The former appears to me to be far more tolerant, eclectic and broad-minded in his orientation and outlook than the latter' (Hasan 2002: 318n1). Rahman Khan might have agreed with this opinion.
36. Suresh Kumar Pillai gives the example of Trinidad and argues that during wrestling competitions, there was rivalry between the two religious groups as 'Muslim wrestlers came mostly from Afghanistan, Punjab or the North West Provinces and were called Pathans and the Hindus wrestlers came from Lucknow and Varanasi'. Yet he adds, 'The religious leaders did not allow it to grow beyond the point of casual verbal remarks' and these Muslims and Hindus 'were united against planters and Africans' (Pillai 2003: 67-68).
37. In India this festival is better known as *muharram.*
38. Pillai (2003: 67) writes, 'But the relations between Hindus and Muslims in Caribbean countries have always resonated the altercations happening in the [Indian] subcontinent but the effects of such incidents were restricted to an extent that they dissolved in front of a common apathetic future the community faced in the larger Caribbean society'.
39. Yet, the Arya Samaj made significant inroads into Surinam's Hindu population and by 1931 about 16 per cent of Hindus adhered to the Arya Samaj (Vertovec 2000: 55). It was especially popular among 'intellectuals' (Ramsoedh and Bloemberg 2001: 137). Compare this to the situation in the United Provinces where 'less than one per cent of the Hindus were followers of the Arya Samaj' (Ramsoedh and Bloemberg 2001: 137).
40. Even for Rahman Khan himself things were not fully settled as on 30 April 1951 he writes a 'religious warning' (in Hindi) in which he alleges that 'some Hindus have diverted from the true path of the Hindu religion and are violating their own teachings of the

*vedas*'. In this critique, Rahman Khan further argues that according to the *vedas* the cow is holy and therefore Hindus should not even consume milk, curd and ghee. He concludes: 'Dear [Hindu] brothers. This is to remind you that we all are sons of Bharat and we have settled in an alien land. It is hard therefore to follow the true path of the *vedas* and our religious customs during such a difficult period. Yet, it is our duty to follow our religious paths as much as possible. Besides, of the three paths, that of the *vedas* [religious rules], *dharm* [duty, destiny] and the country one should at least follow the rules and regulations of the country in which we live and teach love, friendship and unselfishness to our children, who have to live in peace with each other'.

41. Yet, on 20 February 1955 Rahman Khan writes a poem entitled 'War between the Star and the Sun', in which he describes the fight between the 'Sun' [Hindus: Bajrang and Timal] and the 'Star' [Muslims: Ushman and Aligol]. He concludes: 'there are many races settled here but none do fight among themselves like we do. Do not think that, as Muslims are in a minority that they are powerless. We can crush the Hindus any time in the same way as the five Pandavas crushed hundreds of Kauravas in the Mahabharata. This is the justice of God who provides strength to the weak. Religions advise people to live together and abandon self-pride, wickedness, conspiracy and jealousy. I plead to Allah to bless Aligol [Islam] and make the latter immortal'.

42 See for instance Conner (quoted in Safran 1991: 83-84) who argues that those communities are diasporas if they (among others) 'retain a collective memory, vision, or myth about their original homeland–its physical location, history, and achievements' and if they believe that they should, collectively, be committed to the maintenance or restoration of their original homeland and to its safety and prosperity' and if 'they continue to relate, personally or vicariously, to that homeland in one way or another, and their ethno-communal consciousness and solidarity are importantly defined by the existence of such relationship'.

43. The theoretical weakness of the category of diaspora has been the subject of an article by Floya Anthias who points out that the fact that a group of people hails from a particular place does not necessarily make them a valid sociological category (Anthias 1998). Besides, Malkki (1992) presents a critical discussion on 'the rooting of peoples and the territorialization of national identity'. Though we concur with Anthias and Malkki's warnings not to jump too

fast to conclusions, we nevertheless feel that Rahman Khan can be considered as part of an Indian diaspora.

44. In 1949 Hindus and Muslims united in one political party to form a strong front against others. Although attempts have always been made to keep 'religion' out of the party it has to be noted that many Muslims did leave the party, without, however, reorganising themselves in a Muslim Hindostani party. Officially the VHP has always remained a secular party.
45. We here use Bipan Chandra's rather long but very apt definition. Among others it says that communalism is, 'the belief that because a group of people follow a particular religion they have, as a result, common social, political and economic interests' and it is also the belief that, 'in India Hindus, Muslims, Christians and Sikhs form different and distinct communities which are independently and separately structured or consolidated' and that 'all followers of a religion share not only a community of religious interests but also common secular interests, that is, common economic, political, social and cultural interests'(Chandra 1984: 1).
46. Many informants complained that they knew too little about their ancestors, histories. Some pointed out that young people were not supposed to ask questions to the elderly. Others believed that their parents or grandparents wanted to cover up their pasts. Many, however, also told us that the elderly talked among themselves. De Klerk (1998 [1953]: 154) points out that this first generation of migrants was also known as the people with the great longing, 'de menschen van het groote heimwee'. With their death, the yearning disappeared.
47. Mirza Ghulam Ahmad founded the Ahmadiyya movement in 1889 as a reaction to the influence of the Christian missionaries and the Hindu Arya Samaj reform movement in northern British India (Landman 1992: 24). After the death of Ghulam Ahmad the movement split into two: the Quadianis and the Lahoris. Among Hindostani Muslims in Surinam the latter greatly outnumber the former. For further reading see Landman (2002: 23-32) and Mustapha (2004: 127-147).
48. Information provided by Hadja Hafidjan Rahman-Bakridi, the wife of Chote Khan during an interview on 31 May 2004.
49. This depiction of Rahman Khan we received, for instance, from Pandit Mangal Deo 'Jungli' when we interviewed him on 1 July 2003 in The Hague. 'Jungli' had been a good friend of Rahman Khan as he is also mentioned in the autobiography. 'Jungli Kaka'

was also very much loved by Rahman Khan's family.

50. In Surinam we interviewed for instance Bhikhie Safdar Hoesein whose sister is married to one of Rahman Khan's grandsons and Abdul Latif Rahman one of Rahman Khan's grandsons. We also talked about Rahman Khan with the Arya Samji Harridew Sahtoe, who met him on *Janmasti* when Sahtoe was 11 years old. He remembers that it was somewhere around 1954 or 1955 and Rahman had been asked to recite verses from the Ramayana. Faroek Kallan, also from Surinam, knows about Munshi Rahman Khan through his grandfather and remembers him as 'a great expert in Hindi'.

51. In the Netherlands we interviewed another of his grandsons: Naseer Rahman Khan (son of Faiz Khan, Rahman Khan's youngest son) as well as Simon and Albert Rahman, two sons of Chote Khan (Rahman Khan second youngest son) and Hadja Hafidjan Rahman-Bakridi, the wife of Chote Khan. The latter's sad demise on 29 July 2004 at the age of 85 is greatly regretted. We have fond memories of the talks we had with her. We also interviewed Samsoedin, the son-in-law of Mariyam, one of Rahman Khan's daughters. We sincerely thank all those who shared their memories of Rahman Khan with us.

52. This was unlike some other British-Indian migrants who actually disliked the efforts of, among others, Mahatma Gandhi and other members of the Congress Party to abolish 'the system of Indian Indendured Labour'. Congress members in British India and other so-called 'nationalists' felt that the system attached 'the stigma of slavery to the Indian people in the eyes of the Colonies' and that it entailed, 'moral degradation and unhappiness amongst the emigrants' (File February 1917, Prog. No. 22, Dept. of Commerce and Industry, Branch Emigration, National Archives New Delhi). In Surinam however many migrants wanted to continue migration as discontinuation would imply diminution of the contacts between these migrants and their 'homeland'. Related to this some prominent members among the Hindostani community in Surinam, such as the head interpreter Sital Persad, visited, among others, Mahatma Gandhi in India with the request to reconsider his opinion on this form of migration (De Klerk 1998 [1953]: 178-179). Rahman Khan does nowhere comment on this issue.

53. For further reading on gender and indentured labour see Moses Seenarine '*Recasting Indian women in colonial Guyana: gender, labor and caste in the lives of indentured and free laborers*' (26 August 1996)

(http://www. saxakali.com/saxakali-publications/recastgwa.htm).

54. The digital version in Hindi we use spells the name as 'Hors' in devanagari. Compare this with Gautam (1995) who writes 'Horst', which we also feel is the actual spelling in Dutch.
55. This was written on 18 September 1950 after the death of his close but younger friend 'Godan', who arrived in Paramaribo by the same ship, *Avon*. Rahman Khan considered Godan, a Hindu, his 'younger brother' and wrote about him: 'Godan was very generous, religious, tolerant and a real gentleman. I will always remain obliged to him for the selfless help he gave me throughout his life. I in particular admired him as he never brought the differences between Hindus and Muslims in the pen and always respected me like his father'.
56. This refers to the phrase 'Bismillah-hir-Rahman-ir Rahim' (in the name of God, the Merciful and the Compassionate).
57. We have translated Rahman Khan's 'Letter to the Queen' written on 30 October 1955. He also wrote a *doha* entitled 'Holland in distress' about a terrible flood that had occurred in 1953 in the Netherlands.
58. Chickrie (2002: 389) argues that the culture of the *pathan* is based on the principles of 'backbone, hospitality, bravery and honour', which are enshrined in a 'code of honour known as Puktunwali, or the way of the Pathans'.
59. This literally means 'black water' and this is how many migrants perceived the ocean and seas they had to cross in order to reach the place of destination.
60. These are summarized translations.
61. Rahman Khan therefore develops the same unique religious synthesis in Surinam as had already developed in India, using in this case the language not only derived from Hindu and Islamic traditions but also from African and so-called native Amer-Indian traditions. Peter Gottschalk (2000: 136) found that in the Bihar-U.P. regions in India it is quite common for people to model 'their religious lives via Kabir's caustic critique and unique synthesis of Hinduism and Islam' and that 'a great many exercise their religiosity in ways quite dissimilar from the portrait of Indian religions drawn by many scholars'.
62. Migration from India to Surinam officially stopped after the S.S. Dewa took the last batch of labour migrants from Calcutta to Paramaribo in 1916. After 5 years, i.e., in 1921, this last batch of contract labourers had to choose whether to stay back as *freemen*

in Surinam or to return to India. Yet, even in 1931 there still were contract labourers in Surinam, i.e., migrants who had got their 5-year contracts renewed (De Klerk 1998 [1953]: 181). Therefore, (return) migration did continue till at least 1934. We have found that many of these so-called returned emigrants or 'repatriated' got 'stranded' in the Akra camp (Metiabruz, Calcutta) where they remained, 'helpless', 'aged' or 'infirmed' and desperately hoping for the Government of India to send them back to one of the colonies as in India they felt unwanted. Some of them were indeed prepared to take any ship to wherever it would bring them as they felt everything was better than remaining in India (Cf. *Statesman*, November 1, 4, 6, 17 and December 9, 1932; *Amrita Bazar Patrika*, 19 November 1932).

(बिस्मिल्लाह हिर्रहमानिर्रहीम)

(मुंशी - रहमान खाँ)
का
जीवन प्रकाश
पहला काण्ड
जिसको

खुद मुन्शी - रहमान खाँ ने अपने हाथ लिखा है
। अपनी ज़िन्दगी में देखी हुई वारदातों का अहवाल
। उनके ऊपर बीती हुई मुसीबतों का बयान मुफ़स्सल
र परकिया है । [illegible] (चौपाई)
दोहा ।। लखा भारत द्वीप हमेशा । पुनि है निज जीवन परकाश
को है कोह ग्लोब दोहा चौपाई । [illegible] जहाँ तहँ दीन्ह बनाई ।।
(सो.) तीन लोक दश गुरु निगम, ग्रह दिशा मिलि गुरुवार ।
तारीख़ तेरह मई सन् कीन्ह ग्रन्थ परचार ।।

ह० अ० मुं० रहमान खाँ मुक़ाम - देदू लाल नम्बर ४ ।।
(ता.) तारीख़ 13 मई सन् १९४३ ई० दिन बृहस्पतिवार ।।

# Jeevan Prakash

*(In the name of Allah, the Merciful and the Compassionate[1])*

This book is written by Munshi Rahman Khan himself and nobody else. It was written at Dijkveld[2] in Surinam and he started writing the book on Thursday 13 May 1943.[3] It describes the circumstances in which he lived and his life experiences. Some verses as well as a short history of *Bharat* are included[4].

# Preface

I never dreamt of writing a book like this. This is because a man's reminiscence usually perturbs his family. Nevertheless in my case my own sons, the five loving stars[5], persuaded me to put my memories down in writing. However, I appeal to all the readers to pray that *Allah* will forgive an insignificant soul like me, the writer of this book. I also wish that all who read this book, recite the 'Sur-E-Fatah'[6] and 'Darud Sharif'[7] so that their blessings may redeem all my sins and stimulate my salvation. I sincerely wish that my dear sons, and their lovely children, be granted a full and prosperous life by Holy *Rabbul Aalmeen* [the God of the Universe]!

O Holy Allah, let my children and off spring live the same blessed life they now experience, even after my death. May they, in future have the same abundance as You currently provide. May they always remember You and praise Your holy name. O Lord, bless my children and their family and never let Your son be in need of anything, except You Yourself.

Aameen Aameen. Rabbul Aalmeen![8]

**My Address in Hindustan**

Country: Hindustan
Capital: Delhi
Commissionary: Allahabad
Distict: Hamirpur[18]
Thana & P.O.: Biwarn
Village: Bharkhari
Father's name: Muhammad Khan (*jamadar*)

# Introduction: History of Hindustan[9]

I begin this book with the brief history of Hindustan, in the name of the Almighty who is also my *Guru*.

1. Hindustan is the largest country in South Asia. In its north lies the chain of the Himalaya Mountains and in the east are Brahma Pradesh and the Bay of Bengal. In the west are located Afghanistan, Baluchistan and the Arabian Sea while Ceylon is situated in the south. This subcontinent stretches thousand miles from Rameshwaram in the south to the Himalayas in the north and is 900 miles broad from Brahma in the east to the borders of Afghanistan and Baluchistan in the west.

2. The primitive inhabitants of Hindustan were uncivilized and forest dwellers. The Aryans who arrived in Hindustan used to call them black slaves. Some of these tribes, for example, the Bhils, Kols, Santhalis and Gonds, are still found in pockets of certain hills and forests. They used to worship natural elements such as snakes and trees. These customs are preserved in Hindu traditions today.

3. Central Asia is located north of the Himalayas. People from this cold region crossed over the valleys of mountains to settle down in the fertile land of Hindustan. The first among them were the Dravidians who now reside in the plains of southern India, south of the Vindhyachal Mountains and speak a Dravid language. Turks (Mongols) were the next to come to Hindustan and some of them can still be found in the eastern and northern parts of the country.

4. Aryans were next to follow. They settled down in the villages and towns of Hindustan and used to keep sheep, goats, cows, and oxen. For a certain period, they settled down in the Sind river valley and were worshipers of the Sun. When they came to know about the rich and fertile plains of the rivers Ganga and the Yamuna they migrated to those areas and chased away the inhabitants there who sometimes took shelter in forests and hills elsewhere while others became slaves of the Aryans.

5. The ancient history of the Hindus is one of glorious

courageous warriors. Shri Ramchandra is the most popular among them. He was the bravest and strongest in the country. He was married to Sita, the daughter of King Janak. Ram was exiled after a few years of marriage on his stepmother's request. Ram's younger brother Lakshman and wife Sita followed him in the forest.

6. In the forest, the wicked King Ravana of Lanka kidnapped Sita but Shri Ramchandra later killed him helped by Hanuman, the leader of monkeys. Thereafter Sita was freed. At last, Ramchandraji returned to his kingdom and ruled for many more years with fair justice and peace. His life history is mentioned in the epic called the Ramayana.

7. Aryan Hindus spoke Sanskrit, which is one of the oldest languages. It is not spoken presently in Hindustan but it is the origin of most of the present languages spoken in the country. The Mahabharata is another big epic written in Sanskrit.

8. Gautam was not only a fearless warrior but also possessed a very generous and tolerant character. At the age of thirty he renounced the world including his family and went to live in the forest where he spent his time in meditation. When after a few years he returned, he was called Buddha, and since then Buddhism has taken shape. It taught people to be compassionate and caring and to respect mankind by giving up cruelty and sinful deeds.

9. The larger part of Arab is devoid of rivers and lakes and largely suffers from drought. There was an astrologer, named Mohammed, in Arabia, around 600 A.D. His followers were called *Mussalmans* [Muslims].

10. They believed in the holy war against atheists and those Muslims who were killed in such a war would become martyrs and were supposed to attain salvation. Mohammed conquered other countries like Turkistan, Afghanistan and Iran and spread the religion called Islam in all these regions.

11. Mahmud Ghaznavi, the king of Gazni came to know about the riches of *Bharatvarsha* [i.e., east of Ghur and Ghazni, that is present-day India].[10] He thought of waging a holy war against Hindustan and of looting its rich temples. He attacked India seventeen times and during his last invasion in 1042 A.D[11], he reached up to Gujarat in the south west of Hindustan and looted the Somnath temple, known throughout the country for its treasures. He met a sudden death before reaching Afghanistan.

12. Mohammad Ghori[12] too, was a valiant fighter like Muhammad Gaznavi. He spent his life attacking *Bharatvarsha* [Hindustan/India] and his goal was to conquer the whole country. He did not have any offspring and after his death [in 1206] Qutb-ud-din became the ruler of Delhi and most Indian provinces. Life was very insecure during those days.

13. Qutb-ud-din Aibek was the first 'Slave King'.[13] He ruled for 4 years and constructed a high and beautiful *minar* near Delhi, called Qutub Minar. Eight emperors and one empress [Raziya 1237-1240] succeeded him. There also were the four Khalji *sultans*; Alauddin Khalji (1296-1316) was the most powerful and cruel among them and conquered the south. After them came eight Tughlaq emperors. Muhammad was insane but Firoz Shah ruled for 40 years (1351-1388) and did a lot for the development and prosperity of the country.

14. In 1398, Taimur [Taimur of Samarkand, a Mongol] attacked Hindustan with a large army contingent and returned only after looting, plundering and destroying Delhi. He stayed in Hindustan for 5 months. Sayyed and Lodi *sultans* succeeded the Tughlaq rulers and ruled in and around the Delhi-Agra region.

15. After the death of Taimur his kingdom was divided into smaller states. Babar[14], 13 years old, got one such state but he had to flee south because of wars. He was a great warrior and valiant ruler who ruled over Kabul and Gazni for many years. He attacked Hindustan in 1526 and captured Delhi. He ruled there for 4 years only but laid the foundation of the Mughal dynasty.

16. Humayun (1530-1540), son of Babar was a compassionate ruler but not as proficient and able as his father. Nor was he true to his words. He took over the reign with several enemies around him. An Afghani soldier, Sher Khan an Afghan based in Bihar, defeated him and he had to run for his life to Persia [present-day Iran]. After the death of Sher Khan, Humayun's son Akbar took over. Akbar was born in the desert during the period in which Humayun recaptured Delhi and Agra. However, Humayun could not rule the region for a long period.

17. Akbar was the greatest and most excellent emperor among all the Muslim rulers. His rule lasted 50 years, which was approximately the same period as the rule of Queen Elizabeth of England. He befriended Rajput kings and married with their daughters, and their fathers and brothers were given posts of senior

officers in his army. He had good relations with Hindus. He abolished *jizya* and pilgrimage tax. He died in 1605.

18. Jahangir Salim[15], the eldest son of Akbar, ascended the Delhi throne after the death of Akbar. He married Nur Jahan who ruled his state with full authority. Sir Thomas Row was sent to his court by king James I of England to seek permission for English traders to do business in Hindustan. During that period the country was abounded by dacoits and travelling was very unsafe.

19. Shah Jahan [Prince Khurram 1628-1658] was the most powerful of all the Mughal emperors in terms of religion, deeds, money, offspring, might and knowledge. During 30 years of his reign, he constructed beautiful towns, palaces, mosques and tombs. He built the Taj Mahal, the most expensive and beautiful tomb in memory of his Persian wife Mumtaz Mahal. The Jama Masjid in Delhi and the Moti Masjid in Agra are other such examples of his power. He fell sick at the age of 76 [in 1657] and his four sons started fighting for the throne. Aurangzeb, his third son (1659-1707), was the strongest of all and captured the throne of Delhi. He put his father Shah Jahan behind the bars between 1658 and 1666 in Agra where he died.

20. Aurangzeb killed all his brothers and put his father behind the bars during the 50 years of his rule. He removed all Christian and Hindu staff and appointed Muslims in their place. His hatred for the Hindu religion is seen from the destruction of Hindu temples at Banaras and the killing of their priests. He again started collecting the *jizya* [tax] that had been abolished during Akbar's period. He advanced towards the south and after a long battle, captured Golkonda and Bijapur. However, he could not win over the Maratha chief, Shivaji. He died at an old age in 1707.

21. At present, Hindustan is part of the British Empire, and the King of England is called the Emperor of Hindustan. At first, 300 years ago, the Britishers came as traders. They purchased rice, cotton, indigo, spices, coconut, sugar, and opium. They brought woolen clothes, bronze, mercury, iron, to India, which were not available here.

22. The Marathas ruled in the western part of Hindustan, which is now called the Bombay Presidency (Deccan). Shivaji was born there in 1617. He was illiterate but skilled in horse riding, shooting and archery. He captured the fort of Purander at the age of twenty and won several other forts. He defeated the army of the Bijapur Kingdom and killed its leader Afzal Khan.

23. Aurangzeb followed Shivaji and sent his army to check his advances. Shivaji bowed down to the mighty Mughals and presented himself at the court of the Mughal emperor. But Aurangzeb caught him by trick and put him behind bars. However, Shivaji escaped in a basket and reached his state safely. He died in 1680, aged fifty-two.

24. During the Mughal period a total of fifteen emperors reigned. Six of them were very powerful and Aurangzeb was the last among them. Yet he made many enemies because of his unjust rule. Even Governors of his provinces severed relations with him and in turn aspired to become independent rulers. Marathas gained strength during this period. Aurangzeb killed the son of Shivaji, while Shahuji was worthless. As a result the *brahmin* ministers called *peshwas,* inherited the property and ruled the state. There was no peace in the region and Maratha dacoits used to roam around, looting the people.

25. After the death of Aurangzeb, the 30-year old Nadir Khan Shah from Persia ascended the throne. He kept his name Nadir Shah, and conquered Afghanistan. He attacked Hindustan and took away all the wealth and jewellery that Mughal emperors had collected since Babur's period. The Mughal Kingdom then totally disintegrated. Marathas became more powerful and popular all over the country.

26. The war between the British and French took place in 1744. The French Governor Dupleix, who was very clever, attacked and captured Madras in 1746. In 1748 a peace treaty was signed between the French and Aurangzeb that was respected till 1756.

27. Robert Clive was working as a clerk in the English East India Company in Madras. When the French captured Madras, Clive ran away to Fort St. David, which was then looked after by Major Lawrence. Clive fought very bravely and was appointed as the officer in the army. Nizam-ul-Mulk the *subedar* of the Decan, who received the title 'Asaf Jah' died in 1748 and was succeeded by his son Nasir Jang. His nephew (*bhatija*) [this should be grandson] Muzaffar Jang sought help from the French to overthrow Nasir Jang and so did Chanda Sahab in order to rule over Karnataka. Dupleix was more than happy to promise assistance to both.

28. The old Nawab of Karnataka was killed. His son Mohammad Ali fled to Bichanapalli[16] and sought assistance from the British. Nazir Jung, too, got killed and Arcot was taken over by

the British. Clive returned to England and became very rich and famous, popularly known as a brave general from Arcot.

29. The Governor of Bengal died in 1756 and was succeeded by his grandson Siraj-ud-Daulah. He attacked Calcutta with 16,000 army men and defeated the British after a four-day fierce battle. Around 146 British men were held prisoner and out of them 123 died of asphyxia. Their bodies were thrown in a ditch.

30. General [Rahman Khan writes Colonel] Clive reached Calcutta from Madras after hearing the news. He was the commander of the army while admiral Watson was the naval officer. Both wanted to revenge the killings of the Britishers. Siraj-ud-Daulah was defeated in the battle of Plassey and fled. General Clive reached Murshidabad and appointed Mir Jafar as the Nawab. In return Mir Jafar gave away the territory in and around Calcutta to the East India Company. This became known as the Twenty-Four Parganas District. This was the first region in Hindustan that came under the British and announced the beginning of their future rule in the Bengal Presidency.

31. Mir Jafar who ascended the throne of Bengal was a drug-addict and spent time in merry making. He was left unprotected as soon as Clive went to England in 1760. An inept ruler, he was dethroned by the Governor of Calcutta and his son-in-law (*damad*) [should be father-in-law] Mir Qasim ascended the throne.

32. Mir Qasim proved to be a better administrator. He returned all the loans and made a better settlement of his kingdom. He transferred his capital to Munger and thinking himself better equipped, started preparing for a war with the British. He arrested some British traders in Patna and ordered his men to arrest and kill Britishers. He was defeated by major Adams and fled for his life never to be heard of again.

33. Clive again came to Hindustan on hearing the news of the war started by Mir Qasim. However the war ended before he reached here. A treaty was signed at Allahabad, according to which Shah Alam II gave permission to the Company to collect taxes in Bihar, Bengal and Orissa. Lord Clive made amendments in civil services and defence. He died before the age of fifty in England.

34. Ahmad Shah Abdali became the ruler of Afghanistan after the death of Nadir Shah. He captured the Punjab in 1752 and advanced towards Hindustan. Peshwa Balaji Rao (1702-1740) sent Raghunath Rao to Delhi on hearing the advances of Abdali. He

moved west and captured Lahore. Ahmad Shah Abdali proved stronger and defeated the Marathas in the battle of Panipat in 1761.

35. The Marathas again became powerful 10 years after the battle of Panipat, but Scindia, a Maratha chief at Gwalior was more powerful than Peshwa, another Maratha chief at Poona, and attained the title of Maharaja. The Britishers captured Delhi and after they house arrested the Mughal Emperor Shah Alam II, they started ruling over the Mughal Kingdom. When the English took over Delhi in 1800, Shah Alam was freed and was given a pension and allowed to stay in his palace.

36. The East India Company authorized Clive to give the control over Bengal to the people themselves. So he made the son of Mir Jafer the ruler and appointed two ministers to collect taxes on his behalf. But the latter collected excess taxes and returned only little to the exchequer of the Nawab. The appointed ministers were Muslims.

37. Warren Hastings was an able administrator of Bengal. He stopped the so-called Dual Government, which was started by Lord Clive and appointed an English collector and judge for better administration. The Prime Minister of England made Mr. Hasting the Governor General of the whole of British Hindustan, and constituted a council of four ministers to assist him.

38. Lord Cornwallis (1786-1793) was the second Governor General. The son of Haider Ali conquered Malabar, Coorg and Travancore. The king of Travancore sought the help of the Britishers and Tipu Sultan was defeated. Lord Cornwallis appointed a judge and collector in each district for better justice and collection of revenue respectively.

39. The third Governor General was Sir John Shore and he did not have any problem with the local rulers. The Marathas defeated the Nizam in 1795 and took half of the kingdom under their possession and for the remaining half the Marathas were paid taxes. Such loot led to infighting among Marathas.

40. The British became powerful during the rule of Lord Richard Wellesley who was the fourth Governor General of Hindustan. He issued an order to the Nizam, Tipu and the Peshwa to remove all the French and depute British forces in their principality and pay for the expenses. The Nizam agreed but Tipu revolted. This led to wars in which Tipu was killed and the British annexed Srirangpattan [Seringapatnam] and Mysore.

41. Lord Cornwallis again visited Hindustan but he was too old and died within 3 months at the age of seventy. Sir George Barlow became the caretaker Governor General. The sons of Tipu revolted but were crushed and sent to Calcutta. Lord Minto ruled between 1807 and 1813. In 1813, the English Parliament opened the doors for all, to do business in Hindustan.

42. Lord Hastings came in 1813 and defeated the Marathas during his 5-year tenure. Peace prevailed in Hindustan and also the farmers were happy.

43. In 1824 the king of Burma attacked and killed some Englishmen in its border region. The British force retaliated and captured Rangoon. Lord Amherst captured and destroyed the fort of Bharatpur.

44. Lord William Bentinck cleared the way for travellers and opened the doors for Hindustani people to get government jobs. Schools were established. He built Fort William at Calcutta named after him. He was the ninth Governor General of Hindustan.

45. Sir Charles Metcalfe ruled for one year in 1835. Local newspapers started coming up during this period. Lord Ellenborough [should be Auckland] destroyed the fort of Kabul and Dost Mohammad was sent to rule over there. Sind was made part of the British Empire.

46. After the death of King Ranjeet Singh, infighting broke out between the Sikhs and the British in Punjab. Gulab Singh was made the king of Kashmir who paid for all the expenses of the war. Daleep Singh was made king of Punjab but his mother ruled the state till his adolescence.

47. War with the Sikhs again broke out during Lord Dalhausie's period. In 1848, the Britishers annexed the Punjab and Dilip Singh was given pension. Similarly, the principalities of Madhya Padesh and Awadh became part of the British Empire.

48. Railways were introduced in 1853. Business rapidly progressed during Lord Dalhousie's period. Before him, the postal system was not popular because of the high tax on it. Moreover, there were neither railways nor many roads. Lord Dalhousie issued half-anna stamps as result of which letters could be sent to any part of the country. Till 1853, the East India Company appointed Indian Civil Service (ICS) officers from England and sent them to Hindustan. But after that year, apart from Europeans, the doors of the ICS were opened to locals as well.

49. When Lord Canning became the Governor General in 1856, there was peace all around with no sense of insecurity. But a sudden revolt broke out among the Hindustani force that became popularly known as Gadsar. Rule by the East India Company came to an end and Queen Victoria became the Empress of Hindustan. The post of Governor General changed into Viceroy.

50. The first Viceroy was Lord Canning, who ruled till 1868. Two wars with Bhutan and two great famines in Orissa and in the western part of Hindustan occurred during the period of third Viceroy Lord Lawrence. The fourth viceroy was Lord Mayo who came in 1869 and ruled for 3 years. A prisoner killed him during his inspection in the Andaman Islands.

51. A great famine occurred in Bengal when Lord Northbrook was the fifth Viceroy. The eldest son of Queen Victoria Prince Edward was the Emperor of Bharat. There was great pomp and show and big Rajas and Maharajas, rich and poor, came to see the Emperor when he visited Hindustan in 1875.

52. A big *durbar* was held in Delhi in 1877 when Lord Lytton was the sixth Viceroy. Queen Victoria was given the title of Empress of India (*Bharateshwari*) during this Durbar. Two wars with Afghanistan took place when Lord Ripon was the seventh Viceroy. This led to the downfall of Afghanistan and Abdul Rahman was made the Amir of Afghanistan.

53. The British annexed Burma during Lord Dufferin's period. Overall development took place in the field of education, drinking water and health. Queen Victoria died on Tuesday, 22 January 1901. The Prince of Wales, King Edward III of England became the Emperor of Hindustan. He was born in 1841.

54. The grandfather of Queen Victoria was George III. He had two sons. The eldest was the Duke of Kent and named Edward George IV and the second son was named William George IV. When the father of Queen Victoria, Edward George died, William IV ascended the throne.

55. Queen Victoria was born on 24 May 1819. She succeeded her uncle William IV after his death in 1837. She married Prince Edward of Saxenburg, Germany in 1840. He died in 1861 after 20 years of marriage. He had four sons and five daughters. The eldest son was Albert Edward also called the Prince of Wales. He ascended the throne after the death of Victoria in 1901 and ruled till his death in 1910.[17]

# Volume I

## My Family History: Lineage

I, Rahman Khan[19], son of Mohammad Khan, belonging to the race of *pathans*.[20] I came to know that Hindustan was ruled by Hindu kings during several centuries till 1022. The last king, Jaipal's grandson Angadpal ascended the throne in Lahore in 1013. Mohammad Ghaznavi, the ruler of Ghazni defeated him in 1022 and captured Lahore. It was during his time that the strong foundation of the Muslim Sultanate was laid in Hindustan. This conqueror attacked Hindustan seventeen times to accomplish his goal. Thirteen attempts were made in Hind and three in the Punjab. During his seventeenth raid in 1048, he captured the Somnath temple. This temple had fifty-six pillars and fifty-five doors. At Md. Ghaznavi's arrival, the chief priest of the temple pleaded him with folded hands saying: 'Lord, you may take all the valuable jewellery that adorn the idols from me, but please do not harm the statue'. Ruler Ghaznavi replied: 'I am not a seller but the destroyer of the idols'. Saying this he gave two heavy blows with his *gurz* (a heavy weapon) but nothing happened to the idols. A third blow however, smashed the statue into three pieces and all the jewellery offered by the priest, fell out. The *badshah* (ruler) took all the valuables along with the three pieces of the idol and returned. One of these pieces later adorned Shahjahan's throne, another was placed at the gate of Delhi's Jama Masjid and Shahjahan put the third piece near the staircase of his bedroom. There were about 1.25 lakh priests who used to worship in the temple of Somnath during that period. God knows the truth.

Many such rulers kept on invading Hindustan and helped in expanding the territory of the Muslim Sultanate. In 1237 [Rahman writes 1336], Sultana Raziya ascended the throne of Delhi. In 1339 Qutb-ud-din Aibak[21] became the first of the so-called Slave Kings of the Delhi Sultanate and ruled for 4 years. During his reign he ordered to establish a military base under Bahadur Resaldar Jalal Khan near the river Betwa to resist the attacks of the Bundelkhand kings. A thousand horsemen comprising mainly Afghani *pathans* and *mughal* fighters were sent to the base camp under his command. Accordingly, brave Resaldar Jalal Khan left with his men and reached Kalapi, about 200 miles from Delhi. Thereafter, he moved south, to about 15-20 miles from the city where river Betwa flowed.

The Bundelkhand territory lay beyond that river. The troops crossed the river and stationed themselves in two groups. On the right, about 2 miles off the river, the *pathans* took position and the Mughals camped in the dense jungle about 5 miles from there. In this way they hoped to be able to check the enemy who would either attack from the riverside or from the jungle.[22]

## The Naming of Jalalpur

Due to their weakness, the Hindu kings never dared to attack the area, however, and the territory where the two battalions stayed, remained free from any attack. It was a common practice during that time to carry various tents, food, medicines, animals like elephants, horses, camels, donkeys, cows, buffaloes, sheep, goats, labourers, cooks, workers, etc., along with the army. After the establishment of those two base camps, no enemy launched an attack and the troops were also never called back or transferred elsewhere. The two cantonments therefore stayed on and their resource station lay in between them in the 5- mile territory.

Steadily, as time passed by, businessmen and other people began visiting and later resided there. Gradually their numbers increased. A sense of complacency grew and the soldiers began to marry and form families.[23] As the years rolled by, the children of those soldiers grew up and found employment there only. Moreover, the Muslim rulers encouraged the development of a township there. With a growth in business, the small settlement soon developed into a city. It was named Jalalpur after Resaldar Jalal Khan who laid the foundation of this settlement.

## The *Mohalla* of the Respected *Bhattu Pathans*

Initially, Jalalpur consisted of two well-known *mohallas*. One of them was of the Afghani *bhattu pathan* soldiers who camped 2 miles off the river Betwa. It was called Bhattu *Tola* and is still there. Since the *pathans* were the first to settle there, the elders of the community are still regarded with reverence today. The other group of 500 *mughal* soldiers, which had settled in the jungles 5 miles away from the *pathan* out-post, was later transformed into Madar *tola,* which also still exists. Between these two localities, several other *tolas* cropped up in due course of time, e.g., Saidbara, Chaudhrana,

Kajyana, Kasaura, Nalbandhyana, Jugyana, Sukalyana, Chamroara, Puranisarai, Naisarai, Purana Baazar, Naya Baazar etc. I originate from these *pathans* who resided in this Bhattu Mohalla of Jalalpur.[24] Allah has blessed me, Rahman Khan, son of Mohammad Khan. I came by his consent to this island [Surinam][25] and have spread seeds in Demarara [British Guyana] where my eldest son Suleman Khan has settled. I sincerely thank Allah, Holy Rabbul Aalmeen without whose permission nothing is possible. Aameen. Aameen.

## *Jetha Tazia*: Grand Spectacle

In order to honour and remember the *pathan* clan of the Bhattu Mohalla, colourful turban clothes[26] adorn the *tazia* during *moharram.* It is called *jetha tazia* due to its huge dimension and is also known as the *tazia* of the *pathans*. It is made of netted material and its splendor is unparalleled in the whole of the district. People from far-off places come to see it and they wonder about its craftmanship. Though similar *tazias* are made elsewhere too, none can challenge *jetha tazia's* grandeur.

On the ninth day of *moharram*, the *jetha tazia* is taken out for procession from one centre only when all the elite Hindus and Muslims, high officials, other *tazias* of the town and the musicians have gathered around it. The same is followed on the seventh day at the time of Alham. After the gathering, the *jetha tazia* is carried along with the procession with music and much fanfare. This *tazia* then leads the masses and other *tazias* follow it once it passes the *chowk* where they are constructed. The procession, then, marches through the whole city and finishes the next morning when the *jehta tazia* returns to its own square. During that whole period and on the tenth day, the soul of Hazrat Imam Hassan Hussain is remembered in Allah's name. Words cannot express this moment of divinity.

During the night of procession the whole town is illuminated. Fire-works and fêtes are plenty and several thousands of rupees are spent on the festival. The scene is inexpressible but worth viewing. On the tenth day too, the *jetha tazia* is again lifted in the daytime and after roaming through all the streets of the city, it is buried at four in the evening at the square. On this day arrangements are made to feed thousands of poor and destitute with *pulao*, *rotis* and meat in the name of Hazrat Imam Hassan and Hussain. Various games, like wrestling, but also circus and fêtes etc., are organized in different places. People with different types of drums and instruments walk along while some ride camels or pull carriages or carts with heavy drums. The cacophony and noise is typical and beyond description.

If someone is displeased and has not come to witness the *jetha tazia's tazim*, then the *jetha tazia* would not march past his doors. Moreover, if due to any reason the *jetha tazia* does not cross a square, the *tazia* of that square would neithert be lifted nor taken out for procession and the mourning rituals would be performed at the chowk itself. On the tenth day the *tazia* would be buried there in the evening. Similarly, if a wealthy person or official, be it Hindu or Muslim, avoids the *jetha tazia*'s *tazim* due to any displeasure, the *tazia* would not stop to pay its respect at the person's doorstep. This is deemed to be very disgraceful. The procession stops at the gates of the affluents (rich Hindus or others), where dry fruits, sweets and other niceties laden on camels are distributed among them. After partaking in these refreshments in Allah's name, the *tazia* proceeds. The *pathans* of Jalapur are still respected. Even the rich Hindus (*pandas*) highly respect the *pathans* be they rich or poor. The *pathans* are treated well and honored till today.[27]

## The Tomb of Jalal Khan Wali

Thank Allah, Holy Rabbul Aalameen Elahi, for death spares no one. The famous and brave Resaldar Jalal Khan Sahab, on whose initiative and Khuda's grace this small town of Jalalpur came into existence, also met his doom. The place was named after him. After his demise, he was renamed as Jalal Khan Wali. It is said that on the third day of his death, divine flowers were found on his grave. The concrete tomb of Jalal Khan Wali was constructed about 2 miles off the twin cities on the bank of the river Betwa.[28] This place is known as Jalal Khan Wali ka Ghat. During the monsoon, this place harbours the boats and the boatmen recall Jalal Khan Wali before untying the boat and crossing the river. No incident of drowning or any other mishap has occurred here till date. Such is Allah's blessing.

Of the two tombs present there, the first has twelve carpets and houses Jalal Khan Wali's grave. The second tomb adjoining the first one is called Janana Makbara and is devoid of any door. No one knows what lies within. It consists of a small opening under the *gumbaz* from where every Friday evening, a light can be seen and the fragrance of incense can be smelt. A *fakir* is the caretaker of these two buildings and on Friday evenings, prayers etc. are performed at Jalal Khan Wali's tomb.

## Khuda's Miracle or Jalal Khan Wali's Deeds?

I have been a witness to the following incident. A few meters away from Jalal Khan Wali's *ghat* is another *ghat*, which has two parts. One is meant for women and the other for men to take bath. At the first site, three *surahis* have been built for the Hindus where they can do their *pujas* in the name of their deities. Behind this is a garden. Women, rich or poor, come and bath here.

One day, the wife of a famous rich man, Jhaulal Baniya came for a bath. She sat on the steps of the bank and started bathing. The water level of the river was high due to the rains and the wet steps were covered with slippery algae and moss. Suddenly, the woman slipped and fell into the water. The swift current swept her away. The woman shouted and screamed and several boatmen rushed to her rescue. As soon as one of them reached her, she disappeared but appeared after some time a little farther on. When the boats came near to her, she again drowned. Her head became visible soon afterwards a few meters further down. The boatmen came close again only to see her drown for the third time. However, after the fourth drowning episode, the woman was found standing in knee-deep water on the other side of the river. She was brought to the shore assisted by the boatmen.

Many people standing on the riverbank witnessed this whole incident, and by the time the woman was safely taken out of the water, her husband had arrived. He was extremely happy and praised Allah, and after wishing in the name of Ram and Sita thanked everyone present there for the miraculous act and their help. Then the woman was helped back to her residence.

On hearing about the episode, the whole community turned up at Jhaulal's door to see the woman. After consoling her they expressed their pleasure at her safe return. Then they asked her how she survived, since she did not know swimming at all. She feared that the miraculous old man would again throw her away if she said the truth. But after getting assurance from the people, she agreed to speak out the truth. She said thus: 'I slipped and fell into the river and began to sink. The current pulled me down and I could not breathe. As the water filled my lungs and I started to loose my senses, a tall old Muslim with a white beard and dressed in fine fabric appeared. He was a fair man and had clear blue eyes. He came to me, softly caught my hands and pulled me out of the water. When my head surfaced, I inhaled air just before I sank again. This happened three times during which I desperately tried to swim but it was in vain. The fourth time the holy soul caught me again and angrily pulled me out with great force. Suddenly I could feel the ground beneath my feet and when I stood up I found myself in shallow water. The good old man was nowhere to be seen thereafter'. The woman took a deep breath and resumed: 'My Lord and my elders, this old man was my saviour. It is only because of him that I am alive today'.

After hearing this, Jhaulal ran to different *maulvis*, *kazis* and renowned *pandits* of the city and when they were all assembled he narrated the whole incident. He then pleaded: 'My dear gentlemen, please tell me whether this is a spirit's act or God's miracle'. These wise men with various religious backgrounds pondered and came to the conclusion that it was Allah's order, which the spirit of Jalal Khan had enacted because he did not want his name to be tarnished. The *ghat* had not claimed any life before and should not do so ever.

Jhaulal then fed thousands of poor in the name of Allah and Jalal Khan Wali and distributed clothes and money. The next day he gave a big party to all the Hindus and Muslims and invited all the bigwigs of the society including the high salaried officials. Jhaulal was, however, not satisfied. He now desired to repair and reconstruct the Jalal Khan Wali *ghat*, which had collapsed at several places. A few days after the incident, Jhaulal hired workers and began the work.

The lowermost step had not been finished when Jhaulal dreamt of Jalal Khan Wali who ordered him to stop the repair works. 'Do not do this', he said, 'because I do not want a non-Muslim to invest his money on any of my business'. However, Jhaulal thought that it was only a dream and continued with the renovation. The first step was completed. When the second step was being made, he again dreamt of Wali Khan. The man again ignored it and the second step was made.

When work began for the third step, Jalal Khan Wali once more visited him in his dream and sternly forbade him to continue this work. The *baniya* however, was not convinced as his death was nearing and this had subdued his senses. Before the completion of the third step, Jhaulal met his doom. But prior to his death, he told everyone about his dreams and the fatal arrogance of the old man. With his death, the repair work also stopped. Such was the sanctity of Jalal Khan Wali that he would not accept anything from a person who was non-Muslim, be it money or even any eatables or clothes! I like to tell you the teaching of Allah the Holy who wants the Muslim believers to be generous and refrain from greed. Ameen!

*Doha*

*Avoid Wali's resentment*
*Salman wrongs and loses His contentment*
*Man should always act with wisdom*
*And neither hurt others nor should he forsake His Kingdom.*

## The Degeneration of Jalalpur

*Chaupai*

*When the end draws near, intelligence loses sight*
*Right seems wrong and wrong seems right*
*This town once housed the wealthy and the rich*
*Personal interests ruined them, greed did bewitch*
*Ignoring the fakir's plea, they invited the wrath of Wali*
*Muslims lost their minds and along with it their gaiety*
*Therefore, if man acts with understanding and discretion*
*Then neither sorrow nor bankruptcy shall be life's direction*

As long as the Muslim Sultanate lasted, Jalalpur was a flourishing town with wealth, fame, sufficient population and trade. Both Hindus and Muslims were well off and lived in prosperity. Trade took place and businessmen from far and near visited the town. My elders taught me that from this town alone, gypsies (*banjara*s) took 15000 bulls and brought them to other places for business. In return they brought goods that were sold here. Though small, this town paralleled any big city in respect to its business and affluence. But when the Muslim rule ended in Hindustan paving the way for the British Empire, Jalalpur suffered a heavy blow.[29]

As the English established themselves, they decided to bring about a change in the whole country that suited them.[30] New government offices like post offices, police stations, courts, middle schools, etc., replaced the system that had existed under the Muslim Sultanate. It is true that as kismet manifests itself, proper advice looks bad and everything and everyone turns against the place or person. I have already narrated the futile attempt of Jhaulal *baniya* to renovate the Jalal Khan Wali Ghat. About 2 years later, twelve doors of the tomb of Jalal Khan Wali's shrine fell into the river and were washed away. Then the *fakir*, who was also the caretaker of the place, dreamt that Jalal Khan Wali wished that the *ghat* be repaired and the expense be borne by the affluent Muslims of Jalalpur. Jalal Khan Wali had spoken in the *fakir*'s dream: 'Otherwise the manner in which my tomb has become abandoned, so would be my township'. He also had added: 'I wish that those Muslims who are able should donate part of their earnings to reconstruct the place. I do not want any non-Muslims to give money for this purpose because I detest their ill-gotten wealth. The *fakir* did accordingly and spread the word around among the wealthy Muslims, but alas, nobody paid any attention to his sayings. Everyone thought that the *fakir* had fabricated a story to mint money and thereafter they shunned him.

The poor *fakir* went from pillar to post but in vain. Common sense and wisdom deserted the minds of the people who were heading for an economic crisis. When the *fakir* heard that he had been labelled as a liar, a wanderer aiming at making money, he was very perturbed and fell silent. What else could the poor soul do? One single wealthy Muslim household could have contributed enough to do all the work, but alas it was not to be and the decline was imminent. As a result, there is not even a single rich Muslim in Jalalpur today while the situation favours the Hindus.

From that day onward, *Khuda* diposed the Muslims from His virtue and after a few years, the government officer's buildings of Jalalpur began to crack and wither. Muslims had owned most of these buildings and many of them had worked there. The government, then, ordered the new offices to be shifted to Hamirpur[31], about 8 to 10 miles away from Jalalpur, near the confluence of the rivers Betwa and Yamuna. This town has become a district since then.[32] Soon thereafter, the administrative buildings and the court were also transferred to Muskara, 5 miles away on the bank of the river Berma (near its confluence with the river Betwa). Several Muslims held high posts in these government offices.

Later, these buildings were again shifted from Muskara to Maudaha (from where I passed my middle school) and partially to Raath (where Rahim Sai runs his shop). This led to a complete breakdown of the economy and livelihood of Jalalpur, and Muslims of the town bore the brunt. Their houses and hotels now lay abandoned and many have fled to seek greener pastures. They suffered heavily and the economy plunged to even greater depths. The streets were abandoned as its residents left one after the other. One could only hear the cries and barking of the dogs. The huge mansions now had bats and spiders as tenants. Empty buildings became toilets and dumping grounds.

The *fakir's* prediction had come true and the Muslims bit the dust. Their wealth had vanished and they now rubbed their empty hands in repentance. But time and tide wait for none and they do not make a comeback in such situations. This was the story of the rise and fall of the town of the *pathans* and *mughals*: Jalalpur. The story of my elders who migrated to Bharkhari village about 5 miles from Jalalpur must however wait since I first wish to say something about the brave *sher bahadur* [lion hunter] Haider Khan before I embark on that story [about my parents].

## The Brave Sher Bahadur of Jalalpur

My two sisters were married off to two brothers of the Madar Tola (the colony of the *mughals*) in Jalalpur[33]. My elder brother in-law was Sardar Khan who worked for Mohanlal Panda, one of the wealthiest persons of Jalalpur. Allah had blessed him with a huge abdomen. He could not easily move or walk and was even unable to clean himself after defecation! He kept a servant for this purpose.

Fateh Khan was my younger brother-in-law. My sister's sister in–law was married to Haider Khan, a well-known brave lion hunter (*sher bahadur*). They all lived in the same locality and whenever we visited them, we were sure to call on Haider Khan too. Haider Khan was a very cheerful man. People said that whenever Haider Khan wished to eat meat, he would tell his wife to grind and prepare spices before going out for hunting. He would take his gun with him and would shortly afterwards return with a buck or deer.

One day, five of us paid him a visit in Jalalpur. Haider Khan came to meet us and as our talk progressed the topic shifted from one to another and finally focused on hunting. I jokingly said that no one in Jalalpur seemed to know anything about hunting while in our village, Bhai Ramjan Khan was a deft hunter and could kill a deer any time he wanted and we would feast on it. This was enough to instigate Haider Khan who immediately picked up his gun saying: 'you from Bharkhari know nothing about the feasts. I will now show you and return with a deer'. He then turned to my elder sister and said: 'Prepare the spices and make everything ready' and insisted this work to be done before he embarked on his mission. After about 2 hours he returned with the prey on his shoulder. We were surprised and praised him for his effort.

This man was also famous for his duels with tigers. He hunted deer with a gun while he fought tigers with a sharp cutting weapon (*katar*). He had slained a number of tigers with it and the government had awarded him the title 'Sher–e–Bahadur'. Whenever a tiger was to be killed, the officers and hunters of the area would summon Haider Khan. A group of noise making people with drums and other musical instruments from three sides would scare the animal to run in the fourth direction only to find Haider Khan brandishing his weapon. The other hunters did not move till the animal had proceeded towards Haider Khan. On seeing the animal, Haider Khan would shout, inviting it to attack him. He would then challenge the animal, saying 'Hey you, if you are a real tiger, be strong and fight.' The animal would roar and accept the challenge. Eye to eye, they would prepare to attack each other. As soon as Haider Khan winked the animal would pounce on him and Haider Khan would evade it by ducking. Then, before the tiger could turn, Haidar Khan would thrust his weapon into the animal's torso. Doing so, he would move away from the wounded prey, which could not stand up against him again. He had employed this technique to slay several lions and tigers and the people of the locality, as well as the high officials of the English government, all talked a lot about his bravery.

## Haider Khan as the Tiger's Prey

Thank the Almighty for creating such an extraordinary personality like Haider Khan. Yet, alas! He was not given longevity. One day a new collector was posted in the District of Hamirpur. This Englishman was very fond of hunting and heard about Haider Khan's adventures. Once the collector *sahab* got an opportunity to go for hunting, and he summoned Haider Khan, three days in advance to accompany him. On that particular day the collector, along with his convoy of hunters and noisemakers, camped in Jalalpur. They moved into the jungles and as usual with the noisemakers from three sides and the hunters from the fourth.

As the wild animals fled away from the noise, the hunters who had been waiting with guns and ammunition shot at them. Suddenly a huge lion came into view. Haider Khan was immediately conveyed the message and came in action. Haider Khan jumped in front and challenged the lion. The lion roared and the two stared at each other. There was dead silence as everyone watched from hidings with bated breath. The enemy prepared himself to attack at the most opportune moment. Some of the onlookers trembled with fear. The collector *sahab* admired the hair-raising contest while seated on his horseback. He had never witnessed such a thing before: A man armed with only a small *katar* in front of a big wild cat. This was something he had never dreamt of before. But then the inevitable happened.

As soon as Haider Khan dropped his eyelids, his waist belt opened. To fasten it again his hands moved down.... and suddenly the lion pounced upon him just at that fatal moment which did not last more than a second. The fight was over. All the cleverness and deftness of Haider Khan betrayed him and he met his end. A sharp blow by the lion's paw struck Haider Khan with exceptional speed and extracted a pound of flesh and his life out of his body. All the spectators watched the gruesome incident in awe but could hardly move to rescue the victim. Haider Khan left this world leaving behind his wife and children.

Another hunter ultimately shot the winner. The death of Haider Khan spread like wildfire and led to the closure of the school and market of the town. The collector was very perturbed and a 3-day long mourning was observed. The flags flew at half-mast and the collector *sahab* donated Rs. 500 for the upbringing of Haidar Khan's children. The famous *pandas* Mohanlal and Mannilal of the town called upon Haider Khan's widow and met all the expenses incurred during the last rites. They also promised to sponsor the marriage of two of his daughters when they grew up (Haider Khan had four daughters and no son). His neighbours took responsibility to take care of and marry off the remaining two daughters in due course. The *pandas* also gave the widow 10 acres of land for cultivation throughout her life. Thus the bravery of the Sher-e-Bahadur, Haider

Khan of Jalalpur came to an end because of a wild *sher bahadur*. It is true that a swimmer usually dies in the river, a tree climber from a fall and a snake catcher from snakebite. Here lay a lion, mauled and killed by a lion. Haider Khan passed away but his fame and memory are immortal. Aameen. Aameen. Rabbul Aalmeen!

## The Migration of my Elders to Bharkhari Village

I am Rahman Khan, son of Mohammad Khan, s/o Bakshi Khan, s/o Baaz Khan, s/o Shamsher Khan, s/o Afzal Khan, Bhattu Khan, an Afghani *pathan*, who was a lieutenant in Jalal Khan's army. Afzal Khan had been recruited in Afghanistan and got employment in the Delhi Sultanate. He guided a small group of men under Resaldar Jalal Khan and brought the latter to a place on the banks of the Betwa, where later the town of Jalalpur was founded.

When the tide turned against Jalalpur, and its residents were forced out of the town, my father Mohammed Khan[34] became friendly with Chetram Marwari, a *zamindar* of Bharkhari village, about 5 miles away from Jalalpur. They established contact when my father was the head of the fourth grade employees in the court and the government paid him Rs 8 per month. Chetram Marwari, the *zamindar* of Bharkhari frequently visited the court and met government officials on various accounts. They met each other in order to facilitate the work in the advantage of both. When government offices were removed from Jalalpur, Chetram Marwari[35] asked my father to work under him and look after his business and he offered same payment. Chetram was a small *zamindar* and had about sixty villages under him. He was a successful bussinesman. A detailed account of his business activities would take me 25 years.

My father and Lala Kamta Prasad were the two right hands of Chetram Marwari. They managed all the affairs. Due to this job procurement our family shifted to Bharkhari village. Chetram provided us with two ploughs, four bulls and several acres (150 *bighas*) of land for cultivation on a low revenue rate. He also provided two labourers for a year on his expense. After 12 years of cultivation, the land was to be transferred in my father's name.

By Khuda's blessing the business did well and we were quite well off. After 12 years my father started plantations on a small part of the land and grew mango, jamun, mahuwa, plum, guava and other trees. Adjoining this land a small graveyard for our family was prepared.[36] My eldest aunt was the first one to be buried there.

The system of leasing land by the *zamindar* was as follows: A deed was signed between the landlord and the taker (the second party)[37] which was valid for twelve years during which the second party would sow and harvest on the piece of land and pay the *lagan* (revenue) yearly. The second party had the right to build a house, mosque, dig a well, plant trees, etc., and even give it to someone else on lease at a higher rate. The landlord would not object if the payments were regular and on time. If the payment was defaulted by 3 years the landlord had the right to take the help of the government and evacuate the plot. In those circumstances the deed would be dissolved. In the new agreement (if entered into) the landlord had the right to increase the revenue.

If a third person or party was to lease the land from the second party the first party (landlord) had no say provided his payments were being made properly. This third party had no right to claim the land after the twelve-year period had come to an end and no agreement was needed with the landlord in this regard. In case of death of the second party after at least one year of agreement, his son had the right to continue cultivation under the same conditions, and the land would become his property after 5 years only.

## My Birth

My father, Mohammed Khan, was the eldest of two brothers. My uncle, Maan Khan, had four sons and one daughter and lived in the city of Charkhari[38] where Raja Malkhan Singh ruled. Ramjan Khan, Nawab Khan and Imam Khan were my cousin brothers. Dildal Khan was my maternal uncle and Sardar Khan was his son. My second aunt was married to Chote Khan and Badal Khan was their son. Dayam Khan was the son of my maternal grandfather, Faiz Khan, and he had two sons: Bahadur Khan and Pahalwan Khan. They lived in the village Saidnagar Kotra. All the other families mentioned above reside in Bharkhari village. My father Mohammed Khan and my mother Bhulan had three children. My elder sister was Kariman while Hukman was the second and I, Rahman Khan, was the youngest and the only son. (After my migration to Surinam, my elder sister became mother of a son named Gulzar Khan, my nephew).

I was born on 11 August 1874 (according to the Hindu calender this is on Bhado Badi 6 (Tuesday) Vikram Samwat 1931)[39]. During this period, the Hindus celebrate Hari Chat on a grand scale offering various kinds of roasted grains (*bhunja*) to their deities. It was on the very day that this festival was going on that the world heard my first cry. My father asked Pandit Chaturbhuj Vyas of the village (who would later on die in my presence) to prepare my birth horoscope (*kundli*). On the occasion of my marriage, my neighbour, Pandit Mohanlal Dubey read out the day and year on which I was born, which I memorised and mentioned above.

## A School in My Village

Zamindar Chetram Marwari's *karinda* (assistant), Lala Kamta Prasad, was a rich gentleman and his elder brother Lala Mathura Prasad was a government clerk in Bharkhari village. His two sons Badrinath and Kedarnath were of my age. When I was 8 years old, my father decided to put me in school but there was none in the village.[40] So my father talked to Lala Mathura Prasad, Lala Kamta Prasad and a few other village elders and stressed upon the need for a school in the vilage. In order to open a school in a village the government had framed certain rules and regulations being:

1. A clear ventilated house.
2. At least thirty children.
3. Half yearly salaries (of all teachers) are deposited in the government office.

The government would take over the responsibility of running the school on a permanent basis only after 6 month's of its existence. (Otherwise the government only opened schools in the towns and cities).

Accordingly, Lala Mathura Prasad and my father worked hard to arrange for forty students who were required for starting a school. A nice plastered veranda near the well of the village that was built by Chetram Marwari was chosen as a site for the school building [see photograph]. The teachers' 6-month salaries (at the rate of Rs. 7 per month) were collected and deposited in the government office. It was 3 months later, in 1883, that the village Bharkhari got a school. I was 9 years old when I began my study in this school. Baijnath was our schoolteacher. But since the village was small, the study level of the students soon began to dwindle and after about 3 years, in

1886, the school was forced to close down. We were very happy to be relieved from school and studies.

## Studying in another School

It is true that a bull does not die according to the wish of a tanner. Our happiness for being relieved from school was very short-lived. After a few days only, on a fine Sunday evening, my father called us and ordered Kale Khan (my cousin) and myself to go the very next morning along with six Hindu children to a school in Dumari village. Kale Khan was older to me and was very naughty. I tried hard to feign sickness but my attempt failed miserably and my father gathered all the eight children the following morning and set off to Dumari village half a mile away. On reaching our new school, we met Munshi Kaluram Sahab who was to be our teacher there. After a brief talk, my father enrolled all of us in the school register.

During those days the classes were numbered in the opposite order descending from class VII to class I. Class VII had two sections: Ba and Alif. A new student was admitted to class Ba (pre-primary). After obtaining some knowledge, he would be promoted to class Alif. The (government) Deputy Inspector for Education would conduct the exams till class V. The class teacher was not allowed to promote any child by himself and every year each student was examined by the Inspector Sahab. The Assistant Sahab took the examinations of class IV and III. He was a higher ranked official. These examinations took place in a center where students from four or five schools would gather to appear in the exams. The students who passed this rigorous test were awarded books and a slate-pencil. One could pass in one of the two kinds of grades. Those who could answer some questions but not all were passed with reservation while those who made no mistakes at all received first division. The joy of passing the examination was greater than receiving a 100-rupee note, while those who failed were grief stricken and these students were far more depressed over this failure than over their father's death!

Munshi Kaluram Sahab asked us about our previous education and after testing our knowledge, admitted my cousin and myself in class V while the six others were sent to class VI. The medium of teaching in the school was Hindi, because 90 per cent of students were Hindus and only 10 per cent Muslims. Munshi Kaluram Sahab was well versed in Hindi as well as Urdu and in the primary school he had to teach both languages up to class III.[41] The middle school encompassed class II and I. The government provided a stipend of Rs. 3 per month and free boarding and lodging. All village students were provided these facilities during the first 3 years to enable them to pass the middle school. If anyone failed during this period, they had to study and pass on their own expenses as a private candidate. This stipend was not given to the children residing in towns and cities.

This time, my cousin and I began our quest for knowledge in earnest knowing that there was no other way out. Munshi Kaluram also did everythingpossible. Particularly, because my father had secretly offered Kaluram, at the time of our admission, the foodgrain produce of two *bighas*[42] of land. This arrangement would last during our total study period in the school. We did quite well in school upto class III when I was overcome with big-headedness. I failed in class III while my cousin Kale Khan was promoted and went on to join middle school in Kulpahar. He later on also passed the middle school and found employment.

The cause of my failure was as follows: when we began studying in the *madarsa* in Umri village[43], more than the expected number of candidates passed the examination each year. Munshi Kaluram Sahab was initially paid a salary of Rs 7 per month. After one year of teaching in our school he was given Rs. 20 as a bonus and his salary was hiked to Rs. 8 per month. After 2 years he would get Rs. 25 and after three years Rs. 30 were given to him because we all did well in the exams. His salary also increased by Rs. 3 per month after the third year examination. But when I failed in the fourth year exam, no bonus was given to the teacher. Our confidence, developed during the time of passing the primary school, vanished. Though we had prepared well, we were not successful that year.

We were with six students in class III: I (Rahman Khan), Gangadin, Khyaliram, Vrindavan, Udayram and Laxman. Gangadin and Vrindavan were *kshatriyas* (*rajputs*), Khyaliram was a *kayasta*, Udayram a *brahmin* and Laxman was a *dom* belonging to the lower castes. Among them, Laxman had a low IQ and was weak in studies, while the others seemed to be good at everything. Whenever the teacher instructed Laxman to take our help in all matters we would make fun of him. The poor fellow would learn the answers by rote and was unable to independently solve the problems while we were proud and overconfident. During the exams, the five of us wrongly solved the questions yet Laxman, though following the wrong method, reached at the right answer, which he had remembered by heart. As the final answer was taken into consideration during the examination, the five of us failed, while Laxman passed. A year of hard labour had gone in vain.

Yet, the following year (i.e 1890), I passed for the primary school examination and thanked Allah thousand times. I stayed at home for a month waiting for a call from Munshiji, my teacher. When he called me, I quickly obliged and met him. Munshiji asked whether I wanted to be a teacher or a clerk (that is a *patwari*, a registrar of the village land accounts). In order to become a *patwari*, one had to undergo three months of clerical training followed by an exam. One could get the job only after that, provided vacancy was available in the government. I however wished to pursue a teaching career or become a government accountant and therefore was required to appear in another exam to avail a stipend for higher education. If I passed the exam, the government would admit me in a school where I had no relatives and provide me a stipend of Rs. 3 per month along with all the other facilities as mentioned in schedule 40. After obtaining the pass certificate, I would be eligible for a job as *mulajim* (civil servant). I opted for the latter. Munshiji was pleased and asked me to draft an application.

## Passing the Examination with Merit and the Stipend

I quickly began to draft an application in Allah's name. Munshiji made the necessary corrections and forwarded the copy to the Deputy Inspector Sahab for education. After a month Munshiji informed me that my application had been accepted and I was to appear for examinations in Hamirpur district starting on 25 February 1891. The first day of oral tests would be followed by a written mathematics test and a geography test. The standard corresponded to middle school level and not to class IV or III. The government examiner would provide printed question papers, answer sheets, pen, ink, etc. during this test. Munshiji had also explained: 'Please write the right number of the question before your answer and attempt to solve those questions you know in methodical way. After finishing, tie the paper in a bundle and write your name and complete address on it and submit it to the superior sahab present there'. I was to return on the fourth day. I thanked Munshiji, went back home and told my father about my visit to my teacher's place. My father was very happy and took me to the mosque to seek Allah's blessing for the upcoming examination.

The district town of Hamirpur was situated about fifteen miles from Bharkhari village at the confluence of the Jamuna and Betwa rivers. It took us one whole day to cover the distance. I eagerly waited for my examinations. Two days before the scheduled date, my father called my uncle Nazm Khan, who was my stepmother's (she was my father's first wife and with whom he had no issues) younger brother to stay with us. Uncle Nazm Khan was given the duty to accompany me on his horse to Hamirpur next day and stay with me in a house which Chetram Marwari owned till my exams were over. My father had ordered: 'let him take bath in the river each morning and bring him on time after a light breakfast to the examination center along with his admit card. At four p.m you should bring him back to Chetram Marwari's residence. Feed him properly and ensure his well-deserved rest. Bring him back here after the exams'. My uncle did accordingly and we set off for Hamirpur the very next morning. Two sacks of food cooked especially for us by my mother were put on the back of the horse while my uncle walked along on foot.

We reached the bank of Betwa by late afternoon. There we saw a bridge made up of 75 rafts. Every year this bridge was constructed during the monsoon when the level of the river water was high. It was dismantled once the water level lowered during winter. We had to pay 1 paisa per person to a contractor who had been given this job. We also had to pay 4 paisa per horse or a camel and 4 annas per cart. Elephants were not allowed to cross the bridge. Accordingly, my uncle paid 6 paise to the *munshi* who collected the toll on the contractor's behalf. Unfortunately, at the time I had no idea that students were waived from this toll tax. It was only after 4 days when we returned after the exams that I came to know. At that time, we met the contracter himself and he asked about my purpose of visit. When I told him that I had visited the place for taking examinations, he immediately called the *munshi* who had collected the tax from us four days back. The contracter scolded him and ordered him to return our money. The *munshi* apologised to us and I, with folded hands, said: 'May Allah the Holy one forgive you. I am a young student and not yet worth anything. So you too, forgive us'. Then we proceeded. Late that evening, we reached our place of shelter by the grace of God. When we returned home we told everyone about our safe journey and everyone felt glad and happy for us. Aameen, Aameen. Rabbul Aalmeen.

## Boarding at the Middle School

After a few days, Munshiji received a letter from the government in which I was selected for a stipend in the middle school. I pleaded to Munshiji to help me get admission in a school in Jalalpur. He said: 'Rahman Khan, I think the government will not accept your proposal for Jalalpur because your roots are there and moreover, your two sisters are married and settled there. Anyway, I shall forward your letter to the Deputy Inspector Sahab but you shall have to go wherever government thinks proper'. 'Please do so for my sake', I had pleaded and I sincerely prayed in my heart to Allah for Munshiji's and his family's wellbeing.

I received a reply from the government in which my plea to study in Jalalpur was rejected on the ground that I had my relatives there. I was to pursue my studies in the Maudaha subdivisional school [see photograph]. I was asked to report there by 1 July 1891. Munshiji told me to meet master Lala Ishwari Prasad Sahab in the Maudaha School. 'He is a very simple and God-fearing man. He is a teacher par excellence and there is no one else like him in the whole district. He has a 32- years teaching experience in the school of Patwaris. Since the last 3 years, he functions as headmaster in this school in Maudaha. His house is in the town of Mahoba, about 10 to 12 miles from Maudaha where a railway line connects Allahabad with Jhansi. He has six able sons who have studied well and now hold respectable government posts. You will however, not understand Masterji's words during the first 6 months of your studies'. I was taken aback and asked: 'How will I be able to study if I will not be able to follow what he says'. 'You fool' said Munshiji, 'what I mean to say is that the man is old and has a trembling voice but whatever he teaches is very informative. Do not worry and go to him as he has never failed in his teaching mission'.

All the *brahmin*, *kshatriya*, *baniya* and *kayastha* boys who studied with me in the school in Umri had left their studies after class III or IV and had started their own business or other work. Only Kale

Khan and myself went on to study till middle school. The time passed by and the day of my departure for the middle school arrived.

On Friday 30 June, the day of my departure, we offered *namaaz* and my father packed my requirements for the hostel and put the baggage on a cart while I went to say good-bye to my friends. We boarded the bullock cart accompanied by our servant Binda Chamar and began our journey in Allah's name.

The town of Maudaha was about 8 miles from my village. Chargaon, Kargaon, Masgaon, Dhungaon and Mancha were the villages that we had to pass to reach there. When we were between Dhungaon and Mancha, it began to rain heavily and it became very difficult to ride over the wet muddy road. Somehow we managed to reach the house of Dayam Ali, the *zamindar* of Mancha, by evening. When we landed at his doorstep, Dayam Ali was seated in his portico. Seeing my father he exchanged greetings and offered us to stay at his place for the night. My father was hesitant because we were complete strangers. He told Dayam Ali that I was to join school the next day. The kind *zamindar* did not change his offer and we had to conceed to his request. Moreover, he informed us that the weather was bad and that even the bulls needed some rest. He therefore thought it proper for us to spend the night there as the following day was Saturday and the school would be closed anyway.

The *zamindar* then ordered his servants to untie the bulls and feed them in a proper shed while we made ourselves comfortable in his portico. Then we ate and fell asleep. The next morning, we bade farewell to our host. Just before leaving he said: 'Son, go and study well. Whenever you pass through this place on your way back home or to school, you stay here as my guest'. I thanked him and left the place while saying '*inshah Allah*'. This visit paved the way for my marriage, which was to follow in due course of time.

Maudaha was about four miles from Mancha and when we reached there in the afternoon, the gate of the school was locked. After knocking, a boy named Ghasiram opened the gate and inquired about the purpose of our visit. He informed the Headmaster, who resided in the school campus, about our arrival. My father bowed to greet him and I followed him. He was a very old man and had a long white beard. He had no muscles left in his body and was toothless.

We were allowed inside and I presented the government's letter regarding my admission. The Headmaster read it and ordered

Ghasiram to take my belongings into the hostel. If Ghasiram had not been there we could never have understood him. Ghasiram, a *baniya's* son belonging to the town, studied in class III in the school. He immediately took my baggage and we were guided to the boarding house, which was in the compound itself. The hostel had six rooms in each row. The size of each room was 12 feet x 10 feet. The rooms were all locked. Ghasiram opened room number three and gave me the key. He then helped me to put my things inside the room. After finishing all his work he went back home. Our bullocks and cart were tied outside the school while we made ourselves at home in room number three.

The next morning my father took me around the city. We visited several places and in the evening I was left alone in the hostel with loads of advice and eatables while he departed wishing me good luck. I was the lone son of my parents and was never left alone like this before; not even during any party. My father never ate his meal until I had returned from school. This was our first separation and our grief was immense.

## Some notable Features of Maudaha

The city of Maudaha had its own distinct charm.[44] Whereas 85 per cent of its population was Muslim, 5 per cent were Hindus.[45] There was no river but a fortress built by Nawab Nizammudin Khan Sahab of Banda was worth seeing. The government and subdivisional offices of the British rulers were housed inside the premises of the fort. The treasury was situated in the centre of the fort and adjoining it was a nice well-maintained garden and a mosque.

The Juma Masjid and a school were two important monuments built by the Sub-divisional officer Mirza Sahab [see photograph]. Besides the Juma Masjid and *Naya* (new) Bazaar, there was a small lake on the right side of which a small garden was located. On its left was a road leading to the market. The school was on the other side of the road near the fortress. The school building was tall and built on a high platform.

The town had its own magistrate office, a new and old market, Nai Sarai, a post office, a special market for ladies, etc. The *purana* (old) bazaar housed a Shiva temple, built by the *baniya* Mathura Prasad and therefore known as Mathura's Shivalaya. It was a tall artistic monument and a mirror was placed on the steeple of the round *gumbaz*, which reflected the sunrays over a distance of more than four miles.

Another landmark was the tomb of Pir Surkuru at the city center, which lay about 15 to 16 feet deep in the ground. Its boundary was of approximately the same size. A small but cemented house and a neem tree adorned the campus. The campus itself was only open at the top and otherwise surrounded by four walls. Surprisingly, even the heaviest rains did not inundate this area though it was devoid of any drain system. Its entrance was at the ground level. People said that the neem tree had once been a small piece of neem stem, which the Pir had used to clean his teeth. *Khuda* knows the truth. But it was a fact that if an ailing animal was cleaned and some ash was applied on the ailing parts in the name of the *pir* at his tomb, the animal often recovered.

The Mira Taal was one of the three big lakes of the city. It was located in the western part of the town and Mir Sahab had dug it. It was the biggest and the deepest among all the city's lakes. Cemented staircases surrounded all these three lakes. Mir Sahab had also built a huge *idgah* near the lake, which was so big that people from the twelve villages adjoining Maudaha gathered there only to offer *namaaz* during *id and bakr-id.* (One should know that 95 per cent of the rural population in the area was Muslim).[46]

During the month of October, the Hindus celebrated Ramlila around the Mira Taal. A *baniya* had dug the second lake, the Auro Taal, which was situated in the north of the city. The third lake in the eastern part of the town was called the Alhi Taal. During the summer season, once a year and near this pond, a month long fête was organised in memory of Ghazi Mian. Near this pond, close to the gate of Naya Bazaar, a rich harlot had constructed a decorative mosque, yet no Muslim offered *namaaz* there. The same place accommodated a market on every Tuesday and Saturday. Women operated a third market and though men could buy, they could not sell anything that day. On this day, women from the countryside brought vegetables and other crops to sell. The produce used to be fresher and the rate cheaper than the other by-weekly markets as the rural women sold off their things in a hurry to return back to their far-off villages before evening.

## The Story of a Stone Idol

In the south of Maudaha there was a road leading to the town of Banda. On this road a *peepal* (fig) tree was planted under which a stone idol was placed that sat with legs crossed on a pedestral. The arms of the statue were both broken, perhaps already since the time of Mohammad Gaznavi's invasions. The right thigh of the statue contained an Arabic inscription, which no one had deciphered that time.

After a year of study in Maudaha, a new sub-divisional officer named Namzan Muhammad Sahab was appointed. He had two sons for whom he had brought along a *maulvi* named Jafar Ali who had come from the Punjab at his expense. His sons were admitted in my school and all the students were invited to the feast on this occasion.

A few days later, officer sahab chanced upon the idol and the inscription engraved in it. Being puzzled, he returned back home and told the *maulvi* about his discovery.

After a couple of days, the two of them went to the place and the *maulvi* was shown the inscription engraved in the stone. Seeing it he fell silent. When the officer wondered about this silence, the *maulvi* told that he would reveal the contents only in the presence of all the wise men and religious leaders of the locality. The officer agreed. He then ordered his subordinates and policemen to make an announcement in the city that all people should gather near the fig tree on a particular day at four in the evening. The news spread everywhere and when our headmaster heard about it he permitted all his students to witness the event if they wished to.

On that particular day a huge crowd had gathered at the site. Wise and dim-witted, scholars and illiterates, rich and poor, everyone had come to listen to the *maulvi*. Even a blind resident of the town named Hafiz Nizammudin Sahab was present. Though Allah had deprived this man from eyesight right from his birth, he had nevertheless been blessed with an immense knowledge of the Holy Koran. Whenever there was any dispute regarding religion, this man was the one who would surely solve the controversy.

A few minutes after 4 o'clock, a vehicle arrived carrying the two men. Everyone greeted them. Subsequently, the officer ordered the learned few to get closer while the others were requested to stand a few steps away from the idol. Everyone followed his command and did accordingly. The *maulvi* stood upon the pedestal and asked whether anyone could come forward and read and explain the inscription. Yet not a single person moved.

The *maulvi* was in tears and turned to the officer saying: 'My Lord, before I start, I wish to ensure that my family is taken care of after this act of mine which is sure to drive me insane'. The officer asked him what he desired. The *maulvi* had replied: 'Sir, I wish that my family and children are taken care of'. His family lived in a village in Kanpur district and the officer immediately gave a written guarantee that he would take over the responsibility of looking after the *maulvi's* family. He even conferred a village in the name of his family. Upon doing this, all people present applauded for the officer. The *maulvi* too thanked him for his kind deed.

The *maulvi* then started reading the inscription loudly, so that the crowd could properly hear him. During this explanation he suddenly jumped from the pedestal however and started running. 'Catch him, catch him', the people shouted. There was big hullabaloo and everyone started running after the *maulvi.* Somehow, the crowd managed to overpower him and bring him to the officer's residence in his carriage. In the end, everyone felt extremely sorry for the poor soul, but all were helpless. The forbidden writing had led to the *maulvi's* insanity in the presence of everyone. The *maulvi* had been transformed into a mad man and the cryptic epitaph remained a mystery[47] .

## Admission in the Middle School

The school re-opened on Monday and the students began to arrive. They paid their respects to Munshiji and sat in their respective classrooms. I, a newcomer felt lonely in a completely different atmosphere. A village boy amidst the city folk with all new faces and I felt very odd indeed. I hesitantly entered the classroom, bowed and wished the headmaster Munshi Ishwari Prasad. Munshiji called me besides him and then turned to the class to issue a warning. 'Beware', he said, 'behave well with this boy or be prepared for a punishment'. Then he tried to console me and explained that I was like his son. This made me cry. He said: 'Do not worry everything will be all right. Be patient and happy and study nicely. Be friendly to your classmates and you will not feel lonely and if anyone troubles you, inform me at once and I shall straighten him'. I then felt relieved and at ease.

Subsequently, Munshiji entered my name in the school's register and placed me in class II. I immediately obeyed. After some time, Munshiji gave me a lesson to read which I did so in Allah's name but I understood nothing. Munshiji then ordered Salamatullah, a senior student of class I, to help me understand what Munshiji said till I was able to decipher his speech by myself. The boy agreed to this task. By Allah's grace I began to study in earnest and in few days time I was able to understand Munshiji's way of talking. The produce from 2 *bighas* of land that my father had promised as donation made Munshiji pay special attention to me during classes and even after school hours.

As the bell rang at 11 o'clock for lunch break, I went to my hostel room. There I found wheat flour and raw pulses, but no one to cook! I was exasperated, since I was totally ignorant in kitchen matters. I felt very sorry for myself and did not know how to react: whether to cry or try cooking. I had no idea how much pulses to boil and what to do with the flour but since I had to do something, I began with double the amount of flour I could eat and started kneading. Subsequently, I boiled trice the amount of dal I needed. Finally, my meal of half-cooked and half-burnt rotis of different shapes and sizes were nearly ready to be devoured along with a pot full of thick dal when the headmaster arrived. Seeing my accomplishment he shook his head and said something in his shivering voice of which I could understand only a couple of words. Then he chose five or six thin rotis and put them on the fire one by one. He subsequently baked them properly showing me how to do it. After this, he showed me how much of flour, pulses, oil, salt, etc., was required to prepare a meal for a boy like me saying, 'from now onwards, do not use more than this amount of these items to make your meal and cook it well as I have just illustrated. Thereafter, he walked away while I ate my food and kept some of it for the evening.

## Satanic Act

After 6 months, it was announced that examinations would begin on 15 June 1892 and conclude on 18 June. From that day onwards, we hugely changed our attitude towards studies and two shifts of harsh preparations followed. The first was from five in the evening to eleven in the night. The second shift started at two at night and continued upto six in the morning. Relaxation and play came to an abrupt end. I was 17 years old then and very often homesick. The hard routine, study and above all cooking troubled me and to this was added the fact that during this phase I got 3 hours sleep a day only. These all furthered my grief.

It was during that time that Satan struck. He had gauged my weakness. My mind was diverted from studies and I became very sad and homesick. No advice to pursue my studies seemed to affect me though I always prayed to Allah for his guidance. My heart refused to concede to my brains and I could find no way out. Whenever I became very perturbed, I would go out with my friends to the garden or market place but whatever I tried, I could not succeed in my mission to get the clear-mindedness needed for studies. Studies throughout night reduced my sleeping hours. The thought of the easy life at home made me crazy and I begged Allah to make me sick so that I could at least rest peacefully. But that was also of no avail. Daytime would pass while studying along with my classmates, but the nights were terrible. I longed for some sleep but did not get enough.

I had no other problems as every month, my ration and pocket money would arrive in due time. My father did not ask me even how I spent his dough. He supplied me with everything in surplus because his aim was to let me study as much as I could. Munshiji was also very supportive and always guided me. He always allowed me to visit my home for a couple of days whenever I wanted.

Yet when Satan rules one's mind, righteousness is forgotten. Once I happened to be at home on a 5-day vacation on the occasion of Diwali. About 50 metres from my house was Chetram Marwari's Shivalaya [temple], where the priest, Jaganath, lived with his nephew Ramgopal, who was about my age. We were quite friendly with each other. Now my mind had lost its orientation and together with Ramgopal, I planned to go far away to another place to work and earn money. We fixed up a date for leaving secretly and pondered over how to collect enough cash for our adventure. I had saved some rupees from my hostel allowance but it was too little.

During that period, my father kept the little money that farmers had given as *lagaan* for *kharif* cultivation, in a moneybag under his pillow. I used to sleep beside my father. I was completely out of my mind as I was conspiring to rob this money to satisfy my desire. I stayed awake in the night waiting for the right moment to make my wrong move. Being convinced of my father's slumber, I gently pulled the moneybag from underneath his pillow and sneaked out of the room into the darkness. Nobody was aware of my evil plan except Ramgopal and I proceeded to his house and gently knocked on the door to avoid waking up others. Hearing the tap, my partner in sin crept out silently and we together walked away towards the city of Charkhari where the Hindu king Malkhan Singh ruled. It was about fifteen 15 miles from our village and my cousin sister was married there. Our plan was to find some job in that town while putting up at her place.

It was about 2 a.m. when we escaped. We ran and ran for about 7 miles at a stretch till we reached Gahrauli village where my paternal cousin Badal Khan lived. Baldev Marwari of *mauja* (village) Emilia had employed him. The day was dawning. My cousin and sister-in-law were very happy to receive me and took good care of us. When they asked me about everyone back home, I feigned that they were not only well but also that they had permitted me to visit them. After taking bath and breakfast, we talked a little and then walked off saying that we were going to roam about the village. Charkhari was about 8 miles from Gahrauli and we set off as fast as we could towards our destination. It was situated behind a hill and surrounded by a fortress wall. Raja Sahab's palace was beautifully situated on top of the hill and a golden pinnacle adorned its top. We reached there about 4 o'clock in the evening. The gates to the city were open and we entered into the land of our dreams.

The city was very appealing and full of life. We felt very pleased with our decision and walked along the streets admiring the place. Each year, during the month of *kartik* (November-December), this city would organize a big *mela* (fair), during which people from far and near came to sell their wares amidst games, sports, circus and other activities for fun and enjoyment. Raja Malkhan Singh had started this festive season to commemorate the birth of his son a few years before. No other city in the whole district hosted such a huge fête. We enjoyed watching the decorations, the shops, the houses, the king's palace and everything that we came across till we finally arrived at my brother-in-law's residence at 6 p.m. after asking several people. We greeted each other, sat down on the *charpoi* and began talking about people at home. I was careful not to disclose my intention of seeking a job. They had the impression that I had merely come there on a vacation because I was not allowed to go anywhere without any purpose other than studies.

Ramgopal was given flour, pulses, etc., and separate utensils to cook his own vegetarian meal and after a nice dinner we slept merrily. Next morning after breakfast, we ventured out into the city saying that we were going to roam about the place. We walked a lot and tried to see as much as we could in a few hours. The decorated city, the zoo and the animals it housed, (which included lions, elephants, a hippopotamus, wild cows, cheetahs, leopards, monkeys, chimpanzees, crocodiles, alligators, different types of snakes, etc.), the mosques, temples, houses, lakes and many more things that made our trip exciting and thrilling.

At 10 a.m, we landed at the king's court and walked along when suddenly, we chanced upon a holy man who, while seated, was writing something. We approached him and sat down besides him, after getting his permission. In turn he asked us about our purpose of visit. We humbly said that we had come from a far off place in search of employment and we pleaded: 'Kindly guide us to a place where we can find some work. We shall ever be grateful to you for this generous act'. The saintly figure replied: 'if you follow my advice, then by *Khuda's* grace you shall achieve your goal'. We sat and waited while he continued with his work. After some time he turned to us and explained: 'if you seek a job, be careful not to be fooled by fraud and squander away your money. Listen to me and do what I tell you. I have heard that the king is a kind, supportive, and benevolent ruler who heeds to the grievances of the people everyday from noon to 1 o'clock. He knows that the rich can approach him with ease while the poor and needy find it difficult to meet him. Therefore, he has made it a routine to be available to the deprived people of his jurisdiction during that hour. Go there during that period and wait near the big gate of the palace where the guard is patrolling. Do not be afraid of him, he will not say anything to you and exactly at 12 o'clock, when the cannon is fired, he will allow you inside the gate. On entering, you will find a beautiful building with a golden gadget at its top, on your right side. Go there without hesitation and greet the security guard present there. Tell him that you are a poor refugee seeking the king's assistance. He will show you the way to the king's court. Go there with your hands folded and head bowed, wish the king and apprise him of your need'. We thanked the good man for his advice and walked towards the gate from where we were to go in at the sound of the cannon at noon and we started waiting.

## Allah's Blessing

About half an hour later, the cannon went off, the bell sounded, and as the *pir* had said, the guard opened the gate. We went in, met the sentry inside who led us to the king's court. By this time, we had lost our senses and were overwhelmed by the majestic surrounding. The beautifully carved and decorated buildings, the silver chandelier, the soft, smooth carpet, the lovely fragrance in the air, were all terrific and beyond description. High ranked officials and ministers had gathered clad in fine clothing with their arms on their laps. When we were taken in front of the king, we knelt with our hands folded and head bowed. Raja Sahab acknowledged our greetings and motioned us to get up. I immediately stood up and was completely dazed when I saw the radiance emanating from the king's face and his jewel studded crown. I had never witnessed anything like this before in my entire lifetime.

Raja Sahab asked: 'What do you want?' and I replied, 'My lord, I wish to earn a living'. 'Do you know how to read and write', he asked. 'Yes my lord, I have studied till class III in Hindi', I replied. Then Raja Sahab threw a knife and a pen without a nib and ordered me to make a pen out of it. I quickly did as I was told and placed the pen and knife on the table (which was made of elephant tusk) in front of him. Raja Sahab picked it up, examined it, wrote something on a piece of paper and gave it to me saying: 'Write your name on this paper'. I followed his order, wrote down my full address and returned the paper. Raja Sahab gave the paper to his *munshi* and directed him to register my name. He told me to report next morning at 10 a.m. Now it was my friend's turn. He said that he had had no schooling and was illiterate. Raja Sahab saw that Ramgopal was fat and well built and ordered a job in his army for him. He was also told to return the following day. We bowed and thanked the Raja Sahab and left. Happy over our appointments, we made our way back to the holy man who had directed us and narrated our experience. Then we walked back home feeling satisfied at our achievement and could not restrain ourselves from narrating our day's adventure to my cousin sister. We were bubbling with excitement and joy and knew nothing of the tragedy ahead. At night we ate and slept soundly dreaming of our would-be way of life.

What man proposes, God will dispose. Our fate was not to be what we had planned. Back home, when my father woke up finding me missing from the bed, he inquired about my whereabouts from my sister who said that she had not seen me. Thinking that I might have gone to attend nature's call, he waited for some time. But still there was no sign of my presence. Then my father picked up his pillow, and found his moneybag gone. After some time, the priest Baba Jagannath came looking for Ramgopal. Soon everyone realised that the two of us had run away somehere with the money and all were stunned by this act. A massive manhunt was launched to nab us and people were sent in all directions to search for us. The fire in the kitchen was put off and everyone went on a fast.

In the evening, a messenger arrived with the news that we had visited Badal Khan (my cousin), in Gahrauli village the day before and seemed to be on our way to the Kingdom of Charkhari. On hearing this, my father borrowed Marwari Chetrams' fast moving camel and set out immediately though it was already late in the evening. He reached in the night while we were fast asleep. He silently woke my brother-in-law and cousin and came to know about all our activities. After this, they gently picked us up one by one and put us on the camel's back. As the camel moved, we woke up from the deep slumber, but we dared not to say a word as soon as we realised what was happening.

Charkhari was a walled city and had heavy gates on all four directions. As per rule, the gates were closed after 9 p.m. each night and reopened only at five in the morning. At the time of opening and closing, the cannons were fired to apprise the public. As my brother-in-law, Kasim Khan, was in-charge of the infantry, my father had asked him to accompany us and secure our exit during the odd hour. On reaching the gate, the guards stopped us. Kasim Khan got down and explained that the camel did not belong to the regime and was owned by his relatives who were to leave as soon as possible for an urgent work. Once we were allowed exit, my brother-in-law wished my father and returned.

Now we were on our way back home and by dawn, reached our destination. The fire in the kitchen was restored after three days and everyone finally ate a meal after thanking Allah for our safe return. My friends from the village came to visit us and we felt very ashamed of ourselves. Countless bits of advice were showered on us from all angles and several mouths opened to give us a piece of their minds, but my father never said a word. We could not see anyone straight in the eyes. The next day, my father fed the poor as a thanksgiving to Allah for my safety and on that very day itself, put me on a camel's back and accompanied me back to school again.

He neither said anything about my misdemeanors to the headmaster, nor did he ask me about his moneybag. He then returned home. For some time after our misadventure, my father neither spoke a word to me nor allowed anyone at home to speak about the episode. This punishment seemed to be very severe and I found it very difficult to bear my guilt. It, however, opened my eyes and thrusted a sense of maturity into my mind. The moneybag remained with me but the satanic spell, which had influenced my senses during a whole week, vanished.

Aameen. Aameen. Rabbul Aalmeen.

## Class II Examination

I finally began to study hard in class II and gradually started enjoying my school because four more village boys had joined the hostel. One was a *kayastha* named Hubblal who had joined the school 6 months after my admission. The others, who had come before me as government-sponsored students were Matole Singh, Umrao Singh, Parmanand and Shivdayal. The six of us were all aided by the government and studied in either class II or I.

According to the hostel rules, we were not allowed to leave the school campus after eight in the night. Smoking, drinking alcohol and gambling were prohibited. If anyone were caught indulging in any of these acts he would be punished. The headmaster had the right to either give three lashes on the hands or even reduce his stipend. Therefore, no sponsored student dared to make a wrong move. We studied day and night and when we were allowed to go home on holidays, I would stop on the way back home at Dayam Ali's house for a visit.

On my first vacation after the Charkhari episode, I handed over the moneybag to my mother with the 95 rupees, which I had stolen from my father and sincerely pleaded to return it to my father and grant me forgiveness. My mother did accordingly and persuaded my father to grant me pardon. In due course, I became friendly with Dayam Ali's son, Madar Ali. Being assured of my good character, he proposed a match for me with a wealthy *pathan*'s daughter and talked to my father. My would-be father-in-law, Bade Khan[48], also had a son called Badal Khan. My father had had no intention of marrying me before the completion of my studies, but had been very shaken by my running away to Charkhari and decided to chain me. He hoped that my marriage would prevent me from leaving home to seek greener pastures in the future. However, this was not to be since Khuda had different things in stock for me. I was to leave my parents, brothers and sisters, wife and family, and settle in an alien land later on. I also never would get a glimpse of any of them ever thereafter!

It was with this anticipation that my father agreed to talk about my marriage. Earlier he had refused many such invitations. The conversation being over, my wedding was finalized and was scheduled for the next month. I was 18 years old then. After the marriage ceremony and holiday, I returned to school and resumed my studies in a sincere way. The days passed and the examination dates were announced in due course of time. Since I had been very disturbed throughout the year, my preparation for the tests had been inadequate and I was not confident that I would do well, but could not back out either. Altogether ten boys from our school would appear for this examination and all of us began preparing seriously. A week's food and other rations were packed as well as the money for the journey and for stay had been provided and a carriage had been booked.

On 14 June, the headmaster brought us to the district town of Hamirpur. Five out of the ten boys belonged to class II while the remaining four were from class I (middle class). During those days, there were eight middle schools in Hamirpur district. Hamirpur was the examination centre for all the district schools of Rahkul Pahar, Maudaha, Mahoba, Kabrai, Jalalpur, Maruha and Sumerpur. Hamirpur was about 15 miles from Maudaha and we reached there at four in the evening and stayed in a rented house at government's expense. After a good night's sleep, Munshiji woke us up at five the next morning, took us to the bank of the Betwa to take bath. After dressing up, Munshiji took us to a *halwai* shop and we had breakfast there at seven. We were allowed to carry only a small knife into the examination hall.

When we reached our examination center, Munshiji remained at a distance while we took our allotted seats. The invigilation was very strict and a policeman stood between every two candidates keeping an eye on us. If during the test one had to leave his seat for some reason or the other, we were supposed to look down and were accompanied by a policeman. If someone needed anything like paper or ink, he would have to raise his hand and the required thing would be provided at his desk. Pin-drop silence was the norm. Each student was given two *keelaks* (kind of pencil: *bebani kalam*) instead of a pen. We had to sharpen that with our little knife and use according to the language we wrote in (either Hindi or Urdu). Ten marks were allotted for neatness and good handwriting. Those replying in Hindi had to write on the right side of the answer sheet while those of the Urdu medium schools, wrote on the left side while the other half was left empty. This empty half was meant for notes about the student's health (e.g. whether he suffered from headache, abdominal pain, etc.), or any complaint (against the invigilators) or any other problem faced by the students. The empty page meant for remarks also facilitated an easy way of checking results as the Examination Controller could immediately understand the student's difficulties and these could be dealt with accordingly.

During the exams, all that could be heard in the hall was the scribbling of pen on paper. The serenity, the cool fresh air and the atmosphere were inviting a good sleep, and the student who was unprepared for the test invariably felt the urge. What Munshiji had said had been true. Those who did not know the answers fell prey to the god of slumber, while those who had toiled hard reproduced their memories with ease and fluency. At three in the afternoon, after the slogging was over, the bell rang to announce that the time for writing was over and the answer sheets were assembled and tagged. Fifteen minutes later, everyone was supposed to write down his name plus address on his bundle and submit it during the next thirty minutes to the authorities. The bundles were then sealed and put in a bag and collected by the postman at 4 p.m. Being hungry after the whole day's work, we ate greedily and slept soundly only to get up the next morning to follow the same routine once again.

The first day's subject had been Hindi language and literature followed by mathematics (arithmetic and algebra) on the second day. On the third day we had geometry and on the fourth and final day it was geography and science. By the fifth day we were free and could go back home. Those who had appeared for the middle school exams were granted a 3-months holiday during which period the results would be declared. Class II examinees were not allowed to go on a vacation.

## Class I: Course and Middle School Examination

I returned to school after a week's vacation. Three months later, the examination results were announced and six out of the ten who had appeared from our school had passed. (Of these, four students belonged to class II and two were of class I). The remaining four had failed and I was one of them. A whole year of study and hard work had been wasted. Nevertheless, I thanked Allah for his decision and renewed my pursuance for knowledge with greater vigour.

The city of Maudaha had two big lakes, i.e., the Kirat Sagar and Madan Taal, which were dug by the elders of Allah Udal. In the center of each lake was a temple. In these lakes grew plenty of sweet water *singharas* and half a kilo of this sweet and nutritious fruit would cost only 1 paisa during those days. Nearby, a fort and a house constructed by Allah Udal, lay abandoned and deserted. The cattle market was held in the town of Bharuha Sumerpur on Saturdays, while in Raath, it was on Sundays. Hindus and Muslims sold or bought different cattle like cows, horses, buffaloes, sheep, goats, etc. in these markets. The English currency (rupee) was not used in the market of Raath. Nagri, a different currency was in circulation. It was a small square shaped coin that the vendors exchanged for the English rupee by paying some extra money. The unused nagri could be re-exchanged after the marketing was over because the currency was not valid elsewhere.

Days, weeks and months passed by studying and in due course of time, the examination dates were announced. It was to begin on 20 October 1893 and end on the 23rd and therefore would last 4 days. With even greater zeal and commitment we started day and night final preparations for the examinations. This time there were twelve examinees from Class I and II. After the exam, we went home for a few days and when the result was announced, I was among the successful candidates. Five students of class II and four from class I (i.e., nine out of the twelve examinees from our school), had passed. Khuda had rewarded my two years of hard work. I was promoted to class I [final class of the Middle School]. The two years of labour in class II made my preparation for the class I examination easy and 6 months later the notice for the next exam arrived. It was to commence on 18 November 1894 amd would last up to 21 November 1894. Eight students from our school appeared in this test and went home after its completion four days later. This time, I was granted a 3-months leave, which I spent happily with my family. With the blessings of my elders and Allah, my luck favoured me and I managed to pass. Seven out of the eight students from our school had been successful, three from class II and four from class I, including myself.

Munshiji gave us the certificate along with our results. I had scored a total of 370 marks out of 400. Each paper carried 100 marks out of which 10 marks were awarded for neatness. Those who scored 200-275 marks out of 400 were given 3$^{rd}$ division, 275-340 marks meant 2$^{nd}$ division, while students securing above 340 marks received 1$^{st}$ division certificates. I thanked Allah thousand times for my success and after 11 years, managed to free myself from school and study. My parents fed the poor and praised the Lord for his benevolence. Aameen. Aameen. Rabbul Aalmeen.

## The Family of Zamindar Chetram Marwari

Chetram Marwari was a moneylender and in a short span of time owned more than half of Bharkhari's land. Increasinly, he managed to buy land of other villages as well. He then planned to build a concrete house for himself (earlier, he lived in a mud house). Instead of making new bricks out of clay to build his house, my father suggested that Chetram could take the bricks from the mound of an old settlement on his own land. In this way, Chetram would spend less money and time. My father arranged ten labourers to dig out the bricks from the mound.

A *chamar* called Devi was also hired to dig the earth. One day while he was digging with his pickaxe he struck upon a box full of treasure. He looked around and after he saw no one, quickly covered it again with soil and started digging in another place. On being questioned by my father, he replied that proper bricks could not be extracted from there so he had abandoned the site. My father not sensing his motive, believed him. At night, the *chamar* Devi accompanied by his wife plus four sons carried the whole load of treasure to his house, and hid it. The following morning, when all the labourers arrived, they found some of the money and valuables scattered around the place. Those who had come early grabbed these leftovers. Thereafter, Devi and the other men started their work as if nothing had happened. Later in the day, when my father had arrived on this spot, he learnt about money that had been strewn here and there. He immediately asked Devi about these riches being discovered. But Devi flatly denied that anything had been found.

Soon, however, everyone in the village knew about the findings and Chetram called Devi to confess. Yet Devi stuck to his statement despite being beaten with shoes and slippers. Chetram lost his patience and Devi was hanged upside down from a neem tree; a fire was lighted underneath him. As the flames threatened to roast him, Devi cried out and admitted his deeds saying that he was ready to return all that he had found. Chetram ordered him to be brought down immediately. Four huge baskets full of rupees were recovered. Six men were needed to carry one such basket. God knows whether it was the whole treasure or part of it! It was however, more than enough for Chetram to build his elegant mansion.

Chetram Marwari had three sons, Hardasi, Matadin and Dwarka Prasad.[49] A rich, childless *marwari* lady who was the landlord of Umri had adopted Dwarka Prasad. Hardasi had a son named Harlal who had drowned in a concrete well at the age of eleven. A few days after the child's death, Chetram, too, died. This was immediately followed by the death of his wife and his son Hardasi. Surprisingly, even Matadin died soon after. The ways of Allah are unique. Of all the members in Chetram's family, only two widows survived and escaped the shadow of death that swept the family. These two, Kasturi Bai and Rajkunwari, were now left to run the business. In fact, it was Lala Kamta Prasad and my father who had to look after the whole business now.

Two years later, even Kasturi Bai died and Rajkunwari was the only one left. She had no children and did not know what to do with the huge property and wealth of the family. She became very religious and began spending money for the upliftment of the society. She proposed to dig a well for the village and my father readily agreed. She laid the foundation of a well somwhere in the western part of the village and work soon began in earnest. She opened her treasury for donations and charity and sponsored *pujas* in the

Shivalya temple built by her father-in-law, Chetram. Hundreds of poor and destitutes, *brahmins*, etc. were provided with food and clothing. The kitchen of the Shivalya temple fed all those who visited or lived there.

## Digging a New Well

As the work of digging a well had progressed to the depth of a few feets, the men encountered sand. This caused the collapse of all the four walls of the well and Rajkunwari was upset. She called my father and said: 'Hey *jamadar*, if you try and succeed in digging this well, I shall be very obliged and will give you a golden bracelet as a gift'. My father had replied: 'Khuda hafiz, yours will shall be done, because the Holy One always helps the righteous'. The landlady thanked him and wished him good luck.

My father ordered 500 carts of stone chips and 1000 carts of wood. Subsequently, he prepared a large furnace to make lime and lighted it. After one whole month, the lime was ready and bricks could be made from the very site on which the treasure was discovered. My father now started constructing the walls of the well starting from below. By Allah's grace the ploy worked and after reaching a few feet deeper, it was evident that the walls would not collapse anymore and everyone was exhilarated. The diameter of the well however, due to the collapse of the previous walls, had increased significantly and now measured more than forty feet (about 24 forearm lengths).

As a result, there was abundant water in the well. Even if two bulls would have been employed to pull water from the well for a whole day using a large torso made up of cow skin, the well would still not have dried up. Six heavy iron chains were slung from the top to climb up safely if anyone chanced to fall into the well. When after 6 months this well was finally ready, Rajkunwari was pleased. She presented my father with two heavy golden bracelets worth around 500 rupees and thanked him. All rejoiced at the completion of the well.

## 'Marriage' of the New Well

In Hindustan, if a Muslim digs a new well, he gives alms to the poor and feeds them at the time of its inauguration. Similarly, a

Hindu performs a 'marriage' ceremony. Neither do people drink water from the well till this ritual is over nor is it used for any other purpose. Accordingly, Rajkunwari arranged for the 'marriage' of the well and ordered all the necessary items to be assembled. Money was freely spent and hundreds of tons of wheat were milled in every village where Rajkunwari owned land. For each household 5 kilogram of wheat flour was prepared and stored in her house. Sixteen rooms were filled with this flour that was preserved in sacks made of thick new cloth and sealed all around. The roof of each room was removed and flour reached the top, after which it was sealed. When required, the flour could be taken out through a window constructed in every room.

Sixteen cartfull of plates and *lotas* were brought from Kanpur to distribute the alms. Many other things required for the ceremony such as clothes etc., were brought from different places also on carts and carriages. Two *pandits* were called from the western part of the country to perform the rituals and read from the Bhagwat Gita. They were supposedly very learned and deft in their profession. When all the necessary things were collected and ready for the *yag*, a big flag was hoisted which was tied up to a long pole that was attached to the well. A bell was hung from a smaller pole. This bell rang whenever the wind blew. Another flag was hoisted at the Shivalya mandir and during the next 6 months, following the rules in the scriptures, rites and rituals would be performed at both these sites. The two *pandits*, with the help of several other priests, performed the ceremonies and people from all walks of life came to see, listen and feed themselves and accept the gifts and alms, which were in abundance. Every morning and evening, hot *puris* cooked in ghee, two *laddus*, two *jalebis*, a handful of *bundis*, white sugar, a large piece of mango pickle, *pudina* paste, a ladle of curd etc., were given to every person. Even those with a voracious appetite could not eat more than three puris: so wholesome they were.

Each kitchen had six men for every *karahi*. Sixteen women made *puris*, two men put them in the *karahi*, two turned them to fry and two took them out from the *karahi*. Sixteen men were employed to serve every 100 people. Such was the system that for each kind of work, different people were hired and paid a monthly salary. Therefore, during the 6 months of the *yagna*, this small village of Bharkhari attracted more people than any of the cities. The *yagna* took place simultaneously at both the places and people flocked to listen to the sermons and partake in the meals provided. Those aspiring for alms were bestowed with Rajkumari's donations. She visited both the sites day and night to listen, offer prayers and give away gifts.

One day, two men were talking with each other. One said: 'Yesterday night, Madam (Rajkunwari), had come to the well to hear the discourse'. The other responded: 'That can not be true because I saw her at the Shivalya temple last night'. They finally decided that the coming evening they would try to solve this mystery. That night, they were surprised to see her in both the places at the same time during the proceedings of the *yagna*! Those who witnessed this pondered over Khuda's miracle and praised Him.

Six months of *yagna* finally came to an end when the paddy, sowed on the Govardhan hills was ready for harvest. A few grains from the new harvest were needed to complete the last rites of the ceremony. Forty-two and a quarter maunds [1 maund is equivalent to 40 kilos] of paddy was needed to carry out the offerings near the holy pyre. The *brahmins* performed this *hawan* and from a distance of about 30 feet threw the offerings in the fire. At the place where they had assembled, a concrete drain was built in which ghee and other offerings were poured meant to keep the holy pyre burning. The flames that arose attracted the eye. The community kitchen continued to feed everyone for another month after the conclusion of the Yagna. Even travellers from far away places were invited for meals.

The scar on my cheek is a reminder of this *yagna*[50]. When I returned home one day after school, I saw that in front of my house a big crowd had assembled eating from the temple's kitchen. A bitch with three or four puppies was seated not far from them. I threw a stone at the dog and ran away only to trip and fall. The bitch ran after me and bit me in my cheek.

When alms were being distributed, each *brahmin* was given cloths, a plate, a *lota* and one rupee as donation. Thousands of *brahmins* attended the *Yagna* and sixteen carts of plates and *lotas* fell short. When these items were no more, the remaining *brahmins* were given money instead, as compensation. Similarly, when the stock of clothes had finished, cash was provided. This *yagna* had drawn thousands of *brahmins*, sages and learned men and women from far and near. Everyone admitted that such a grand spectacle had never been heard of or seen before. After the the ceremony, all the volunteers who had helped in making the function a great success were showered with gifts and presents. Later that evening, my father asked Kalua, a *dom* [sweeper], who was a leader of his community: 'Kalua, how much *puris* did you manage to collect during the whole period of *yagna*?' He replied: 'Jamadar Sahab, if famine occurs today, we can survive during at least the next 3 years on the *puris* and *ladoos* amassed from the ceremony'.

## The Demise of Rajkunwari and of her Wealth

Till her death, this generous lady left no stone unturned to donate and to give alms to the destitutes and needy. Whenever a girl (rich or poor) from the village was married, she gave 10 rupees as a gift and provided free wood, grass, wooden poles, flooring, etc. for the occasion. At a boy's wedding, she gave 5 rupees and the necessary items. She would call school children to her residence, distribute sweets and one rupee to each of them and talk to them, lovingly. Throughout her life she had arranged for food and donations at the Shivalya temple. When the lady died, her manager Lala Kamta Prasad Sahab kept on throwing coins all along the cremation procession up to the burial ground. A commendable feature of the Marwaris was that this procession, rather than by woes, cries and silence, was marked by the singing of bhajans, religious recitals and the playing of music. These pleasant sounding hymns were however, beyond my comprehension. The deceased was put upright on a nice chair and her face was uncovered during the march. The body was cremated in a garden near her palace and behind the Shivalya temple. About twenty other members of her family had been cremated there earlier. During the next three days the poor used brooms to clean up the place hoping to find more coins. They picked up all the coins that were strewn during her funeral procession. Neither dust nor dirt could be seen on roads through which the caravan had passed. Every soul was moved and grief-stricken by the death of this exceptional character and no one could hold tears. May Khuda bless such humane and generous people who lived for the benefit of the entire community! Lala Kamta Prasad spent heavily on her last rites. I cannot find words to praise his effort. May Holy Allah repay him for his generosity!

Since Rajkunwari had no issue, the government confiscated her property. Yet, Dwarka Prasad, the youngest son of Chetram Marwari, who had been adopted by a Marwari of Umri village, now claimed the possessions. Hearing this, his paternal cousin, Lachiram challenged him in the court. This was the beginning of a bitter rivalry between the two and several lawyers profitted enormously. Apart from them some local goons supporting either side also enjoyed themselves with the wealth of these two brothers. Eight bodyguards, four in front and four behind, always surrounded both Lachiram and Dwarka Prasad even when they went to the fields to attend a call from nature.

The case at the High Court in Allahabad continued for 5 long years. By the time court case had ended however, due to heavy expenses incurred on fees for lawyers and the court, witnesses, bodyguards, goons, etc. both brothers were bankrupt. To meet the expenses, they had also sold off their land and property. By the time of the third hearing, all their land, except for that in Bharkhari had already been sold. On the last hearing, the court ordered five elders of Bharkhari to act as government witnesses. Accordingly, following the order of the Session Judge, Ram Prasad Dubey, Muhammad Khan, Khushali Pathak, Panch Kalar and Tijwa Chamar were selected and summoned to the Allahabad High Court. On the basis of their confessions, the verdict was finally passed in favour of Dwarka Prasad. But what did he get? He had floundered his wealth and possessions in this show of strength. As a last show off, he now could only curl his moustache while his heart wept.

## Prediction of Hakim Nawab Ali Sahab: My Fate decided

With the blessings of Allah and to my satisfaction, my father's dream that I would pass middle school was fulfilled. I now wished to seek a job but the real decision was to be made after my return home. After this return, I lived happily with my family and looked after our business and property. The Marwari had still employed my father and we had sufficient income to thrive on. One evening I sat with my father who smoked hucca in the portico. We chatted about our business and other activities, when I suddenly put forwards the proposal of applying for a government job. My father did not like the idea and asked me what had made me want such a thing.

'What else do you want? Tell me and I will get it'. I replied that I was content and did not require anything. He then asked: 'why do you wish to join government service? Khuda has provided me with only one son who can look after us and after our assets when we grow old. You have 150 *bighas* of land, which others cultivate and give you a share of the harvest. You can keep a couple of servants if you wish. Why then, do you aspire for employment elsewhere when you are self-employed and well off? We are growing old. Your mother and I shall be devastated if you leave us. Never let this thought enter your mind again. The Lord will provide your needs. Here upon, I fell silent.

My father was about 70 years old and my mother[51] was sixty then, while I was twenty. Though my father had received no formal schooling, he nonetheless was intelligent and knowledgeable. He also was very punctual in his *namaaz*. I followed his advice and continued to take interest in our business.

As told earlier, Lala Kamta Prasad was the right hand of the *zamindar* Chetram Marwari. One day he fell ill. Despite all modes of treatment his illness could not be cured. Finally, he called my father and said: 'Jamadar Sahab, I am now fed up with this disease and have a feeling that it will kill me. If you have any idea of a cure for me I shall be highly obliged to you'. Hearing this, my father said: 'Lala Sahab, if you permit me, I shall tell you my opinion'. Lala Sahab agreed. Then my father said: 'I know a Hakim called Nawab Ali Sahab who lives in village Khamot near Jalalpur. Maybe his treatment could cure you if God desires so'.

Lala Sahab immediately summoned Hakimji. He came and stayed at our house. He examined Lala Sahab and said that he would arrange and prepare a medicine after one day. He then returned to our house and after his meal told my father that the next day, he required a big tortoise. My father quickly called a fisherman and ordered him to catch one the following morning. Next morning, a large tortoise was brought before Hakimji who then turned to my father and said: '*Bhai* Sahab, make this turtle urinate'. My father was puzzled at Hakimji's remark. 'Hakimji, I cannot do this'. 'Please try it', he replied. 'Doctors know how to make others urinate or pass stool and examine them. How should I tell this animal to urinate?' They both laughed and I smiled.

Hakimji then turned to me and told me to fetch a stove, a pan and some firewood from my mother. I quickly ran and brought everything. Hakim Sahab now lit the fire and put the pan upside down on it. When it became hot, he placed the tortoise in the pan and pressed it firmly with his shoe. This made the tortoise urinate and Hakimji immediately collected the product of excretion in another utensil. Then he ordered me to dig the earth and bring him three earthworms. I did as I was told. Hakimji then took two and a quarter of the earthworms, baked them on the hot pan and then powdered them when dry. He then mixed this powder with the urine of the tortoise and prepared three small tablets from it. My father and I were surprised. Lala Kamta Prasad was given these tablets to swallow, one every day for three consecutive days in the mornings. By the grace of God, Lala Sahab was healed after three days. Lalaji was extremely happy and showered Hakim Sahab with gifts. He was presented with a luxury chariot, fully adorned and covered with a fancy umbrella, a couple of bulls, and a generous sum of money.

Lalaji accompanied by my father and myself escorted Hakim Sahab to the outskirts of our village. We were about to return when Hakimji shouted and called Lala Kamta Prasad. When we reached him he warned: 'Lalaji, listen and remember one thing. For the next 6 months, you must not touch milk or any of its products like ghee, curd, sweets, etc. If you ignore my advice, your life will be at stake'. Lalaji promised to follow his advice. Later, Lalaji hosted a grand party to celebrate his recovery, fed people and distributed alms and clothes to hundreds of poor.

It is true that wisdom takes the back seat when death announces its arrival. Lala Kamta Prasadji lived a healthy and happy life for 3 months after this episode of illness. One day, he had to present himself at the Collector's office in person and though he was quite weak due to his long sickness, he had to go to Hamirpur. By the time he reached there on a *doli*, carried by four men, it was eleven in the night and he was extremely hungry. Lalaji immediately sent a man to fetch something to eat. The man set off to the marketplace, which was closed that time. He found only one sweet shop open. The shopkeeper was preparing sweets and had nothing to offer except for *rabri*, a milk-based sweet. Finding nothing else, the man bought it for four paise and returned. Lalaji could not resist and took a mouthful of it before he realised that it contained milk, and since he was very hungry, swallowed it fully down.

The inevitable had occurred, and Lalaji again fell ill. The poor man had to return home that very night. Early next morning, news of his relapse spread soon in the whole village. My father came to see him and Hakimji was summoned at once. But Hakimji came only to warn him for the impending doom, which was to come in a couple of weeks. He said: 'Lalaji, you have but two weeks to do whatever you want in this lifetime, I am unable to do anything for you'. Saying this, he left the place. Surely, Lala Kamta Prasadji died after a fortnight.

During the first visit of Hakimji, when he successfully had treated Lalaji, I was playing at my doorstep with some of my friends one Sunday afternoon. My father and Hakimji were sitting in the portico talking, when my father summoned me. I obeyed and sat down in front of them. Hakimji held my right hand and examined my palm and its lines closely. He read, counted and calculated the lines of my palm and forehead and after some time turned to my father and said: 'Bhai Sahab, this boy will not stay with you. His fate will lead him to a foreign soil from where his return seems impossible. Moreover, he will marry twice. He will have five boys and three girls. He will also be intelligent and wise and will not be dominated by his boss at work. His childhood and youth will be blissful but he will face some trouble in his old age. He will have three encounters with death in his lifetime. The first at the age of 10 or 12 years, second between 35 to 40 and the third around 50 years of age. If he survives these three ordeals, he shall live to become eighty. He will earn handsomely, but shall not keep his wealth. However, he will not be bankrupt and will have people working under him. He shall own a horse and shall build a huge house [see photograph]. He will also either construct a mosque himself, or make a big contribution for its construction. He will have few enemies and many more friends. He will possess a mild and kind attitude and will rarely be irked. He will receive co-operation from the people around him'.

When Hakimji made these predictions about me, I was 13 years old and it was true that I had escaped death when I was eleven. At eighteen, I had married. Later, I was to leave my wife and go to a foreign land. Four years after my immigration, my first wife died and one by one Hakimji's prophecy came true. The only one forecast, which still remains to transpire, is the horse.[52] Maybe he meant that after my death, my body would be carried on the back of a horse. After hearing this prediction my father had raised his arms up to the sky and had said: 'Holy Allah, I shall abide with your wishes'. He shed a tear and wiped it off while I ran back to play with my friends. They continued with their talking. Aameen Aameen Rabbul Aalmeen!

## The Demise of Nawab Ali Sahab

Nawab Ali Sahab was not only a renowned *hakim*, but also very generous and kind-hearted. He would make all efforts to treat and help poor patients even at their homes without charging any fees and he would even arrange free medicines for them. He would also ask patients on the road whether they were taking medicine and if not he would prescribe them or provide the required ones free of charge. Once, a rich butcher, named Sera of Jalalpur, developed a sore on his hand. This man did not want to seek the advice of Hakim Ali Sahab because there was some dissension between the two. He thought that the Hakim might not treat him well or charge in excess due to the animosity and therefore avoided him. Hakim Sahab however, saw him many times with his hand in a bandage and felt sorry for the man. He knew what the butcher thought, but did not want his wound to grow out of proportion and harm him. 'This rich man is a fool and will make himself a handicapped person if I do not help him', he opined. One day, he finally broke the silence and called Sera as he was passing by his home. Hakim was smoking his *hukka* [waterpipe]. Sera came and wished him. Hakim Sahab greeted him and asked: 'Sera, what is wrong with your hand?' Sera replied: 'I have a sore, which is not healing since the last one month. Rather it is getting bigger day by day'. 'Then why did you not come to me for treatment?' Hakim Sahab asked. 'I was afraid', said Sera. 'What?' retorted Hakim Sahab, 'you were frightened of my being biased due to our strained relationship? A Hakim and a Muslim would never do such a thing. It is a big sin to harm deliberately. You brush aside these feelings and open your bandage'. The rich butcher was ashamed. He then let the Hakim uncover his wound and examine it. Eyeing it carefully, Hakim Sahab said: 'Go and fetch me the roots of *jagdhakkan* ['world's roof plant', does not really exist] and I shall prepare a paste for your boil. If Khuda wishes, you will be cured'. Sera nodded and told him that he would do accordingly and left.

Sera now began his search for the medicinal plant but could not get hold of it in Jalalpur. He then sent some people to the cities of Hamirpur, Raath and Maudaha but still could not find it. Finally, he came back to Hakim Sahab empty handed. Hakim Sahab laughed: 'Oh, so you could not get the roots of Jagdhakkan? Why? Did you not spend money to acquire it?' Sera replied: 'I did spend the necessary amount to send my men everywhere to buy it but they all came back empty-handed'. Hakim Sahab smiled and said: 'Sera, you are a novice. You could have spent a fortune in vain if I had any malice against you, but it is inhuman and sinful to do so. I was only testing you to make you understand that one should never ever breed a feeling of disbelief and unfaithfulness against a Hakim. Now go and fetch the bark of a cotton plant, make a fine paste of it and apply to your wounds and if God wishes, you shall be cured in a week'. Hakim Sahab refused to take any fees from him.

When the sore of Sera had recovered, he came to Hakim Sahab and pleaded for forgiveness. Hakim Sahab told him that since Sera had not done anything wrong to him, Allah would be merciful. Sera the butcher was now indebted for a lifetime. When he asked Hakim Sahab about the root the latter told him that it was only to test him. 'Listen, "Jag" means the earth or world and "dhakkan" stands for cover. Now can you tell me, what covers the earth?" Sera acknowledged Hakim Sahab's intelligence. Throughout the district the *hakim* was well known for his humor and gentleness. Such good men are not allowed however, to reside for long on this earth. Hakim Sahab had four wives. The first three were childless and therefore he kept a fourth wife. They all lived together in harmony. Khuda had blessed him and his fourth wife with three sons, i.e., Hussain Ali, Nivajis Ali and Afzal Hussain. Hussain Ali and I were schoolmates.

Stones in the urinary tract made Hakim Sahab very weak. He was an able physician but could not cure himself. When my father heard about Hakim Sahab's illness, he took me along to see him. After inquiring about the sickness, my father asked him why he had stopped taking his medicines. Hakim Sahab replied that though he had cured others with similar problems he had failed to treat himself.[53] Yet he named one Abdullah, who lived in Kalapi and who might possibly have the remedy for his problem. My father pressurized Hakim Sahab to write a letter to Abdullah explaining his illness. At once, a servant carried the letteron horseback to Kalapi, which was about 10 miles from Khanaut. Hakim Abdullah read the letter and then turned to the messenger and said, 'you seem to have come here too late. According to the features of the disease, your master's days are numbered. I cannot heal him but shall explain what is to be expected shortly'. He then wrote down a reply stating the course of the illness. 'For 3 consecutive days the stone will block the urinary tract, after which it will be expelled. Following this, a long threadlike tissue will come out and urination will resume. Three days later, the threadlike substance will also cease to be excreted and during the next 3 days there will be spasm causing extreme pain. On the ninth day however this all will stop and death will be imminent'.

The servant brought this reply back in the evening. On reading the letter, everyone became sad and surprised. My father decided that we should stay there for the next nine days and see what happens. I consented. Every word written in Hakim Abdullah's letter became true during the nine days that followed and on the ninth day when the dribbling of urine terminated at about nine in the morning, Hakim Sahab took his last breath. Hakim Sahab's death cast a shadow of gloom in every house of the city. I doubt if there was a single soul who did not shed a tear during this time of mourning. Today, Hakim Nawab Ali is no more with us, but his name will live on forever on this earth. May Holy Allah receive him in Paradise! Aameen. Aameen. Rabbul Aalmeen!

## Registrar Syed Tafazzul Hussain Sahab and His Brother

Registrar Syed Tafazzul Hussain Sahab and Fazaluddin Sahab were brothers and relatives of Hakim Nawab Ali Sahab. They lived in the prosperous Saidvara neighborhood of Jalalpur and were known for their richness. These brothers lived together and while the elder, Fazaluddin Sahab, was God-fearing, the younger was an intellectual. Fazaluddin was unmarried while Tafazzul Hussain had three sons and a daughter. Fazaluddin was a devout Muslim and a man with a heart of gold: pure and perfect. I witnessed the following miracle that took place at his house during the *jetha tazia*. I have written earlier about the *jetha tazia* and the procession, which followed it in Jalalpur. This march would stop at the doorsteps of the rich and poor and at Registrar Sahab's residence it waited for a longer duration because cold milk was served there. All the *ahirs* of the nearby area provided free milk to the Registrar Sahab who would distribute this on the day of *tazia*.

Hindustan has three seasons: winter, summer and the monsoon. During the summers (*baishakh* and *jeth*), the weather is very warm and due to this, the milk collected at the Registrar's house for the *tazia* that year was only four barrels. This was far less than the required amount to quench the thirst of the people participating in the procession. At 9 a.m. the march began and moved slowly from one locality to another. They were offered water and fruit squash at various points. By the time they reached Saidvara, it was about 11 o'clock and everyone was dehydrated. They stopped at the door of Registrar Sahab. *Brahmins* had been appointed to offer refreshments to all amidst music and fanfare. Due to the dry and hot climate, drinks were immediately consumed and people still wanted more. The men rushed to Fazaluddin Sahab and reported the shortage of milk. 'What? Is there no more milk? Come and show me'. Saying this he lifted his arms in the sky and prayed to Allah. Fazaluddin Sahab then asked the *brahmins* to show which barrels were empty. They pointed to the four barrels covered with lids. Mir Sahab opened them, one after another in the name of Allah and lo! All of them were filled to the brim. Everyone was surprised to see that miracle. That afternoon, as the temperature soared, people drank to their satisfaction for an hour but the supply of milk did not finish and even when the procession had left, the barrels were still full. Everyone across the region soon came to know about this unbelievable occurrence.

Fazaluddin's holiness and goodness led to the increase of wealth in the house of Registrar Sahab and every evening Tafazzul Hussain would receive lots of money [as bribes], which I have seen with my own eyes. When Syed Fazaluddin Sahab died, the whole town observed 40 days of mourning. Soon thereafter, Khuda took his hands off from Registrar Sahab's house. Money had spoilt the minds of Tafazzul's sons with pride and haughtiness. They would eat a thin layer of rotis made of wheat flour smeared in ghee with fried meat and throw the rest from their mansion into the streets. Hence, during mealtime, the poor beggars would wait expectantly below the window for the left overs that were thrown away by those boys. Behind their mansion, lived a poor barber whose wife was called Indu. These boys called on Indu and asked her what she had cooked that day. The poor lady replied that she had made rotis of gram and some gram spinach. The children remarked that they disliked rotis of wheat smeared with ghee, pulses and fried mutton. Indu kept silent.

The registrar lived in a four-storey mansion and inside the visitors' room if one looked up, he could see hundreds of images of himself on the multi-mirrored ceiling. The whole building was beautifully carved and decorated. Each door of the house costed about Rs. 300 (Mulchand Panda bought the same door for Rs.150 after it got damaged). The haughtiness and selfish attitude of Registrar Sahab was apparent in his behavior as well. One evening, Mannu Sai, the younger brother of Roop Sai, who was a *fakir* and caretaker of Jalal Khan Wali's *makbara*, came to meet Registrar Sahab for some official work regarding a small plot of land that he cultivated. The office was crowded with people to bribe the Registrar Sahab to get work done in their favour. The poor *fakir* sat in a corner observing the transactions. The shower of rupees finally came to a halt at about 7.15 p.m. when all those who could afford it had paid for their work and had left. The poor fellow got up slowly from his corner and approached the Registrar Sahab with folded hands. 'What do you want?' asked the Registrar Sahab. The *fakir* explained his problem. On hearing it Sahab was highly irritated and blurted: 'Ya Allah, when will a day come when I shall be relieved from my job? It is already eight in the night and I am still plagued with work'. The *fakir* thought to himself: 'O what a thankless man is he. He has been filling his pockets during the last few hours with ill-gotten wealth and he refuses to heed to my pleadings just because I am empty handed. O Holy Allah, do justice to your subjects'. Praying thus, the *fakir* left.[54]

The Holy Allah heard the problem of the *fakir* and within a fortnight, the government ordered the suspension of Registrar Sahab who had to hand over his charge to another man. Tafazzul Hussain now felt the might of Allah. His sons became drug addicts, and turned out to be gamblers too, leading to the draining of all the wealth in a short time span. Soon they lost their house and other possessions and while the daughter was married off, the father and sons became homeless and destitute. All this took place when I had completed my primary school and was promoted to the middle school in Maudaha.

After this turnaround of fate, Tafazzul Hussain Sahab somehow managed to acquire a job as a *munshi* in the subdivision Tehsil of Maudaha where he earned a few paise by writing applications and filling up forms. While I was pursuing my studies in Maudaha, my father once asked me whether I recognized him. My father then told me about his past affluence and its decay due to his sinful ways. 'If by chance he pays you a visit, do treat him well. Feed him and offer him whatever money you can spare because he is old now and has paid dearly for his wrongdoings. Allah has already punished him severely'.

*Doha*

*To be proud in this world is a crime*
*It destroys human beings in no time*
*If you do not appreciate the food God serves*
*You will get the life you deserve*
*You will become a man who has to beg*
*With cloths not more than rag*
*Common men asked for many things as he was rich*
*And the fakir did just this*
*Yet pride deprived him of mercy and see*
*Taken away was all his wealth provided by Goddess Laxmi*

## Experiences of a God-fearing honest Man

When I was in class III in the primary school, there was a Sub Inspector, named Ijaz Hussain Sahab, who was in-charge of the police station in Jalalpur. He received a very low salary of Rs. 75 per month but was very honest and law-abiding. He neither took any bribes nor would he harass anyone. He even refrained from accepting any *ghee* from a Hindu, let alone milk or curd. He was religious and had a soft spot for the poor. Unlike other arrogant and ill-mannered policemen, Ijaz Sahab was well behaved and good-natured. He never seemed to get angry and always had a smile on his face.

There is a saying that a dog licks the mouth of an upright man. This was true for this man whose righteousness had antagonised him from a certain section of the society. These people tried to falsely implicate Ijaz Sahab and complained to the Superintendent about the former taking bribes. However, no action could be taken against Ijaz Sahab because there was no proof of his alleged malpractices.

*Doha*

*Nobody can harm those who are protected by the Lord.*

Inspector Sahab could never prove Sub Inspector Ijaz Hussain's guilt but still reported the rumor to the Collector who in turn noted it down but could not do anything against Ijaz Sahab due to lack of evidence. A few days later, the Collector decided to tour the district and sent the message that he would be arriving in Jalalpur on a particular day. On receiving the notice, the Sub-Inspector immediately began preparations for the Collector's reception. Ijaz Hussain along with others, on the day that the Collector arrived with his tent and lodgings, came to receive him and presented himself before him. Since the Collector was to stay at Jalalpur for a couple of days, it was decided that he would go for hunting the next day and Ijaz Hussain, along with a few men would accompany him. Even though the *thanedar* refrained from hunting, he could not refuse to accompany the Collector. The Collector had wanted to see Ijaz Hussain's reaction to his order.

Early next day after breakfast, the team left for the jungle. As the drums began, the animals ran to the open fields fearing the cacophony. It was here that the hunters waited for their preys. However, whenever an animal ran close to *thanedar sahab,* he would open fire on the sky and frighten the animal away rather than aiming at it. Seeing this happen frequently, the Collector asked him the reason. The *thanedar* replied that he was only following the government's orders and he could not go against them. He added that during riots, the police was required to frighten away the mobsters by firing blank before embarking on taking aim. Only if the mobsters persisted, police were allowed to shoot. Hearing this, the Collector smiled but said nothing.[55]

## Test of Truth through a Horse

After the hunting was over, the Collector went to his tent in the afternoon. His stable-man took his horse, tied it and gave it food and water. On the other hand, the *thanedar* tied his horse to a nearby tree and attended the Collector without giving his horse any food. The poor animal continued to be without food and the Collector noticed this. When he finished his meal and after his siesta, he came out of his tent in the evening and sat under that very tree where the *thanedar's* horse was tied. The *thanedar* walked up and down waiting for his orders. Suddenly the Collector recalled what the Inspector had said about the *thanedar*. He summoned Ijaz and asked him: 'I have heard that you accept bribes, is it true?' Hearing this, the *thanedar* beseeched him with folded hands and replied, 'My Lord, what you say is always true as my post is that of a *daroga*, which means liar in Arabic. If I tell you the truth, I shall be treated as a liar because of my rank and you will not believe me. Khuda himself is my witness. What can I say about myself? Even my horse will refuse any ill-gotten thing. You may test him now if you please'.

The Collector was stupified over this revelation. He called a Constable and asked him to fetch some stolen food (grams) from a shop for the hungry horse. The policeman quickly ran and brought it. In Hindustan, two spiced ladoos and soaked grams twice a day were given to horses for their health and strength. The Collector ordered a feeding bag filled with grams to be tied on the neck of the *thanedar's* horse. The *thanedar* then spoke to his horse. 'Son', he said, 'Eat this, if you ever have consumed ill-gotten food before. Otherwise do not even dare to touch it'. The starving horse bowed its head and stood steadfast as if there was nothing to eat at all. This was very touching indeed. The Collector fell silent. The *thanedar* subsequently called a *chowkidar*, gave him two paise from his pocket and told him to bring some stale grass. When the *chowkidar* brought the dry grass, the *thanedar* removed the feeding bag from the horse's neck and offered it to the starving animal saying: "Eat it. It is the wage for your labour'. The horse immediately complied.

The Collector could not control himself. He rose, shook hands with the *thanedar* and even embraced him. He then wrote a *hukm-nama* in favor of Daroga Ijaz Hussain and transferred him to the city of Rath that was the most lucrative place in the whole district of Hamirpur and increased his salary to Rs. 150 per month, which was far more than what any *thanedar* received during those days.

## The simple Lifestyle of the *Thanedar* and the Gift

Rath was about 12 miles from Jalalpur. The *thanedar* lived there with his old mother and had two younger brothers who studied in an English-medium school. He was unmarried and very religious. He shifted to Rath and took charge of the police station there. He became very popular and the people were delighted with his posting in their city. The rich fed the poor and gave donations. Fireworks and celebrations marked his arrival. A free kitchen was opened in his name and the *thanedar* himself donated Rs. 75 from his salary to help increase the food supply while he continued to live on the same amount of salary (Rs. 75), which he had received earlier. In fact, Rs. 75 was insufficient to even maintain his two young brothers who studied in English-medium school in Hamirpur. The *thanedar* lived a very simple life. He would cook the meals for his mother and himself and if he was busy, his mother would do the cooking. Whenever he went on a tour or patrolling, he took with him only two dry rotis and was satisfied with it. His duty and his God were his only passions.

His monthly expenses would usually amount to Rs. 100 to 125 just because he was very generous to the poor and needy. However, somehow or the other, all his expenditure would be met with each month by the grace of Allah. Gradually, the fame of this man spread far and wide like the fragrance of *kasturi* and people from different walks of life aspired to see him and share their problems. He fixed up a time every day from four to six in the evenings to listen to the problems of hundreds of them. Soon he became showered with gifts and donations. He would touch each gift made by an affluent Muslim and give it to run the free kitchen. He never touched any gift donated by a Hindu but nevertheless always thanked and blessed them saying: 'May the Lord provide you in abundance. Go and donate your money to some temple or to the poor'. Every day, the *munshi* of the community kitchen came for two hours to present his accounts to the *thanedar*.

By the grace of God and the heavy expenses invested in their education, the two brothers of the *thanedar* managed to pass their B.A.H.L. examination in the English medium school and soon got employment as highly ranked government officials in different places. The *thanedar* now came closer to Khuda and acknowledged his blessings.

## Death of *Thanedar* Ijaz Hussain

*Allah is one.*[56] *His word is one. The Holy Book says that the old order changes and gives place to a new one. Aging is universal. Everything happens with Allah's consent.*

Since the arrival of the *thanedar*, the populace of Raath enjoyed a secure and peaceful atmosphere. There was no untoward incident and no sign of robbers or anti-social elements. The tree of bribery had been uprooted. All those involved in such crimes feared the *thanedar*. Every government employee appreciated his way of work and themselves avoided unfair means. During his period, if a culprit would be arrested for an offence, the *thanedar* would try to reform him rather than punish him. A Muslim offender was made to confess his crime and had to swear by Allah never to repeat it. On the other hand, a Hindu criminal had to swear in the name of Gangaji and promise to turn over a new leaf. Whenever there was a confrontation or fight, he used to mediate between the two parties and if anyone would be injured in a scuffle, the *thanedar* would arrange for proper treatment and adequate compensation. In case of murder, he made a proper investigation before handcuffing the accused and pleaded on his behalf if one was repentant. He would hand over the culprit to the law if it were beyond his jurisdiction. He however, did not refrain from appealing for a criminal if required, in a court of law. The government knew about *thanedar sahab's* judgment and paid heed to his pleas. Very few cases from the peaceful city of Raath reached the courts for justice during Ijaz Sahab's reign. The ideal life of this man made him famous and revered and everyone prayed for his immortality. Yet, Allah's decision is binding and his followers have to accept it willingly. In this world of sin and evil, the Holy One does not allow His beloved ones to live for long. It is His nature.

A day arrived on which the *thanedar* fell ill due to some stomach ailment. He started taking medicines as a cure. This disease would subside at times only to flare up later. After some days, he was struck with fever, or rather his doom. Two days later, on a Friday at 1 p.m., he succumbed. A shining star of Hind disappeared into the darkness of death. The news of his demise spread like wildfire throughout the region through letters and by mouths. Soon every town and village knew about this sad event. The whole town condoled his death. All the offices and schools of the district were closed and the flag hoisted at half-mast as a sign of mourning.

On hearing about the death of Ijaz Hussain, his friend *zamindar* Chatri of Antrauli village, about 9 miles from Raath, fainted. When he regained consciousness, he asked whether the news was true or just a rumour. Then he mounted his pony and set off to Raath to attend the burial ceremony. Ijaz Hussain was about 50 years old when he died. His face shone like the *kaba sharif*[57] as his spirit departed. His body lay on a bed when *zamindar* Chatri arrived crying incessantly. The old friend looked up to the sky with folded hands and prayed: 'Allah, allow me to meet my dear friend'. He then turned to the corpse and as he looked up towards the door he saw Daroga Sahab standing there. Seeing this the *zamindar* again fainted. When he gained consciousness, he again started crying.

Thousands turned up from government offices, cities and villages to pay their last respect to the departed soul. Even though the rain poured the whole day, the streets of the town were crowded with people. The drizzling continued throughout the day and seeing no respite, it was decided to hold the funeral despite the drizzle. Then the old mother of the deceased spoke: 'Son, look so many people have come for your sake and are facing this bad weather, pray to Holy Khuda to prevent them from getting drenched'. The near ones lifted the coffin and the procession headed towards the cemetery while it was still raining. When they reached there, everyone was surprised to find that those who had carried the coffin, and those who had dug the grave were completely dry! Everybody wondered and praised Allah for his miracle. The 'Bara Maulvi' [senior *maulvi*] of Rath conducted *namaaz* at the burial site and then the coffin was lowered into its grave and everybody put earth on it. After the rituals and final prayer for the departed soul, everyone walked back to their respective homes with a heavy heart.

The mourning that followed the death of *thanedar* Ijaz Hussain Sahab was exceptional. No words from my pen can ever describe the grief, which the whole society experienced that time. The memory of that day still makes me cry. Later it was heard that on the third day of his death, when the *thanedar's* relatives went to offer flowers on his grave, they found that it was already decorated with three flowers of a kind nobody had ever seen before. (In Hindustan, on the third day of a person's demise, at about 8 or 9 a.m., flowers dipped in oil are strewn on his/her grave. The ritual is called *phool utarna*. Thereafter, everyone sits on a clean floor and participates in a meal of boiled or baked grams or peas in the name of Allah. In the evening, the *fakirs* are offered a sumptuous meal also in the name of Allah. Days later, people began to recall Ijaz Hussain as a saint and every Friday evening, a *shirini* and a small fête was organised near his grave. I sincerely pray to God to accept this upright and honest man in his Heaven. Aameen Aameen. Rabbul Aalmeen!

*Doha*

*The world is like a platform*
*People arrive and people go*
*During good times, mother, father, son and wife are all friends*
*Yet in adverse situations only God will save you*

## The Game of Fate

*A person cannot change his fate as this is in the hands of Ram.*

I have earlier mentioned that after passing my middle school, I began to look after my house and business at Bharkhari village. Days passed off peacefully. One day I decided to apply for the job of teacher in a government school as a trial. I secretly drafted an application and sent it to the Deputy Inspector of Education without the knowledge of my father. A few days later, I was offered to join a primary school in the village Atrauli on a salary of Rs. 9 per month. I was supposed to start my work on the first of April 1891. This made me very happy. I showed the letter to my father and explained what it said. He was very distraught at my move because he did not want me to leave home and pursue a career elsewhere knowing well what Hakim Sahab had predicted about me. But after showing his displeasure, he allowed me to do whatever I wished, saying that I was old enough to make my own decisions and that he did not want to be an obstacle in my way and damage my aspirations. 'Khuda will do his wish and I shall accept my fate', he said. 'Who am I to question His will?'

I had reached Atrauli even before the date of my joining. Half a year passed by happily, but afterwards I became bored with the routine and began to think about my next step. I tried hard to persuade myself but in vain. After all, my heart wanted me to be tossed about. It shunned all good advice. All of a sudden, a notion of taking a month long vacation to meet my relatives and friends struck me. 'Maybe a tour of this kind could pacify my straying thoughts', I said to myself. With this in mind, I applied for a month's leave stating that I needed a break to recoup my deteriorating health as it had been affected adversely in a new place. Therefore, I stated that I required some rest at home and some medicines. I sent this application to the Deputy Inspector (Education). Two months later, my holiday was sanctioned and another teacher was deputed in my place for a month. I returned home. When my father asked me the reason for my return, I told him that I was not keeping good health and therefore, had come on a vacation. Two weeks later, on 14 August (*bhado*), on the occasion of *anand chaturdasi* (a Hindu festival), I left home forever. Only Khuda knew that it was going to be my farewell day, because then I had no intention of going away! I walked aimlessly like a moron without luck at six in the morning thinking to return after a stroll. I had no fight or altercation with anybody at home and food, clothes, etc. were not a problem. There were no enemies to be afraid of, I had no credits or debits, and government had not put a price on my head. If anything was wrong, it was in my destiny. The time had come for me to seek a livelihood elsewhere and Holy Khuda had passed his verdict, which no one could stop.

I walked alone to my elder brother-in-law, Sardar Khan's place at Bokhar. He served under Mohanlal Panda of Jalalpur and was posted at Bokhar, about 25 miles from my village. I reached there at four in the evening. My brother-in-law was very fond of me. I stayed at his house for four days but did not tell him about my desire and destination. What could I say? I myself did not know where I was going. On the fifth day, I took leave and came to Jalalpur where I had lots of Hindu and Muslim friends and relatives. There I stayed for a whole week after putting up at my sisters' home. I did not spill the beans at them as well. All they knew was that I had just come to visit them and would return home afterwards. On the eight day, I walked off to Chandpur village, in the district of Kanpur. Here lived my maternal uncle Nazm Khan's son. Nazm Khan had accompanied me to Hamirpur when I had gone there to appear in the test in which success had promised a government stipend. I had never come here before. I stayed there for 3 weeks but ate at my uncle's house for one day only. The rest of the days, all other relatives who lived nearby invited me.

It was here that I heard that the *ramlila* was being organised at Kanpur.[58] I longed to see it and requested my cousin Mustafa Khan to allow me to go to Kanpur. He flatly refused, saying that I was prone to fall prey to the unwanted elements of the city since I was new to the place and had no experience of travelling to a town like Kanpur. 'I am afraid that you might be lured away by a deceitful person and lose your way', he said. I protested: 'Bhai Sahab, am I a bird to be caught by a man in his net and sold off?' But my wise cousin stuck to his 'No' for a long time. However, after my continuous pestering during 3 consecutive days, he finally permitted me to go. He explained in great detail about my journey, the railway station and the place where the Ramlila was being held. He came with me to the station, bought my ticket and helped me into the train while cautioning me about everything that he could and then he left. I was glad to be on a train for the first time in my life. Though I had read about the railways in my books, I had never travelled in one before. In our district, there is only one railway track that connects Allahabad to Janshi via Mahoba but I had never had the opportunity to see it. I had no idea about how to board or embark from a train. The bell rang and the whistle blew. The train began to move with a 'Chhuck, Chhuck' sound and it surprised me as I saw how everything around me was changing with the moving train. I pondered over my family and my country from where I was going far away.

Three hours later, at four in the evening, the train reached Kanpur. I got down with the other passengers and surveyed the station full of people resting or walking here and there. Everyone went to the exit hall of the station and then their ways parted. I also walked off to the place where my cousin had directed me to go. I asked several people on my way. My cousin had briefed me that the station was in Collectorganj [see photograph] and close to it there was a small rivulet. I was to cross it, and ask about an inn that lay straight ahead of the bridge over the brook. The inn was to be my abode because it was very close to the site where the ramlila would be held [see photograph]. I had been allowed a 3-day-stay and watch the ramlila and the city, after which I was supposed to return on the fourth day by the same route to Chandpur and by the same train. My cousin had said that he would receive me at the station on that day.

I did as I was told and walked down the road leading into the city from the bridge. I asked for the inn, which was about an hour's walk from the station. The flag of the Ramlila, which was hoisted in front of it, was its landmark. At 6 p.m., I checked in, took bath, had my supper and went off to bed. Next morning, after refreshing myself and after my breakfast, I went off to see the city. I returned at 11 a.m., took lunch and rested for a while. At two in the afternoon, I went to see the Ramlila. It was the day of Lanka dahan [the burning of Lanka] in the play. The programme was worth watching. The scenario of Lanka was made of golden shining paper on a bamboo framework, which was filled with fireworks. The door of Lanka was adorned with various decorations. A wooden ape was tied to the end of a rope, which connected a tall tree to the door of Lanka. On its tail, gunpowder and oil was tied. At seven in the evening, when the burning of Lanka was to commence, a man climbed the tree, lighted the wooden monkey's tail and pushed him along the rope towards the door of Lanka. The monkey was pulled back after Lanka was lit. As soon as the fire spread, different types of fireworks began to explode with a bang. As the fire engulfed the decorated door of Lanka, the lights and colours that it emitted, were a treat to watch. Hundreds of rupees had been spent by the *mahajan* to prepare this spectacle.

For 3 consecutive days, my eyes were treated to these shows. The day of 'Bharat Milap' was the best of all the exhibits. On that day, the whole city of Kanpur was decorated and lighted up. On the fourth day, I checked out of the inn early in the morning and walked back towards the station. When I reached Collectorganj, I strolled into the market place that was the biggest in Kanpur. Then I slowly but steadily inched towards the bridge over the stream adjoining the station, thinking of boarding the train at 8 o'clock and returning to Chandpur.

## Admission in the Depot

I was standing on the bridge when the clock in the marketplace struck seven. From nowhere, two Muslim men, with feminine faces, approached me. I guessed they were money minded and wicked men. Yet, they were well dressed and looked like gentlemen, so I wished them '*Salam-ala-kum*'. They reciprocated my greeting and asked me to be introduced. I said I was staying in the Parade Inn and planning to catch the 8 o'clock train to Chandpur. Then they lied to me and said that the train had been rescheduled and was now to leave at noon according to the new timetable. I was trapped in their net. Thinking them to be knowledgeable men from the city, I believed them. As I had some more time left, I decided to visit the marketplace again and take some breakfast. 'Are you interested in doing a job?' one of them asked. 'What kind of job?' I inquired. 'A government job', one said and then asked me if I had any education. I told them that I had passed middle school. They responded happily and said that I could be made a *sardar*. 'You shall be paid twelve annas each day and your work would be to supervise labourers in the sugar business. You will travel on a government ship loaded with sugar once in 3-4 months. If you have any doubt regarding your payment you may come and get registered yourself at the government office. If you follow me then I can show you the labourers who would be working under you. If you agree then your boarding and lodging shall be free from today onwards and the chief will bear your expenses. You will have no problem at all. You will enjoy life, and if you work honestly, you shall be duly promoted'.

Such sugary talk swept me off my feet and I forgot everything: my family, my country and myself. I started daydreaming and believed those evil minded men. Twelve annas per day meant Rs. 24 per month, and this amount was very difficult to earn here. I started to convince myself and said to myself: 'Why not work for some time? If it doesnot suit me, I would quit. If I am registered with the government, everything should be allright and my salary would also be ensured'. With this one-sided thought in mind I consented to go with them. On the way to Babu Ramnarayan Singh's depot, they kept on luring me with future prospects of my new career. Babu Sahab was present in his house that time. The three of them talked in privacy and then called me in. They took me to the verandah and showed me some men and women who were present there and would be working under me. One of them said: 'Babu Ramnarayan is a government worker and he will register you with the Magistrate Sahab Bahadur'. Then both evil men left me there and went off.

Ramnarayan babu turned to me and said: 'Stay here and look after these men while I am away'. I agreed and began to stay in the depot. The bird was trapped and caged. I asked myself: 'What can be done now?' If only I would have had the guts to cancel my agreement in front of the Magistrate, I could have come out of that mess. But I did not know about this possibility and even if I had known I still would have remained there because Holy Allah had picked me out and I was destined to leave Hindustan and earn a living in Surinam. I was to become the black sheep of my family in Hindustan. Very sad indeed!

## A Tale to Tell

There is a bird called, red robin, which some people keep as pets. This bird is very beautiful and chirps in a melodious manner. On the other hand, there is another bird called a crow, which is black and ugly, but clever and vicious. One day, a bird catcher netted several birds of different feathers, e.g., *mynah*, *bulbul*, etc. and along with them was caught an unlucky crow despite his smartness. A red robin seeing this scene from a tree nearby asked: 'How come you have been trapped with the other birds?' 'I have been caught due to the chattering of these birds', replied the crow. Hearing this, the red robin flew away while the poor crow was left at the mercy of the hunter. I met a similar fate as the crow. My inquisitive ability left me like the red robin that flew away. I stopped wondering about alternatives and accepted my fate. What remained was my clever mind that of a crow. My reasoning had failed me and the 11 years of study proved futile. I stayed on at the depot.[59] Occasionally, I went off to the city to roam around.

One day, while passing through the market of Collectorganj, I saw two different varieties of rice piled up for sale. One was the one we normally ate, while the other was flat-rice, which I had never seen before because it was not available in my home district and region (Bundelkhand) to which I belonged. However, I had heard about *chura* from my elders, being eaten in Antverd and in the east, but I did not know that this region between the Ganges and Yamuna rivers was called Antverd [the *doab*, the tract of land included between two rivers as in the Ganges and the Yamuna]. I stopped in order to better observe it. I asked a shopkeeper about the flattened rice and he replied that it was called *chura* and eaten along with sugar. Urged to taste it I bought sugar and *chura* for 1 paisa each, and went to the riverside to taste the new stuff. The *chura* was tasteless like a morsel of wooden chips. Regretting my decision to buy that item, I threw all *chura* in the river, ate the remaining sugar and went back to the depot.

Kanpur is a famous city spread over more than 15 miles in all directions. It is densely populated and the only one of its kind in the whole region. It is the centre of cotton and textile factories, flourmills, has a big market, flourishing business houses and major government offices, all employing thousands of people, apart from a military cantonment. Flourmills run by windmills and hydel mills were also there. One day, I wandered off to another market called Phula Bazaar, where I heard a peculiar sound emanating from a huge building. When I peeped inside, I saw about eighty men working on a strange machine that I had never observed in my home district. I enquired from a man working there and he replied: 'It seems that you are from Bundelkhand, across the river Yamuna?' I nodded. 'Well, this is not available in your region because there is no rice granary in that area. This system to remove the husk from the grain to extract rice is called *dheki*. Then I understood that it was a tool to mill the rice grain and it required a good amount of labour. Later on in Surinam, I encountered this very *dheki* on numerous occasions and there it pressed sweat from our bodies.

I lived in Kanpur for three months during which I did not even write a letter to my father fearing that he might come and take me back. When we were about to leave for Calcutta, I sent him a letter saying that I was well and on my way to Calcutta. I did not mention my admission into the depot and my whereabouts in Calcutta. I and sixty other men were sent to Faizabad from Kanpur for 3 weeks. Faizabad and Ayodhya are close to each other. Only a guava mangrove separates the two cities. One day a recruit ran away from the depot in Faizabad. Babu sent me to Lakar Mandi to search for him. This place is across the river Saryu that had no bridge because it was very wide. The railway station was at Lakar Mandi and the railway track connected it to the town of Bahraich. I went to the station to find the missing man. To cross the river Saryu, I had to walk over a bridge made up of 95 boats. The ghat of the river was well constructed. Ayodhya city housed more *sadhus* than common folk and was thickly populated. Hanuman Gadi, Lakshman Gadi, Ram Bhavan, Sita Rasoi, etc. were sites worth seeing. Raja Ramchandra was born here and it was the capital of his territory. Faizabad boasts of Chowk Bazaar, a museum and other such places but it is not as big and densely populated as Kanpur or Ayodhya. There are agricultural fields inside the township itself where potatoes, cauliflower and other vegetables are grown.

After three weeks, 150 people were enrolled and sent off to Calcutta from Faizabad, including myself. We boarded the train at 4 p.m. and reached Lucknow where we stayed overnight in an inn. During the short stay I could witness very little of the beauty of this city situated on the banks of river Gomti. But I caught the beauty of the huge well-decorated buildings, the cleanliness and lighting of the city. I also saw the *sarai* that was built by Nawab Wajid Ali Sahab who had also constructed the *imambara* here. These two buildings and the government railway platform were superbly constructed. We left Lucknow next day at eight in the morning and continued in the train to Calcutta; we stopped en route at Mughalsarai where we had to change and board another train. Mughalsarai has a big station and is a railway centre. Business concerned with the railways flourishes here. The railway tracks form a dense network.

We boarded another train at Mughalsarai and proceeded for Calcutta. We were given *bhuja* (baked grains) and sweets to eat every now and then. After 2 days of travelling in the train, observing people, fellow passengers and different stations, we finally reached Howrah station situated on the banks of river Bhagirati (Ganges). It was four in the evening. Across this river lay Calcutta. The rush of people and the huge crowd there could upset even the most intelligent. Moreover, the number of trains, platforms and railway lines was very confusing indeed. We were completely dazed due to our village background and stood there staring at the activities going on. The two *brahmins* who had brought us here went off to arrange boats while we waited. Soon a few boats were brought to the shore and six men climbed into each of them. We reached the Surinam depot in the evening and were lodged in a camp near its entrance. We ate rice, *daal* and vegetables to our satisfaction and slept soundly after our tedious 3-day journey.

## Behaviour of Upper-Caste Hindus in the Calcutta Depot

Till we reached at the depot, we had been allowed to cook our own meals in the manner we wanted and were given the necessary ingredients. Besides, everyone followed his own rituals and systems. One would wear the *janau* [sacred thread], a second a *tikka* [sign on the forehead] and a third the *kanthi mala* made out of flowers, etc. People acted according to the rules and regulations of his or her caste and religion and followed the system and recognized high castes and labelled the untouchables, etc. They had thus managed to preserve religious sanctity.

In the depot we got up at 8 o'clock and the *sardar* [supervisor], who was a fat *brahmin*, gave each of us soap, oil, etc. and ordered us to refresh ourselves in the river Bhagirathi. They told us that after return in the depot we had to wear the government uniform and enter the camp. The two *brahmins*, who had accompanied us from Faizabad to Calcutta, were the sons of the *jamadar*. They brought us to the river for taking bath. It was ebb tide and all the men and women began to wash themselves. The *brahmins*, *kshatriyas*, *vaishyas* and others laughingly began to throw off their threads and necklaces into the river saying: 'Mother Ganges, we offer you our belongings, if ever we return, we shall adorn them again'. They then oiled themselves and took bath and thus became one with the sudras. The two *brahmin* escorts stood at the banks observing, but not uttering a word. How could they say anything? They were themselves the least bothered about caste and religion. If their brothers had agreed to become converts, why should they bother?

After this bath that removed the caste barrier, everyone returned to the camp. The fat *jamadar* also did not ask why the *brahmins* had discarded their holy thread and necklaces. He was t not bothered, in his own interest, to try and maintain the sanctity of caste and creed. He provided a yellow *kurta* and *dhoti*, and a red *dhussa* [scarf], to each one of us. Wearing this we all looked like yogis emprisoned in a camp. At 10 a.m., the food was ready and the *jamadar* now distributed a tin plate and an earthen pot. From the plate we had to eat food while the pot was used to keep water for multifarious activities like drinking, washing hands and face, and washing after defecation, etc. This was highly unhygienic and especially against the habits of the *Sanatanis* [orthodox Hindus] who had earlier followed their beliefs rigidly. I later on asked these followers of the Sanatan Dharma in Surinam[60] why they had not resisted such force in the Calcutta depot. These were exactly those people who later on were to cause unrest and division in Surinam.

As soon as the bell rang and announced lunchtime, every person, now looking alike in his or her dress, lined up. There was no distinction anymore between an uppercaste person and the lower castes. No Hindu wore the sacred thread or had put *tilak* on their foreheads. No other Hindu symbol was to be found among them. All Hindus had become *sudras*. There was no differentiation any longer between *brahmins*, *kshtriyas*, *vaishyas* or *sudras*. However, the Muslims with their beards and *topi* could still be singled out. They also offered *namaaz* either on their beds or under a nearby mango tree.

In order to get food, we had to line up in two separate queues, one for men and the other for women. There was no separation based on caste, religion or class. At this point in time no *brahmin* or *kshtriya* protested that they would not sit along and eat with Muslims or *chamars* [lower castes]. This is because they all had become *sudras*. A smaller depot adjoining the one in which we stayed, housed the kitchen, dining space and the dispensary. It was here that we all lined up with our tin plates and earthen pots. There was no demarcation between caste and religion among the recruits. No upper caste man or woman complained about this system. The servers now brought rice on a cart, and *daal* and vegetables in buckets. A Bengali named Hari Babu, wearing English boots, served rice with a big tin ladle beginning from one end of the queue to all those present regardless of his or her belief and status. Following him were others with buckets-full of *daal* and vegetables. God knows to what religion these servers belonged!

Everyone started eating greedily at the same time and side by side and forgot all about religious rules. Nobody said a word about anyone being untouchable or of another religion and all shared one mess and the food. Neither did a Hindu ever complain about having to sit next to a Christian nor did he object to the fact that the food was served by someone wearing shoes. They never objected to their plates being used by different castes and therefore had made the food impure and destroyed their religion. Later on, in Surinam, one could wonder how these same people had suddenly become *brahmins* who boycotted Muslims and created division in all households. It was rather surprising therefore to find these same people proclaiming to be pure and faultless and wanting to separate themselves from the Muslims and others, and which behaviour caused a schism between Hindus and Muslims. The *brahmin jamadar*, who was the chief of all *sardars*, wore his holy thread and offered his prayers regularly with *tilak* on his forehead. He could have requested the government to arrange for separate lodging and provision for everyone according to his or her religion and caste, but he did not bother. He was more concerned about himself and his own family than his religion and society. However, only he cannot be held responsible since he could not have done anything to change the situation singlehandedly.

The government did not interfere with anyone's religion. It was secular and everyone was free to follow or abandon any faith he or she wished. The culprits were the Hindus themselves who discarded their sacred belongings and practices after arriving here. On the ship, it would have been difficult to observe these practices but in the depot of Calcutta, it could have been done. These uppercaste Hindus should have preserved their religion upto Calcutta at least. I was offended by their attitude, because the government had not imposed any restrictions on any religion here. The breach of religion did not end here and these people resorted to infidelity. They had not brought their wives along and they did not hesitate to have other women from different castes and creed to keep them company. They also were very close and intimate with the untouchables, and ate, drank, and had fun with them, and started relations with their womenfolk. Their company was therefore, those very people who ate pigs, cows, etc. and they even impregnated their seeds in these women. These men who later on proclaimed to be staunch followers of their faith did not at that time avoid one single act of sin.

In the past, renowned and true *brahmins* who would make, drink and sell alcohol were jailed. I do not know whether these activities were considered to be acceptable to their faith or not. The epic of these Hindus describes Ravana, the grandson of Pulasth Muni and son of Vishshrava, who though being a Brahmin, was nevertheless condemned and treated as an evil spirit. However, Ravana had never prepared, or sold alcohol and had never been jailed for anti-national activities. He had never sold milk, curd or cows. Yet indeed, he ate meat, drank alcohol and abducted Sri Ramchandra's wife Sita. For these reasons he was declared to be a devil. Yet take the example of the so-called *brahmins* of Surinam, who distilled alcohol, sold and drank it, sold milk and cows, ate every conceivable non-vegetarian dish, and slept with women of different castes and religions to attain their 'salvation' by producing offspring from them. They committed all the sins mentioned in the *vedas*. Despite committing all types of sins, they still claimed to be chaste and pure! This I call the height of hypocrisy! Be they and their followers be blessed! This is what people label as an eyewash. Throw dirt into others eyes and blind them for your own benefit! In my opinion, the *sudras* were thousand times more god-fearing as evident from their manners and their way of life than these hypocrites.

I remember a story mentioned in the Bhagwat [Gita]. Once, Lord Sri Krishna and King Yudhistir, along with his younger brother Arjun, went to invite a sage to grace an occasion. Seeing them, the holy man welcomed them warmly. On getting the invitation, the sage could not refuse to accept it but since he did not want to go there, he began to weep. King Yudhistir could not contain himself either and joined him. Sri Krishna followed suit and Arjun did not hesitate to do the same thereafter. Nobody said anything there and then but when returned home, Arjun asked Sri Krishna the reason of his crying. He queried, 'the saint may have had some reason. King Yudhistir may have joined out of compassion. Yet you O Lord, you are the Supreme One. What made you weep?' Sri Krishna replied: 'Listen Arjun, the sage cried because the *vedas* do not allow a sage to accept any offerings or food from a king. Since it was therefore against his faith to accept the invitation, he wept. King Yudhistir lamented because he was hurt knowing that though he was so wealthy he could not buy a visit of a true *brahmin* to his home. And I wept because there are still such *brahmins* who maintain their faith and sanctity. However, in *kaliyug*, there will be *brahmins* who shall disregard these teachings of the *vedas* and become alienated from their religion. But you, you wept for no reason at all.' I fully acknowledge Sri Krishna Chandraji's prediction about the *kaliyug*. Every word he uttered has become reality. I have seen this with my own eyes. The *brahmins* of Surinam have started behaving according to the way aspredicted by Lord Sri Krishna. Tulsidas has veritably written:

*No matter how much affection is bestowed on a crow, it will not refrain from consuming flesh*

The *brahmins* acted in similar manner as these crows[61]. A week had passed and Sunday arrived. Goats and sheep were slaughtered and mutton and rotis were cooked. The bell rang for dinner and everyone ran with his or her tin plates and earthen vessels in their hands towards the mess. At that moment, *jamadar sahab*, Raghunandanji, the chief of all *sardars* announced that all the vegetarians should be fed separately. It was during that period that I noticed there were only ten to twenty Hindus who were vegetarian.

## Aboard the Ship

After 3 months of our arrival in Calcutta the final list of immigrants was made. During those 3 months, I had not gathered enough courage to write to my father. Just before our departure however, I sent him a letter telling him that I was on my way to the island of Surinam. We had come to know that our departure by ship was due in the first week of *phagun* (February) and that we would be with about 750 men and women. A few days later, we heard that the ship would be ready for sail the very next day. We were given our kit which included a tin plate, a tin *lota* [utensil], two blankets (one red and one black woolen one), two *dhotis*, three shirts (one black, one coloured and one white), two caps (one warm black one and the other coloured), and a bag to keep our new belongings.

The atmosphere in the depot, after this distribution, became very charged and people became anxious about their journey to an alien world. Our excitement and joy deprived us of sleep and the very next morning, at 10 a.m. when the bell rang for our meal, nobody seemed to be hungry at all. At 3 p.m., we were all aboard the ship on the deck and at 4 p.m. the anchor was weighed. A big steamer pulled the sailing ship out of the harbour into the open waters. It was somewhere in the month of February 1898. We left Calcutta behind and saw nothing more than water around us. At 5 p.m. we got something to eat. We received three buiscuits each and a big spoon of sugar. I had never seen let alone eaten buiscuits and wondered what to do with this food. One of my friends, Abdullah who had returned from Demerara [British Guyana] and now had become the chief, explained how to eat these buiscuits. I had to break them in pieces and mix them with water. I was still unable however to eat those buiscuits.

At dawn, the dark ocean surrounded us and the only land that we could discover was the place of the sacred temple of Jagannathpuri. The ship's mast and sails had been hoisted and they fluttered in the strong winds of *phagun*. The wind and the waves toyed with the vessel, which swayed to and fro in nature's hands. Excited and happy, we looked around us intently and experienced something that our parents and grandparents had never even dreamt of. In books it has truly been written that on a ship in the ocean, one is turned towards the Supreme Being, because it is there that

His works are manifested and all one's senses are focussed on Him. The vast stretch of water, the horizon, the playfulness of nature, all seemed so miraculous. The only things that we could see apart from these, was the ship and ourselves. When we still had been on the shore in Calcutta, I had been told about the experiences I would face aboard. However, I still had the impression that land would be more or less visible throughout our journey! But already on the very next day I realized that I had been completely wrong. Many of us became dizzy and had to vomit. Even I was not spared and was seasick for nearly 3 weeks. As a result I could not eat properly and only one roti with tamarind chutney was all that I could digest.

The food on the ship was far better than the food that had been served at the depot in Calcutta. But the nausea prevented us to feed ourselves well. On our ship, more than half of the passengers hailed from West Punjab and South Bundelkhand. Therefore, rice and rotis were served thrice a week while on Sundays we were given chura or biscuits. Every fifteenth day, fresh sheep meat and rotis were given to us. *Daal*, vegetables, tamarind chutney, tinned meat and limejuice were also provided daily.

Everyone, be it Hindu or Muslim, was forced to eat what was served. If anyone resisted, he would have to fast. On board, there were no distinctions between high castes and low castes, Hindus or Muslims, or other racial distinctions. Each of us had to eat the tinned meat fried in ghee to our heart's content. Persons, who were rigid in their religious practices, had not been allowed aboard of the ship to Surinam. No *brahmin* could remain chaste among us in Surinam since everyone had to eat meat, etc. This was unavoidable. There was provision of medicines and dressings for the sick and all of us were well cared for. Every week each one of us was supplied with a bar of soap to wash our clothes and take bath. If our clothes became worn out or were torn, we received new ones. The strong winds facilitated our journey and we crossed Cape Town (South Africa) after 4 weeks. Within 2 months, we reached Satlina, where we harboured for 24 hours to refill our food stock: sheep, vegetables, cucumber, potatoes, onions, drinking water, etc. The kind ruler of the place gave all of us pears to eat which were very sweet and delicious. A doctor checked our (medical) fitness and prescribed two pears for each of us including the 150 black men who worked on our ship and looked after its maintenance and safety. After 24 hours, we again set off.

A week later, the captain announced one evening that a storm was anticipated after a couple of days and after 3 p.m. we all became concerned and were disturbed. Yet who can avoid Khuda's orders? On the third day, dark clouds were seen high up in the sky. The captain ordered everyone to abandon the deck and go indoors one hour before the scheduled time. (Normally, we were to go inside at nine every morning and three in the evening for our meals that were served at 10 a.m. and 4 p.m. each day. After meals, we would again climb up and stay till 6 p.m.). When we were all inside, the captain ordered his men to pull down all the sails except the one in front. The sailors immediately set out to work, but before they could finish assembling the heavy cloth, the storm struck. Two of the three masts had been untied, but the third, which was in front, was still manned by a sailor who was trying to untie the sails. The force of the storm broke the tip of the mast and the sailor atop it fell into the waters along with the broken end. The captain immediately ordered to cut off all the ropes of the masts. The sailor who fell down could never be traced again. The ship tossed about dangerously and every now and then we felt as if we were going to drown and find our watery graves. Ropes were tied along the corridors and passages to hold on to while walking because the ship was shaking vigorously and it was difficult to stand still. The food served that day was biscuits and we ate inside with great difficulty amidst the turbulence. Things began to fall here and there and there was commotion everywhere. This storm lasted for 3 hours and we were extremely shaken and frightened. Khuda then commanded it to subside and the wind's velocity decreased. The Captain then ordered his men to hoist the sails again. Everyone thanked God that the ordeal was over and that they had survived. We were a happy lot.

The ship started sailing again with albeit two masts only, which remained functioning however, and we finally arrived at the shores of Surinam. The water was cold in the morning when we were told that our destination was now visible as we watched a thin streak of darkness at the horizon ahead of us. We learnt that this line that we could see, was the jungle of Surinam. The captain commanded that the sails be lowered to slow down the ship. As we drew near, this thin line seemed to grow broader and taller and by the afternoon we had neared the shore. Only two sails remained untied. The captain then sent an officer who was a European, along with four sailors in a boat to fetch the lineship (which guards the shore). The officer aboard this vessel knew the way to the harbour. As a rule, no ship was allowed into Surinam without the consent of the officer in charge at the shore. This rule is still being followed.

It was 2 p.m. and the wind was strong when a boat with five men on it was lowered to go and fetch the lineship. However, due to the winds, this boat was steered in the opposite direction towards where we had come from. The sailors desperately tried to guide the boat to the lineship and to beat the waves, but all was in vain. The boat kept on going in the wrong direction and within an hour or two we lost sight of it. The captain, the doctor and others now picked up their binoculars to trace the boat. A buoy with a white flag was now dropped into the sea. It was tied to a rope eased off by two men. Several long ropes were tied to each other to make a real long rope that was attached to this buoy. The captain intently watched as the buoy made its way towards the lost boat and it was five in the evening when he ordered the ropes to be pulled back. A rewind machine was used for this. It was eight in the night when the seamen were finally safely pulled aboard the ship. Everyone was grateful to God for this rescue action. Later that night, as the waves receded, the boat was again lowered to bring the government officer posted on land. At 8 a.m. the next morning, the boat returned. Now the charge was handed over to the officer of Surinam who guided our ship towards the shore. After about 3 hours, our ship finally arrived on the shore of Surinam after a more than two and a half month, long and tedious journey. The ship was anchored in front of the fortress for 2 days. On the third day, the Head Immigration Officer [also called *Agent-Generaal*[62] in Dutch] arrived. Sheetal Prasadji a very popular interpreter *(tolk)*[63] accompanied him. They climbed aboard, met everyone and announced the rules and regulations that were to be followed in Surinam. Then they left. After some time, a steamer parked next to our ship. Half of us were taken to the city of Paramaribo on this steamer, which after bringing us ashore returned to collect the others. The ship's captain took us to the Combé depot in Paramaribo. All in all 750 young men and women from Calcutta had reached Surinam on 13 April 1898. We thanked God for the successful journey. Avon was the name of the ship on which I reached Surinam.[64]

## The Coming of Indians to Surinam[65]

Initially, the *habsis* [blacks][66] from Africa were brought to Surinam to work as slaves. Later, on 1 July 1863 they were freed from bondage. Ten years later, i.e., on 5 June 1873, the first batch of 408 Indian immigrants, were brought to Surinam from India by the ship named the Lalla Rukha. These Indians had come to work on a 5-year contract (*girmit*). During the same year, four more shiploads were brought from India. Thus during the very first year, 1501 men, 556 women, and 390 children were brought to Surinam from India. By 1926, 64 ships laden with workers had arrived in Surinam from India and till 1938, 41 ships were sent from Surinam to India. Out of the total of 34,024 men, women and children who had come to Surinam, 11,659 returned to Hindustan.[67]

# VOLUME II

## The Depot in Surinam[68]

The depot at Paramaribo was more comfortable and quieter than the one in Calcutta. The food was better and the nice thing was that we could meet new people and make new friends. On Sundays, people from outside were allowed to visit the depot and meet the inmates. People from our country who were already working on the plantation came in search of men from their own village or hometown or in search of their relatives. When somebody discovered a known face, they cried out in joy, wept, embraced each other and talked at length. The place was charged with nostalgia. Such event was a normal phenomenon on every Sunday and the depot would be full of old and new immigrants meeting each other. A small get-together took place. During weekdays, men were dispersed to different plantations as per requirement. My friends signaled me to join them when they were assigned their place of work. On the first day of such an allocation, my friend Subhan (from Allahabad District)[69] and I sat among the crowd of recruits. Even though people on our ship who had been in Surinam before had warned us not to sit there on the first day since the place of appointment would be Nickeri[70], we left it to Allah who would decide upon our destination. After all, we had to work somewhere.

With Khuda's support, on that first day the first six, including the two of us, were allotted work on the plantation 'Lust en Rust' [in Sranan Tongo this plantation was called Skerpi]. The next six were sent to the 'Vredenburgh' plantation and another batch to the 'Peperpot'. That was all for that day. This routine continued during 4 weeks and at the end all men and women had been assigned their place of work. During our 4-week stay in the depot in Paramaribo, nothing worth mentioning occurred and we spent our time in peace and comfort. When we returned to our camp, people enquired about our assigned working place and those who knew the place, said we were lucky to get work on such a plantation because the *garamsara* [the owner of the plantation] [also called papa] was very kind and gentle. Then, after we all had been allotted a working place, each of us was sent to his or her posting.

## Off to the Plantation Skerpi [Lust en Rust]

On our first day, Pandit Sheetal Prasad, a translator, read out instructions and rules in the presence of the *Bara Sahab* [Head Immigration Officer] and said: 'You are to work on your plantation for 5 years, after which, you shall be free to go and work anywhere you wish. If you decide to go back to your country, the government will sponsor your journey'. It was Friday when people destined for Skerpi were summoned at 8 a.m. We were four Muslims, one Hindu man and one Hindu woman. Pandit Sheetal Prasad told us to take breakfast and be ready by 11 o'clock. We nodded approvingly. Around eleven, two men came to escort us to our new destination. We said goodbye to everyone at the depot and headed towards the plantation. We had stayed a month at the Surinam depot in Paramaribo.

Across the coffee garden, where we had left our steamer, was a government bungalow and opposite to it in the harbour, was the residence and shop of our landlord Dolf Horst[71]. We were brought inside and made to sit in a room. At about 2 p.m., when the water level of the river receded, all six of us were put in a boat rowed by three oarsmen and one oarswoman. Before we left, we were given a large loaf of bread (which could not be eaten by one person alone), and some sugar. We gladly accepted it and ate as much as we could while looking out of the window and appreciating the scenery around.

One of the three oarsmen was a *brahmin* named Chandrashekhar[72]. He had brought the Ramayana and kept it in the boat. I chanced to see it lying there and felt an urge to pick it up and read from it. But as I reached out, the *brahmin* scolded me harshly saying that it was not a book belonging to my religion and I was not to touch it. Since I was a newcomer to the place, I immediately pulled back my hand in shame. It was wrong to touch anyone else's belonging without his or her permission. But I thought to myself that when I reach my plantation, I am surely going to procure and read this book. After all, what was this *brahmin* going to read in it anyway?

It was four when we reached our plantation. On seeing the boat, the *sardar* [supervisor] of the place, a *chamar* named Harangiram, came to receive us. Chandrashekhar, however, had told us that the man was a *brahmin* and that we were to salute him when he would appear. The *sardar* wore wooden slippers (*klompen*) and had draped a green cloth around him. We disembarked and said: 'Maharajaji, salaam'. He greeted us and replied that he was not a *brahmin* but a *chamar*. I said to myself: 'how a *chamar* dares to wear things meant only for *brahmins*? In our homeland, one would have been beaten with shoes till all hairs of the head would have fallen out. This man must be joking'. The *sardar* introduced us to *Meneer* [Sir] Bhusman and brought us to his bungalow. We saluted him and he seemed happy at our arrival. (The owner Dolf Horst, the manager Bhusman and the foreman Harangiram seemed all very nice and kind-hearted. The assistant-manager also known as *skreeman* was also a good man).

The manager ordered us to be given a lamp, oil and one room for every two men in the colony. We were five men and a woman who was without a husband. Seeing this, the manager asked the lady who her husband was. I do not know what happened to this bitch but she alleged that I was her husband. (Maybe she found me more youthful and handsome than the others). I was stunned and immediately refuted her allegation. But despite all my pleadings, the manager refused to heed to my clarifications and warned me of dire consequences if I refused to lodge with the woman. I was extremely exasperated. The government had made provisions for two persons to stay in one room and I could not be given a separate single room. I prayed to Allah to relieve me from this burden. Had I known about such a possibility, I would have brought with me a beautiful young *brahmin* or *kshtriya* girl from Kanpur of my own choice[73], because there would have been so many such girls who had wished to accept Islam and stay with me. But I had not wanted to keep a woman with me in a foreign land because I had planned to return to Hindustan after the completion of my 5-year contract. The manager ordered the foreman in the local dialect (*Nengre*) to put me along with the lady in one room. When we reached the street full of small houses and the foreman started allotting the rooms, I tried to slip along with Subhan inside the room meant for him. The foreman quickly grabbed the luggage from my head and put it in another room where the woman's baggage was kept. Then he turned around to me and said: 'If you dare to disobey the manager, I shall put you in a dark cell near the hospital and lock you up there'. Miserably, I stood in the corridor and contemplated my next move. If I quarrelled, I would be jailed and if I kept silent, I would be accepting a chain around my legs. The foreman had left us alone by then.

My friend Subhan, who was elder to me, came to me and consoled me. He said: 'this is a foreign land and you should think well before you act. As for today we have no one here but later on thousands will know us. Have patience, abide by the rules and bear with this lady. You have nothing to lose and everything will be okay after some time. There will be a way out sooner or later and now live according to the time. This period will be over in course of time'. I gratefully accepted my friend's proper advice and went inside my room. I put my things on the second bed. Every room had two beds consisting of three wooden planks each. I ate the remaining bread given to us on the boat and crept into my bed.

The next morning, the *sardar* took us to the shop and bought us the necessary cooking ingredients and utensils, a basket, a chopper [a sharp, sword-like tool to clear the forest], and a shovel for digging. He then ordered us to clean our rooms and cook for ourselves. It was Saturday and we were to start work in the fields on Monday. We returned and did as we were told. The newcomers were not allowed to mix with those who were already working there. We were not to visit their places. On Sunday, the *sardar* sharpened our choppers and shovels, and took us to the river to take bath. He also provided soap and some lime. Finally the weekend ended and the first day of our contract work had arrived.

## The First Day of my Contract Period in Skerpi

By manager's order, the night guard woke us up at four in the morning to cook our meals and get ready for work. We were to report for work at 6 a.m. We hurriedly cooked whatever we were able to, ate some of the food and kept some rice in our saucepans for lunch. We picked up our choppers and tiffin and walked off with the *sardar* when the bell rang. He took us to the cacao fields and allotted a bed each for every couple. A woman was to work with me. We were to cut about 10 feet of grass and collect it in the centre. For the cutting of grass of one bed, we would get Rs. 1.50 each[74]. The *sardar* then left us. I had never expected such a job. It made me cry. 'Did I deserve this?' I thought. I had spoiled my life for nothing. But now it was too late to regret.

It was rainy season and the ground was very wet and muddy. Mosquitoes were everywhere and in great abundance. Seeing this I said to myself, 'my soul, this is a foreign land where no one is known to me. Who will come and support me? The only one to whom I can turn to is Khuda who has cared for me and will take care of me in future as well'. As per government's law, we were to work on a minimal salary during the first 3 months, but had to be provided all living expenses. After this, each person would be paid according to his or her job. If I could not work under these conditions, how could I earn to fend for myself and save something? My days of easy living were now over and I had to resort to physical labour and face the tune of destiny. Thinking likewise, I picked up my chopper in Allah's name and started my work. Soon my hands became sore due to blisters and my arms hurt. I was confounded. I tried to do as much as I could and returned to my room at four in the evening when the day's work was over. Once more the *sardar* gave us some lime and liquid soap (*groene zeep*) for our bath.

Every day we followed this routine while the *sardar* guided us in our work. Finally the weekend arrived and on Saturday, we received our first payment. I had managed to cut more grass than the rest of my colleagues during the first week. I had cleared two and a quarter of beds and was given 25 paise (one fourth *du anna*)[75] extra. The owner took 25 per cent of the total amount we earned. However, a minimum amount of Rs. 2 was paid to even those who could not do the work properly during the first 3 months. Utensils and shoppers were freely provided. Therefore, newcomers were a liability for the government during the first 3 months. I was happy to get the money and thanked Allah for it. I saluted the manager and walked home. Week after week, Subhan and I received some extra money [above the minimum allowance].

## Decision not to touch the Ramayana

I now like to write about the *brahmin* Chandrashekhar, who had stopped me from touching the Ramayana on the boat to Skerpi. On Tuesday, during the very first week after our arrival in Skerpi, Pandit Janki Prasad, the *guru* of Chandrashekhar came to his house for *katha* and *gurumukh* recitations. In just 3 days, people of the place had learnt about my ability to read and write Hindi. Word about a Muslim well versed in Hindi had spread without my knowledge. Our lane was behind that of Chandrashekhar's lane. On Tuesday night, all invited people from the plantation had come to attend the occasion while we, the six new faces, lay quietly on our beds since we had not been invited.

When the *katha* and *gurumukh* ceremony was over and food was about to be served, Pandit Janki Prasadji asked his disciple Chandrashekhar about the new recruits in the plantation. 'Why do I not see any one of them? He inquired. 'They have not come', replied his follower. 'Did you not invite them?' *baba* asked. Chandrashekhar pleaded guilty and said he had not called us and then his guru ordered him to immediately invite us. 'The new immigrants from Hindustan deserve to be called first to such a gathering because they are like our guests. If you had not invited ten men who have been living here since long, it would not have mattered much. Go, bring and feed them', he commanded. Chandrashekhar quickly ran and requested us to join dinner. Then I said: 'Maharajaji listen. When we were in Hindustan, we (Muslims) did attend these gatherings, ate and gave a few paise for *aarti*. Yet here after just a day's work and no pay, we have nothing to give and since we are not invited, cannot partake in the feast. You may take the two lower-caste Hindus: a *koiri* [agriculturist] and a *garrerin* [shepherdess] but we four Muslims cannot come with you'. The man felt ashamed and begged not to refuse his invitation saying that he was extremely sorry for his mistake. His repeated attempts to coax us succeeded as we thought that being introduced to old batches of workers would be a nice and pleasant thing. Therefore, we all attended the function, greeted everyone, talked and ate with them in our old but clean clothes, which had been provided on the ship.

Our dress made us look different and we felt awkward in the company of the others and therefore decided to leave as soon as we had finished eating. But that was not to be because Panditji asked me to sit besides him and offered me some tobacco to smoke, which I refused politely. Then he asked me: 'I have heard that you know Hindi very well?' I replied that I had studied but how well, I could not say myself. Hearing this, he placed the same book, i.e., the Ramayana, which Chandrashekhar had brought on his boat, in front of me and asked me to read. I refused to touch it. Panditji asked me the reason. I told him to ask his disciple the cause of my refusal. Chandrashekhar did not say anything so I narrated the whole incident to Panditji who laughed with the others and scolded his follower who apologized for his misdoing. I then opened the book and asked Panditji which portion to read. 'Read about

Ramchandraji's marriage', he replied. 'Alright', I said, 'I shall read the *chaupai* and you explain'. Yet, Panditji asked me to do both things. When I began my reading and explanation, everyone present there was surprised. Panditji praised my *guru* for teaching me so nicely. For 3 hours in a row, I read the Ramayana and everybody sat silently during the whole period. After I finished, Panditji offered me a pajama, a jacket, a cap, a vest and a rupee folded in a handkerchief as gifts. He then summoned Chandrashekhar and told him to accept me as his *guru* and learn from me because I could teach him hundreds of *mantras* while he had been able to teach him just one so far. Saying this, he turned to me and requested me to accept Chandrashekhar as my pupil because though he was a *brahmin*, he was as ignorant as a *sudra*. 'Maybe he will learn something about his religion and be indebted to you for it', he told me. I said: '*In shah Allah*' [May Allah be with you].

From that day onwards, Chandrashekhar regarded me as his teacher and I began teaching him and a few more men who also had shown interest. This man had come here two and a half years prior to my arrival and had completed half of his contract. During his remaining days he learnt quite a lot and even went to a few places to recite the *katha* himself. When he became a *freeman*, he decided to go back to Hindustan. One good day he came to me and said: 'Munshiji, I wish to return to Hindustan. Please teach me *gayatri mantras* because if anyone ever asks me to recite these I shall be embarrassed. 'How many do you want to learn?' I asked. 'How many are there?' he queried. I said: 'Twenty-four'. He then pleaded with folded hands and requested me to teach him all of them. I picked up a small copy, and wrote down all the twenty-four *gayatri mantras* and gave it to him to take to India. He had come as an illiterate from Hindustan but went back as a *pandit*. He had no money when he returned but he acknowledged that he had acquired enough knowledge to make a living back home. He said that he would be grateful to me throughout life. By now I had learnt that the only craze of learning in Surinam revolved around the Ramayana and no one was bothered to know about mathematics, geography, science or any other subject. I therefore thought: '*Jai Ganesh Uma Mahesh*, so be it, let's see what happens later'. I did not force anyone to learn anything else. Soon, everyone in the plantation did know about my acquaintance with the Ramayana.

## Separation from the Woman and the Organization of a *Maulud*

We started following the same routine every day. The older workers had become used to us and we became increasingly familiar with Surinam, the new place. We started understanding how to cope in Surinam. Though the government was to support all new immigrants during the first 3 months, not everyone was bound to accept this support. When I learnt about it, I refused to accept this provision and after just 4 weeks, I paid off my debts to the government. I now was to be paid according to my labour. I returned home and equally divided the money, which the woman and I had received from our allowance. I gave her half, collected my belongings and went off to my friend Subhan's room. Now the woman was bewildered. She began to scream loudly, shouting: What will I eat now? How will I survive?' Not wanting to pursue the matter any further, I gave her even my share of money and told her to be happy with it. However, she went to the manager and complained, 'my husband has deserted me. Who will now look after me and bear my expenses?' Hearing her complaint the manager inquired from me and when I denied her allegation, he ordered to give one fifth of my earnings every week to the woman till her expected son would be six months old'. My whole body burned with ire and I replied angrily: 'I will teach a lesson to the person who dares to touch my salary' and then I walked off. Till today she has not given birth to a son and not a paise has been deducted from my earnings. The chains that had bound me broke and I was set free. I began to work, earn and live happily with my friend Subhan.

That week, Subhan also stopped taking the government's allowance. He was a workaholic and stronger than me. He worked like a woman in the house, did everything from cooking to cleaning and did not allow my helping-hand saying that he was still alive and I need not bother. He never did anything without consulting me. Whatever he earned, he gave it to me to keep without any accounts whatsoever. He had immense faith in me. Whenever his clothes would tear or fade, I would ask him to buy new ones. He would inquire whether any money would be left after our purchase of food, etc. When I bought anything for myself, I was sure to buy the same thing for Subhan. Both of us lived like blood brothers.

Gradually, more and more people from the neighborhood became friendly with us. Besides Chandrasekhar, I now had four more persons who I taught how to read the Ramayana. People now highly respected me and offered money, clothes (*dhoti*, *kurta*), etc. in exchange for my recitations and teachings. Though I objected to such gifts, they pressed hard and I had to concede to their pleadings. Subhan and I spent the days together earning our dough. One day, we both decided to organise a *maulud* [prayer meeting] at our place. We fixed up a date four months in advance and began our preparations in earnest. We did not know much about the other plantations. Some men from our ship had been employed at plantation 'Fargorgu' [Voorburg] and on a Saturday, I visited Bhikan and Durbari[76] who worked there. People of that plantation had also come to know about my ability to read the Ramayana and the *sardar* of the place, Basau, and his subordinate Shivnarayan, met me and asked me to stay. That night, I was requested to recite verses from the Ramayana at the *sardar's* residence. In the evening, people from the area gathered and Sardar Basau told me to start the *katha*. A *babu* who was illiterate, but had been in good company, began to explain the meaning. Though he could not read or write, he could explain it quite well. I recited about the burning of Lanka when a man asked him: 'Babuji, who was Megnath's father?' 'Ravana', replied the Babu. 'Who was Ravana's father?' he again asked. 'Vishesharwa', said Babu. 'Who was Visheshwarwa's father?' the man persisted. Babu could not bear him any longer and exclaimed, 'you yourself, idiot!' Everyone laughed.

The *katha* lasted till 11 p.m. and everybody appreciated my skills. A man called Hussain was among those who had gathered there and we became friendly with each other. Since we planned to hold a *Maulud*, I, therefore, went to him to ask for advice and to arrange somebody to recite on the occasion. Hussain told me about Paigambar Sai of the *kothi* 'Sur' [plantation Zoelen] who was very knowledgeable, decent and skilled in his task. The two of us thus went off to meet Paigambar Sai. He greeted us warmly and inquired about our wellbeing. He then accepted our invitation to conduct the *Maulud*. During those days, Hindus and Muslims both had only *puris*, vegetables, curd, etc., that is, only vegetarian dishes on their menus and on no occasion meat was served. Hence, we made our preparations accordingly. *Maulud* was read in the presence of all those who were invited and everyone had a good time. We thanked Allah for all his blessings. My mission was fulfilled and everybody went very satisfied to his or her respective home.

Aameen Aameen. Rabbul Aalmeen!

## My Second Marriage

One year passed in this way: working and teaching people on my plantation. I wrote several letters to my father and also sent some money during that period.[77] At times he replied and asked about Ashraf Khan, who was my brother-in-law's son and had left India before I was even conscious of my surroundings. His old mother and wife lived with us in Bharkhari and my father cared for their necessities. They had still been alive when I had left my home.[78]

When Chandrasekhar Maharaj had hosted the *katha*, a man called Ganpat Singh had attended the meet. He had worked in Skerpi before I joined and had left the plantation to settle on the land donated by the government. We had not talked much that time, as I had newly arrived but he had asked me about my religion, caste and background. Because of my knowledge of Hindi, very few men believed that I was a Muslim and most of them thought I was a *brahmin* who had fled the country and that I had adopted a new name to hide my identity. Many would therefore touch my feet in reverence. Some would even insist that I become their *guru* but I politely and firmly declined their requests. If I had agreed only God would have known where I would have been now. I could easily have gathered more disciples in Surinam than the great Jatadhari Baba Balwant Singh (a renowned *sadhu* of Surinam) or even Bhaggan Das Kumhar (Kabir Panthi) of Saramacca.

While I was in the Kanpur depot, Babu Ramnarayan Singh had indeed asked me to change my religion and caste and declare myself a *brahmin* because in that way it would have been easier for me to earn money in Surinam. But I deemed this to be a sinful act. I had no intention of cheating my disciples. I was afraid of Khuda and did not convert as was asked from me. I also refused to accept any payment in return for my teachings and told the Hindus to seek some other teacher if they wished to pay for their lessons because I hated to accept money for my teaching. Hearing this, they would keep silent and gave no reply. But increasingly, people came to know about my abilities and Babu Ganpat Singh spread this information in the plantations 'Lalkondre' [La Rencontre], 'Laluiki' [Laarwijk] and 'Domborgo' [Domburg]..A few days later, a man called Bihari, a *chamar*, who used to study under me in the plantation, hosted a *katha*. Apart from others, he invited Ganpat Singh and Gajadhar, who had been a *sardar* in Skerpi and had his own land in Domburg. The latter two men both attended the meet. On this occasion, we talked at length and I showed them my father's letter to make them believe that I was a Muslim. On hearing about Ashraf Khan, Ganpat said that he stayed in Domburg and had come to Surinam 12 years ago. Ashraf had acknowledged that he had a younger brother called Rahman whom he had left behind in India. I told them that I would visit Domburg on the day of the *tatil* [farewell] of the *tazias* [the last day of *tazia*] and meet him.

On the day of *tazia*, I thus went as scheduled and met Ashraf. Though he was not my real brother, he nevertheless showed great affection for me. We got along well and visited each other often from that day onwards. He had started his contract in plantation 'Firajoint'[79]. Two years before his arrival Ilahi Baksh had come to work on the same plantation. This gentleman had a daughter of fourteen and two sons named Karim Baksh and Imam Baksh. The eldest, Karim Baksh had died at eighteen years of age and Ilahi Baksh had died even before him. The responsibility for the care of his daughter had been given to Ashraf. Ashraf was concerned about the daughter's marriage and made a proposal to me. I however refused. I told him that I wanted to go back to Hindustan. Ashraf did not give up hope, however, and visited me trice for the same purpose but I remained adamant. One day, Ashraf visited my house along with another cousin of his who had come with him from Hindustan. They again made the same proposal, which I, as usual, turned down. This time however, the two brothers stayed overnight and brainwashed me by explaining the ups and downs of life in a foreign land. I found some truth in their explanation about the necessity of marriage while staying in another country, which would give some stability to my life. I therefore finally agreed to marry the girl. After all they were my elders and would not mislead me.

Two months later, I was married for the second time.[80] Later on, by the grace of Khuda, my eldest son Suleman Khan was born on 8 January 1901, a Tuesday. Since I was a contract worker that time, I sent my wife to my in-laws during the last days of her pregnancy and Suleman Khan was born in his (maternal) grandmother's home. My in-laws belonged to the *sheikh* community and registered him as Abdul Baksh. Later on, I re-named him according to my community of *pathans* and he became Suleman Khan. Truly speaking, it was this boy who prevented me from returning to Hindustan when my contract was over. By Allah's blessing, this was my first son whose affection has till today made me breath the air of Surinam. He has now settled in British Guyana (earlier called Demarara). Only Khuda knows whether he will return to Surinam or stay there throughout life.

## My first Confrontation with the Authorities

As I have already written, I came to the plantation when Mr. Bhusman was in charge. Two years later, he was transferred and Stukuru Sahab [Mr. Stark] took his place. I was still a contract labourer then. One day in the morning, cacao was being plucked and collected. It had not rained adequately and the produce was not much. If it rained well, the fruit would be plenty and we would get five annas for one basket of cacao. Yet, if it remained dry, only two annas were paid for one basket. The fruit was plucked, collected and carried over quite a distance by foot with the basket on one's head because the ditches would not contain enough water to allow for boating. I also plucked and collected cacao.

The new manager built a new container (*tobbe*) in which cacao could be stored, which was about 20 *duim*[81] long and its width was also 20 *duim*. The old container had been 18 *duim* long with a width of 12 *duim*. In the dry season, the old container was used as a standard measure. Yet when the rains came and the cacao production increased, the manager ordered the supervisor to tell the men that the new container would be used from the next day onwards. The rate for one full container was fixed at one rupee only because, he claimed that the diameter of the container was less than the earlier one. We previously had received 9 *du-annas*.[82] At the time, nobody commented.

Next morning we all–means Javanese as well as Hindustani labourers–went to the fields. There we started talking among ourselves regarding the new rate, which was less than what we had been getting earlier. We thus decided to protest against the lower wages. I was supposed to lead the team by posing as the first one who would get his cacao measured, and while I would protest against the new way of measurement the rest would support my reaction. After a whole day of work, we collected our cacao and deposited them in a boat. As a rule, the person whose baskets reached the *kasi* [storehouse] first, had to measure his toil first in the container. Since I was the one who had to take the initiative, somehow my load had been put in front. I was at home when they summoned me for measuring my freight. All were waiting for me when I arrived. The *sardar* and the *skreeman* waited at the door of the storehouse. The poor *sardar* was an *ahir* and had never attended school so he did not know how to read or write. He said: 'Come on *Ustad,* measure your cacao. (Actually, nobody ever called me by my name during that time but he had christened me as Munshiji or *Ustad*). I said: 'Alright', and entered the storehouse and saw the new container and asked the *skreeman sahab*: 'How much will you pay for this full container?' He asked puzzled: 'Has the *sardar* not told you about the new rate?' I replied: 'He has indeed told me about the rate. Yet, I will not use this new rate. I want 18 annas for the new container'. The *skreeman* said that this would not be possible. I replied however that the other option was not possible either. Finally, both the *sardar* and *skreeman* went away angrily. I piled up my cacao, covered it with *bakoven* (banana) leaves and went home. Later I came to know that the other workers had done the same with their loads.

The following morning, we again went to the fields and collected the fruits. In the evening the measurement had again started and the same thing was repeated. The manager then sent a message by wire to the police inspector in which he complained about us. In the evening of the third day Major Sahab accompanied by a policeman called Kanhai, came over. During those days, the fort accommodated only 300 military police men. The office of the District Commissioner was located in Kanophro and had only six policemen while the Major was posted at 'Pulpungi' [Poelepantje]. All pleadings from Hansu to the Fort of Nieuw Amsterdam were forwarded to the Commissioner of Combé while those from Sur on the other side of the Suriname River, were forwarded to the Commissioner of Kanophro. When at 4 p.m. we arrived at the storehouse with our cacao loaded on a boat, the manager and the major and others welcomed us. The manager pointed to me and said something to the major in the local dialect. Probably he had told him that I was the one who had started the problem and had instigated others. Policeman Kanhai (who had some land in Kamsairi but is no more now) always accompanied the Major and acted as an interpreter for him.

Through Kanhai, the Major asked me why I had had a fight with the *sardar*. I said that I had never fought with anybody. I had neither beaten nor abused anyone. I worked for my living. 'In that case, why do you not than measure your cacao?' he asked. 'Well, I shall not use the new container as an instrument of measuring'. I then turned to Kanhai and told him to keep quiet if he did not know about mathematics and calculations, and I would discuss the problem directly with the Major, albeit in a broken language. The poor chap replied that he knew nothing about maths and was employed as an interpreter only. I told Major Sahab then that I was willing to use the old container as a measurement instrument at the same rate, but would not consent to measurement through the new container even if the rate would be one rupee per container. Major Sahab asked for the old container. I said that the manager knew about it. The old container was brought and the Major took out his yardstick when I asked if he had one. I requested him to compare the two containers. He did accordingly, and the old one was 18 x 12 (216) square *duim*, while the new was 20 x 20 (400) square *duim*. I asked Major Sahab whether it was appropriate to give someone one rupee for 400 square duim while already 18 annas were received for 216 square *duim*? Was it right? Hearing this, the Major Sahab turned to the manager and said, 'if you take this man to court, you shall be fined Rs. 500 as a result. It will be better if you increase the wages for the new container'. The manager was stunned. He now had to give more for the new container. We saluted both of them and went home after measuring our cacao. This was my first encounter with the manager.

## My second Confrontation with the Authorities

It is maybe superfluous to remark that the owner (*garamsara*), manager, *skreeman* and *sardar* were all addressed as *sahabs*. Our owners were four brothers: Frans Horst, Dolf Horst, Diderik Horst and Louis Horst. Their father's title had been Horst and he had been in charge of Skerpi for 52 years. He had ordered that no worker, be it a *freeman* or a contract labourer, should be troubled or jailed because they were here to earn for themselves and their families.

His sons followed the advice of their father, and even if they had to suffer losses, they did not put anyone in prison. Only an obvious offence like robbery or fighting could land one in jail. If someone went against the rules of the plantation, he was ordered to do heavy work. The plantation itself was a jail for such men.

Of the four brothers, Dolf Horst was the cleverest and deft in running the plantation. He was well versed in the Hindustani language. It was due to him that Tulsi Kurmi[83] of our plantation had been appointed as an interpreter (*tolk*) though he only knew Nengre and he talked in Nengre to the Commissioner. Dolf Horst was a nice man and very extrovert. He mixed with the Indians. When news of my activities reached him, he came down to the plantation to look into the matter personally. He found no fault with me and told the manager that I was good enough to become a *sardar*. But the manager vehemently objected to such appointment.

To avenge himself, the manager ordered that I along with three others should remove grass and other vegetation from an old and big dyke[84], which lay abandoned in the jungle. It was about 30 feet wide and we were to get 12 annas[85] for every 6000 square feet of clearing. The poor *sardar* could not even make calculations of 600 feet and 6000 was too much for him. In the morning, the four of us went to the site and sat down. At 9 a.m., the *sardar* came and scolded us for not having started the work despite being on contract. Then I told him that he had not assigned our part of work in the field. 'All four of us do not want to work in the same place at a time and wish to make our own separate contributions.'

Hearing this, the *sardar* lost his temper and said: 'Alright, I shall measure your part separately at once'. He soon brought a ten-feet long stick and dropped it on the thicket to break it in two. As soon as he dropped it the third time, a large snake hissed at him and he fled saying that he was going to do some other work and was not bothered whether we did ours or not. Seeing this we laughed heartily and I said: '*Saarhu bhai* [brother-in-law], you are good for nothing. We shall manage it ourselves'. This *sardar* was called Akkal and had taken over from the old *sardar* Harangiram who had returned to India along with 800 other men by the very same ship that had brought me to Surinam. Akkal's mother-in-law and my mother-in-law had come to Surinam by the same ship (before my arrival), and therefore my wife and his wife were like sisters, hence I had called him *saarhu*.

After the *sardar* had left, we began our task. In two days time, we had cleared the dam from one end to another. On the third day, an easy job was assigned to us. After clearing the dam, I used the same stick that the *sardar* had used to measure our work. The place was 354 sticks long and 30 feet wide, i.e., 354 x 30 = 106200 square feet. The remaining 1200 feet were not measured. On Saturday, I asked the *skreeman,* 'how much work have we done?' The *skreeman* replied that it were 1625 units. I argued they were 1725 (106200/6000) units. When he disagreed, I took out a pencil and paper and showed the calculation. The *skreeman* would not listen and said that there were 17 units less than what I claimed. He was angry and started talking to me in the local dialect. He said: 'Hindustani coolies do not know anything'. In reply I told him: 'Even your father does not know more than I. Your father knows only about Surinam but I know about big places like Calcutta, which have many things that Surinam does not have. I have seen both countries: Surinam and India. So you better do not order me about. I am not like sweetened water that you can drink to your satisfaction. The *skreeman* then went to convey my words to the manager. The latter listened to his complaint but did not comment.

Thereafter I was assigned hard and treacherous tasks but the manager could not find any fault in me. He might have hoped I would do something against the rules and regulations of the plantation. Yet, he was unable to take me to court, as he could not find any reason. One day, he ordered me to cut trees in Mariënburg as the wood was needed for the construction of a fence. I would be paid 12 annas only for 30 thick pieces of wood. Due to the rains, the jungle was flooded at the time. The water level was so high that we could only rest on trees and high roots, which were dry enough to sit on. Besides, there was always the possibility of coming across a boa snake in the jungle and there were too may leeches. For these reasons, we [my friend Subhan and I] had been told to work there. The manager must have thought that we would not be able to complete our task and he would then have sufficient ground to send us to prison. We searched over a distance of 20 *ketting* [400 metres] but could not find any thick trees that could be cut. Actually there was a law, that if a person did not earn more than 12 annas on 3 consecutive days, he would be jailed for 3 weeks. Yet, by the grace of Allah we could finally achieve more than we ourselves had expected. After all, no one can harm a person if God is on his side.

At last, I was given easier jobs to do. I did more work than the others and if anybody dared to deduct from my earnings, my friend Subhan and I would go with a huge stick to collect my money. Seeing this, the manager would immediately ask the *skreeman* whether he had not paid me or had cut our earnings. ' Pay them because they are not lazy', he would say. The manager had tried every trick to test us but had failed. Finally, one evening he called me to his residence. My true friend Subhan Khan said: 'Brother, not you but I shall go instead. The bloody man may again play tricks and cheat you, or beat you up'. I was not in the least perturbed however and asked: 'Brother, you are very ignorant. Am I an ant, which he can crush without you knowing about it? *Khuda hafiz*, I shall go myself. You need not worry'. Saying this, I put on my *kurta* and *dhoti* and made my way to the manager's house.

I saluted the manager and saw that the *skreeman* and *sardar* were also present there. Keeping away from them, I asked the manager as to why he had summoned me. The manager asked me to come closer to him. I said that I was not hard of hearing and could hear him from a distance. I was afraid that the three of them might suddenly attack me and beat me up. I thought: 'If I stand at a distance I can at least beat one of them up if any one of them attacks me'. I therefore told the manager to speak from a distance. (Besides, my dear friend Subhan had followed me secretly and had hid himself behind the netted gate of the house and with a huge stick in his hand was listening to our conversation). The manager spoke: 'I wish to make you a *sardar*'. I said that I did not want it but the manager would not listen: 'You are under contract and must go where I depute you and do whatever job I tell you to do'. I said that he was correct: 'Yet, I have been brought here from Calcutta to toil as a labourer and not to work as a *sardar*. I can earn more in the fields than as a *sardar*.[86] What will I do with that kind of job?' The manager replied: 'I cannot force you, but the owner has ordered me to promote you to the post of a *sardar* and even I wish that you take up this duty'. Hearing about my *garamsara*, I had no choice but to accept his order. *Garamsara Sahab* had recommended me so how could I refuse? 'Yet if you want me to work as your *sardar*, I have three demands before I start, otherwise I shall back out', I said. 'What are these demands?' queried the manager. 'Firstly, I should be allowed to decide how much has to be paid to someone.

I want to judge according to the severety of the assignment and I must have the right to raise the amount paid upto 12 annas if needed. Secondly, if somebody does not do his work properly, you may deduct from my allowance but not from the worker's wages. You should allow me to decide upon his or her renumeration. Thirdly, your behaviour towards me should not be like that meted out towards your other *sardars*, because if I am treated badly, I shall have my own solutions'.

The manager asked me: 'Why have you made such demands?' I replied that 'all the fighting and tussles, which take place here revolve around payments and favouritism. The *skreeman* and the *manjha* (manager or manager) favour those people who work less but spy on others. These men always get their full share while those who labour hard have to bear the brunt. They are reprimanded for even minor faults, which they indeed make at times. Because of these, money is deducted from their wages, which is given to the less deserving. This is unjustified and I am dead against such practices because it breeds ill feeling among the labourers and at time even causes in fighting. A *sardar* has to face these situations every now and then'. This opened the eyes of Manager Sahab who admitted that I was right. 'I had never thought that much', he said, 'the *garamsara* and I will grant what you demand and everything will be done according to your policy. Yet you should be careful and do not allow any mischief'. I said: '*Inshah Allai taalaa*' [Thank God].

## Sardar in 1901

When we had finished our negotations, the Manager Sahab turned to the old *sardar* and told him to read out my three demands to everyone on the plantation. He also told him to add that whoever would act against these rules, would be liable for imprisonment for upto 6 weeks. By Khuda's consent, I began my new task. By now after 2 years of stay on the plantation, I had learnt to speak Nengre and Javanese[87]. This helped me a lot in my new job and since most men respected my friend Subhan (or rather feared him) and myself, I had no trouble in asserting myself as one who had to be acknowledged. Many men were anyway also my students! Everyone therefore obeyed me and work soon became orderly and streamlined. I also was honest and humane in my approach. The owner had been informed about my promotion and the demands I had made. Dolf Horst, who was more intelligent than his brothers, visited the plantation a month after my appointment as *sardar.* It was dry weather and about sixty people were busy digging ditches. I had fever at the time and was not in good physical shape. I looked thin and weak due to the illness. The *Garamsara Sahab* and the manager visited me at around 10 a.m. They had seen the work going on but had kept quiet. God knows whether they liked it or not! The owner looked at my face on which my illness was written and inquired whether I was sick. I saluted him and replied that I was having fever every fourth day (malaria). The owner understood, as he knew Hindustani quite well. He asked me whether I ate *bachhaun* [*bakkeljauw,* a kind of salted fish][88] or not. I answered with a 'no'. He then asked me whether I ate *elen sansan* [*haring*][89] I again replied in the negative. 'Do you drink brandy, gin, cognac, or champagne?' 'Never', was my reply. He then said to me that he would have died in Surinam: 'I know that you are a Mohammadan and that your religion prohibites the drinking of alcohol. Yet fish is not forbidden and you must eat it otherwise it will be difficult for you to survive here'. He then talked to me for an hour as if I were his own son. He told me that drinking was a way to stay healthy. I did not agree with him however. When he saw that I would not yield, he planned, without my knowledge, to give alcohol to me as a medicine. He asked: 'Do you not take medicines from the hospital?' I replied: 'Yes, I am taking quinine but it has not helped me'. Then *Garamsara Sahab* promised to send other medicines against malaria from the city through the *manjha.* I was supposed to drink that medicine every morning and evening.

Suddenly, *Garamsara Sahab* put his hand in my pocket and pulled out my notebook. He flipped through a few pages and saw some diagrams (triangles, rectangles, etc.) drawn in it. It was related to last week's work. Seeing these diagrams he asked me what they meant. I replied that it showed the work done at different sites during the last week. The magnitude of the task performed and the payments made for the work were also mentioned in it. I told that the *skreeman* could confirm the data if he wished. The owner smiled and said: 'Rahman Khan, I believe in your honesty and truthfulness. I know that a Muslim like you is absolutely trustworthy. Do not worry about anything and work here as if it were your home. Run the plantation as you think proper and pay the wages according to your assessment. We four brothers will not obstruct you'. He shook my hand and left.

*There is nothing wrong with the original but nothing right with the duplicate.*

Honest people should not fear. These people were Christians but acted as promised. The owner, throughout life, never failed to remember his promises. If the plantation needed new labourers, the owner even allowed me on his behalf to go with the money and the register to the office of the Commissioner who had to sign the labour contracts. When summoned, I also attended the courts as a representative of the plantation. I was indeed trusted so much, that the Commissioners Uiten (*Sahab*) and Granada (*Sahab*)[90] would refer to me at times as 'the owner of Skerpi'. The story that tells how this all happened is written in the following sections.

Work on the plantation progressed well. When the owner had returned to the city after his visit, he had arranged for a big earthen bottle (*kruik*) of jenever, which strongly smelled of *jeera,* a kind of spice. He also sent a small glass containing *kwasibita*. When the jenever, mixed with the medicinal plant, was poured into a glass, it would turn bitter within five minutes. It was worse than quinine and a really obnoxious medicine. I had to drink it after ten minutes of its being poured into the glass. It gave me neither pleasure nor caused intoxication because it was terribly distasteful and smelled strongly of cummin. Nevertheless, by the grace of God, I was fully cured in 3 weeks time.

A few days after having become a *sardar*, my friend Subhan was appointed as night watchman. The *skreeman* was suspended from his post after 3 months and all the work in the fields was conferred on me. I however requested two more assistants to help me in my work. Accordingly, a *sardar* named Sakhawat Khan and a junior assistant named Ribo of Malaysia were assigned to work under me. My own work was now limited to seeing that everything went right, guiding my assistants, distributing the payments every Saturday and submitting my reports and accounts to the manager. The owner would come occasionally to supervise the works. My days passed comfortably in this manner.

## Demise of my dear Friend

I now have to narrate the story of the demise of my dear brother and friend Subhan. Subhan (Subai) was a *julaha-maybai*, whose profession it had been to paint houses. He had come from the village Bharatganj in Allahabad district. He had opted for contract labour in Surinam after some feud at home and it was in the Calcutta depot that we began our great friendship. Though I had left my home for a different reason altogether, we got along well. (I had gone to Kanpur to watch the Ramlila and was to see Surinam lila in a land of *kafirs)*. Subhan told me his own story as follows:

> My dear brother, I have a wife and two sons. The four of us lived along with my parents. I had a small job. I did not know how to read or write but knew about the Holy Allah. I respected Him, His Holy books, His Prophets and observed *roza* and *namaaz* as much as I could. I worked together with my father and we painted houses. I had two older brothers who lived separately from us and had their own business. My faith in Allah gradually grew so strong that whenever I went to the mosque to offer prayers, I would stay there for long periods and even spend my nights there. As a result, my work was affected and at times I would even skip my duty for *namaaz*. Most of the time, I spent in Allah's presence and did not feel hungry or thirsty. Whenever I went home, I ate whatever was served and returned to the mosque as soon as possible. My activities made my parents angry. Their ire was justifiable because my old father had to labour hard to feed a family of six. I knew that I did the wrong thing by putting this burden on my old father's shoulders, but somehow I could not break free from the chains formed by my faith. My wife was also furious. She tried to make me understand that I needed to work for my children and family and should not depend on my father. However, I would tell her that the One who had brought my children to this world would take care of them and left her, crying.
>
> Once it happened that for 2 consecutive days, my wife told me that there was nothing to eat for me since the children had been too hungry and had eaten my food. By this time, my parents had stopped talking to me. I now began to ponder about

my two children and their hunger. I did not care for my food, but I could not be responsible for their starvation. I compared my condition with a snake with a *chhuchundar* in its mouth. This animal looks like a rat but has a long snout and smells horribly. If by mistake or due to hunger, a snake catches it in its mouth it can either swallow it and invite death, or spit it out and become blind. My brother, I contemplated hard and came to the conclusion that the Lord's work was important for both worlds, while labour on earth was only for this world. What man proposes, God will dispose. Thinking likewise, I returned to the mosque and became engrossed in prayer. When I offered my morning *namaaz*, I pleaded to Allah saying that he is *Rabbul Alamin* (*Aalmeen*)[God of the world], *Sattar, Gaffar* and *Roszinshah* [attributes to God the provider for everyone, the shining, the forgiver]. I begged him and said I was a sinner but did not want Him to turn me out empty-handed. Saying this, I raised up my hands to the sky and as soon as I looked down on the floor again I was surprised to find an 8-anna coin lying there. I thanked Khuda with my whole heart and picked it up.

I took the coin home and gave it to my wife who bought ration and prepared food for the whole family. We ate to our heart's content and thanked Allah for his blessings. When the day passed, I again went to the masjid and was drowsy after eating so much following a two-day fast. Laying down on the *janamaaz* I felt sleepy. Half asleep and half awake, I dreamt that a holy sage, clad in clean robes and having a white beard, told me not to disclose my blessing to anyone else otherwise I would be punished and would never be blessed again.

As Subhan had finished telling this story, he slapped himself as now he had told the secret, which he had been forbidden to utter. I was dazed and began to cry. He resumed his history after some time: 'Truly my friend, I have been punished for my misdeeds'. I asked him how and why and he replied:

My brother, this miracle of my receiving a coin became routine and I received it each day during the morning *namaaz*. I gave it to my wife every day and we had an easy life. Yet my wife got suspicious and asked about the secret behind my earnings. Those who were jealous of our prosperity might have influenced her mind. One day she angrily demanded that I tell her from where I was getting the money. Had I taken a loan from somebody or did I get it through some sinful means? Why was I forcing my children into debt? She asked how I could return my credits without doing any work. I was upset and told her to shut up. 'Khuda is with us and he will care for us', I said. 'What has this to do with you', I also queried. But the stupid woman retorted, 'how will I return this amount? Should I resort to robbery?' I could bear it no longer and I walked off to the *masjid.* That evening, after the *namaaz*, I went home. Dear brother, the day had arrived on which my destiny was reversed. At night, when we went to bed and took each other in the arms, my bitchy wife asked me for a favour, which I promised not suspecting her intentions. Then she questioned me lovingly about my source of income. She asked me who had provided me with a loan. She had questioned: 'If something happens to you, how should I know from where this money has come?' It is true that when calamity is in the offing, the mind becomes functionless. I could not hold myself back and told her that this money was not borrowed from a moneylender. 'Then how do you make money or do you rob it from somewhere', she persisted. I felt that there was no other option for me but to tell her the truth. How wrong I was! I was truthful and told her everything, forgetting the warning of the *pir* who had forbidden me to do so. When I returned to my senses, I was very annoyed with myself, but I had already committed the mistake and was now a culprit in my own eyes. Nothing else was left for me, but to cry. But [I wondered]: What is the use of rains when the drought has already killed the crop?

I immediately got up, took bath and hurried to the *masjid.* That morning, after *namaaz*, I sincerely prayed for forgiveness. But when I looked under the *janamaaz*, there was nothing but the floor. As a punishment, no more money was gifted. I was very ashamed of myself and returned home empty-handed, said nothing to my wife and ate my meal. After I had finished, my wife asked for the day's money. I kept quiet. She then began to complain that this was a ploy that men employ to tease their women. She said: 'I know from the very beginning that you were taking credit from someone and now my children will have to pay for it. Where is the help that you were getting from Khuda?' This comment broke my heart. I said nothing and walked out of the house. I left my family. I went to Allahabad and enrolled myself, which brought me here. Now whatever Khuda has in store for me I shall accept.

Subhan had still not arrived in the Calcutta depot when I was staying there already. He joined two weeks later and occupied a bed that was four beds away from mine. I had kept a bronze *lota*[91] from which I drank water and I used the earthen pot to carry water to the toilet. Poor Subhan had nothing there. He was a *namaazi* and had trouble in performing *vazu.* I would see his problem from my bed itself. He offered his *namaaz* on his bed every morning and night and on other times he offered it under the nearby mango tree. On the third day of his arrival, he approached me in the evening. After an exchange of greetings, he said that he had come to me to seek a favour. He said: 'I have difficulty in performing my *vazu.* May I borrow your *lota* for the purpose? I shall be very obliged to you'. I replied that he was most welcome and that there was nothing to be obliged for. I offered: 'I only wish to share it with you while drinking water after meals. The rest of the time you may keep it in your possession'. Hearing this, he promptly picked up his bed and laid it alongside my cot. From that day onwards till his death, he lived with me like a brother. He never said a word against me. This *lota* was the foundation and binding force of our friendship, which grew in intensity day by day from that time onwards.

Subhan did not know of anything else than work and earn money. He gave all his dough to me and did not shop at all. He never smoked tobacco and he did not know about alcohol and cannabis. He stayed with me for 4 years but I never saw him sleep soundly throughout the night even once. Nobody else saw this either! He was a straightforward and truthful man. If by chance he wronged anybody, he would go to him, slap himself and apologise for his misdeed. He never spoke harshly and did not abuse anyone. Whenever I happened to be awake in the night, I would find him humming or singing in praise of Allah. He was so simple that he would believe anyone and not think of the consequences of doing so. Many a time I had scolded him and explained things to him, but he would not listen.

*Doha*

*A leopard never changes his spots. A man cannot change his nature. The neem cannot become sweet, no matter how much sugar you mix.*

Subhan was no exception.

One day, we ran out of vegetables so I went and bought a pumpkin. It was a Sunday and when Subhan asked me whether to cook it or not, I said: 'Yes, and cook rotis as well'. Subhan made nice and soft rotis, good enough to shame many ladies. He peeled the pumpkin, prepared the spices and then asked me how much water to pour in the utensil. Jokingly, I said that one *lota* would be enough to cook the pumpkin. The simple soul had no idea that there was no need to pour any water and he quickly added the water and started to knead the flour in another utensil. The excess of water in the *karahi*, the cooking utensil we used, had not dried up even by 10 a.m. while the dough of flour began to melt. I was feeling hungry so I asked him for food. Subhan said that it was not ready yet. When I asked him why, he replied that he had burned all the wood that was needed to cook for 4 days, but the water in the *karahi* with vegetables was still the same. I asked him how much water he had added. He said one *lota* only, not more. I laughed and said: 'Subhan, you are weird. Don'tyou know that you need not add any water while cooking pumpkin'. 'But it was you who told me to do so', he answered. I then asked: 'Will you jump into a well if I told you to jump'. 'Of course, I can give my life for you dear brother', he replied. I told him not to think like that and use his brains in such situations. 'The dough has also become watery, what should I now do', he queried. I told him to make *gulguley* out of it. Then he threw the dough in the *karahi* and cooked *gulguley*.

Another day, during the harvest season of cacao, Subhan and myself were assigned to pluck and collect the fruit. Two men were supposed to assist each other in this case. One person would pluck and pile up the cacao beans while the other would crack them, put them in a basket and take them to the dam. I was busy plucking the cacao from the tree and piling them up, while Subhan was doing the rest when he said: 'Bhai, I wish to drink the juice of this cacao but am afraid that the bloody *skreeman* might notice and drink it himself as he always does'. I told him to clear a place surrounded by tall grass near the cacao beds and put the fruits there. 'But what should I do to extract juice from it', he asked. Thinking of the pumpkin episode, I told him to dig a clean hole and place a basket full of cacao in it. 'At about 10 a.m. pick up the basket and drink the juice that has accumulated underneath it', I said. Subhan nodded and did as he was told. He dug a hole, smeared it with wet mud from the ditch and placed the basket in the hole. He forgot however to put banana leaves, as I had not told him about these leaves. At 10 a.m., Subhan felt thirsty and said: 'Come, brother, let us go and drink the juice'. Since, I knew that no juice could be collected from there, I said: 'I am not thirsty, you go and drink it all by yourself'. He protested: 'I cannot lift the basket alone without spilling the cacao, so you have to accompany me'. I therefore went along with him and helped to pick up the basket out of the ditch. What we found was only a few millilitres of juice on the base of the hole because the mud was wet. Seeing this, Subhan was furious and shouted: 'Bloody *skreeman* is a big thief. I shall teach him a lesson if he comes this way today. I had secretly tried to extract cacao juice, but still he managed to locate and devour it'. Hearing this I laughed. He became more infuriated and asked, 'why do you laugh? Did you have to carry loads of cacao on your head? I am damn thirsty and you are laughing'. 'Then leave the *skreeman* alone and beat me up instead', I said. 'The fault is yours, not the *skreeman*'s. You have not spread any leaves in the pit. It did not cross your mind that the earth cannot hold any juice or water by itself. You are an idiot and have not heeded to my teachings. Have you forgotten the cooking of pumpkin? You had done something similar that day'. Subhan realised his mistake and replied softly that he had not put leaves there because I had not told him to do so. I said that whether I told him or not he should have done it since he was not insane. 'You did not use your brains and if you beat the *skreeman*, I shall testify against you and send you to jail for six months. Our relation would sore', I said. Subhan cooled down, cursed himself and went back to work. I followed him. There were many such instances, which showed his ignorance and simple nature. A complete detail of each would fill this book! Therefore, I shall continue no further.

Though he was silly, Khuda had blessed him with immense strength. Near the river in Skerpi, there was a large iron *koker* [cylinder, shaft]. Two strong men could manage to lift and remove it in about half an hour. But Subhan could lift it up and carry it on his shoulders to the riverbank, which was five *ketting* away, all alone. My dear friend would never complain about my choice of ration, vegetables and even clothes, which I bought for both of us and he never asked about the receipts, which I kept. He sincerely offered his *namaaz* all five times a day. I wrote our accounts with great honesty and when his savings would reach upto 60 or 70 rupees, would tell him to send the money home to Hindustan for his family. He would say that if he had not enough money to feed himself, how could he send them anything? I would give him his money and coax him to go to the city and post it to his children along with a letter.

We continued with our jobs as usual when one midnight, while on duty, Subhan noticed that a fire-like thing floating on the river was coming towards the plantation and the waterlevel rose tremendously. He thought it was a ship on which they had made a fire and as it was very dark, the fire looked very bright indeed. The darkness and high waterlevel had forced the ship to pursue a course along the banks, he thought. So he went to the riverbank with a lantern so that the captain of the ship might see the light, and steer the ship towards the middle of the river and in this way he would avoid a crash into the bridge. However, when the light approached him, he saw that it was not a ship. It was a boat with four rowers and a navigator who shone like a fire. The boat also seemed to be alit. Seeing this, Subhan ran to the manager's bungalow and said that something amazing was happening in the river. As soon as the manager opened his window to face the river and saw what lay ahead, he immediately shut it because he belonged to the country and knew what it was. He then ordered Subhan to go and let it be. Hearing this Subhan fumed and shouted that the men of Surinam were cowards who pissed inside their homes at night [instead of going outside and help others in need]. He then returned to the riverbank to see what was going on and returned to the bungalow only when the boat could not be seen anymore. He passed the night in tension and the next morning narrated the whole incident to me. I scolded him for disclosing the happenings he had perceived on the river because it was improper to do so. Subhan pleaded his innocence: '*Khuda hafiz*, what will happen, will happen', he said.

The evening following the incident, Subhan went to make his rounds as a watchman but came back at 8 p.m. with fever. It stayed with him throughout the night. The next morning he was hospitalised and given a laxative. This worked like a poison however and incessant diarrhoea ensued. After 3 days he began to bleed from his rectum. I suspected some black magic and consulted a *Negro* named Bachau. During the time of slavery, men from Africa had been brought to the plantation and though slavery had been abolished now, these blacks still lived on, on the plantation. Bachau was one such person. He was an old man, skilled in his task. He had lost his right leg, from thigh downwards. I requested him to do something for my friend after telling him about his problem. He lived in a small hut on his own piece of land. When I had finished my query, he pulled out seven thin branches from the fence surrounding his hut and counted them thrice in different manners. He then said, "*Basia*, I cannot do anything for you because the thing your friend has seen was not evil and would even have been beneficial to him, provided he had not told anyone about it for at least one week following the incident. One is in real trouble and can even die if one opens one's mouth before a week has passed. I was shocked at this revelation. He then told me to go to Subhan and ask him what to do because the day Subhan would dream of the same thing again, he would die. 'I cannot tell you anything more than this', he said. I saluted the holy man and left.

Now my turn had come to serve and care for Subhan. Every morning I went to the hospital, collected all his blood stained clothes, washed them in the river and spread them out to dry on the banks. Then I would sponge his body with wet cloth and clean it thoroughly. Next, I would clean his bed and room and help him lie down on the bed. I fed him with bread, cacao, porridge, etc. My young brother-in-law Imam Baksh was deputed to look after him during my absence. After nursing my friend, I would go to the river to take bath and used soap to remove the stench. Only after that I would take breakfast and attend to my duties. Again, in the evening I would first visit Subhan, clean and feed him before taking a bath and return home. My routine during Subhan's illness was as mentioned above. Khuda had inflicted Subhan with such a horrible disease that the doctor had to send all the other patients away because the pungent smell emanating from him was difficult to bear with. Subhan was the lone patient admitted there. Those who came to the hospital for medications in the morning or evening would cover their nose and mouth with cloth to reduce the stench.

While caring for Subhan, the smell of his body would fill my mind and no matter how much perfume or lavender I sprayed, I could not get rid of it. Eating was a challenge and swallowing was not easy. The odour seemed to fill my clothes, my body and my mind. Even the hospital, which was cleaned twice a day with a chlorine solution, could not suppress the strong smell. Neither the diarrhoea ceased nor his odour. Neverthless, I continued to nurse him because the poor man had treated me like his own younger brother and had not even allowed me to pick up a bucket full of water when he was healthy. He had always done everything himself, from gathering wood for the fire to cooking our meals. He would always say that he had nobody here except me.

Every evening when I asked him what he wanted to eat, he would cry and tell me that I cared for him like a brother indeed. One day he said: 'Beware, after me do not ever befriend anyone in Surinam to this extent anymore. Do not fight with anyone and live a simple life. Believe and trust in Khuda and his works. Do not rely too much on anyone. Make Suleman study well and teach him about Islam. When I am gone, inform my family. I wish that a clever learned man would perform the *namaaz* at my funeral. Pray for my soul and feed the poor in Holy Allah's name. This is all that I have to say. I also have a burden to carry with me to the other world, as I shall no more be by your side in person as I had thought earlier I always would. However, I will always be near you whenever you need me and surely meet you once more. Do not be afraid, the Holy One will take care of you. Ask a good man to read the *namaaz* at my funeral and you should be the first one to throw earth over my coffin. I have nothing else to say'. Hearing Subhan speak this way was very pathetic and sorrowful. I wept. He saw me cry and told me to be strong at heart and praise Allah for He would not leave me in need and would bless my children and me. 'Now go and look after your business', he said.

I obeyed him and went to work. In the evening, I had to submit my report to Hussain on plantation Voorburg. I told him about Subhan, his illness and his wish regarding his funeral. Hussain assured me he would do accordingly and said that I need not bother about the *namaaz* and expenses. He said, 'you know Ali Baksh (Hukka Mian) quite well as he reads our *namaaz* and is quite good at it. I shall get hold of him'. 'But he has still not finished his contract and may not be available on weekdays', I said. Then Hussain told me that he was in the *garamsara*'s good books and would request him to allow all the (Muslim) contract workers and *freemen* to attend the burial on that day. 'You should not worry about it', he said. We ate at his place and I then returned to my place.

When the doom's day drew close, Subhan stopped eating and drinking. His bleeding also stopped during the last 3 days that he was still alive. On the fourth and final day I found him up and about, his face looking very fresh. On other days, he had not been ableto get up by himself and had even needed support while sitting. Moreover, his characteristic stench had also vanished. I was glad and asked him how he felt. 'By the grace of God, I feel great today', he said. 'I want to brush my teeth and wash myself', he said. I immediately ran and fetched warm water and a clean towel for him. After he had changed his clothes, I asked him what he wanted to eat. 'Coffee', he said. I quickly went to the bungalow and brought hot coffee and bread for him. I sat besides him and fed him the bread with my hands. While he was eating I thanked Khuda for curing my friend and thought that he was out of danger now. Suddenly, Subhan began: 'Bhai, yesterday night I dreamt about the same phenomenon that I had seen that day'. 'If Allah wishes, you shall be completely cured', I answered. Yet I recalled what the old *kafir* had told and my heart skipped a beat and gloom descended on me. Believing that we were about to be separated soon, I left for the fields.

During the whole day, I kept on thinking about Subhan and could not concentrate on my job. It was 2 p.m., the sun was shining brightly and the atmosphere was heated by its intensity. I returned from the fields to my home. The road ahead was clear. As soon as I crossed the fields and reached the clearing, I felt very hot and therefore sat down under the shade of a maple tree. Suddenly, I became drowsy and could not resist lying down. I had just shut my eyes when a voice at my right rang into my ears: 'Bhai Sahab, *Salaam walekum*. I am leaving', someone said. I was startled. I looked around to see who it was but found no one. Then I realised that Subhan was no more. I got up and walked home at a brisk pace to find Imam Baksh, who had looked after Subhan during my absence, standing on the bridge near the fields waiting for me. As soon as I had reached and asked him about Subhan, he began to cry: 'Elder brother-in-law, Subhan is dead', he sobbed. I stood there and cried, and cried. 'He was a true friend who bade farewell when it was his time to leave', I thought, and kept on weeping bitterly.

I went to the hospital and found Subhan without a soul. I remembered his friendship, his ways, his God-fearing attitude, and the days we spent together and lamented. I then thanked Khuda for His deeds because whatever He does, He does for the benefit of His subjects. When I had composed myself, I set off to inform others about Subhan's demise. As soon as Hussain got the news, he collected all our acquaintances. That day, work was suspended on our plantation. Ali Baksh, (whose fields are in Leiding 8) took the pulpit during the funeral and carried out *namaaz*. I was the first to throw earth on the coffin of my friend Subhan as he had wanted and we all prayed for his wellbeing. On the third day, the *fakirs* were fed. The poor and destitutes were given a feast 40 days after his death (*chalishwan*) and I invited everyone known to us. I tried to do as much as I could to make Subhan's soul rest in peace. May Holy Allah provide his heavenly abode [Paradise] to such pure souls like my friend Subhan.

In fact, the death of Subhan posed greater problems than my being separated from my family and homeland, because Subhan was my right hand in an alien land. Due to him I had feared nobody. I did not have to worry about my chores and household tasks. During the contract period, people have to face lots of difficulties and troubles, but Khuda knows that all my problems seemed small in Subhan's company. Now, I woke up as from a dream and could truly see all the problems around me. I thanked Khuda for it.

It should be remembered that Subhan had promised to meet me at least once after his death. I started thinking about this all the time. I wondered where and how we would encounter each other. I thought that he might come to me in the jungle and not at home. Thinking thus, I would wander about in the jungle alone, everyday from 11 a.m. to 2 p.m. after having finished my job to provide him an opportunity to make an appearance. One day, as I drifted towards the ditches I was lost in my thoughts. The sun shone hard and the jungle emitted a typical sound in the calmness of the surroundings. My clothes were wet with perspiration, when all of a sudden, I chanced to see a big deer which came out of the jungle and approached me from near the dyke. It came close and stared at me.

I blurted, 'Is that you Subhan? Have you come to meet me? I greeted: '*Assalaam walekum*'. The animal sped and leapt across a 10 feet wide trench and ran into the forest. I waited for some time and then walked back home.

In my dream that night, Khuda commanded Subhan to appear before me. After greeting each other, I asked him where he lived. But instead of replying, Subhan told me not to roam about in the forest to meet him. 'If ever we meet, it will be in your dreams', he said. 'I shall tell you the place where I live', he added. 'I live in a house on which the "Alif" letter is written in a city that you will see in your dreams only'. Suddenly I woke up. The thought of him made me cry and I could not sleep again that night. After a few days, I dreamt about a beautiful city. When the sun's rays fell on the fabulous buildings of the city, they sparkled and I could not look straight towards them. I had never seen such a place in my life-time or in my earlier dreams. I wandered through this lovely city when all of a sudden I remembered what Subhan had told me about his address. Looking for his house, I arrived at a locality where all the houses were spotlessly white and glittering. There were a thousand of these and I am unable to describe the magnificent sight, which lay ahead of me. I walked into the corridor of one such house and peeped through the door into its interior. Lo behold! In glistening golden letters 'Alif' was written there. I thought by myself that this must surely be Subhan's abode. I then saw Subhan clad in fine attire coming out from the interiors. He said '*Salaam walekum*' and forbade me to ever try to meet him again. 'We cannot meet again', he told me. Saying this, he went inside. At once, my slumber was fully gone and I found myself next to my bed. There were neither city nor houses and there was no Subhan around me. I felt very sorry. From that day onwards till date, I have never again met Subhan not even in my dreams. May Khuda give him a place in Paradise! Aameen Aameen. Rabbul Aalmeen!

# VOLUME III[92]

Subhan died in 1902[93] and my contract expired in 1903. On Monday 13 April 1903, *Manjha Sahab* called all of us. He gave us certificates by which we became freemen (free from the bondage of the plantation contract).[94] The manager told us: 'Now that you are released from the contract of the *garamsara* you are free to go anywhere you please. However, if you wish you may enter into a new contract'. We thanked *Manjha Sahab*, took the papers in our hands and said: 'We will not renew our contracts, we rather prefer to be *freemen*'. *Manjha Sahab* again tried: 'If you want a contract here in Surinam once again, you will get Rs 100 each for a fresh five-year contract and you once again will work as an indentured labourer under the same conditions as you did before. For each one of you the owner of the plantation spends Rs. 166, out of which you get Rs. 100 while the rest of the amount will go to the government'. We just nodded but did not comment further.

## The Cacao Disease

Cultivation of cacao in Surinam was akin to gold mining. This was because cacao once sowed and looked after properly for 5 years, promised enough income for the rest of one's life. The only thing needed was weeding twice or trice a year. Costs involved were thus very minimal and it was considered a lucrative business. Cacao cultivators in Surinam were an affluent lot, until diseases affected the cacao. During the season, cacao trees would be heavily laden with fruits. Cacaobeds were 10 *ketting* long and 30 feet broad and would accommodate three rows of trees. Such was the abundance that two labourers could not pluck and collect all the fruits of even one bed during a whole working day. The labourers would earn as much as Rs. 1.50 to 2 rupees per day. In those days if a planation would sell its cacao at Rs. 1.25 per kilo, the farmers would get 1 rupee out of it. If the planation rate were 1 rupee per kilo, the farmers would be getting 75 paise per kilo. This cacao was an important reason for Surinam's prosperity. Every man, rich or poor, earned, ate and was at peace. During those days cacao trees were treated as if they were made of silver, and silver they were! But alas, when a plague hit the cacao, Surinam shrank.

In 1898, the year I arrived in Surinam, our Queen Her Majesty Wilhelmina married and ascended the throne on 31 August. She was only 18 years old then. The occasion was celebrated with much glamour. We all got 4 days holiday and there was a lot of merriment. At that time the cacao cultivation was at its peak. Earlier only small sheds had been built to dry and prepare the cacao fruit. But when the quantity increased these sheds could not accommodate the fruits any longer. Besides these sheds, the hospital and even the bungalow of the plantation owner were also being employed for this purpose. If space for drying the cacao beans properly were limited, 2-4 weeks of rains would spoil the cacao. The space for storage on the plantation was indeed limited and hence much of cacao would start rotting and ultimately was thrown. The fruits left on the trees would meet the same fate. Rains would not only prevent the collection of fruits from the trees but would also prevent those already collected to dry, which was necessary for its processing. All this led to the building of large warehouses and machines to accommodate the great quantity of cacao of the plantation and to facilitate the drying and processing of the beans. This proved to be very lucrative. As far as I can remember, in 1900, Surinam totally produced 2,500 sacks (*zakken*) of cacao of which 900 sacks came from Skerpi.

Yet in 1900, Surinam faced a 9-month long drought and this was the beginning of its fall. The exceptional rainfall that came after the drought completely ruined the cacao cultivation in Surinam as due to the excessive rains a cacao disease had broken out. Saramacca was the first to be affected. Our *Manjha Sahab* visited Saramacca to assess the character of the disease. Skerpi was not spared and it affected the fields where I previously had been employed. The owner Dolf Horst was informed and he immediately came for inspection and then returned. The news about the disease spread like wildfire. Every now and then authorities from near and far would come and take stock of the situation. The disease first affected field no.10, also called *koeli guruwan*. One day the manager ordered me to tell that all those involved in 'cacao-killing' (the destruction of diseased cacao) should get an empty sack in which they had to collect all the diseased branches. These sacks had to be dumped near the river and all had to be burnt in a big fire. 'Beware', he had said, 'not a single infected branch should be left behind'. I did what sir (*meneer*) had told me to do.

Yet God's wish was otherwise. This 'treatment' only led to a flare-up of the disease. Branches and twigs of cacao trees were cut and collected, and piles and piles of them were burnt. Yet the plague spread even faster. More and more men were employed to curb the menace but in vain. Besides, the problem was that many people who were not skilled in cacao plantation were also involved in trying to fight the disease. The disease now began to take great toll and affected the trees in their entirety including fruits. Black spots would develop on the fruit making it hard as stone. The seeds inside were not spared either and they would turn black and rot. Though the trees bore plenty of fruits every season, alas, it was only to rot and decay. Cacao was no more profitable. The economy slumped to great depths.

One day *Manjha Sahab* called and said: 'Do not go to the fields tomorrow till the ship arrives at 7.30 a.m. A doctor and other officers will be here to make an assessment'. I said: '*Sahab*, doctors do ask patients as to what is their problem. If the sick say they have fever, the doctor tells them to open their mouth and show their tongue and then the doctor prescribes medicines. Will the doctor ask the cacao trees as to what is wrong with them? I do not believe any doctor has a remedy for this. This is God's wrath and no one can do much about it'. *Manjha Sahab* was very angry and said: 'I do not care what you say', and then he left. I thought of questioning him again somtime later. The next morning I accompanied the manager to the shore. The ship arrived in time. Our *garamsara*, along with a doctor and three other men from different plantations arrived and went straight to the diseased fields. The doctor inspected the trees while another dug up some soil and gave it to the doctor who tasted it and remarked loudly: 'Uhh, very salty'. I laughed and thought: 'What else would one find in a land so close to the sea'. The doctor then thrust his stick into a small drain. He pulled it out and said: 'This stinks'. This was very funny indeed. I asked myself whether it was so strange that wet, decaying cacao trees and fruit remnants, which were rotting, had a foul smell. Only a fool would expect a lovely aroma in these surroundings. The doctor then ordered: 'Each big and small drain on the plantation should become at least 1 to 1.5 foot deep'.

What was the result? Just add water to the *daal* and see.

That evening an order was circulated throughout the plantation which stated that every male, whether skilled or not, was to work in earnest to comply with the doctor's prescription and finish the job at the earliest. A lot of money was spent to accomplish the task in record time. Along with this, the cutting and removal of infected tree parts to far-off jungles and the burning process was also ensured in an effort to control the disease. The pluckers were told to even bury the covers after removing them from the fruits. The disease named *krullotenziekte* by now had spread all over the plantation and the same treatment was employed everywhere. Every Hindostani or Javanese, irrespective of working under contract or being a *freeman*, worked accordingly. At that time, almost no land was cultivated. The little cultivation that was there concerned cacao and a little bit of banana cultivation. At that time, there was no rice cultivation whatsoever.[95]

Within a few days all drains had been dug as ordered, but the cursed disease had overcome every hurdle with uncanny ease. Cacao trees had started to wither and die, and once green fields, gave way to barren lands. Only a few *kofimamabomen* and five-ten cacao trees had been spared. The doctor again visited the site and found his order being followed. After further thinking he said: 'The main ditch should be dug two feet deeper because more space is needed for a better flow of the water to the smaller ditches. As for now the water is stagnating'. Soon we were assigned the new job. The work was completed within 4 weeks and the report sent to the authorities. The same doctor came for the third time, now accompanied by the plantation owner. The scene they encountered blew their heads off! The extent of destruction was beyond their imagination. After surveying the situation, the doctor visited the creek He eyed the iron *koker* and blurted: 'Take this iron *koker* out and increase the depth of the trench by three feet and then reinstall the *koker*'. This was enough to drive both the manager and the owner crazy. In the evening when I reported and asked the manager about the doctor's opinion he retorted, 'to hell with the doctor. The whole problem was created by him'. I said: 'Sir you were mad at me when I first told you this was not what any doctor could deal with. Look what happened today'. The manager now realized the truth of my words and said: Anyway, let us now do whatever we can to solve the problem'. Thereafter two-dozen shiploads of medicines were brought. It resembled white lime. Three-feet big holes were dug in each cacao tree and fixed doses of medicine were encrusted in them. Yet this experiment did not yield results either, and no answer could be found as to how to free the plantation of this cacao plague. *Freeman* workers soon lost their jobs. They were allotted shelter but were told to search for work elsewhere. During these 3 years, the plantation had economically been drained to the limit. Only contract labourers remained.

The government now announced that anyone who wished to get a treatment for the disease could ask for government aid. But there were no takers. The same offer was then made to the people of Saramacca and the 'Muses' plantation [Susannesdal], which was located near plantation Voorburg. The costs of this project were unimaginable. All branches of each cacao tree had to be chopped off until only the main trunk was left. The trees were then washed with a copper sulfate solution and tapped water. After this a brushing of the trees followed and in some places this had to be done with limewater. A good production year followed a year of heavy expenditure. Yet, after that the disease struck again. This depressed everyone and business again slumped. The plantation could now only afford to keep those working on contract basis and that too at lower rates. The *freemen* were left to fend for themselves. On the four government plantations (Alkmaar, Domburg, Laarwijk and Lalkondre) only cacao could be cultivated and other crops were rarely cultivated.

It was during these testing times that the plantation owner requested the government for help. The then Governor-General Lord Lely accepted the challenge and laid the foundation of a railway network in 1904 in a bid to usefully employ the jobless.[96] The *freemen* were paid Rs. 1.25 per day while those on contract received one rupee. In my opinion, his act of benevolence and wisdom must be written down in history books in golden letters.

## As Freeman in Lalkondre

When I had become a supervisor (*sardar)* I had been promoted to a higher pay scale. The manager had said: 'Your contract decides the level of your payment but when you become a *freeman*, you will get your full payment'. Later when my contract had expired, I reminded the manager of his commitment. He replied that since the economic depression due to the cacao disease was persisting, I had to wait for some more time. After 9 months, I reminded him but in vain. There was no sign of the disease having been controlled and my pay hike seemed a far-off dream. I therefore thought it better to leave the place and with this in mind I went to Asraf in Domburg. After consulting Asraf, I bought plot no.119 at Lalkondre, which was not far away from the sluice near the river across the cemetery. I bought it for Rs. 200. I brought my family and belongings from the plantation and started living in my own place. I had however not informed Dolf Horst, the owner of Skerpi. When he came to know about it, he inquired about the reason of my hast decision. I said that I had no grievance and that it had been my own wish to leave. Dolf Horst did not comment on this. These happenings took place in 1904[97].

I owned nine cacao beds, had also cleared the forest and planted banana trees, cassava and other crops, which could help me to make my living. My father-in-law had some land in 'Laluwiki' [Laarwijk] near the river Suriname but he himself worked in the railways. On his request, I consented to go with him. The three of us (i.e., my father-in-law, Asraf and myself), used to cut the jungles for the construction of a railway track. I was able to save Rs. 22 after 3 weeks of work there. I returned home for 2-4 days and was planning to return when *Meneer* [afterwards Mr. or Sir] Weijtink, the Commissioner of Domburg, summoned me. He had a good sense of humour and was a caring man. He told me that the late Jahangir, a translator/interpretor (*tolk*) who had lived across my newly purchased house, had also been the lock-keeper. Sir Weijtink therefore requested me to take up the job now that Jahangir had died and I had started living near the sluice. He gave me the keys and said that I would be paid Rs. 100 per year for this work. I thanked him respectfully and accepted the offer. Mr. Niboer, who was the manager of the place, had also been present there. With great pleasure I started my new government job.

On Saturday, 1 April 1905, Allah blessed us with another son, Karamat Khan. This child was so prone to illness that a whole book could be written describing the poor soul's sufferings. He was the weakest among all my children. Plantation workers of Domburg received their wages every Sunday. On one such day Sir Weijtink, the Commissioner, and physician Dr. Haren along with the manager had gathered at the latter's place. The distribution of wages being over, the Commissioner asked me: 'I heard you are well read' and I replied: 'Sir, I cannot say so'. In order to test me, they then started posing questions to me. I enquired about the gentleman who was asking most questions. I was told that his name was '*Meneer* Niboer' and that he was a graduate from Holland. I then agreed to answer his questions. They asked me nine questions out of which I could answer eight correctly. I then asked them one question each and they, together, could answer only one. From that day onwards they started calling me *Meester* [teacher, master, sir]. Even later on when the Commissioner had been promoted to the post of *Agent-Generaal (Roshfail)*, he remained respectful to me.

Hanuman Singh and Balwant Singh were two brothers who had arrived in Surinam by a ship called *Jandevi*[98] [John Davie]. In Surinam, Hanuman Singh had married a *brahmin* lady who had some property there. The woman had a son called Ramanand who had been born in Hindustan. He now lived with his aged mother near the sluice, which was given in my care. Their land was in fact adjacent to this sluice. Hanuman Singh had already died while his brother Balwant Singh had become an ascetic. Regarded as a sage, he had thousands of Hindu followers. These two brothers had started off as contract workers in Saramacca but within a few days had been transferred to the 'Hansu' [Meerzorg] plantation, which was, during that time, a flourishing centre of sugar cane production. These brothers had completed their contract there. Balwant Singh was invited to grace various occasions in Hindu and Muslim families alike. They called him Hansu *ke baba* or Jura *baba* because he had long hair tied in a bun (*jura*). Whenever I was in Kanara and when Baba Balwant Singh visited the Jachtlust plantation, he would ask me to recite from the Ramayana. He greatly appreciated my explanations of the verses. He would tell me: 'I have been very close to many *sadhus* in Hindustan but no one could recite and explain the meaning of the Ramayana like you. Great is your *guru* who has taught you so well. I have never heard the Hindus in Hindustan speak such fluid and properly pronounced words and give such splendid explanations, leave aside Muslims'. I sometimes thought about this.

During that time in Lalkondre, nobody was used to the recital of verses from the Ramayana. With my arrival there, Ramayana recitation along with explanation of the verses became very popular. I was invited to each and every Hindu family. The Singh trio comprising of Babu Ganpat Singh, Kanhai Singh and Dalganjan Singh along with me, formed a team that went to recite Ramayana in the area. Ganpat Singh's wife was an ardent follower of Jura *baba* and whenever the *baba* visited Lalkondre, he would come to her place. Then, during his stay there, *baba* would every day ask me to recite from the Ramayana and explain the verses to him. When I was made in-charge of the sluice, the *baba* had also been in Lalkondre. He said that he had been informed that I had taken charge of the sluice and when I confirmed he said: 'You have a family and children, please return the keys'. When I asked why he explained, 'this sluice is under the spell of an evil spirit. I have seen him with my own eyes. Jahangir, the translator, has become a victim of this devil [he has died due to it] and hence I forbid you to carry on this job'. I then said: 'Babaji, whatever God does, he does for the good of mankind. What can we do if it is my fate that the devil catches me? What are we afraid of? I am grateful to the Lord for his kindness. The Commissioner Sahab himself called me and handed over the keys to me. How can I return them now? Let fate decide my life pattern. I am not perturbed'. Hearing my words, *baba* kept quiet. Yet, deep in my heart I valued *baba*'s warning, as I knew he would never lie.

## Fake Ghosts!

On hearing Baba Balwant Singh's warning, I was sure that there was something sinister about the sluice. The cemetery was also adjacent and many people confirmed the presence of evil there.[99] I became very careful and every evening during my checking routine I carried a lantern and a chopper. One day I saw that, during daytime, one *sadhu* of the Kabir Panthi sect[100] had come to visit Ramanand Maharaj's house, which was located near the sluice. That same night the moon shone brightly and at 1 a.m., I had to close the sluice. I had set my alarmclock at 12 mid-night. The sound of the bell woke me up and I lit the lantern, took my usual equipments and walked towards the sluice that was about five *ketting* away from my house.

Mango trees planted on my land prevented any view of the sluice from my house. After walking a *ketting* or two, the sluice became visible. That night the sight was different however. A tall shadow clad in a white robe upto the knees, stood on top of the sluice. Baba's saying had come true. The devil was standing in my way. I was tempted to run back home but then I thought, 'that would be a coward's act and why should a youngster like me do such a thing? I decided to face the devil and leave everything in Allah's hands. I kept on walking towards the shadow thinking, 'what can the evil spirit do to me? I know the *Khudai Kalam* [words of Allah: The Koran] that will drive away the evil'. When there were only forty paces left between the lurking spirit and me, I started reciting my verses. When I crossed my land and did proceed to the government's dam I repeated my recitation but the devil was unmoved. I thought that this whole exercise was futile but nevertheless kept on reciting. I thought that in case these prayers failed, I could always use my chopper. I would hit the thing whatever it was and not care about the outcome. Thinking about my next step I approached the shadow and behold! There stood the Kabir Panthi *sadhu* clad in his long white gown with his large protruding eyes as still as a statue. I scolded him: 'You idiot, what the hell are you doing in the middle of the night on top of government's property. People come and go here and you keep just mum? Cannot you say something or cough when somebody draws near? Move and give way! The *sadhu* did not reply to what I had been shouting but instead said: 'Mother *(mai)* of Mariënburg and Father (*baba*) of Alliance'. Hearing this, I realised that this man was under the influence of cannabis (*ganja*) and therefore talking nonsense. I closed the sluice, returned home and fell asleep.

Next morning I called Ramanand and told him that I was going to sue him. He politely asked me: 'Bhaiya, please let me know my mistake'. I told him that he invited these strange *sadhus* to his place, creating terror by their awkward behaviour. I then narrated the whole incident. Ramanand was very ashamed. He apologised with folded hands and said: 'I shall at once tell this *sadhu* to leave. You are correct. This man had no cannabis with him last night and so filled his *chilam* [pipe] with *dhatura* seeds. It is due to the great intoxicating value of these seeds that he must have gone to the dam in the middle of the night. I am very sorry for this and I assure you that this will never happen again. Your bravery is unparalleled. Anyone else would have fainted out of fear'. I fell silent. The *sadhu* was immediately given marching orders. I also informed Baba Balwant Singh and he seconded my acts.

Lalkondre had not always had an irrigation system. This particular dam guided the boats that would come and go. When the water of the river and the dam were at the same level the sluice would be lifted. Boats arriving later or earlier had to wait till the dam water and the waterlevel in the river were the same, after every twelve hours. Here, near this dam, lived an old and big *trapoen* [a type of fish] just underneath the sluice. This fish would sometimes jump up and down and the splashing of water would frighten the boatmen who would then seek shelter at Ramanand's house. The place where boats were tied up was a big wooden shed made of bamboo. It was always dark inside, even on a moonlit night. This along with the mysterious splashing of water made up the theory that there was a ghost in the vicinity. Yet this myth was uncovered when Babu Ganpat Singh's neighbour Bhola Maharaj was blessed with a child and we were all invited for a feast on the occasion of *barhi*, held 12 days after the birth. It was dry weather and I was asked to recite from the Ramayana that day. The sluice was closed and the waterlevel of the river was high. When the water pressed on the sluice, two gates that were probably moth-eaten crashed open and the force of the current broke the brick wall below the sluice. The bricks were thrown away over a distance of about ten feet and this uprooted the 'ghostfish'. He moved to another place where later on the water receded however. As the water in the newly formed dam had now vanished, the poor fish was rendered homeless and trapped on land with no water. It could go nowhere and succumbed. It was six feet long and three feet broad. Yet no one ate its flesh because it had become bitter. This 'ghost' was also never again encountered!

## About the Question asked by the Manager of Satliyon [Plantation Groot Chatillion]

Dr. Mr. Haren had narrated the 'question and answer episode', which had occurred between the Commissioner and the doctor himself, the district secretaries and me in Domburg, to the government manager of Satliyon. Dr. Haren was a *kafir* [black][101], but very sharp, intelligent and kind-hearted. Once, Sir Weijtink called me, and five others, for some work in Satliyon near the river Suriname. That morning when we were on our way to do that work on the plantation, while crossing the bungalow of the manager, the manager who had heard the story about me from Mr. Haren and who was from Holland, called me by name. I turned around and heard: 'Rahman Khan, this work is not according to your standard'. When I asked why, he replied: 'I have heard that you are a very talented man and this job is not appropriate for you'. I retorted: 'Sahab, no one can conquer fate. If it were Hindustan, I would be in a higher post than you. But destiny has placed me under you'. Hearing this the manager said that I was right. After this short encounter we proceeded to work. In the evening, on our return from our duty, I was cooking my meal like the others. Having prepared the *daal* [pulses], I was making rotis when the manager came to me and said: 'Please do not mind me asking you just one question'. I said he was welcome and I had no reason to be angry with him. The manager then asked, 'there are two taps of a container. On opening one top, the container can be filled in five minutes, while on opening the other the container can be emptied in ten minutes. If both these taps are opened simultaneously, how long will it take to fill the container?' I said: 'Sahab, please wait for some time. Once my rotis are prepared and my hands washed, I will tell you the answer'. The *sahab* said that I could give the reply the next day as well but I said that I would let him know as soon as I had finished cooking. 'Very well', said the manager and went away.

After the cooking, I wrote down the question and its answer on a piece of paper and I walked to the manager's bungalow. It was 8 p.m. *Manjha Sahab* was at his dining table eating his supper. He stood up and gave me a chair. I sat near the dining table besides the lamp, took out the paper written in English and handed it over to the manager. The answer was 'in ten minutes'. The manger was pleased. He took his hat off and said: 'You are as good as I was told'. I stayed at Satliyon for 4 weeks and the manager behaved very well with me. Hassan Khan was the government chef at Satliyon. He and his son cooked food for the patients there. They were very good cooks. I had the opportunity to eat his rotis and meat everyday, and due to them had to prepare my meal only once each day.

## Skerpi revisited in 1907

When I had left Skerpi, its owner, Dolf Horst, had searched for me and had suspended the manager there. He took over the charge from him. After some time, he wrote a letter to manager Mr. Niboer Sahab asking him to send me to the plantation. Mr. Dolf Horst and Niboer were friends. Mr. Niboer called me and said, 'your *garamsara* wants to talk to you. I can give you 3-days leave. Go and listen to what he has to say'. When I went to Skerpi, Mr. Dolf Horst and his wife were very pleased and they behaved nicely. On hearing about my arrival, people from all walks of life in the plantation came to meet me. We talked with each other at great length. When all were gone, sir told me that he was having problems with the contract workers on the plantation. They had become rebellious and were out of his control. He needed me to run the plantation. 'I am growing old', he said. 'I am not as strong as I used to be. Come back here. You will have no trouble at all'. I then told him that I was very happy at Lalkondre because the Commissioner was very kind to me and that I would be unable to resign. On hearing this he became sad. Mrs. Dolf Horst also tried to persuade me. I felt sorry for them because I could not comply with their wish. I said to Mrs Horst: 'Mama, I can do nothing, please ask the Commissioner'. After our talk, we had dinner and went off to bed. I stayed there for another day and in the morning tried to convince the contract workers that they should give up their agression. Some understood that my effort to pacify them was for their own benefit. 'But', they said, 'a good shepherd looks after his flock properly, otherwise the sheep wander here and there, cause problems and are beaten up for it'. I knew they also wanted me back, but I said nothing in this regard and told them to do whatever they felt was right.

When I took leave from *Garamsara Sahab*, he gave me a dollar and the to-and-fro fare for the ship and again requested me to think about coming back. Back home I narrated the whole incident to *Manjha Sahab*. He felt very sorry for his friend. A few days later Mr. Dolf Horst sent a clerk to Commissioner Weijtink. The Commissioner then called me and we talked at length in presence of manager Niboer Sahab and the clerk. Finally, the Comissioner said: '*Meester* Rahman Khan, you are indebted to Mr. Horst. He now is old and the contract labourers are not afraid of him. Without you it will be impossible to run the plantation. You must return and control the situation there. I will see that you have no problem'. Mr. Niboer was of the same opinion. I had no choice. In 1907, I again joined the plantation in Skerpi and got paid fully. Work began as usual and everyone did his bit to resume normal routine under my orders.

On Tuesday 22 July 1908, my daughter Mariyam was born and by Allah's grace Dildar Khan came to this earth on Saturday 10

December 1910. Dr. Koch who was on duty at that time had predicted that this boy [Dildar] would be very stubborn and short-tempered. Whenever he would cry, he would faint and the only medication he required during such episodes was a bucket-full of water thrown over his body. He proved right. Nobody would therefore beat Dildar or tease him. When Suleman Khan was 10 years old and Karamat Khan was five, I gave a big party inviting about 500 men for a 3-day feasting on the occasion of *sunnat* in 1911. Friday was a night of waking while on Saturday it was Dildar Khan's *mundan* and *sunnat* was on Sunday. For the feast I had rented 200 large plates from plantation Voorburg. I however decided that at the marriage of my two sons I would serve food on lotus leaves. I therefore brought lotus seedlings from plantation Mariënburg and planted them on my big plot in Skerpi: they are still there!

I have mentioned earlier that my *garamsara* had three brothers. The eldest, Frans Horst had a son named Didi Horst. Both father and son had migrated to America ten years before, after which the father left his son there and returned with a 22-year old German wife to Surinam. He was 65 years old then. Their return was celebrated with grandeur. The day after their arrival in Surinam, they proceeded to the plantation Skerpi by ship. The poor German soul had had no idea as to what awaited her. She had lived a life in great comfort in a well-developed civilized nation (America) and had never imagined she would land up in a jungle! The new mistress of the cacao fields was afraid to venture out of her bungalow and would cry every now and then. Though *Mevrouw* [afterwards Mrs.] Dolf Horst was a real Dutch lady (*echte Hollandse*) she was very considerate and coaxing. Yet she could not help the girl to do away with her misconceptions and fears about the place. This girl knew only trees and plants growing in parks and gardens and had never seen a forest let alone jungles with the wild animals that were ready to pounce at her as soon as she came out. The more she thought of her plight, the more miserable she became. Mrs. Dolf Horst once invited her to visit a factory to which she agreed, though reluctantly. The distressed lady wandered at ease with her guide when, all of a sudden, she saw an army of bats. She shrieked in panic and sat down crying with her head in her hands saying: 'Let us run away otherwise these vampires will suck my blood out'. She then ran back to her residence and would not yield to any explanation. In the evening Frans Horst took her to Paramaribo. Such was the incident of the day.

The father of the Horst brothers had been from Holland while their mother had been a black. Three of the brothers were married. Frans Horst and Louis Horst had a son each while the other had no issue. Following the death of his wife, Frans Horst took his son Didi Horst and went off to America. At that time the cacao disease had not struck as yet. This disaster came after his departure. Dolf Horst and I somehow made ends meet for 5 long crisis laden years. When money from the city to meet the expenses would not come, I would spend my hard earned money to facilitate work and avoid any hindrances. I lost about Rs. 200 in all this. Dolf Horst and I had expected that the runaway Frans would soon return and help to revive the production and the economy of the plantation. But it had turned out otherwise as he had fallen ill in America. He had been admitted to a hospital there, where he had met the [German] girl, who had been working as nurse there. The bald fell for the beautiful and he trapped her with a spell of smooth tempting speech. He was lucky as she fell for him. He told her that he was a landlord in Surinam and had two plantations that yielded plenty of fruits. He also had a place in the city and he said that Surinam was a wonderful country. 'Would you like to come with me to this paradise', he had lured. The lady had been enticed and agreed to accompany him to this unknown heaven. However, it was illegal to go to a foreign land along with a woman who was not one's wife. This old fellow of 65 years old therefore got married to this young innocent girl. Thus began her miseries, which doubled once they came here. At times he would also beat her up. Enduring no more she sued for a divorce and got it. The poor 'orphan' worked for some time in a Christian institution to earn her fare back, while Frans Horst lived the remaining part of his life in Surinam. While Frans Horst had been in America, his three brothers had run the plantation with great difficulty and believed him by what he wrote from there. But once he returned with a wife and not his son, he lost his status among the family members. They thereafter cared less and less for the plantation. The cacao disease had already indebted them and moneylenders pressed hard for money.

## Off to Hansu [Meerzorg]

The four brothers fought over the debt. They also owed me Rs. 200. Seeing all this, I told Mr. Dolf Horst that I could not continue there any longer because the sale of the plantation could land me in trouble. Dolf Horst was a clever man. He understood. 'You are right', he said, 'everyone must change with time'. Saying this he gave me a box of medicines and made me write the name, dose and use of each medicine on every bottle and container in Hindi. 'I have nothing else to give you but these medicines will surely be of great help in the fields. Surely, if you wish you may take some planks of wood with you'. I was happy to receive these necessary items and thanked him for his goodness. I collected whatever was permissible and left for Hansu. Before leaving Skerpi however, I met my friends who had become like brothers to me and then proceeded to my *garamsara*. The couple was very sad. They wept as if I was a member of their family. They said that even if the plantation was sold I must come and visit them. I said: '*Insha Allah*' and Mrs. Horst wept bitterly. She had cared for my eldest daughter Mariyam when my wife had been ill and expecting, and Dolf Horst had himself cut the cord because I was not at home that night of her birth. Mariyam was named after Mrs. Horst [Marie]. Both of them would drop in at my place now and then and always gave some gifts to Mariyam or me. Mrs. Marie Horst died 10 years after her husband Dolf Horst. She had treated Mariyam as her own daughter and Mariyam inherited several clothes and a heavy golden necklace. The couple was fond of my spicy meat preparations and would call me to their bungalow to cook stuffed chicken and eat for a week from that. Once I prepared the head of a goat, which they liked very much. They said that they had never eaten anything more delicious than this before and would remember it till their death.

I bought two fields at Hansu for Rs. 350. A small house with a tin roof and premises with a boundary was all that I needed. This and a cowshed as bonus came along with the land. Many other Hindostanis lived in the locality and I was greatly respected there. At first only people from Jagtlust had bought fields there. As a matter of fact, they were the pioneers of farming there. When they landed there, the government had owned the land. Then the owner had given them farming land on lease. This man was very nice and soft spoken. His nature and speech were very enticing. I came to Hansu in 1912. That year, after a 10-months drought, the rains came with a cyclonic storm, which devastated the plantation. Roofs were blown off houses and thick trees in the jungle were uprooted. Godan,

Durjan, Ganpat and Rahim helped me in settling in Hansu and I had no trouble whatsoever. All my works were accomplished in a proper manner and we lived in great harmony with each other. Every night I would educate my sons. Basic necessities such as food were not so expensive in Hansu during that time. Their staple meal consisted of *puris* and vegetables while rice and pulses were unknown commodities. There were about forty houses in Hansu. All lived peacefully together. I was glad to be a part of it.

We also ran a kind of bank in Hansu of which I was the headman and the cashier. Every weekend 100 rupees would be given to one person each. One man was appointed to monitor the collection and distribution of money. Once it was the turn of Khedu, a *chamar* and my neighbour. I told him in the evening to collect his 100 rupees. He asked me to keep it for him till the next day when he would collect it before going to town. I kept the money in my jewellery box. That same night, one Malay person who worked in my house, robbed me of the cash, a clock and utensils but left the clothes and jewellery. The following evening all the members, on hearing about the theft, gathered to decide what to do. I told them about the burglary and assured them that I would return the lost money. Everyone, however, dismissed my proposal saying that since I had not stolen the money, I should not be punished for this. Each member contributed to compensate the loss. Such was the understanding and cohesiveness amongst us in Hansu.

By Allah's grace Chote Khan was born on Wednesday 21 May 1913 in the big hospital[102] because his mother was ill during that period. His *barhi* and *mundan* were celebrated in a grand manner. After these ceremonies the Hindustani Durjan, an *ahir* left for India by ship.

The plantation Skerpi had been sold. Mr. Toni Nassy had given them a loan of 10.000 rupees and the Horst family had been unable to return the sum. They had to give up their father's place, which they had kept for over 52 years, and give it to Mr. Tony Nassy. Mr. Nassy was a businessman. He had no idea about farming. When the plantation became his property he contacted his friend Mr. Niboer, the government manager in Domburg. He wrote a letter to him, asking for help in this regard. Mr. Niboer replied that he should look for Rahman Khan (contract no. 452/Aa) who could run the plantation smoothly. Neither Toni Nassy nor I knew each other. So he sent an application to the Emigration Department in search of me. Mr. Leon [Lyon] was in-charge during that time. He asked his translator Pandit Sheetal Prasad about my whereabouts. The *tolk* explained that I now lived in Meerzorg. The *Bara Sahab* immediately sent me a letter requesting me to report to him. I was glad to receive such a summon thinking that my application for reimbursement of the sum I had spent in the Skerpi plantation (Rs. 200) had been accepted because the plantation had been sold now and I thought that could compensate the loss. The next morning I reported to the *Bara Sahab.* He said: 'Lust en Rust has been sold. The new owner wants to meet you'. I pleaded: 'Sir, what about my money'. He replied, 'the sale of the plantation could only pay off the debt to the new landlord. You were the fourth in line and so will not be paid, like all the others'. I said: 'Sir, how can a poor man like me bear such a loss'. He said: 'You as well as the others who still have claims will not get anything'. I thought it to be useless to pursue the matter any longer. I consoled myself that the money I had earned had at least been spent on the upkeep of the plantation. So I shelved the subject and asked: 'Sir, I do not know Mr.Toni Nassy or where he lives'. The police then escorted me and brought me to his residence.

Mr.Toni Nassy was at home. He quickly came out to receive me and invited me in. He gave me a chair and we sat down to talk. He told me all about his acquisition and the problem of managing the plantation. I said I had my own field and cows to look after and was unable to return. He asked, 'is the land registered in your name? I answered in the negative. He said, 'do not worry; my men will take good care of your cows. The contract labourers will cut grass and do whatever is necessary. Your orders shall be followed here as it was during the days of Mr. Horst. Come let us visit the plantation and meet the manager'. We were still talking when the *memsahab* [Mr. Toni Nassy's wife] laid the table. I pulled my chair away from the dining table thinking Mr.Toni Nassy was to eat his meal. But instead he held my hand and asked me to join him saying I was his guest and knowing that I was a Mohammadan, he had ordered nothing that was against my religious code. I could say nothing, and sat down. After dinner, as we sat down to smoke a cigarette, he took out Mr. Niboer's letter and read it aloud saying that he had come to know about me only through this piece of paper. He said: 'I hope you will neither disappoint Mr. Niboer nor me and take charge of my plantation'. I told him that it was not possible for me to decide at once and needed a couple of days to decide. He agreed.

## My third Return to Skerpi in 1913

When I was about to leave, Toni Nassy gave me a box full of biscuits for my son and 1 dollar [2.50 Dutch cents]. I took the boat home. I narrated the whole incident to my family and friends. Nobody wanted me to return to Skerpi: 'Why do you want to go there again?' they asked and added that if I needed anything they would try and give it to me. They did not like me to leave. I however replied: 'Allah has provided all I need but since I have given my word I must go'. Accordingly, on the promised day I went to the *garamsara's* house, which was in the town. After the formal greetings we sat down to talk. At 9 o'clock a lavish breakfast was served and we ate together like before. After food we had one glass of cognac, two-three buiscuits, some tangerines [sweet lemon] and oranges. Smoking followed.

We then proceeded to the Morgenstond plantation by a horse-driven carriage, as there were no automobiles at that time. Four people were waiting with a boat to help us cross the river. We reached Skerpi and there the new manager, Mr. Gomes, had come to receive us. We greeted each other and went to his bungalow. We sat down and talked for 2-3 hours about the situation. They knew how I had managed the plantation single-handed when Mr. Horst had been in hospital and that none of his three brothers had taken care of the plantation during his absence. They said they had received this information from the elite white (*bakra*) residents in the city who knew about my honesty and sincere approach. They referred to incidents that had taken place in 1909 when the cacao season had started and harvest work had to be prepared. Rainfall had been adequate that year. Mr. Dolf Horst had come to inspect the fields one day but someone had thrown a mango peel and Mr.Horst became its victim. He slipped and broke his left arm on three places, and lost consciousness. A message was sent by wireless to the doctor who came and immediately referred him to a big hospital. Mr. Kori, the manager of the plantation 'Belwatra' [Belwaarde] also received the message about the accident and came to see him. Mr.Horst asked him whether, during his absence, he could collect the reports from me on every Friday and could give me money for the maintenance of the plantation on every Saturday. He also requested Mr. Kori to send a monthly report based on information provided by me concerning plantation matters to his brothers in the city. Mr.Kori asked who would distribute the wages on Saturdays and allot the work to the labourers. 'Do not worry about that', Mr.Horst had said: 'my *sardar* is capable of handling all this. You should just take the reports, pay him and he will manage the rest. Whenever you wish you may inspect his handling'. Mr. Kori was highly surprised and had remarked: 'How can you rely so much on a Hindustani'. But Mr. Horst said that I was more honest and intelligent than the natives in Surinam. Mr.Horst was then admitted to a hospital, but just before that he had briefed me about what was to be done during his absence, which as it turned out lasted 4 months. Horst had told me that whatever money I needed, I could collect from Mr. Kori every Saturday after presenting the report on Friday. During the time that Mr. Horst was in the city hospital, I had to manage all the work as Mrs. Horst was also absent from the plantation to look after her husband in the hospital. One Saturday, I went to the office, opened the register and found a note of 25 rupees. I left it on the place where I had found it and kept an eye on it. Mr. Kori trusted me with all the work including all financial matters. Mr. Horst' brothers did not even once visit the plantation to check my work. I had not touched the 25 rupees. Actually, I later on came to know that it belonged to Mr. Horst and that he had forgotten where he had kept the money. When Mr. Horst returned from the hospital after a period of 4 months, he asked me to show the accounts and explain how the money had being utilised. I handed over the reports to him and his wife and also brought the register of the contract workers. The latter also contained the 25 rupees note, which I handed over to them. They were satisfied and happy with my work and gifted me the 25 rupees as a reward for my honesty. They said nobody else would have returned the sum as I had done, and that it was difficult to find an honest person like me.

Mr. Nassy and the manager had been pleased to learn about this incident and said that they had not heard anybody speak against me on the plantation. In fact, an enquiry about me had convinced them of my spotless character. I was a unique person, they thought. After this encounter we took our meal and rested for a while. When

I was about to leave, Toni Nassy gave me a 5 rupee note and asked me to join plantation 'Lust and Rust' (Skerpi) as early as possible. I took leave and walked back to Hansu. When I told my family and friends about the meeting and my decision to again join the plantation, it hurt them as well as myself.

In 1913, I sold my land in Hansu and once again started working in Skerpi. Manager Gomes was easy-going and as promised, Toni Nassy took care of my cows. Both of them were kind and helpful. When my sons or I were ill, they took great pains to procure medicines for us and ensure our wellbeing. We were treated as family members. After recovery, I presented a cow to the daughter of manager Gomes on her birthday. This sickness had been the second encounter with death that had been predicted by Hakim Nawab Ali Sahab during my childhood days. Yet, once again Allah ordered it to pass. I shall narrate the story about my illness later on.

After a year, Mr. Gomes, our manager, replaced Mr. Currie of the Belwaarde plantation. Mr. May succeeded Gomes. Mr. May was a true *kafir* but he behaved like a white man. He had married Paula Sai of Umra whose father was an honorable man among the Muslim community. She had had a *kafir* mother and she looked more like a black. Yet her face resembled that of a full-blooded Hindustani.

## Failure of Black Magic (*Voodoo*)

***Doha***

*If someone plants thorn-bushes in your garden*
*You should plant flowers in turn*
*Because a flower remains a flower*
*And thorns form a trishul (trident)*[103]

The satanic disease that struck my family was the result of my goodness. It all began during my residence in Hansu. I had a close friend whose wife's intention was not good. My friend was unaware of that, however. The woman had no son and badly desired one. She, like her husband, belonged to our circle of family friends. One day she pleaded and asked me to give her a son. I said that it was Allah's domain and that it was he who decided over everyone's fate. I told her that if it were her fate she would be blessed but only if it were God's wish. I asked her to collect certain items to make a talisman and she assured me she would get them. My friend knew what had transpired between us that day but did not know what followed later on. I do not know why this woman carried out such an evil act, which made our lives so miserable. During the time that my wife was pregnant and in her eighth month, this woman with evil intentions was very close to us indeed. She would give bath to my children, cook food for us and also help in other household chores making life very easy for my pregnant wife. I had no reason to suspect any foul play and she was the wife of my close friend. Yet one day this woman decided to destroy my wife's pregnancy and implant her own womb by using black magic. For this purpose, she went to Lalkondre where her brother and sisters lived. In Lalkondre, she contacted a black man called Johnny, who practised *voodoo.* He was my friend and clever too. When I had resided in Lalkondre, I would help him whenever he needed any food or other assistance. This woman told him about her desire for a child. She thought of terminating someone else's pregnancy by black magic and become pregnant herself. The *shaman* (witch doctor) asked her who would be the victim. When he came to know it was my wife, the good man flatly refused. The woman did not give up, however, and coaxed her brother to take the man to a liquor shop and make him inebriated. Her plan worked: Intoxicated, the man gave her the medication she wanted without him being aware of its use. Her brother named Katwaru was a *timmerman* [carpenter] who worked together with black workers. Through them she carried out her evil design. The woman had all forgotten about our warm friendship. Yet I advise: Do as you would be done by.

It was the month of *phagun* (March-April) and in the morning of *holika dahan* she prepared cacao for us and poured the evil potion (a mixture of certain spices) into the pot. She served every member of my family but refrained from drinking the cacao herself and emptied the pot for us. We did not suspect a thing. The drug did its work, as the woman had desired. Next morning at 8 a.m my wife asked me to take her to the hospital because she was bleeding and was afraid that she might have an abortion. I said that since it was Holi, my Hindu brothers had been invited for the festivities so I told her to wait till the next day. I told her that if it were Khuda's wish nothing untoward would happen. Saying this, I tied a *tabeez* in Allah's name around her waist. This greatly reduced the pain of her abdomen and the bleeding also decreased. Early next morning I took her to the hospital. Four weeks later my wife delivered Chote Khan by God's grace but my wife remained ill and kept on having stomach problems. Besides, my three sons also fell sick. Mariyam had not drunk the potion as at the time she had been living with Mrs.Horst.

Suleman Khan became so sick that he could no longer walk as his thighs and legs had swollen to a great extent. I took him to plantation Jagtlust and met its manager named Mr. Poelman. I requested him to admit my son in the hospital. The manager said: 'Sardar, this is not a government hospital and is meant only for those working on this plantation. Yet since I know you and your history of good deeds at Skerpi, I shall consider your case. I shall arrange for the medicines but you will have to pay the doctor's charges. Dolf Horst was a friend of Mr.Lyon, the Head Immigration Officer who had also become the *eigenaar* [owner] of Jagtlust. I thanked the manager and asked him what the doctor would charge. He said it was up to the doctor. The doctor visited the hospital every week on Mondays, Thursdays and Saturdays. It was a Monday and the manager first talked to him in Dutch and then introduced me and told him about my problem. The doctor remarked: '*Sardar*, when your son recovers I will take a cow from you'. I said: 'Sir, I am a poor man and have nothing else to satisfy you besides a cow, but even money is nothing compared to the good health of my son'. Upon this the doctor laughed and said: 'I just tested you because Hindustanis are in general so miserly that, even though the life of their son might be at stake, they are not prepared to give even a cent for his cure. Yet you are different. Just pay me today's consultation fees and I shall not charge you anything until your son is cured. I know your close association with Mr.Horst, and how Mrs.Horst loved and look after your daughter Mariyam'. I thanked the doctor and did as he ordered. With Allah's consent my son recovered after 3 weeks. It was during this period that I left Hansu and moved to Skerpi for the third time. After this however, Karamat Khan and Dildar Khan became very ill. They could not even digest a few crumbs of food. Eating led to severe pain in their stomach and they would turn over in agony. These two sons and their mother were still suffering when we shifted to Skerpi.

As far as I was concerned, during 9 months I regularly found blood in my stool and severe pain in my abdomen had forced me to tie a cloth around my waist before going to work day in and day out. I would refrain from eating my meals and would distribute my lunch among the workers to avoid pain. I was so troubled by my illness and my sons' sufferings that once I even thought of the extreme of ending our lives in the river. I could not sleep that night and it was already 11 p.m. I kept on thinking of suicide when suddenly I remembered the words of Hakim. Hakim had narrated the story of a place where cannibalism was prevalent. People would eat the sick, and once he had also been asked to accept human flesh. Hakim had told them, however, that Allah was the Master and would heal the sick and make the healthy sick as He desired. Hence it was improper to take these decisions [about life and dead] in one's own hand. I was ashamed of myself and at once I realised that Allah had been testing me. I prayed to Him for forgiveness vowing never to think negatively again.

Since I was new on the plantation and not in good health, I had felt sad and angry most of the time. I had also stayed aloof of the manager and his wife. Yet after the night of my realisation I visited her at her residence the very next morning and told her in detail about our physical condition. The good woman promised to arrange the required medicnes from the very next day onwards. My ordeal now seemed to be over. We were given medicines the taste of which was so bitter that I would not even prescribe them to my enemies! It also had a very horrid smell and we all had a tough time gulping it down. Yet by Allah's consent we were cured in about 4 weeks. I gifted a cow to the daughter of Mr.Gomes. My dear wife however, remained ill.

## Goodness never goes unrewarded (God's Justice)[104]

With God's will and the black magic, the vixen that poisoned us did become pregnant and she gave birth to a boy in a hospital. The Lord is the Supreme Judge and He moves in a mysterious way. I had no enemies and had never imagined that someone so near and dear to us would do such a thing. My wife suffered for 3 years due to the effect of the poison, which however, did not kill her. After 3 years the poison had lost its efficacy. However, the woman who had caused our sufferings died just 6 days after delivering her child. God had not given her even a year after her misdeed, while my wife lived on. Someone else looked after her son but he too passed away after 9 months. My son, however, survived and is still alive. Both mother and son died but the woman's victims were spared. It is true that one cannot mock God.

As I have written earlier, the manager Mr. May, who replaced Mr. Gomes, was black while his wife's parents were of black and Hindostani origin. She was the daughter of Pola Sai and her mother's name was Naseeban. Her skin colour and hair were those of a black while her face was Hindostani. The manager and his family were very gentle and kind. They were not arrogant and helped others whenever need arose. Man should always do well to others even if he gets nothing in return. Khuda sees everything and will prevent that any harm is done to those who do the right thing. One should not listen to others and take revenge if someone wrongs you. Let Allah pass the judgement. We only reap what we sow.

During manager May's time one Saturday, a festival was celebrated on the plantation. It rained cats and dogs till 2 o'clock in the afternoon that day. Due to this unfriendly weather, a poor black man named Willem who lived near the river Korina, close to plantation Constancia, was held up in Skerpi. This farmer had arrived there on a small old boat. He was drenched when he arrived, tied his boat and enquired about the way to my house. He called for me from a tin shed outside my house at around 11 a.m. Hearing someone shouting, I came out. He greeted me and said shivering: '*Basia* [friend], my tobacco and matchbox are wet and I too. I am feeling very cold, please give me a cheroot and a match to smoke and get warm'. I felt very sorry for the man and said that I had no alcohol to give but would try to arrange something for his cold. I quickly brought a big glass of warm milk for the half-dead soul. With trembling hands he accepted this and then closed his eyes for a moment. When he felt better he opened them again. I offered him half a packet of cigarettes and a matchbox and asked from where he had come. He thanked me and replied that he lived in Constancia near the river Commewijne, where he had a small field. He said that it had rained throughout his journey and that he was very indebted to me for my warm and kind hospitality. I replied: '*Mati* [friend], there is no reason to be so obliged. I only offered what there was in my house. I do not drink and so have no liquor to offer and just gave you warm milk'. He said that he presumed milk was a thousand times better than wine. After smoking, his chill vanished and I then gave him a plate of steaming rice and pulses cooked in my home. He ate to his heart's content and fell fast asleep in the yard in his wet clothes. When the rain stopped he washed his face and hands and again began to smoke.

I sat on another bench beside him and watched his activities intently. Suddenly he spoke: '*Basia*, I want to work under you'. I asked him whether he had come here seeking a job. He replied: 'No, I was on my way to the city to find some work but the rains and cold weather forced me to stop here. Your kind attitude has changed my mind and I no longer desire to go to the city. I now wish to work for you'. I said: 'You are a native of Surinam and will expect Rs. 1.50 per day for your work, which is not possible here because here the contract workers get only twelve annas and *freemen* are paid one rupee for a day's labour. You can earn much more in another way and place'. He told me that as far as he was concerned a good work environment was more important than money. I asked him whether he was single or married. He replied that he had a wife and children. I said that I had to take *manjha*'s permission and went off to meet him as soon as the rains stopped. I then told the manager that a native wanted to work in Skerpi for a rupee a day. He said: 'As you are the *sardar,* you do as you think proper'. After my return from the manager's bungalow I told the *Negro* about our talk. He said he would come after a couple of days, as he had first to dispose off his field. On the third day he was indeed back with his family. He began his work in earnest and became very close to me. He would get one rupee while his wife earned eight annas each day.

By now, my sons and I had fully recovered form the mysterious disease but my wife still suffered. Towards the end, the pain became unbearable and my wife was bed-ridden. Suleman nursed his mother every day and attended to her needs. It was Saturday and around 10 a.m., and while I was writing something on my notebook, somebody pushed me from behind. I had finished the report and was to check the accounts. It was in the middle of an empty field (no. 23) that this incident happened. I nearly fell down. Nobody was to be seen. I was puzzled. Notwithstanding, I expelled all fears and continued with my work. I thought of proceeding to the next field as I had finished my work in field no. 23 but suddenly saw the manager who was returning from the field. We met and he asked me where I was going. I replied that I was going to make an account of the labourers' work, as it was payday. He told me to postpone the work till next Saturday and go home instead. I returned home with the manager at 11 a.m. and found Suleman crying. I asked him what it was that made him cry and the poor child cried: 'Mother is rolling her eyes and talking all nonsense'. I thought her end had come and called the manager and showed him my wife. He recognised the plight and told me that it was the result of black magic and that he did not know a cure. Saying this he left me stunned: 'Who could do such a thing to us'. I wondered. I had no enemies, whom could I suspect? I was in a fix. The whole day I tried to find a solution for this life-threatening problem.

All at once, Willem flashed in my mind. He is a black I thought, and maybe knows some way to help my wife. At four in the evening after the payments had been made, I called him. He at once diagnosed the evil spirit and went home to fetch some medicine. After about half an hour he came back and smeared it on my wife's forehead. No sooner had he done this, she got up and started talking loudly, which she had not been able to do earlier. With her eyes popping out she narrated the whole episode of mishappenings and diseases, which had plagued my family since the last 3 years and explained its cause in *Negre* [Sranan Tongo]. At this, Willem asked the devil to leave my wife alone. The evil spirit, which had possesed my wife, replied: 'I shall take this woman along with me when I go because only 3 days are left'. Willem asked: 'Will you surely kill this woman'. The reply was: 'Yes'. 'Then why did you spare her child and why did you kill the woman and her son in Lalkondre who brought you', Willem asked. The evil spirit laughed loudly and said: 'Willem, why do you ask? You can do nothing to me. Nevertheless I will tell you the reason. After mixing the potion with the cacao I began to destroy this lady's pregnancy but her husband tied a *mantra* written on a paper around her waist and the spirit in it did not let me do my work. It was stronger than me and displaced me from my site. I tried to act from another place but could not succeed. Wherever I approached, this woman would tie the thing over that area and my attempts went in vain. I could not snatch the child and so I killed the woman who called me as well as that I killed her son'. Willem asked the spirit (through my wife), 'you were brought to kill the child only, why did you trouble the entire family?

What will you gain by killing this woman'. The spirit replied: 'I have been working thoughout Surinam and never failed and no Hindustani labourer had the guts to defy me. But this woman's husband nullified my attacks by his cleverness and saved his child from me. How can I take this easily? I will avenge my failure. If you heat one end of an iron rod the other end will also get hot'. Willem asked: 'you said that you would not leave this woman. Tell me then where will you be pleased to be sent to'. The spirit replied: 'Only when you can control me you can pack me off to another place'. Saying this it left the body of my wife and she again was laid up and started coughing like before.

This incident shook me and I praised Allah for his protection and kindness. Willem then asked me as to what would be our next step. He asked, 'should I send this spirit back to the person from whom it came? Or should I throw it in the river? I pleaded that I did not wish to take revenge since Allah had already done justice and I did not want to cause any misery to anyone. It could again cause troubles for me. Willem was very pleased with my reply and said: '*Basia*, very well said, anyone else would have opted for revenge but you are an exception. Now if you do not want to send this spirit to someone else you must yourself take it at night and throw it into the river when the water turns black. I cannot do this myself'. I said: '*Inshah Allah* [with God's will], I will do it with my own hands. God will help me'. Willem then said: ' Let it be tonight itself because further delay might lead to a sinister outcome'. I immediately gave my consent. At ten in the night Willem began his rituals and completed all his activities by 11.30 p.m. He had put the evil spirit inside a big bottle and gave it to me saying: 'Throw this into the river and do not look back on your return or else you will find no cure'. I assured him to do as he had said and at midnight, when the water turned black, I took the bottle in my hands and went off to the river. The bottle was empty but weighed about 5 kilos. When I reached the riverside I threw away the bottle with all my strength. I then turned around and following Willem's warning I did not look behind on my way back home. My wife seemed better early next morning but weakness and abdominal pain remained. Then Willem undertook a long journey beyond Koffiedjompo in Para district to fetch some herbs, which were not found on the plantation and added those herbs that were readily available and made my wife drink it and take bath in water mixed with the potion. Khuda allowed my spouse to be cured after a week's treatment.

Later on I took my wife to Toni Nassy whose elder brother was a doctor. He gave her some medicines against her weakness. When I asked Willem what he wanted in return for the favours he had done for us, he declined: 'I do not want anything'. Thus, with the help of the All Mighty, we proved stronger than evil spirits and made them bite the dust.

My third tenure in Skerpi began with manager Gomes who stayed for a year. Mr. May succeeded him but he left for Nickeri after about a year as well. During his time in 1914, World War I broke out in Europe between England and Germany. In the month of October in 1914, our *garamsara* Toni Nassy visited the plantation with his family for a change. During that time it was a fad amongst the affluent to go away from the city for a month's vacation to a plantation. Our *garamsara* did this as well and stayed with his family and creole maidservants for a month with us. The bungalow was filled with noise and commotion.

Near the water stood an almond tree under which the *garamsara* would pass his time in the evenings with his family and the maidservants. One evening at around three, two of his sons took bath in the nearby river. The river was full of water and there was a strong current. A small boat was tied to the landing place. The boys enjoyed themselves in the water when suddenly the younger one got pulled down by the current and began to drown. Seeing this, the elder brother jumped in to save him and began to sink himself. When Meneer Toni Nassy saw what had happened he immediately ran and jumped in the water in a bid to pull them out, but in vain. He also had not noticed the boat tied there. The water near the shore had formed a whirlpool and all three of them were entrapped in it. Now huge shouting and shrieking started near the riverside. I was on my return from the field with manager May when we heard this commotion but not knowing the cause, I went back home. The manager however, walked to the shore and seeing the situation jumped into the water wearing his heavy field gear. The boat had also missed his attention and commonsense had failed once more.

The noise near the shore increased considerably. I had not even changed my clothes when I heard the turmoil and I rushed to the site wearing the same dress. I could only discover three circulating heads just above the water and a fourth one moving away. I immediately blew my whistle. The boatman was there within a second with his boat. I ordered him to rescue the three heads while I would rescue the fourth one after loosening the small boat that was tied up near the landing. Three heads were pulled out while we were closing in on the fourth victim. He was about a foot inside the water. I had no inkling that it was the manager who had been with me a few minutes earlier and now was on the verge of losing his life for others. I thought he had gone home. He had short hair so I grabbed hold of his jacket and pulled his head out of the water. I tried to pull him onto the boat but I could not he was short and fat and had his heavy clothing on him. I immediately ordered the men to stop rowing and to lend me a hand. They helped me by taking him aboard by holding his legs. Only then did I recognise the manager. He was unconscious and half-dead. We quickly brought him to the shore and then took him to his residence and sent a wireless message for the doctor. The doctor arrived shortly in his horse-drawn carriage and removed the salty water from the manager's body through his mouth until he regained his senses. He then gave medicines to the father and two sons who were very shaken by this incident. Thus the lives of the four drowning men were saved by God's grace. It is true that one cannot increase nor decrease one's period of life. God decides when it is time to go. Till their deaths the manager and his wife were grateful to me. Whenever my children would visit them, they would take good care of them. The manager also would tell his own children how I saved his life and how he was indebted to me.

## From Skerpi to Cabbelbuiten in 1916

When manager May left for Nickerie, Mr.Warner replaced him. He had been a clerk on the Constancia plantation from where he had been ousted. He had then joined the Mon Tresor plantation also as a clerk but due to his bad behaviour was removed from there as well. He was of mixed origin (*mulat*) and was very short tempered. He showed no kindness to the poor and downtrodden. He would not listen to anyone and was aggressive and arrogant. It was very difficult to bear this man and I was having a horrid time working under him. Nobody liked him.

One day, we were busy cutting trees in the jungle near the

plantation to plant tangerine trees. (These trees are still there). I, along with a Javanese worker, was measuring the newly cleared fields as we had to dig new gutters there. I was about 3-4 ketting away from the road towards the new field. Another Javanese, a contract worker who had done the measuring work, had gone home for lunch at noon and returned at about 2 p.m. At that time, manager Warner was on his way home for his meal when they both met. I saw them exchange words in a heated manner and sensed some punches were to follow. I quickly hid myself behind a tree trunk and told the Javanese who was with me to hide in the drain so that we would not be witnesses to this incident. I knew that the manager was at fault and my presence would prevent the Javanese to beat him and if he did so, I would have to play witness in court to protect the manager and against the Javanese. I had good reasons to avoid this unpleasant task as nobody (neither Hindustanis nor Javanese), liked the manager. Seeing no one near, in particular not me, the Javanese got hold of the manager and threw him on the ground. He then kicked him and gave some blows that made the manager bleed from the face. He cried out for help in his language: '*Basia helpi mi*!' [Help me!]. It was only then that I shouted from my hiding place: 'Hey, who is there? I am coming'. On hearing my voice the Javanese ran to his place of work. The manager lay in a pool of blood still shouting when I arrived and asked what had happened. 'That Javanese fellow named Pawiro has beaten me up', he shouted and added: 'You are an eyewitness to this'. I replied: 'Well, I did not see anything, so why should I act as a witness? I cannot lie in front of the judge'. The manager retorted: 'I do not care whether you have really seen it or not. You must help me'. I declined however: 'Sorry, I can only help you with money or any other requirement but cannot lie to anyone. That is not my cup of tea. Moreover, it is probably your own fault'. 'What is my fault?' he barked. I answered: 'Listen Sahab, every man works in different capacities to earn his bread. People even kill others in order to get their daily meals and suffer for it behind bars. We, labourers, left our country to work under you here in Surinam to earn our living. The government does allow one-hour lunch at 12. The Javanese availed of that right. There was therefore no reason to find fault with him even though he is a contract worker. Afterall he also must fill his stomach to survive'. The manager getting very upset replied: 'He should have brought his lunch with him to work' Yet, I flatly replied that no government or contract rule specified this. However, if a daily wage labourer would not return to work in time, the manager was at liberty to deduct money from his payment accordingly. Yet I added that he should not talk roughly or abuse someone. The Javanese was on a contract of 12 annas per day and if he worked less for 3 consecutive days, the manager was allowed to sue the labourer and he would be sent to jail. A manager was not entitled to do anything more than that as far as I knew. I told him all that and added: 'You are free to take any step regarding this incident, but I shall not give any false evidence. Hearing this, the manager fell silent and went home. I returned to my work.

When this manager had come to Skerpi it had been dry season. By that time, he had already lost his first finger of his right hand. This had happened when he had been working as a *skreeman* on the Constancia plantation. A contract worker named Alopi Singh had chopped off his finger. Reason was the manager's irksome and rough behaviour. Pride and anger were his companions. It is said that anger diminishes one's strength and makes one prone to beatings. One day in plantation Constancia Alopi Singh and Warner had had a tussle over work. Warner Sahab had pointed his index finger to Alopi and threatened him with dire consequences and had said, *Luku bung boi, mi go sori yu*[105]. The *kshatriya* then had lost his temper as he did not like to be treated in this way by a *dogla*[106]. He was a wrestler and had no difficulty in overpowering Warner. He then snatched the chopper from Warner's hands and cut off his index finger saying: 'From now onwards you shall not point this "look you finger" at anyone'. He then left Warner and straight went to the Commissioner with the cut finger and narrated the whole episode. Warner Sahab was sent to the hospital. After Warner left the hospital, the court decided to put Alopi Singh in jail for 9 months, while Warner was ousted from the plantation. Warner then joined the Mon Tresor planation as a *skreeman*. I do not know how long he stayed there but his next posting was as a manager in Skerpi.

When Alopi Singh finished his term in jail, the owner of plantation Constancia refused to take him back, and since he was still under contract he was, as the rules confirm, he was sent to the *Agent-Generaal* of the Immigration Department. The Bara Sahab would then decide where he could complete his contract work. He tried various plantations but no plantation owner accepted Alopi

Singh. Finally Mr. Lyon sent him and another contract labourer with a similar history to Skerpi of Mr. Dolf Horst. The other person was a *fakir* called Sikandar, who had been working on plantation 'Piprapat' [Peperpot] and had been charged with having caused trouble there. It was on a Friday that these two not so obedient men arrived at Skerpi by boat. They handed over their appointment letters to Mr. Horst along with a letter of recommendation written by an older brother of Dolf Horst. After having read these letters Mr.Horst sent for me and said, 'this is the horse's burden on a monkey. Bara Sahab has sent these two useless fellows without me asking for them. My brother is an idiot. He does not even know how to run the plantation and has forwarded this duo to complete their contracts here. They are not my workers and nobody wants them. Let them go wherever they wish but I will not take them.' I then requested him not to be angry and give it a thought. Why Mr.Lyon, an old friend of his, would have sent these men to him? I reminded Dolf Horst that Mr. Lyon had once also extended help to him by giving a job to lazy Tulsi who earlier had worked under Horst but had eloped with his female cook. In order to stay with this woman, Tulsi had even agreed to work as a *freeman* for just a glassful of rice. He finally married her. Mr. Lyon made this man a *tolk* in his office even though Tulsi knew nothing but the native language. The Agent-Generaal had only done so as Mr.Horst had recommendated this fellow in order to help his cook. I told Mr.Horst, 'how can you even think of sending these men back to your friend? He will think we are useless. You must do a favour to your friend as he has done a favour to you. It will not be a big problem to keep them and Bara Sahab would be very pleased indeed'. Dolf Horst had listened carefully and finally decided that I could do whatever I thought was good: 'After all, you are the one who has to make them work'.

After this agreement, I called the two men and said: 'Listen Alopi Singh, you are a *kshatriya* and I am a *pathan*. In Hindustan we are both of equal class. Do not think too much of yourself and cause problems here. It will be better for you to work in harmony here during the time that remains according to your contract. You will be paid 12 annas and that will be enough for a decent living. You are rooted in a good family. Why should you do something that causes disrepute? Work and live in peace like other people of your class'. I then turned to the *fakir* and said: 'As far as you are concerned, you beggar, do not think you are strong enough to cause trouble all the time and get away with it in Surinam. Many bigwigs have come and died in their prison cells here. You do not stand a chance. What are you? If you need, you may ask someone for a cup of rice. Begging will not degrade you, since it is in your blood. But resorting to theft will be a shameful act. You will also get 12 annas per day during this last phase of your contract. Work properly or else you will be in big trouble here. Live like a good Muslim for your own good if not for that of others'. These two men felt ashamed and pleaded: '*Sardar*, you are like a father to us. We have had enough of this bad behaviour and we promise you to be disciplined from now onwards. Bara Sahab had already told us that the *garamsara* and *sardar* of Skerpi were kind-hearted and that we would not get any better place to complete our contract in Surinam. The Bara Sahab warned us not to do anything wrong. We shall therefore abide by your words, and do as you wish'. I then allotted them a place in the lane and they began to work and worked well till the end of their contract period. Thereafter, they went their own ways. Alopi Singh now owns a field in Skerpi while the *fakir* is nowhere to be found.

As I have already mentioned, when Mr. Warner came to Skerpi, it had been dry season. The monsoon followed and the water in the drains began to rise. One day during the reporting hour I told Mr. Warner not to lift the iron cover from the *koker* near the river during my absence. Yet he retorted: 'Do you think I do not know how to operate the *koker*?' I replied: 'No sir, I did not mean that. You may know a lot about *kokers* and sluices elsewhere, but this one is different. Sluices are the same everywhere but this *koker* is different. Please inform me when the water of the drain crosses the danger mark and reaches the level of the plantation. Otherwise, the stone pipe might collapse'. The manager said nothing and I went home. Four days after that, when I had gone to the field the proud manager ordered four men who worked in the shed to remove the iron cover. No sooner had they lifted the cover, it crashed and was swept away by the currents. It was high tide and after some time the water spread throughout the plantation. I was in the field, supervising cacao cleaning, when I saw a white salt-water flow into the canals and drains. I knew the manager had exactly done what I had asked him not to do. I immediately walked to the lock chamber and saw the manager with four men trying to retrieve the cover. He had taken off his jacket and was attempting the impossible. I stood and watched but said nothing. The damage had already been done.

At four in the evening I rounded off the work and went home. Later, when I went to report the day's activities to the manager, I showed my displeasure, as his act had caused damage to the iron cover. He snapped, 'how dare you accuse me, *a no mi schuld'* [I am not responsible]. I replied: 'Sir, I am not accusing you, but despite my warning you broke the cover and now refuse to accept the responsibility. *Sa no yu schuld, suma schuld, mi schuld*?'[You are not guilty? Who is then responsible for it, I?]. I added: 'Why, one day you will set the whole plantation on fire and say that you do not know anything about it. What will Mr. Toni Nassy say? I knew the condition of the *koker* since the last 20 years because it was built in my presence. You have come here just a few days ago; how could you learn so fast about it? You are about 36 years old, and have only experienced fighting and discontent'. I further told him about many other bad incidents in the past, which had only happened due to his wrong management. He said nothing. Finally I told him that I could not work any longer under a hardheaded manager like him: 'I am not one of those *sardars* who is unvoiced. I am one who listens to his manager but also expects the manager to listen to him. Yes, if the law of the plantation forbids advising the manager, I would refrain from doing so. Now you better find another *sardar* of your liking. I shall leave by next week'. After this I returned home. When news about this row between the manager and me reached Hansu, people from the village invited me to join them again in Hansu. I was very eager to return but told them that this had become impossible now as two of my sons were engaged there and living near in-laws is not proper.

I then moved to the plantation 'Cabelboiti' [Cabelbuiten] near Charlesburg[107] where my mother-in-law and her son (my brother-in-law) lived. I bought a field for Rs. 22 and settled there. This neighbourhood belonged to a Chinese named Chin Ko Fat. The rent was high here (i.e. Rs. 9 per *ketting* each year). The land was good for the cultivation of sweet potatos and vegetables, yet paddy was only cultivated in the lowlands. However, the fish there would eat half of the paddy. When Toni Nassy came to know that I had left Skerpi due to the *koker* incident, he himself went to the plantation to have a first hand impression of the situation there. He was very disturbed, and a month later fired manger Warner.

I went to Dijkveld to talk to *babu* Mahabir Singh about some land I wanted to buy. I knew him well from the time he had worked on contract in Jagtlust. He took me to Shri Bhawani Bhikhwhom whom I also knew from before. As a matter of fact, he had been my student in Jagtlust where he had spent half of his contract time. We talked about the land in Dijkveld, which belonged to a black man [Creole]. This man agreed to sell the plot for Rs. 125 to me. I still live there [see photograph]. Then I went to Hussaini and told him about the deal. He quickly agreed and the very next morning, he paid the *kafir* and gave me the land papers, which were in my name. He also gave Rs. 25 to two blacks to get wood from Leiding to construct a house. I sold off my plot in Cabelbuiten for Rs. 160 and therefore could return Hussaini his money. I then shifted to Dijkveld with my family and once again began to lead a peaceful life. On Tuesday 19 August 1920, Faiz Khan was born and Hakim Nawab's prediction concerning the number of sons had become true, due to Allah's blessings.

## Bhawani Bhikh the Charlatan

Bhawani Bhikh had come with his sister from India and had started his work as contract labourer in Jagtlust 15 months before my arrival. He was young but very evil-minded. Babu Arjun Singh was an honest and intelligent man and also lived in Jagtlust. He had studied Urdu upto class III yet his Hindi was not so advanced. We had become close friends and whenever I went to Jagtlust to meet my countrymen, I would surely visit him too. Babu Arjun Singh also taught Hindi to Bhawani Bhikh, Bhulan, Lallu and Gharbharan. One day Babu Arjun Singh requested me to teach them Hindi whenever I visited Jagtlust. I agreed and would go three evenings a week to teach them Hindi. Bhawani, Bhulan and Gharbharan worked directly under the manager in his bungalow. Manager Dhiksar was a very strict man. He would not allow any drums or merry-making after eight at night. Everyone therefore stayed indoors and complete silence was maintained.

Bhawani Bhikh had been cunning right from his childhood and lived with the manager in his residence. The manager had no wife and when he developed a dangerous disease of the throat, he lost his voice and had to seek the services of Bhawani at night. When Dhiksar died one night, Bhawani had been alone with him in the house. It is believed that he took this opportunity to steal some of the manager's property. This was proven when he had tried to change 100 rupees that he had stolen. He was imprisoned for a couple of days but he maintained that the manager had given the money to him before his death. Everybody welcomed the death of the manager, except for two Hindostani women who wept. People of the plantation played on the *dhol* once again. Rameshwar, a *chamar* and a *freeman* with only one eye who worked under me, was so happy that he distributed sweets (*laddu*) that day saying: 'Brothers, I had a miserable time under Dhiksar and had vowed to distribute sweets (*prasad/mithai*) if Dhiksar would die during my lifetime. During his time, two of my countrymen, Bhikhari Pandit and Baldew Maharaj had been taken into custody for 3 days because they had been narrating the *katha*'. Dhiksar Sahab was buried in Jagtlust and as a ghost he troubled the people in the plantation continuously. The ghost would disguise himself as a *skreeman* and would beat lone labourers in the fields. Once a fellow Hindustani, Durjan an *ahir*, was beaten so badly that he was bedridden for several days. Later on, the new manager called a *lukuman* [exorcist] to get rid of the ghost and after that every thing turned to normal.

When this Bhawani Bhikh had become a *freeman*, he began to live with his sister in 'La Phondro' [Livorno]. Yet after a few days, his own sister ousted him from there due to some differences between them. He then started wandering here and there. During that time I lived in Lalkondre (La Recontre). About 15 *ketting* away from my field was Pandit Ram Pratap's plot. I had taught this *brahmin* to enable him to recite the *kathas*. He was very religious and kind to his fellowmen. He was well mannered and would take good care of every visitor. Each time I paid a visit and taught him something, he would give me a dollar inspite of my refusal. He had only one bad habit. He ate dry clay. He kept a stock of it in two big barrels during the rainy seasons. When the cacao disease crippled Surinam, America proposed the cultivation of *congo bacoven* instead.[108] America offered 5-year contracts to those plantation owners who opted for this. Yet, *bacoven* have never been able to push the economy fowards. The Maasstroom plantation was also selected for *bacoven* farming and a clerk from Jagtlust had taken charge there as the manager. New contract workers were hired and the manager also required an intelligent *sabelman* [excavator]. Pratap Maharaj [i.e., Pandit Ram Pratap] of Lalkondre who was adept in this work was appointed for the job. He had worked together with the manager in Jagtlust and was very popular. Pratap Maharaj was made the *sardar* and ran the plantation successfully. Bhawani Bhikh also made his way to the Maastroom plantation and requested Pratap Maharaj to give him a job. This spotless soul recruited him since he was of his own caste and in need. Alas, he did not know that he had given milk to a viper that later on would sting him.

Bhawani Bhikh began to work on the plantation and soon became very friendly to Pratab Maharaj. He then asked him to allot him the shop that a Chinese used to run under the *sardar*. The poor Chinese was shown the door and Bhawani took charge. The plantation was flourishing and the shop also thrived well. Bhawani now minted money. He however, did not refrain from cheating people and did so whenever an opportunity arose. As his wealth grew, he became intoxicated with greed and pride. One day, following an altercation with the *sardar*, he thought: 'Pratap Maharaj earns a lot as *sardar* and on top of that also earns money through the recitation of mantras during various occasions. Why not deprive him of his living? I can take his place if he vacates his post'. Bhawani Bhikh developed some friendship with the manager and found two aides, namely Nurmohammad and Khemchand Maharaj, who assisted and advised him to carry out his evil plans. These two acted as false witnesses in favour of Bhawani in all his cases of swindling and forgery, and justice was denied to the victim in the court of law. The District Commissioner of Kila (New Amsterdam) had registered many accusations against Bhawani Bhikh but due to these two witnesses they were always turned down. One day when Mr. Granada was Commisioner in Kila, Bhawani made a bundle of 500 rupees, a few dollars, and silver coins and told Nurmohammad to bury it near the *sardar*'s house when he was not there. He had registered the numbers of the notes, which were to be hidden. He then secretly pulled down part of his shop's door. Thereafter he sought the manager'spermission to go to the city by boat. 'I will be back tomorrow', he had said and indeed left. He returned the next morning. Feigning his ignorance about the broken door of his shop, he complained to the manager that he had been robbed. The manager at once sent a wireless message to the police. A major and the police arrived immediately and started an enquiry. Bhawani spun a tale of burglary and quoted the amount he had put in the bundle as his loss. On asking about whom he suspected, Bhawani said: 'the *sardar*'. The major ordered a search into Pratap Maharaj's house. Nurmohammad took charge of the search and ordered digging. He asked people to dig here and there to prove his ignorance about the site but soon hit on the place where they themselves had hidden the bundle and exclaimed: 'Sir there is something here which makes a sound'. The Major said: 'Dig there'. The hidden treasure was soon unravelled and the findings and allegation confirmed. The *sardar* was put behind bars. There was rejoicing in Bhawani Bhikh's house while the truth was confined in a cell. Nathuram the poet has accurately written that because of the bad deeds of some, even good people suffer.

Destiny plays a game, however, and ensures that justice is imparted sooner or later. Khuda transformed Nurmohammad into a new leaf. The manager was very sad, as he had trusted his *sardar*. Besides, the *sardar* was so disturbed that he neither brushed his teeth nor did he take bath, let alone ate. Commissioner Granada Sahab, however, suspected something fishy but could not go against the law. Yet then, on the third day of this injustice, Nurmohammad narrated the whole act to the manager who was very stunned indeed. Immediately the Major was summoned. He arrived with the police and they asked Nurmohammad to again narrate his story. They then arrested Bhawani Bhikh while the *sardar* was freed. Yet the culprit still had not admitted his sin in front of the Commissioner. He then was hanged upside-down and beaten till he finally confessed his recent and all previous misdoings. They also recovered the six coins that he had earlier stolen from Baniji Singh of Jagtlust. The Commissioner carried out an elaborate enquiry into Bhawani Bhik's activities and sentenced him to 3 years of rigorous imprisonment. His associates were condemned to one year each. When Nurmohammad had completed his prison term, he asked me for work. I consented and he stayed under me for several years. He was the one who narrated the whole story to me.

When Bhawani Bhikh was in prison, the able Commissioner Granada told him that Surinam was too small a country for him and that the laws there were too lenient. He should have lived in France [i.e., French Guyana] where punishment was severe and enough to change people. He was right, because as soon as Bhawani had left jail, he had gone to his sister in 'La Phondro' [Livorno] and had started his evil deeds again. He victimized many a poor man who lost their homes, their fields and whatever he desired. As he had made a number of disciples there, his work was facilitated, as these disciples would always play witness in his favour.

Once he even filed a double complaint against my wife and me. He had threatened me with dire consequences following an altercation saying that I would suffer the same fate as two other of his victims namely Sukali and Sahuniya of Dijkveld. I responded, 'look up as Allah is there to decide my fate. Who are you?' During this period, Mr.Fanaras was the Commissioner of Combé and Mr.Granada had become Agent Generaal. Bhawani accused my wife of robbery while I was to be tried for fraud. He had assembled five witnesses who would argue in his favour while I had Khuda on my side. I was nevertheless worried and went to meet the *Agent-Generaal.* Pandit Sheetal Prasad was the *tolk* in charge. I explained the whole case to him. He then advised me to tell the same thing to the Commissioner and if he would not take any action he asked me to return to him. I followed his advice and reported the whole incident to the Commissioner who became furious at me and said, 'you will go to jail for robbing Bhawani. I cannot help you. The court will do its justice'. I wished him and returned to Pandit Sheetal Prasad. He asked me to present myself before the Head Immigration Officer. The latter asked: 'Well, what makes "the owner of Skerpi" come to me today?' Sheetal Prasad narrated my case to him. He asked me whether I had met the Commissioner regarding this. I confirmed and said: 'In fact he told me that my wife had robbed Bhawani and that I had not returned his belongings'. I added that the matter was to be heard in court and that I would be jailed. I also told that the Commissioner had said that he could not help me. The Bara Sahab was startled and exclaimed: 'Bhawani Bhikh of the Maastroom plantation!' I replied: 'Yes sir, it is about him'. This was enough to make him angry. He immediately sat at his desk and wired the whole history of Bhawani Bhikh's dirty tricks to the Commissioner who got the shock of his life. The Commissioner quickly ordered the Major from 'Pulpungi' [Poelepantje] to send the police for Bhawani and his aides and to collect all the court summons and papers within a few hours. The problem was solved even before I had returned home. At 3 p.m. on my way home, I met Tribhuwan Maharaj who lived near the shop in La Phondro. He told me that the police had come to take away all court summons. I was surprised and said that I did not know about it.

Bhawani Bhikh's associates had run to Bhawani and had shouted: 'Baba, the police has confiscated our summons'. Baba the charlatan spoke calmly, 'the judge might have fallen ill and the court might therefore have been adjourned. We shall soon be informed of another date'. Yet Khuda and the Bara Sahab called off any further calls and it seems Baba's judge is still sick. It was a big relief for me and I always pray to Allah to show similar kind of mercy to all God-fearing men and women. The chief of all leading criminals, Bhawani Bhikh, was notorious throughout Surinam. When he was finally arrested in 'La Phondro' [Livorno], the discovered ill-gotten gains were shocking. A huge pile of looted goods was displayed in the 'Pulpungi' [Poelepantje] police station ranging from gold and silver to useless items. A government circular was issued that whoever had been cheated or robbed by Bhawani, should come, identify and collect his or her belongings. The police station was crowded with Bhawani's victims. The pile vanished shortly. Bhawani, his sister, and his associates were jailed for several years. Allah has dealt with him and I am not aware of his whereabouts now. It is rightly said that illgotten gains never prosper.

## Diseased due to the killing of a Snake in 1925

A whole book could be dedicated to Bhawani Bhikh's activities. I have only briefly mentioned a few of his deeds to throw some light on this exceptional character. Yet now I will narrate the story of my illness. Nothing happened during the first 6 years of our stay in La Phondro. Later, while cutting grass, my daughter and daughter-in-law noticed a big snake (python) in my field. They ran to me and complained of its presence. They were afraid that it might attack them and refused to further cut grass for the cows there. I immediately went to the site but could not discover any snake. Besides, though others started to complain about this snake regularly, I did not see it. One day the ex-*sardar* of La Phondro, Durga, an *ahir*, came for some grass for his cow. I told him to go and cut it himself. While returning with the bundle of grass on his head he encountered the python. He dropped the bundle and fled. Still panting he reached my house and said: 'I will never again come to your field. There lives a big python in its vicinity. I believe it is the same snake that Dukhi had tried but failed to kill. Instead, he lost his vision for about 6 months. He had to resort to black magic and *dansi*'.[109] I thought it was only foolish talk since I had killed thousands of snakes in Hindustan as well as in Surinam before, and nothing had ever happened to me. '*Inshah Allah,* I shall kill this snake whenever I encounter him', I said to myself.

After a few days, paddy was being sown in my fields and most of the grass had been cut, from all places except for a small patch of lowland. It was two in the afternoon and I was on my way to work with a French chopper in my hand when I saw the big python crossing the field and heading for the meadow. One-third of its length lay over the dyke while the rest had already reached the lowland. Thinking that I could not fully cut the snake in two halves with only one blow, as the snake was very fat and my weapon light, I pounced and slashed at it where it made an angle over the ridge. I had cut the snake into two unequal parts. It made a loud sound and its head and upper two-thirds disappeared into the grove while its lower one third lay on the dyke. My sons Suleman and Karamat rushed to me when they heard the yelling and asked what had happened. I told them about the carnage and showed them the part of the snake that lay on the field. They were about to look for the other two-thirds in the thicket, but I forbade them saying that the injured snake might harm them and will soon die anyway. We threw the cut portion of the python into a ditch in the jungle. We then resumed our work. After sowing the paddy, I met Durga and told him about the snake's killing and that he now could come to cut grass from my field. He said that he would decide.

Durga told the news about my achievement to Dukhi saying that I had killed the snake, which he had worshipped. Only God knows what led to my sickness, which followed after this incident. Yet, the *kafir* who later on cured me, told me that someone had done some black magic and had transferred the plight of the cut one third part of the snake, which I had thrown in the jungle, to me. It could have been avoided if I had buried it like its head, which had indeed been buried 3 days afterwards when my sons found it in the grove. This could have been the cause of the pain in one particular part of my body, since the part of the snake that was cut but not buried comprised that particular part of the snake's body [i.e., the lower part]. I had five different complaints: 1. Severe itching starting from my thighs and ending down to my feet. 2. Tingling of both my legs. 3. Intermittent micturition during a single act. 4. Pain in abdomen and bloody diarrhoea. 5. Unwanted discharge of semen. The body above this level was healthy. Initially, when the itching began, I would rub it hard with a maize stem till it was red, and then smear the area with limejuice because otherwise the itching was unbearable. Then the itching ceased for some time. There were two dogs in my house that also got this itching in the same way. We three would start scratching simultaneously and cry with displeasure. These dogs lost their hairs and looked terribly. The cows were also affected and I asked my sons to take away the dogs thinking they were the cause of my pruritus.

The crops of my field were also not spared and the produce was very low either due to the disease, or due to Allah's decision. Earlier, we would reap more than 80-90 sacks of grain every year and only 60 sacks were needed to feed my family. The rest would be utilised to meet other expenses. But this time we harvested only 20-25 sacks. Moreover, the grain had a pungent smell and the stink had not entered the grain only, it had also entered my life. During those days, we had to make rice from the paddy by grinding it at home as there were no mills. The rice that season was so bitter that one did not even want a second helping. My sons felt bad but still praised Allah for everything knowing fully well that these bad times would change into better times one day and therefore they did not complain.

### *Doha*

*The darkest hour is the one just before the dawn*

With this belief, my sons continued their business. We had rice, flour, banana and cassava and the other items were bought from the market. My boys had however one worry and that was my illness. I had to feed a family of twelve members and these two young sons of mine worked very hard to sustain all of us. My illness demanded also lots of money, and with no income from the fields the problems they had to face to earn were tremendous. I am proud they did not falter and proved successful. They never borrowed money to meet the expenses and worked hard to provide proper clothing, nutritious food and drugs for others and for me. Even if I were hungry at midnight, my daughters-in-law would prepare warm porridge (Quaker Oats[110]) and milk. But the illness did not respond to any amount of food and medication and grew in intensity as time passed. My boys loved me so much that they could not bear my sufferings and fell ill whenever my troubles increased. I had warned them not to consult any *voodoo* specialists or black magic practitioners lest they unnecessarily extorted money from them. They said they would not fall into their traps, but secretly they kept on trying various alternative medications but in vain. Later on I came to know that just in order to get information about the whereabouts of one such quack, they had spent one whole day's payment (12 annas). They then had been informed that the witchdoctor just lived next door! When I enquired why they had taken such a step, they replied that they felt my life was more important than money.

One night I developed a micturition problem and asked my sons to take me to the hospital. It was raining and difficult to venture out alone in the darkness on the muddy streets. My sons dared to fetch a donkey-driven cart from Khalu Wazir who lived at the street, called, Beekhuizenweg. It was very early in the morning when we reached the hospital. My abdomen was swollen and painful. The doctor immediately ordered the compounder to make me sit in a hot water bath. Whenever I remember what happened next, I pray to God never to let it happen to even my enemies! The doctor then went away and the attendant took me to the bathroom where there was a big tub. He filled it with hot water, undressed me and made me lie in the tub covered with a thick bed-sheet from head to toe. He then put a wet and cold cloth over my head leaving only my eyes, nostrils and mouth open. The water in the bathtub was so hot that it made me writhe like a cut hen. I was told not to get up before the water would cool down. The attendant came every 15 minutes to see me. As the water was cooling down, my urge to urinate reached its peak. The attendant helped me to come out of the tub and gave me a pot to urinate. I completely emptied my bladder into it. 'Thank God! What a relief!' I said to myself. The pain in my abdomen disappeared but the rest of the disease continued. The doctor tested my urine, stool and blood but found no cause that could explain my illness. I was catheterised every 2-3 hours since I could not micturate myself.

My sons grew very tense and they could not digest what they ate and were always on the lookout for some cure by hook or by crook. Their search finally ended when they came across Belforos who was a black witchdoctor and lived in the city. He was a knowledgeable man. He did not charge even a cent, and listened patiently to my sons' narration of my miseries from the very beginning till the present state. He analysed the problem and told my sons to ask me what occurred during their absence from the hospital. This is because he used to predict my suffering beforehand. His prediction about my activities in absence of my sons was confirmed to be true. However my sons did not disclose the matter to me fearing my wrath. One and half day elapsed in the hospital but the doctor failed to cure me. However, the witch doctor could sense what was happening to me every moment without even seeing me. On the fourth night, I developed high fever and my urine became thick and white in colour. When I passed urine, the few drops that fell on the sheet, looked like lime water. When the witch doctor noticed my deterioration, he told my wife and children that if they wanted me alive, I should be taken out of the hospital the very next morning and by Allah's grace, he could cure me. Then he told them about the change that had occurred in my urine and about the fever that I had got that night. He explained: 'When the colour of the patient's urine matches that of the snake's stool, it means that the disease is stronger than the patient's resistance and that the patient is now about to succumb to the disease. You must therefore not delay any further and bring him out of the hospital as soon as possible. I shall take him out myself, if the doctor does not release him, and that is my own responsibility'.

Next morning, my boys hired an automobile for 5 rupees from Kadir Baksh of Poelepantje. Belforos accompanied my children and wife to the hospital in that car. He remained in the car while my wife and Suleman Khan came to me and said: 'We have come to take you home'. I protested, 'but I have not recovered yet. If I am unable to urinate, you will again have to bring me here. Let me stay'. Suleman then explained and asked, 'you had high fever last night and the colour and consistency of your urine suddenly changed into something similar to lime water. Am I right?' I was surprised: 'Yes, but how did you come to know about it?' He then said: 'I have heard that much. You must come home with us. If you are saved by Allah's grace then all very good, if not, we shall arrange for your *kafan*. Yet, staying here does not make sense'. I changed my clothes, bade farewell to all and left the hospital. Inside the car, I saw a *Creole* and thought him to be another passenger. Nobody told me he was the new doctor who would soon be treating me. Everyone in the house had been strictly prohibited to disclose his identity because they feared that I might not comply with his medications. When I asked my sons about the black man they said he was just someone who had come for some work. He came home with us. I thought he had something to do with Karamat Khan, who sold milk. At seven in the evening, the witch doctor asked for a tub filled with water and mixed several herbs and medicines in it. He then told me to stand naked in the tub and took out a small book from which he began to chant something and simultaneously washed me. After the bath, I was given clean clothes to wear and made to lie on the bed. In one night a mere black had accomplished the healing, which had seemed impossible to all the doctors of repute, of high salary and high post, and who could influence the government. The Lord had allowed a *Negro*, hated by the Europeans, to free me from all my five symptoms by 5 o'clock next morning. Only diarrhoea still drained me. The witch doctor told me not to worry about it.

My ordeal being over, a new problem came to the fore. I developed an insatiable appetite. I wanted to eat all different items and in huge quantities and was never satisfied. Even during the night, I would wake up at eleven and trouble my daughters-in-law for food despite having eaten more than the others 3 hours before. They never complained, however, and would prepare a pot full of porridge with milk and serve it on a big platter. This happened every night. Doctor Belforos knew about this. One day he told my sons, 'the evil spirit inside your father is very strong. Though it has spared his soul, it has occupied his stomach and appetite. I have healed many sufferers in Surinam (without charging anything), but have never come across such a case. You must do what I say but do not let your papa know about it. I shall give you a *calabash* [gourd] filled with water that you must ask your father to hold one evening while you enquire about his tastes and prepare a menu accordingly. However, the person noting down the items must hide himself from your father's presence. When he finishes, throw the water at a distance'. My sons followed his advice and one evening, Suleman embraced me and made me sit up. This was not something unusual, as very often during my illness they would hug and console me. He then trusted the *calabash* full of water in my hands and started asking me what I desired to eat. He held on to my hands because they were shaking due to weakness. Suleman said: 'I shall get the things from the city if needed and prepare the other items at home for you so that you may eat to your satisfaction and get rid of your weakness'. My desires soared and I even aimed those items for which I had never developed taste. All that time, Karamat Khan stood hidden behind the door, noting down the things I mentioned. I listed things that could be cooked at home and those that were available in the market like bread, biscuits, etc. and various types of drinks. Then Suleman took the *calabash* from me and threw away the water.

Later that day all the food items had been prepared. Rice, pulses, *puris*, vegetables, stuffed rotis (*daal bhari puris*), pudding (*khir*), sweets, mutton, chicken, and many more different items had been cooked and the items from the market had also been brought. The witch doctor arrived in the evening. When it was time for supper, all the items were brought and kept in the veranda in big pots with spoons. All the twelve members of my family were told to sit in a line and were given a plate each. I was told to divide and serve the food and dine along with them. The doctor warned: 'Nobody should leave his place before your papa finishes his meal'. All except my daughters-in-law agreed to this, and they said, 'how can we sit and eat along with our father-in-law? It will be improper to do so'. Dr. Belforos replied however: 'what is the harm? Well, if you do not want him to be cured you then may excuse yourselves'. They were, however, very fond of me and therefore overcame their shyness and also sat down with me to eat. Belforos sat down and looked around. I was given a spoon but due to severe weakness I could not serve by myself so Suleman Khan held my hands and we filled everyone's plate. We prayed 'Bismillah' and began to eat. The doctor, however, did not touch the food at all while the rest ate to their heart's content. When every one else had finished, they waited for me to finish. I felt even hungrier now and kept on eating incessantly. I was puzzled at my own appetite and scolded myself for eating so much. Finally, when every bit of every item had been consumed, I stopped and all of us went to bed. That night I did not get up due to hunger. After this episode Khuda released me from the clutches of this insatiable evil spirit. Now only diarrhoea and weakness remained with occasional pain in the abdomen[111].

## *Sardar* in Satbarwa [Sint Barbara] in 1926

After Bhawani Bhikh's attempt to lodge a case against me in court failed, I married off my eldest daughter [Mariyam] to Karim Baksh, son of Nirhu. The following year, my wife's brother died and on his *chalisa*, Faiz Khan underwent his *sunnat*. As I have already mentioned, there had been four owners of the Skerpi plantation who were brothers. The eldest, Frans Horst left for America with his son Didi Horst when his wife died. Didi had been 12 years old then and I the *sardar* at Skerpi.After that, Skerpi was sold and later another plantation (Blauwgrond) was also disposed off. Ramadhin bought the plantation Ornamibo, which had belonged to Dolf Horst, and now the Horst family had no property left in Surinam. Diderik Horst, who was a bachelor, died, and Louis Horst, who was a government schoolteacher, followed him soon after. His wife took her son and went off to Holland where she later died. Only Dolf Horst and his wife remained alive and in Surinam. Fate had snatched away everything from them and had rendered them penniless. Who would ever have thought that this landlord, who once owned two plantations and also a gold mine, would land up in such a pitiable situation? They had employed hundreds of workers and when I was on contract under them, a male nurse named De Vries, had worked under them for 3-4 months before getting a government job. Promotion in government jobs was time bound and soon De Vries became the head nurse and was posted in 'Kofijumpo' [Lelydorp]. When Dolf Horst' situation became from hand to mouth, he also applied for a government job. He was appointed as a nurse under this very De Vries at Kofijumpo. The Lord had reversed their positions.

## *Chaupai*

*It is true: If the Lord wishes, He can turn the Sumer (a mountain in Hindustan) into dust, and re-transform it again into a mountain. If*

*He wishes, He can make a beggar king and the king a beggar. The poet says that Khuda only expects us to pray and obey Him. If He wishes an elephant can be tied to the foot of an ant and be pulled across the ocean. God moves in a mysterious way.*

Indeed God's ways are unique and an example lies before our eyes. Dolf Horst, once as strong and active like a horse, had now turned into a worker under someone who a few years back had saluted him. The 'ex-Meneer' now bowed for his 'Meneer' and followed his orders. After about 6 years, poor Dolf Horst was terminated from his job and he died shortly thereafter. His wife, Marie Horst followed him 10-12 years later. They had no children and only Didi Horst of this family remained alive. Several years later, Didi Horst who had settled in America decided to become a plantation owner once again. He launched a company in America and came to Surinam in 1926. His aunt, Marie Horst was alive that time. He stayed at her place and one day inquired about me, whether I was alive or not. His aunt told him about me, that I had bought some land in Dijkveld and that my children and I frequently visited her and helped her whenever necessary. Glad to hear this, Didi Horst sent a telegram and called me. During that period, I was suffering from diarrhoea and abdominal cramps (as told earlier). I received the message and took a bus to Saron from where I caught a train to 'Kofijumpo' where he had been put up. He was expecting me and immediately got up from his chair and shook hands with me. I then shook also hands with his aunt and we sat down. The formalities being over, he asked me whether I recognised him or not. I confessed: 'Not very well' and he answered: 'But I recognised you. You have just grown old. I am the same Didi Horst for whom you would pluck guavas and other fruits and one day you had slapped me for some mischief. Do you remember anything of all that?' I replied, 'you were small then and now have grown up and become a young man. You had left for America with your father 20 years ago. How could I recognise you? Yes, I remember slapping you once when you disobeyed me and intercepted a beehive and you got stung as well'. We both laughed.

Then Didi talked business: '*Basia*, you are right. You are like a father to me and have supervised the plantation since the days of my father honestly and sincerely for which you deserve more praise than I could give. It was our bad luck that our family lost the plantation'. Saying this, both aunt and nephew wiped the tears that had appeared in their eyes. It happened as God wanted. Now He has again sought to retrieve what He took. I am representing a company, which has decided to buy a plantation in 'Satbarwa' [Sint Barbara] and you should go there as *sardar* and look after it. I cannot rely on anyone else except you. Me, my uncle, and my aunt have known and relied on you for so many years and I feel deeply obliged to you'. I replied, 'well, there is nothing to be thankful for. I have done my duty. You provided my living in return. I owed you for your salt. I thank you for making me a *sardar* and I pray to Khuda to honour me likewise again and again. But now I am an old man, how can I bear the responsibility of a *sardar*? I am not strong like before and moreover, I have not yet recovered from my illness of which your aunt knows. Your father and uncle were nice and knew how to behave with others. They would listen and follow my advice and I was given a free hand to manage the plantation affairs. I worked according to my capabilities and no one questioned me. But nowadays, men are not so well mannered and straightforward any more. I am afraid that if a person of mixed origin or low caste becomes my superior, I shall not be able to tolerate it. What will happen then?' Didi answered, 'do not worry *Basia* and listen to me. I shall return to America soon and another American will be appointed as the manager here. You will work with him. He is very clever, learned, social and good-natured. He will not resist your decisions. He knows little about the plantation and how it is to be run. Moreover, he does not even know any other language than his own. As for your medicine, it will be taken care of. You just sit and order what is to be done to run the plantation. I firmly believe that even if you do not do a single thing, and be present in the plantation, things will be fine and nothing will go wrong. After I leave, the manager will arrive here by the next ship. You meet him and take good care of the plantation as you did during my father's and uncle's time'. We ate some snacks after this and talked about other things. When I was about to leave, Didi Horst shook hands with me, gave me 3 rupees and again requested me to join his plantation. I bade them farewell and left.

I narrated our meeting at home. Six weeks after Didi's departure, the manager Mr. Makola arrived. He landed at the old Marie Horst's residence and asked for me. I was still unwell but had to meet him, so I went. Mrs. Horst introduced me to the American and translated our talk because she knew English. Then the American and I went off to meet Mr. De Vries who had been appointed as the assistant of the American. He later became a government representative. We exchanged greetings and talked about running the plantation. It was decided to start work next week. I then wanted to return home yet the American Sahab took out a packet of cigarettes (brought from America), a notebook, a matchbox and a 5-rupee note and handed them to me. I then went home and began my preparations for my Satbarwa journey.

When I had been ill, all my children and my wife took good care of me and they provided all types of food and medicines. I had no remorse and all my desires were being met. My decision to join the 'Satbarwa' plantation was accepted under protest since no one wanted me to leave due to my illness. I persuaded them: 'Sons, why refuse Laxmi the Goddess of wealth when she is at our door? Moreover, I have given my word and if I back off now, I shall be treated as a cheat. Do not worry about me Khuda will take care. You look after the household properly in my absence'. They agreed reluctantly. I knew they were worried about me and prayed to Allah thanking Him for these caring and good children of mine and hoped that His blessings would be bestowed on them too. Suleman Khan prepared my journey and settlement at 'Satbarwa' and deputed his younger brother Dildar Khan to look after me. Food, clothing and money were all packed; Dildar Khan had nursed me well since the beginning of my illness. He had been instructed to immediately take a boat and two boatmen and bring me back home if my health would deteriorate. They warned him not to delay in case any problem arose. Though Dildar Khan was quite young when we left for the plantation, he was intelligent and clever for his age. He had taken good care of me during the 9-month illness. I can never forget the trouble this poor soul had to bear for me. My blessings fall short of his dedication. Allah knows. Amen! May His Holiness, Allah shower His manifold blessings over those who care for their parents, and provide them good health and prosperity.

Now my belongings and things were loaded on a boat and I was given a touching farewell. Suleman Khan and Kallan Khan rowed the boat to the Satbarwa plantation. The manager (*manjha),*

Mr. La Para, had already arrived before us. La Para had stayed at Chedi Mahajan's plantation in Pitsak Borgu [Petersburg] for some time. When our boat reached the shore, the manager and I exchanged greetings. I was allotted a house and my belongings were transported from the boat to my room. Thereafter Suleman Khan and Kallan Khan returned back home. Dildar and I were left behind. It was Saturday when the American Sahab came by ship and was introduced to everyone. After that he briefed me about the work and returned by ship on the same day. This happened every Saturday. Six weeks later *manjha* La Para was dismissed. Each weekend the American would come by ship and the manager and I would receive him at the shore. He would hand over the bag of money to be distributed to me, and his bag of clothes to the manager to carry. After payment of the wages, he would hand over the key of his room upstairs, where he kept all his things, to me. The manager was given the key of his room downstairs. He forbade me to let the manager have the key, which I had been given, while I was allowed to take from the store whatever was required. He told me that Didi Horst had warned him not to rely on anyone else except me.

Gradually the production began to increase. I, however, was still very weak due to my illness. I could not even jump over a 2-foot broad canal and needed a wooden bridge to cross it. I would walk slowly to work and come back home whenever I felt like returning. We were with very few people on the plantation: Dildar Khan, a cook, ten Javanese workers and myself. The *Garamsara Sahab* lived in the city and came on Saturdays only. One Saturday, Mr. De Vries and the *garamsara* also went to visit the fields. I myself had not even seen all the fields! When they returned and asked me about my assessment of the yield I told them that I had not surveyed the fields. I asked them how many fruits had been seen on an average per tree. They pointed to a tree full of fruits and said that all trees were similarly laden. I enquired: 'How many fields of coffee trees were there?' 'Four', they said. Then I said: 'Sahab, if all the trees produce as much fruit as this tree then about fifty sacks of fruit will be collected'. When the fruit was ripe, it was plucked and sent to the 'Lalsusu' plantation for further assessment. There were fifty-two sacks. The American, who had seen everything, did not comment. Slowly and steadily, work increased and produce began to progress.

Long before I arrived in 'Satbarwa' [Saint Barbara] one of the dams in the river had broken and the crack was more than a *ketting* long. *Manjha* La Para had a few times tried to repair it but in vain. The owner had shown me this damaged dam on my first day on the plantation. Whenever the water level rose, La Para Sahab would get it repaired by stuffing the hole with huge bundles of weed mixed with thicket to make it heavy. This had become a regular feature and I asked La Para what sense it made to repeat this method again and again without the desired result. The Sahab would say that it prevented the river water from entering the fields. This answer amused me.

Once, large holes had developed in the dam and the *manjha* ordered two Javanese to fill them up the very next day. Early morning the following day, I sent two men for the job. I knew they would repair the holes by the same faulty method, which would last for only a couple of days and I followed them. I watched them cut weed and fill the holes with it. I interrupted them. They said that the *manjha* had told them to do likewise. I said: 'I want you to dig and cut through the centre of the dam and fill it with clay only and press it'. These workers replied: 'That will take a long time and the *manjha* will be furious'. I said: 'Never mind, I will talk to the *manjha* if he gets mad'. As expected, the *manjha* came at about 10 a.m. and found that not even a single hole had been sealed. He scolded the labourers for not closing even one hole. I asked him: '*Sahab*, how many holes can two men close in 3 hours?' The manager replied, 'it should not take a whole day's work to do this. Why did you not put weed and cover it up with clay in each hole instead of wasting time?' I then told the workers to do as I had ordered and they would get the whole day's payment for it and turned to the *manjha*: '*Sahab*, I have neither done, nor will ever do such a deceitful task. If you wish, you may send your men to do it your way tomorrow'. I then left them behind. In the evening when I came to report the day's work, the *manjha* asked me whether I was angry. I replied that there was nothing to be angry about. 'If the *sardar* is incapable, the *manjha* has to take over', I said. He then accomplished the closure his own way. When De Vries and the *garamsara* came on Saturday, I showed them the repair work and told them that I could not tolerate this swindle. I said that this way of working was useless and that the *manjha* wasted money and that I was fed up of that. After *manjha Sahab*'s departure, they asked me whether I could undertake the repair work of the broken dam.

## The Story about the Repair of the Dam

The owner had asked me: 'if you can repair this dam I will bring all the materials required from the city. How much do you think it will cost?' I said: '*Sahab*, with God's support, this will not be a tough task. I only need ten good diggers and full payment for their work. I shall calculate the total expenditure and let you know by next week because without measurement and calculation, I cannot say anything regarding the cost'. They agreed. The American always used to inquire about the cost of any project or work to be undertaken before starting it. He would ask detailed written information to avoid oral estimations. Therefore I needed some time to prepare the project report. By next Saturday, I had measured and calculated the amount required to cut weed, dig the gutters and trenches, to carry the clay and all other approximate expenses. The grand total was about Rs. 350. The American agreed. News about the broken dam had reached the city long time back and the government had given the repair work to a contractor. When he learnt about our efforts to rectify the dam, he approached the American thinking to milk some money out of him. He thought the American had no knowledge of Surinam and the work here, and would require his services. The American refused however: 'I have an old *sardar* here to do the job and only if he fails I shall give you the job. Without his permission I cannot let you work on my plantation'. The contractor persisted: 'How can an Indian ever know about dam construction?' The owner answered: 'I do not care whether he has any knowledge or not, but without his acknowledgement I cannot allow you to proceed'. The meeting ended, but the owner did not tell me about it.

## Repair of the Dam

Ten diggers were called from the plantation 'Laluiki' [Laarwijk] and the work began. During the first week, the weed was cut and drains were dug. When the *Garamsara Sahab* and De Vries came that Saturday, the digging of the trenches had indeed started. They were surprised to see an 8-feet broad trench being dug 15 feet away from the drain, which had clay that came from the drains. Mr. De

Vries was a city man and knew nothing about such works while the American was no better. They began to think: 'what is the purpose of digging two drains and fill one with the material of the other. Was one small trench not enough to drain out water from a small piece of land? Why the 8 feet broad trench? *Basia* has spent unnecessarily on this'. They could not understand what it all meant. Then De Vries called me aside and asked: '*Basia,* do not take it otherwise, but we fail to understand the idea behind digging two drains and filling the smaller one with the clay of the bigger one. Was the small trench not enough to drain the water?' I then explained: 'The small drain is not for drainage, but it is a *bilandar*'. 'What does that stand for?' De Vries asked. I replied: 'like the human body, the dam also has a stomach in its centre. This is called a *bilandar*. When it is dug and refilled with clay, all the crevices, holes, dead decaying roots and wood are eliminated and the new packed soil provides strength to the dam. It prevents any leakage. If it is not dug, the small gaps underground will form holes and destroy the dam after some time'. The two men understood and left with great relief.

Three weeks later the construction was completed. Mr. De Vries along with the American owner and the contractor came to inspect the work. The contractor asked me: '*Basia*, did you dig a *bilandar*?' I denied yet before he could reply, De Vries spoiled my plan to deceive him and he said: 'Yes it has been dug'. I then asked: 'Would one ever prepare a dam without *bilandar*?' The contractor answered: 'Yes, some people do that'. I said: 'Yes but sir such a dam will not last for a long time'. De Vries and the owner smiled. Then the contractor asked De Vries: 'what were the costs involved?' He replied: 'We do not know, ask the *sardar*'. When the contractor questioned me I said: '*Sahab*, the total amount spent was Rs. 222'. It surprised him: 'Man, how did you manage to repair a dam with such a low budget?' I then asked him: 'Sir, how much did you expect that it would have costed?' He said: 'Your dam is going to leak in the near future'. 'We will see', I said. De Vries and the *garamsara* smiled as they left the place.

It was during this period that the American kept a black woman (*mulattin*) and began to live on the plantation with her. After some time he returned to America and gave me full responsibility. He left the black woman behind in Parmaribo. Only Dildar, a few Javanese labourers, and myself were left behind to run the plantation.

After 9 months the American returned and started his business again. Earlier a Chinese had managed a shop in Satbarwa. When his contract ended, the shop was handed over to Suleman Khan who managed it very well. This took place in 1928 and in this very year, on 27 December, Dildar Khan and Chote Khan were married on a Friday in 'Lalkondre' [La Rencontre].

## New Foundation for the Sluice

A few days after the return of the plantation owner from America, the 30 feet long and 20 feet broad foundation for the sluice of Satbarwa near the Surnaukreek broke down. It was 11 feet deep. The sluice had been washed away from its foundation and nothing remained to support it. The American was desperate and asked me to make an estimate of the costs involved to make a new foundation. I said: 'you will not believe me. You better ask Mr. Arends, the manager of 'Watralanti' [Waterland plantation]. He has worked as a manager on many plantations in Surinam for long periods. He is clever and knowledgeable, and moreover, he is your friend. We have known each other since my contract period when three of them had come from Germany to Jagtlust. You better ask him first and then I shall give you my opinion regarding the costs'. The American then quickly drove off to the Waterland plantation to meet Mr. Arends. He returned after an hour with a letter from Mr. Arends for me, in which it was stated, 'you are an old experienced *sardar.* I have known you since I was a clerk in Jagtlust. You know how this work should be done, so do it properly and avoid unnecessary expenses on this American'. I wrote back telling him not to worry and I would do as much as possible in favour of the American. I wrote: 'I shall not imitate your *sardar* Mohammad who has spent double the amount for a similar job under you. I am not like him and will not harm the American. I shall complete this work with the smallest budget possible'. I asked the American what Mr. Arends had calculated and the latter said: 'He told me it would not cost less than 700-800 rupees. The filling itself would require more than hundred sacks', said the American. I nodded: 'Mr. Arends is indeed an experienced manager and has done many such important works in Surinam. If I had quoted this amount you would not have believed me. The total costs may be as high as a 1000 rupees'. The American was stunned and disheartened, and asked: 'Will the expense be so much?' I laughed and told him not to be depressed, 'you will not have to spend more than 400 rupees for this. The *garamsara* was then elated.

The Holy One, Allah, can turn a mountain into dust and dust into a mountain! With his blessings I was finally cured. The horrible disease had left me. This had been the third life-threatening danger, as predicted by Hakim Nawab Ali Sahab and I had defied it.

The work near the sluice had begun in earnest. The diggers were paid Rs. 1.25 while the porters who had to carry the clay were given Rs. 1.00 per day. There was no mud nearby and this had to be brought from quite a distance. The 30-feet long hole was fenced with huge pillars and planks and when a large amount of clay had been collected, the two sides of the hole were filled with it to the brim. Only one portion remained. The water was not less than 7 feet deep and the current was strong. Since a part of the sluice had been filled, the water in the remaining part rose and the force increased. The most difficult and testing part of stopping the flow of the river at 10 feet deep was still ahead. I then told the American that I needed empty sacks and he asked me how many. I replied that I needed at least twenty-five sacks. The owner was puzzled and said: 'But Mr. Arends had said that about hundred sacks were needed, so how will twenty-five suffice?' I answered: 'If more are required we shall see later'. Accordingly I received twenty-five sacks. I filled twenty-two of them with clay and sealed their openings. I then said: 'I now need two men to go into the river to place the sacks in proper place'. The Sahab protested and did not allow anyone to go inside the water, as there was a strong current. He said that nobody would be able to hold on to the riverbed in more than 7 feet deep water. He therefore proposed to throw the sacks into the river from the shore itself. I then replied: 'Alright, Karim and I will go in the river'. The owner was taken aback and said: 'No, not you. I shall go in. You are old and if anything happens to you I will never forgive myself, moreover your services are more important for the plantation than mine. My Company will not tolerate this. Hence I do not want you to take this risk. The government and your family will not spare me if you die due to this. If I drown, the business here will be least affected. Besides, you shall not be held responsible for it'. I then said: 'Sahab, let Khuda alone decide everything. Why to worry? However, you should not go into the deep because you are not accustomed to such a task. You do not know how to place the mud–filled sacks underwater and if they are washed away by the current and misplaced, the purpose will not be served. Hence Karim and I must go in while you monitor the shore'.

Saying this Karim and I tied ropes around our waists while the other end of each was tied to some strong beams. Two men on the shore were deputed to hold the ropes and pull us up immediately when we would pull. They were to be very cautious and careful. We jumped in and told the men to throw down four sacks filled with clay. We then dived underwater, placed all of these sacks on the river base and pulled our ropes. We were pulled up. This sequence was repeated again and again till twenty-four sacks were placed in the riverbed and it took us over 2 hours. Now the flow of the water decreased considerably by Allah's grace and then clay was thrown over the sack-filled area. In 2 weeks the sluice was ready and only Rs. 352 was spent.

In the third week, Mr. Arends came to see the sluice. He was pleased with the work and surprised at the low costs involved. He praised me and said, 'Well done *sardar*. I knew of your works since your days with Dolf Horst and how you managed the plantation for 5 years during its decline, and therefore I sent you the letter. I hope you did not feel offended'. I replied that there was nothing to be angry about. 'It is important on the plantation to teach *sardars* new techniques and improve their knowledge. I therefore must thank you'. Mr. Arends was delighted. 'My *sardar*, Mohammad, was not of your class', he said. 'He betrayed me and made me suffer losses. I therefore dismissed him'. Thereafter, Mr. Arends returned to his Waterland plantation and I to my own business.

## My Stint on the Rubber Plantation

There were plenty of rubber trees in Satbarwa but the American was unaware of there qualities and use. Moreover, a jungle had developed over the area where they were planted and people avoided venturing in to it. One day the American ordered me to take two men with me and make an assessment of all the trees in the field. I was to prepare a list of the fields, how many beds they contained and the number of rubber trees planted in each bed. He also asked me to measure the girth of every rubber tree. The next day, two other men and I surveyed each field from one end to another. We measured the circumference of each rubber tree with a tape and I then calculated the diameter of all of them using the formula (circumference×7/22). I made a detailed account of everything in a notebook. Two weeks later my report was ready. I presented it to the owner and it stated that there were 1492 rubber trees and I had analysed all of them as required. I said: 'You may read it in my account'. The owner indeed took it and read it at night, and the very next morning he said: 'I will send your report to the company in America. How can I be sure of your calculations?' I asked him why and whether he did not believe my report. The Sahab then replied: 'Listen, I am a farmer's son. My father owned a ranch with many horses and cows and fields for cultivation. I was responsible for feeding and milking of the cows and the transport of the milk to the city. Though I attended school, I was unable to continue for long because of my work and have studied less than you. When I reached the age of fourteen, I was bored with my routine work and I left home. I took up an apprenticeship in a factory where iron and steel machine parts were manufactured. After a few days I left and joined another job. In this manner I worked and learnt about various machines in different places in America and abroad until I finally landed here. Do not mind my query about your calculations. I am not capable to analyse them and without knowing about it I am afraid to send it to America because if anything wrong is detected, I shall be hanged. There are several knowledgeable men in the company who are sure to notice any fault in your account and therefore I am very apprehensive'.

I assured him: 'Sir, do not worry about any miscalculations and errors. Mathematics is the same throughout the world, even though the languages are different. If Khuda wishes, no honest person shall find anything amiss in my report. I am confident of myself'. Though the American was not highly educated, he was intelligent and I therefore said: '*Sahab*, as far as the verification of data provided by me is concerned, you can come along and note down the measurements yourself after seeing it with your own eyes. I can assure you that they are absolutely correct'. The American agreed. Close to his bungalow were several betel nut trees. I measured the girth of one of them with a tape and showed it to him. It was 9.05 *duim*. I asked him to multiply it by 7 and then divide it by 22. It came to be more than 3 *duim*. I told him to cut through the tree as perpendicularly as possible. When the diameter of the tree was measured along the centre of the stem, it read exactly the same as calculated. I then asked the *sahab* whether he now believed me and he replied: 'Boss! Well done. The authenticity of your work has been proved. I said: '*Sahab*, here is the mathematical relationship between the circumference and the formula of 7 divided by 22'. My report was translated in English and sent to America. In reply, the Company showered lots of praises to the presenter for such accurate reporting!

## Satbarwa: Land on Lease and Installation of a Flour Mill

When it was observed that the turnover of the plantation was not as high as desired, while acres of land good for farming lay waste, we decided to lease out the unused plots. It would not only give the plantation some returns but would be of benefit for some farmers also. Thinking likewise, De Vries, the *garamsara* and I talked about it and spread the news that we were prepared to give the land on lease. People from all places such as 'Pitsburg' [Petersberg], 'Firaelant' [Freeland], 'Lalauki' [Laarwijk] and 'Mahtim Borgu' [Mariënburg] started pouring in. A long queue was formed and within 3 months all the free land lying between the Surnaukreek and the Satasi plantation was leased out. Many people settled in St. Barbara. Jungles gave way to paddy fields. When I saw that production of rice was now on the rise, I knew a mill was necessary. I conveyed my thoughts to the American. He was dexterous and interested in machinery and was soon convinced. He bought a second-hand mill-plant from a Chinese (Chin Kon Fat), which had been installed opposite the post office in Paramaribo. He then dismantled the whole plant and brought it to the Satbarwa plantation. Construction of the mill began in earnest. This American was very bold and determined. He would not back out and handled situations requiring heavy manual labour. He even involved himself, and did not let others do it for him. Even when I prevented him from undertaking dangerous operations asking him not to go somewhere or climb high altitudes, he would stop me instead of stopping himself. 'No, not you', he would say. 'I shall do it. If you are injured, it will be a loss to me while my injury will have little implications. You just stand here and supervise the whole work because when I was working for a cable factory I used to sweat it out on far greater heights than this'. He would not allow Dildar

Khan to do such jobs either. He stuck through thick and thin during such procedures and never gave up.

The machine looked new after cleaning all the parts with gasoline and removing all rust out of it. He mended or replaced all those parts that were worn out or weakened. He toiled hard to renew the complete machine and now it seemed to be fresh from the factory. All seemed well and the mill was ready to start working amidst delighted spectators, but to the astonishment of everyone it began to rotate in the opposite direction! The American worked hard for a whole week to rectify the fault but to no avail. A whole barrel of oil had been consumed in trying to correct the rotation. The American was puzzled and depressed. Everyone felt sorry for him because there was no mill in Surinam that looked so well maintained and good. Even Commissioner Simons who had come to St. Barbara to see the machine had certified it to be the best in Surinam. He was all praise for the American. But alas, the motor rotated round the opposite way. The mill had two parts. The lower segment contained the engine and the rice/product collection unit where weighing could also be done. The rest of the work was accomplished in the upper section. The milling of grain took place here while the rice and husk were collected below in different compartments so that it was not apparent where the husk disappeared. A 15-feet huge box tilted and fixed above the grinder could accommodate 15 sacks of grain at a time and would empty itself completely. The rate of falling of the grain from this box into the grinder could be controlled as desired. Three filters were placed between the box and grinder. The first would filter off all large particles, the second allowed the grain to pass into the grinder while the third separated all the dirt and mud from the grain. These filters shook automatically to do the cleaning, and all that was required was to clean the filters from time to time. The only visible aspect of the whole plant was its end product, i.e., rice. All other functions lay hidden from the exterior. Sacks filled with grain were pulled up by a rope to a platform 20 feet above. It was from here that the grain was poured into the big container. With proper care there was absolutely no wastage! The workmanship seemed perfect.

The American and Dildar Khan stayed below and managed the affairs there, while I placed myself on the platform above and controlled the opening of the grain container. I also weighed and measured the grain and rice before and after milling respectively, apart from collecting money. The American would not receive a single cent and would point out to me to take the money. People wondered at this. During his stay in 'Satbarwa', the American neither distributed wages nor did he ever inspect the distribution of payments on Saturdays at my house. However, during Mr. La Para's tenure he had come every Saturday to make the payments himself. If Mr. De Vries had come on a Saturday for a visit, I disbursed the wages at the American's bungalow. Once when he asked me why I did this, I replied, 'this man is a native and these blacks never believe in others and therefore distributed the money in his presence'. But the American protested, 'this plantation and the money belongs to me and I believe in you. Why bother about the others?' I said nothing. It was the same with the supervision in the fields. He also refrained from handling any cash and I was responsible for the collection and had to keep an account of it. When 100 or more rupees were collected I handed them over to him along with the details of the money received.

## The Rice Mill and Black Magic (*Obiya*)

As I have written earlier, the American had kept a black woman with him. This woman was spendthrift and wasted all the wealth of the American whom she brought to the brink of bankruptcy. Many had warned the American against this woman but he could not free himself from her clutches. When all efforts to rotate the mill in the right direction failed, this woman approached me in the American's presence and said: 'Basja, someone has done black magic to prevent this machine from running'. I asked her what should be done to change the situation. She replied: 'We should resort to dancing to appease the evil'. I was taken aback: 'Does dancing have effect on machines also?' They confirmed but I tried to resist: 'But madam, it would cost no less than 150 bucks and will be of no use'. She was adamant, however, and said: 'Dancing is a must to dispel the jinx'. I finally agreed and the owner said: 'I shall inform the villagers and arrange for the dance to be performed on Saturday and Sunday'. I asked, 'who will bear the expenses? The reply was: 'Take it from the Chinese shopkeeper'. I then called the head of the *Ingis* [Amer-Indians][112] and told him about the dance proposal. He was glad to accept the offer.

It is said that the sick opt for their healers. On hearing about the dance, many black medicine men and *voodoo* specialists from various places gathered on Saturday with their instruments, drums and other equipments, which I had never seen before. Liquor flowed out of the Chinese shop that also provided food for all. They ate and drank to their satisfaction and then filled a bowl with molasses that was stirred and sprinkled all around the machine. Chanting of verses amidst drumbeats and dancing continued the whole night and lasted even the next day. On Sunday evening, the festivities ended and everyone returned home. The next morning Dildar Khan was ordered to heat the engine of the mill. When warmed, the motor was switched on. Defying all expectations the rotation remained in the wrong direction. I quickly remarked: 'Madam, the spell has not gone yet. Now what?' The woman was no easy meat and said: 'This time call the coolies [Hindostanis] to dance and perform their magical rites'. I consented and sent word about it to the plantations 'Lalauki' and 'Firaelant'. The following Saturday, the Indian sorcerers arrived with their sets of instruments. They were also given drinks and they ate and smoked as much as they liked. Another night of chanting and recitation in various manners passed with no positive result. The only result that confronted us was the expenditure involved in the whole operation of 'spell-unbinding' and the money was wasted.

When the fault in the mill could not be detected, Dildar Khan and I asked the American whether it was possible that a machine had been constructed that had opposite settings by mistake. The American said: 'Boss, there is no company in the world, which would do such a thing. All motors rotate clockwise and not the other way round. Before exporting it, a thorough check is made to exclude any defect in it. This mill was produced in Germany and surely must have been through stringent tests and trials. But I fail to understand why it rotates in the opposite direction'. The following weekend Mr. De Vries came and lamented about the expenses incurred for dancing and witchcraft. He commented: 'Only the government engineer can resolve the matter and he should be summoned'. The straightforward American agreed to his proposal as he usually did with our proposals. He was also very kind and would always send a raincoat to me in the field whenever it rained. He would tell Dildar to immediately give it to me lest I may fall ill. He never lost his cool. The next morning he took Dildar Khan with him to the city on his motor. Dildar usually accompanied him during such visits. Before leaving, he instructed me to assemble all his tools to facilitate the inspector's work. When they were gone I did accordingly and prepared all his tools and instruments as required. The inspector came. The mill was warmed and started. It went the wrong way as before despite all his efforts. He could not detect any fault with the machine. When he saw the display of tools he was surprised. He had never seen so many instruments and had no idea about their use. He accepted his failure and left with his fee of 10 rupees. The problem stayed. We were depressed and the American's sorrow knew no bounds.

One night, at 9 p.m., the American called me and said: 'Boss, tell Dildar to light the fire and heat the machine tomorrow morning at six, and if God wishes, I shall operate it successfully'. I was delighted. In the morning, after making all arrangements to run the mill, Dildar lit the fire. Sahab came early without even having taken his tea. After assessing the situation he pulled out a pin from near the oil pump and pushed it back in the same place in the reverse direction. He started the engine. By God's grace the shortcoming was overcome and the rotation was corrected. It was a day of rejoicing on the plantation. The mill now began to run in full swing and money rolled in with ease. Yet, the new source of income led to further spending by the American's mistress. She was exactly the opposite of the American, be it her colour, her nature, or behaviour. She was proud, ill tempered, and had bad manners, while the American was modest, cool and well behaved. He was also a workaholic and would work seven days a week, even on holidays. His fondness for food and work was well known.

## My Departure and the Sale of the Plantation

When the contract of the Chinese shopkeeper had ended, I requested the plantation owner to sell the shop to me and I bought it for Suleman Khan by paying 250 bucks and procured him a license. This was in 1928. As has been told already, the lady of the plantation was a spendthrift. The income from the mill and the fields was enough to run a family of five comfortably. But unfortunately this was not to be. This woman had no limits in squandering away wealth and in a short span of time laid the foundation of bankruptcy. I have seen many big landlords falling prey to such acts of the fairer sex, rather darker in this case! Once bitten, they could not recover and their children were forced to beg for a living or work as labourers. Wastage of money destroys an individual and his family. Many a times Mr. De Vries and I had warned the American of the consequences of this woman's company but he paid no attention. Even his elite friends tried to persuade him but in vain. They told him to come to various occasions alone and not bring the woman along. She was not welcome to dine with them. The Company also declined to offer monetary assistance to the plantation seeing the amount of expenditure. This woman had turned the tide against us single-handedly. She bought things at exuberant prices. Instead of 2 annas, she would give twelve for some wood and be happy with the bargain. If one could buy tomatoes for 50 paise per basket, she would take four tomatoes for 2 annas.

She would heat 20 pounds of sugar at a time, mix guava into it to prepare jelly and invariably spoil it. Later she would either throw it away or give it to me to distribute it to others, and order for more sugar. Very frequently one could find bread and other eatables thrown outside her house. No matter how costly the cloth was, she would cut it disproportionately short the very first night and show it to me saying, 'Basia look, the fitting was not proper earlier'. Knowing her intentions, I would exclaim: 'Yeah madam, it now seems better'. She would say that the design was nowhere to be found and that she had searchedthe whole plantation. She did the same with the clothes of her family members and then bought new ones after spoiling them. Whenever a wandering merchant came to the plantation, she would buy items at twelve-fold its worth and compliment herself for the bargain.

A tin-full of cooking oil did not last even 3 weeks in her kitchen. All the time, she would order a labourer to wet the clothes and then burn them later saying that they had developed fungus. When a costly pair of shoes was brought from town for her sons, she would invariably cut it small and remark: 'These boots are no good'. I was perplexed the way she wasted money. The American was bewitched by the vixen's charms and consented to her demands without resistance. He had surrendered his senses and danced to her tune. This tendency to show off and live lavishly at another's expense is not new. There is a story of a horse trader. This horse trader always asked his clients as to whose money he was spending to buy the horse(s). If one said it was their earning, he refused saying that you will not be capable of buying my horses. However, if a customer said it was his father's, he knew the deal was made. Once a client came and when he asked the same question, the man said that it was his earning. The trader told him to forget about the horse. The man was bewildered, 'Why? I have the cash to buy and will surely take one. I have not come here to borrow or ask for free'. 'Alright then', agreed the trader and took him to the stable. The trader quoted a horse of 1000 bucks worth, for only 500 bucks and that of 500 bucks for 250 only. 'It is very expensive', said the buyer. In the meantime, another client arrived. When the seller asked him the same question, he replied that it was his father's earning. The dealer said that he could easily buy a horse. They came to the stable and the trader showed him the horse of 1000 bucks saying that it was worth 1500 bucks. The customer willingly paid the amount and took the horse. The first buyer who had toiled for his money was dumbfounded. The seller now turned to him and said, 'See? You did not buy it because it seemed costly. I offered you the same animal for only 500 bucks and you declined, while this man happily paid 1500 bucks for it because the worth of hard-earned money is not known to him like it is to you.'

The lady of the plantation dealt with the American's money in a similar manner.[113] This led to gross misappropriation of the plantation's income and my salary was delayed by several months. Our shop also credited them to a great extent and the payments were irregular and incomplete. The plantation ran into debt and it owed me also about 500 bucks while there was no account of Suleman Khan's shop credit. Still, the ways of the woman did not change, the loans multiplied each day and the company refused to provide financial assistance any longer. Seeing this I concluded that it was now impossible to run the plantation any further and I therefore resigned. The American asked me why and I replied that I could not work on credit anymore. He assured me: 'Boss do not worry, you will surely get your money. If you leave, I shall sell this off'. I replied: 'well, it is your property. You may do as you wish. I have already lost 200 bucks on plantation Rust en Lust when it went bankrupt and I spent my own money to run the plantation. I have never been able to recover it'. Despite the pleadings of the American, I left 'Satbarwa' and returned home. During the 5 years of my tenure in 'Satbarwa', the American neither spoke a harsh word to Dildar Khan nor to me.

After some time Suleman Khan also shifted his shop from Satbarwa and started his business at the Surnaukreek crossing on Sarju Maharaj's land. About 3 years later, he moved to Boxel where he bought a plot and built a big house. Around 5-6 years later he sold it and settled in Paramaribo doing good business. On 1 December 1941, he took his wife and children to Demerara [British Guyana] following some family problems.

Three months after I had left 'Satbarwa', the American sold off the plantation for 13.000 bucks and returned all the money that he owed me. I thanked the Almighty for this. The American then, suffering at the hands of the woman he kept, worked as an auto mechanic for 100 bucks per month under Mr. Van der Voet. He gradually collected money for the fare and then took his family back to America.

# VOLUME IV

## The building of a House in Dijkveld in 1931

My dear young children and I took 7 years to construct this house. It took quite some time to accumulate all the materials required and while I was away at Satbarwa, several items already collected had rotten and were wasted. When I returned I told my sons that since our family was now growing, we needed a bigger house. I told them, 'if you do not wish to stay together, you may divide all that I have and settle wherever you think proper. Just give me a small house to spend my remaining days. I will not impose upon you to live jointly. It is up to you all to decide where and how you will live'. The boys talked it over and concluded that they wished to live jointly and in harmony. This made me very happy. I thanked Allah for their thoughts and said: 'Alright do as you wish'.

Faiz Khan was still very young and it was his four elder brothers who laid the foundation of the house in Allah's name. Fortunately, three of them knew some carpentry and masonry-work. Suleman Khan had better knowledge regarding all this and he supervised and directed how things were to be done. Karamat Khan and Dildar Khan worked under him while Chote Khan carried out the milk business for financial support, because Suleman Khan's shop was at the Surnaukreek when the actual construction took place. After 8 months later, the building was completed and Hakim Nawab Ali Saḥab's prediction regarding a house had therefore also become reality.

## Beginning of the Boycott: Rift between the Sanatanis and the Aryas

Between 1873 and 1929, the government of Surinam had employed migrants from Hindustan. It was aware of only two communities among them: Hindus and Muslims. The two religious communities lived together in peace and there was no sign of the Arya Samaj. Even in Hindustan people did not know this organization. The details regarding Swami Dayanand's birth and his activities were highlighted on 24 May 1929 by the *Shri Venkateshwar Samachar Patre*[114], a newspaper published in Bombay by Tahalram Girdhari Das Samant, and was located at 73 Nagdevi Street, Bombay – 3. A summary of the article has been included here because it was this Dayanandji who sowed the seeds of hatred and separation between the two communities in Surinam, which finally caused their disintegration. A complete profile of the Swami can be obtained from the above-mentioned newspaper.

In 1880, Swami Dayanand who was 59 years old then, secretly published his autobiography in an English Theosophist magazine. He rejected all other languages and prefered to write his book in English. He also purposefully concealed the name of his village, his parents' identity and did not disclose some of his misdeeds and sins, which he committed during his childhood days. Instead, he very cunningly presented himself as a pious and truthful character. Lala Dalpat Rai of village Jagrao in the Punjab translated this English autobiography into Urdu and published it in Vikram Sammat 1945 [according to the Hindu calender, i.e. 1888 A.D.]. After that many articles about the Swami have been written and were published all over *Bharat* in different newspapers and magazines. There was a vast difference among these stories and what they said about his holiness. This surprised people and they realized that some secrets had to be discovered, which explained the controversies among these stories about the Swami. A probe unearthed his birthplace. He was actually born in the state of Morvi in a village called Rampura[115]. Swami Dayanand had claimed that his father had been a reputed landlord in Morvi. Yet, a *dewan* explored papers and files of the last 100 years, which were available in the government office and found that many of Swami's statements had been false. It was in fact proved that Swami Dayanand was born in Rampura village and that his father's name was Haribhajan. A birth certificate confirmed that Shivbhajan was the son of Haribhajan. Accordingly, Swami Dayanand alias Shivbhajan was born in the month of *bhado* on the 9$^{th}$ day of *shuklapaksh* a Thursday in the middle of the night (as per Vikram Sammat in 1881 and according to Shaka Sammat this it is in 1746) [that is 1824 A.D.]. I had preferred to skip the discussion of his horoscope. One may read, translate and circulate this. A detailed horoscope is published in a book named *Dayanand chalkapat darpan* [Mirror of the fraud Dayanand] written by Kaluram Shastri.[116] Shivbhajan belonged to the *kapri* community of the Bhat clan which make a living from singing and dancing.

Changing times in Hindustan promoted Swami Dayanand to create an Arya Samaj as an offshoot from the Sanatan Dharm. The basic philosophy behind it was to criticise other religions and present itself as the true way of life. An organization that looked down upon people professing other religions, highlighting their drawbacks and thus tarnishing their image, was thus established. The Swami taught his disciples to be strict and this extremism caused a rift between them and others, especially between Hindus and Muslims. Consequently, riots broke out in Hindustan between these two religious communities with bloodshed and the death of several innocents. It was through the newspapers that we learnt about it.[117]

In Surinam, the *Bharatvasiyon* had lived like brothers and sisters and in harmony with each other for over 60 years. When Mehta Jaiminiji from India arrived in Surinam in 1929, Hindus and Muslims alike welcomed him warmly. He delivered several lectures and gave talks at different places. He laid the foundation of the Arya Samaj in Surinam and within a few days only also the seeds of discontent and ill will amongst the communities. He then returned to India. When the preaching of the Arya Samajis began, the followers of Sanatan religion boycotted them. No person of either community welcomed each other in their gatherings. Even if one person of the other group were invited during a function, the Sanatanis would refrain from attending it. Moreover, fighting ensued if an Arya Samaji greeted a Sanatani. A number of such incidents occurred making people of both organizations feel hurt and start lawsuits against each other. Initially this friction took place between the Arya Samajis and the Sanatanis while the Muslims befriended both these groups. Yet soon it became evident that the Arya Samajis could not conquer the Sanatanis and the two groups therefore resolved their differences and calmed down. They then again accepted each other's company and even allowed marriages among their children. Yet, the dictim of the Arya Samaj is to criticise others during their meetings and this frequently has resulted in conflicts. The Sanatanis were the first victims while the Muslims escaped. Besides, though after some time relations between the two groups seemed to have become cordial, the cold war between them continued.

## Altercation with the Arya Samajis

When I still lived in 'Satbarwa' [St. Barbara] and Suleman Khan ran the shop there, this division between these two Hindu sects had already commenced and Mahabir, a *baniya* of the Surnaukreek had become an Arya Samaji. He had invited Hindus and Muslims for the *katha* [prayer meeting] at his place. All attended this gathering yet after the programme and dinner, a local Arya Samaji leader called Shukdev, who lived in 'Lalauki' [Laarwijk], began to talk disparagingly about the Sanatanis. He even remarked that the Koran (the holy book of the Muslims) did not have the ultimate truth and was incorrect. I received this piece of information the next morning from Raghuni, a Sanatani from the Surnaukreek. I told him that I could not defend other religions, but if the Arya Samajis would allow me to be a moderator, I would not object to a religious debate. Yet, I told him that I could not go there until they invited me to talk about my own religion. When Raghuni had left, Mohammad Islam, my shipmate Mangal's son, narrated the same story and elaborated on the allegations made against the Koran. He requested me to go and explain matters. It was Sunday so I immediately got ready to go to the Surnaukreek. When the Sanatani Hindus of the plantation heard that I was going there, they wanted to accompany me. I, however, declined their offer explaining to them that the arrival of too many people might cause a commotion. Yet, they insisted on coming and followed me in three boats.

Suleman Khan closed his shop, took the *Koran Sharif* and *Satyarth Prakash*[118] and accompanied me to the Surnaukreek. We met Sukhdev at Mathura's house (who was Raghuni's own brother and had accepted the Arya Samaj[119]). When Suleman Khan asked Sukhdev about his comments the night before, he straightaway denied his remarks about the Koran. Suleman persisted: 'there is no need to deny it. The wise must rectify their mistakes, if there are any, in the holy books and one should be honoured for it, it is their duty to do so. Here, take this *Koran Sharif* and find fault in it if you can. I shall give you one buck for each wrong word. I also have brought the *Satyarth Prakash* and if you accept my challenge, I will point to the mistakes in this book'. Then Sukhdev said: '*Bhaiya* [brother], I do not have much strength and knowledge to do so. I said that the Bible contained many flaws. I did not even mention the Koran'. Suleman Khan took out a piece of paper from his pocket and gave it to Sukhdev saying: 'Brother, if you can decipher the meaning of this verse I shall give you 100 bucks as a prize'. After this our meeting was over and we returned. I had no idea which verse Suleman Khan had given to Sukhdev. I neither knew from which book he had quoted it, nor did Suleman talk to me about it.

He had given Sukhdev 3 days to explain the verse. The Aryans sent their reply by letter on 30 March 1931. Their interpretation of the verse was as follows:

*On the ninth planet, during the first month, in the ninth ocean and on day six (Monday), in the dark half of chaitha, people will achieve true happiness on the seventh day of chaith, 1919 A. D., during the dark hours of Monday.*

This meaning was wrong. The poet Bihari Lal[120], who had written this verse, had described the date of completion of his *satsayi* in it, and the Arya Samajis had therefore wrongly translated the verse. The actual meaning was:

*In the year 1719, during the dark hours of chaith (March/April) on Monday the 6th, the Satsayi was completed.* (i.e., planet 9, shashi 1, saladhi 7, chitijh 1. This written the other way round stands for 1719 Samvat)[that means in 1662 A.D.].

In return, the Aryans had written a few lines in Sanskrit and now challenged us to decipher their meaning. 'If explained correctly, I shall accept Islam', someone had written but had hidden his identity. A child had signed below and thus even if we provided the correct answer, no one would convert to Islam since we did not even know the name of the sender of these lines. This was the Machiavellian ploy. The Aryans had devised this and selected both sides of the coin in the toss up. Suleman Khan wrote the following reply:

*(786)*

*3 April 1931*

*I request Janab Man Meherban, Kadardan and Man Salamat to please accept our greetings. We are all well here and wish the same for you in Allah's name. I was glad to receive and read the letter sent by Shri Yut Mahashay of the Arya Samaj. The following is the explanation of your query mentioned in your letter. I hope it will satisfy you:*

***Chaupai***

*The small poem that you have sent, keep it at home as it has evil intent*
*A verse which breaks a nation, should not be aired, it will breed dissent*

*You sent a letter with no name, is that not a shameful thing?*
*A thief does acts of this sort and goes to jail with suffering*
*The contents of the letter disclose that you did not write it yourself*
*If you had been decent, the delay could have been avoided itself*
*One who does not know the meaning of his own language dares himself an Aryan proclaim*
*The interpretation of my verse was improper, the letter did wrongly explain*
*Without knowledge of your mother tongue you quote shamelessly*
*You have shown your righteousness by taking a month to reply*
*Knowledge of Sanskrit is for the Hindus, for the Muslims, Arabic*
*I could answer, if you had asked to decipher something in Arabic*
*I gave you a verse in Hindi, which you were unable to understand at all*
*One who knows how to debate, doesn't write Shlokas and prove himself small*
*I am a Muslim, keep your blind faith to yourself do not teach*
*You do not know what 'Arya' stands for? How can you venture out to preach?*
*If you knew the meaning, you would be humble and bow before the others*
*Who has framed your rule, which teaches you to be intolerant to your brothers?*
*You celebrate death and toast at every meal to satisfy your desire*
*If a child is your guru, let him reply and face our ire*
*Come to the city of Parmaribo and talk about all our difference(s)*
*Decide and publish it in the newspapers: the day and date of your preference*
*After three such notices, we shall present ourselves personally*
*Do whatever pleases you we shall comply with it whole-heartedly*
*Please forgive my mistakes like the wise forgive the insane.*
*My art is without knowledge, as I am neither poet nor intelligent.*

*Letter to the Aryans, dated: 12 April 1931*

*Whoever has sent this letter on behalf of the Arya Samaj has not responded to my reply, sent one week ago. I am still waiting to know the sender's identity. Since I could not trace him, I sent my reply via the leader (panch*[121]*) of the Arya Samaj, Mukhiyar Durbali Sahab who resides in Lalauki. Let the Arya Samaj know that if they wish to hold a religious debate then rent a hall in the city of Paramaribo*[122] *on a*

*prefixed date and notify it in the newspapers. If you are unable to pay the rent mention it and the Moslims shall hire the place because we are not afraid to face you. Yet please state your intentions in the newspapers.*
*Munshi Rahman Khan, Dijkveld, No. 4*

## The Message of Maulana Ahmad Khan

The formation of the Arya Samaj caused social unrest in the country. One of the elders of the Muslim community, Hafiz Maulana Janab Ahmad Khan, sent a message to me via Janab Kazi Ahmad Ali, stating that he was unable to attend the Bharat Uday Committee[123] meeting on 19 April 1931 because he was sick. Therefore I was requested to give a well-written letter in Hindi and send it first to him so that he could talk to the Chairman Janab Ramprasadji and isolate the person(s) responsible for the conflicts among the Hindustani community. He thanked me in anticipation. I then penned a letter in verses and sent it to him via Janab Kazi Ahmad Ali. My reasons for writing it in Hindi was to address it directly to the Chairman Ramprasad who did not know Urdu while Maulana Hafiz Janab Ahmad Khan knew Urdu but not Hindi. These two were heavyweights in the Bharat Uday Committee.

*11 April 1931*

*To the respected Sir and Chairman Janab Pandit Ramprasadji Sahab*[124]

*I give my greetings in the Lord's name. Everything is fine here and I wish the same at your end by the grace of the Holy One.*

*This is to comment upon the sorry state of affairs in our country. We received the news that rioting has troubled us. Regarding this I wish to throw some light on the situation through a few verses hereby included. I request you to kindly send your reply via the messenger (Ahmad Ali) who brings you my letter.*

***Chaupai***

*Dear Chairman, Speaker and Pandit please think about the following link:*
*You three are religious heads of your own, then why is this animosity shown?*

*Till the time Sheetal was living, Maulana in your meet, was willing*
*Until then no grouse was heard, affection in every caste increased*
*When Sheetal left for the Heaven above, Maulana lost his share of love*
*Hostility in the country began then and three religions now had fighting men*
*Everywhere you can hear them say, Aryans and Sanatanis accept the way*
*To despise Islam and be it damned, the Swami had thus given command*
*We ask, 'who is this man? Doing sinful acts no other can?'*
*'Spell out the name of this enemy, be he a Muslim or a Hindu identity'*
*An evil man is a villainous lout, why then do not kick him out?*
*If you do not judge honestly now, the culprit will escape somehow*
*The oldest religion, Sanatan, says that every religion has a place of its own*
*Islam, Khuda's creation, is true the world over, is known*
*The Arya Samajis are very moody and have their asperity shown*
*Thus says Rahman (your humble minion), do not be vain,*
*It is a shame, think thus use your own brain.*

*(Maulana Ahmad Khan, Mukam Kila)*
*(Munshi Rahman Khan, Dijkveld no. 4)*
*(Note: Dear gentlemen, for your kind information I like to tell that till date the Aryans did not bother to reply to any of the two letters written by Suleman Khan or me)*

## Hindus Boycott the Muslims

The wave of hatred that began in 1933 spread all over and engulfed the whole of Surinam by 1934 turning the two communities into bitter enemies.

### *Doha*

*The Almighty is shapeless. His works are incredible*
*Everyone remembers Him, be it Rahim or Ram we call*
*Shapeless Lord, accept a Form I earnestly pray*
*Have mercy on Your subjects! Pray do not turn away*
*We choose the path we wish, to heaven or to hell*
*One's fate is, however, scriptured by 'mahakaal'*

*But man is not afraid and his works are amoral and evil*
*He accuses others and defends his sinful will*

### *Chaupai*

*The Creator made the earth, the sun, the moon, the star,*
*Every kind of living being, known and unknown, be it near or far*
*Amongst which man is supreme, knowing and responsible*
*Acts of goodness lead to heaven, while the wages of sin is hell*
*One reads the scriptures everyday, but follows the path of his own will*
*While the natives of Surinam sleep in peace, Hindus and Muslims go for the kill*
*Why scorn the Muslims? The Lord shall punish the wrong*
*I shall continue to write, let others realise reading this song*

### *Doha*

*In 1934, the Lord allowed the bad to thrive*
*Who did the 60 years of love divide?*
*Hindus and Muslims were like rice and dal admixed*
*They were separated as repeated clashes were fixed*
*My letters were boycotted and the guru's post did bow*
*When 1934 passes, men will read and realisation will grow*
*One who cares and preserves his religion is a clever gentleman*
*Please pardon my mistakes, think it is the raw Rahman*

## The Wedding of my youngest Daughter and the Beginning of the Boycott in 1933

It was apparent that the Hindus had thought of a boycott against the Muslims for quite some time and this had led to several clashes between the two. But since the Muslims were not at fault, the Hindu extremists could not convince all others who lived harmoniously with the Muslims. These extremists therefore kept this thought to themselves. Yet, they lost no opportunity to add fuel to the fire of hatred and contempt between the two communities. Master Nathuram in his second book on the Hindi language accurately said:

### *Doha*

*The wicked acts to disarray, the genteel to unite*
*Soon after his entry, the bad controls the tide*[125]

The extremists of 'La Phondro' [Livorno] started a huge commotion following a small incident that was then blown out of proportion. The commotion engulfed the whole of Surinam leading to the fraction between the Hindus and Muslims. The scars of the friction are still in the minds of our children. If this continues, the future of the two communities will be gloomy and the generations to come shall not prosper. Our offspring will never forgive us for our deeds and be sorry for it.

On Friday 23 March 1933, my youngest daughter[126] was to be married. Both Hindus and Muslims were invited and had all gathered. According to the custom of my household, some amount of the food was kept separately in a room. I knew Hindi well, and had befriended several high caste Hindus, who used to visit me regularly and on special occasions always happily had eaten whatever vegetarian dish was cooked. I had no differences with anyone and we all got along well. Never did a Hindu brother leave my house without having eaten something. On this particular day of marriage, brothers of both communities were dining together. I had requested all the vegetarians to go upstairs for their meal. While I was busy managing the affairs, our Imam, Kallan Mian and Babu Puroshottam Singh got involved in an altercation of which I was unaware. As a result, four people left without taking their dinner. When I came to know about it, I called a couple of them back in earnest but could not reach all because they stayed quite far away.

Later, I enquired about the cause of the incident and found that it had been Kallan Mian's fault. After 2 weeks, I invited both the parties at my residence to sort out their misunderstanding. Jangli Bahadur, Subhag Chotelal, and about twenty people from our neighbourhood were present when Kallan Mian acknowledged his mistake and apologised to Puroshottam Singh. Puroshottam Singh publicly forgave him and they both shook each other's hand. Everyone was pleased. They all then drank tea, smoked and left satisfied. I was happy. As the trouble had started in my house I had felt particularly bad about it. However, now the trouble had ended and that also in my house. Yet, the thumb of injustice rules the senses.

The extremists could not digest the peaceful outcome of this episode. How could they allow this opportunity to slip out of their hands? They demanded that Kallan Mian should ask for forgiveness from the whole Hindu fraternity. They said that Puroshottam Singh was not the one who could grant pardon in this case. When this bizarre demand was not fulfilled, these men geared themselves up against the Muslims. They visited each and every Hindu household in 'La Phondro' [Livorno] and started spreading the fire of animosity in people's hearts. About one or two weeks after this event, my eldest daughter's sister-in-law was to be married. Her father-in-law, Nirhu Mian had invited both Hindu and Muslim guests on the occasion. When the troublemakers came to know about this, they went about on bicycles during the dark hours and persuaded all the Hindu invitees to return the invitation. In the end only two Hindus, Nagesh and Sahati, graced the event. This led to the punishment of Nagesh and Sahati at Bahadur's house when they attended *katha* there. They had to hold their ears and do sit-ups in front of the gathering. Thus began the boycott of Muslims by the Hindus from the day of Nirhu's daughter's wedding ceremony. No Muslim was now welcome to any Hindu gathering and no Hindu dared to accept any Muslim's call. These louts circulated the rumour among the Hindus that the Muslims always mixed beef with mutton in their cooking and hence it was a sin to partake in their feasting. Besides, they also narrated that beef was a customary item in every Muslim family. This absurd thinking was sowed and watered in all the Hindu minds. Hindus of 'La Phondro' now sided with the extremists and refrained from interaction with the Muslims.

During this period, several committees were formed to resolve the situation. The Muslims said that if anyone was caught in such harmful activities that hurt the feelings of either of the two communities, the two communities should both exclude that man. A single man's doing should not cause injustice against everyone. The Hindus retorted: 'Then ban Kallan Mian'. The Muslims were unwilling: 'How could this decision be made now that Kallan Mian had already apologised for his misdoings? He is now freed of his guilt'. Yet, the Hindus were adamant and did not want to change their mind regarding this. The Hindus then proposed that the Muslims should invite the Hindus openly if at all they wished to summon them. Moreover, a separate food store had to be provided, with meals prepared by a Hindu cook. Only then would the Hindus accept an invitation. To this the Muslims agreed, but said that one half of those in the food store should consist of both communities. The Hindus did not like this idea. Pandit Dhirja Maharaj said that if the Muslims invited the *brahmins* to a feast, these *brahmins* should be given separate food grains, a Hindu cook and separate utensils. Muslims agreed to these demands but with the condition that there should be an equal number of Muslims and Hindus in each of their kitchens. The Hindus outrightly rejected this. Then Pandit Dhiraj Maharaj said that if they were provided dry foodgrains, they might think of attending the feast. The Muslims retorted that if the *brahmins* refrained from eating or accepting gifts from the low caste communities, stopped keeping their women, stopped eating meat and eggs, stopped selling their bulls and cows to the butchers and stopped taking alcohol, the Muslims would do as they wished. 'Is there anyone in this gathering who adheres to the religious conduct mentioned in the Shashtra Manusmriti', it was asked. Nobody was there. Some Muslims therefore told these Hindus that their discussion thus had had no value. It had only been to instigate the two communities against each other. After that, everybody remained silent. Such meetings to reconcile the two communities, however, proved time and again futile, and the cold war spread far and wide. There is a saying: 'The more medication, the more flaring up of the disease'. This became reality. The Hindus now openly came out against the Muslims and their means to promote friction between the two communities increased day by day. A village saying goes like this: 'When a man wishes to denounce his wife he says: "Hey bitch why did not you put some turmeric in the spinach today?"' [A staff is quickly found to beat a dog; Give a dog a bad name (and hang him)]. The blasphemous Hindu scoundrels did the same thing to the Muslims.

Meanwhile, Nanku Singh's mother-in-law died and a couple of Muslims were invited to attend the *terahvi* that would take place 13 days after her death. Yet, the *brahmin* society of Livorno called a meeting and decided to leave out the Muslims on this event. And so they did.

When the Hindus started the boycott against the Muslims, there were still 9 months to go before our festival of Id would take place on which animal sacrifices were to be made. It was a fact that till then no cow had ever been slaughtered in Livorno, though the Hindus alleged that this had happened. Pandit Shrikant went a step ahead and proclaimed that the Muslims ate only beef while the *chamars* [low castes], not only ate the meat of dead cows but also pork hence both of them should be renounced. Everyone in the meeting agreed. This meeting took place in Babu Nanku Singh's residence and he did not even try to nullify the unjust decisions that were made there. He was a *kshatriya* and should have known that the *brahmins*, *kshatriya* and *vaish* belonged to the same upper castes as the Muslims and there was a feeling of equality among them. They belonged to the same class and were equal in matters of business, invitations or festivals. They only avoided food cooked inside a Muslim home, but had no other reservations whatsoever. The upper caste society avoided the people of the lower strata and even talked to them from a distance. If this *brahmin* society had not passed this absurd and provoking resolution that was completely against the scriptures, this fire of discord (*phut ki aag*) [communalism] would not have burnt Surinam to ashes as it happens in the rest of the world.

Following Pandit Srikant's proposal, the Muslims and low castes were castigated from the rest. But denouncing the low caste Hindus was no easy thing to do for the phoney *brahmins* whose earnings dropped considerably. This was because every pandit had no less than 20-80 followers who belonged to the lower castes. Soon the ban against the lower caste society was lifted and only the Muslims remained a segregated lot. It is justly said: 'Even though the house of in-laws is 80 miles away, still one opens the windows for them'. Likewise, even though Id was 9 months later, the Hindus already accused them of slaughtering cows without any evidence. This was plain injustice. Day by day the feeling of hatred grew and the Muslims bore the brunt of the isolation. All decisions and actions went against them. Several efforts to end this conflict failed and the day of *bakr-id* drew near. The Muslims had now lost their cool and contemplated the sacrifice of a cow on the day of *id.* When the unethical Hindus came to know about this plan they went berserk. The upper caste Hindus collected donations among themselves and bought a pig to be slaughtered close to the Masjid on *bakr-id*. They went through with this unceremonial act and God knows what they did with the swine's body. While the Muslims sacrificed the animal according to their rituals, the Hindus of Livorno acted against their religion.

Yet, it is not against their religion to sacrifice an animal during a *yagya*. In the *shashtra manusmriti* (chapter 5, shloka 39 and line 156) it is stated that it is not a sin to kill an animal as an offering. The Lord (Prajapati) himself created an animal to be sacrificed in the fire for the prosperity of the earth hence this act is not considered to be sinful. Therefore, according to the Hindu scriptures, the Muslims had not slaughtered the cow [but sacrificed] and were therefore guiltless. On the other hand, the Hindus had not killed the animal to please the Gods. In fact, they had slaughtered the pig. Their aim was to annoy the Muslims and therefore they had gone even against their own rules of religious conduct. Moreover, they accused the Muslims of having performed a wrongful act, which they had not. Yet this episode only helped them to add more fuel to the fire and indeed the Hindu extremists took full advantage of it. The boycott against the Muslims, which was pre-planned, had now gotten enough mileage to come into the fore. It is rightly said: 'Do not believe the deceitful man, his inner self will be exposed in time'. [127]

## Muslims Boycotted

One cannot hide his thoughts in his heart for long as it spills out some time or the other. In 1933, the year in which the Muslims had sacrificed a cow and the Hindus had slaughtered a swine, the Hindus also organised a huge convention to get rid of their guilt feelings over the killing of the animal. They gathered at chairman Pandit Paltan Maharaj's residence. Here it was decided to enhance the means of the boycott and a resolution to enforce it was passed. The active members of the sect then went from one village to another to spread the fire of enmity in order to isolate the Muslims even more.

By 1934, the whole of Surinam was engulfed in the fire of the boycott. The Arya Samaj orator Mehta Jaimaniji, as described earlier, sowed the seed of hatred in Surinam in 1929. Though the initial rift had been between the Aryans and Sanatanis, as time passed the tide turned the Hindus against the Muslims and on Monday 26 March 1934, the Hindus took out a procession with flags and killed a pig near the Masjid. They did this just to irk the Muslims on the occasion of bakr-id. They had planned to culminate the proceedings in a riot but by the grace of God were unable to convert their dreams into reality. The just and able government of Surinam deserves merit in this regard. It prevented the occurance of any wrongful act. Under this government, both the lion and the goat shared the same river to quench their thirst. Sensing the evil intentions of the Hindus, the government had sent its troops to control the situation at the site of slaughter. They forced the mob to disperse within minutes leaving all their drums and flags scattered. On seeing the police, these mobsters fled to an unknown destination while the dead animal was carried off to the police station. If the government had not taken such a prompt action, the story would have been very different and bloodshed would have been inevitable. Government troops however guarded the places of sacrifice everywhere and the Hindus felt defeated.[128] They could not create any trouble and harm the Muslims.

When the news of boycott became known everywhere in 1933, the Sanatanis employed a new method to harass the Muslims by announcing the 're-conversion' of illiterate poor Muslims by 'cleansing'[129] them. I wrote two *chautals* (verses) to them in this regard questioning their behaviour. One of these verses I sent to my ship companion (*jahazia*), my countryman *bhai* Godan of Hansu. I learnt that he became furious after reading my verse. I then wrote a letter to him saying that I would come the following Saturday to meet him and announced: 'You keep your sticks and rods ready to beat the person who is at fault'. I also penned the whole story of the boycott and the devious activities of the Sanatanis of Livorno and took the paper to Hansu on Saturday. That evening, Hindus and Muslims gathered there to discuss the matter. I read out what I had written and explained to them about why I had written the two *chautals*, of which one I had sent to my 'brother' Godan.

## The religious Note read out at Hansu

*Subject: The duties of the leaders of the Sanatan Dharma Mahamandal Sabha of Surinam*[130]*, Dutch Guyana*

*Author: Munshi Rahman Khan, Dijkveld no. 4.*

*Date: 10 March 1934*

*My dear Hindu and Muslim brothers, mothers, sisters, sons and daughters,*

*Please accept my regards and greetings*

*This is a humble request from me, a humble and insignificant individual not capable of presenting or teaching anything to you. You are wise and clever and can understand the situation. In these testing times I, a man of little knowledge, wish to say something. Please be considerate to my mistakes and pardon me. Kindly lend me your ears and let us join hands to fight this destructive menace. It is our duty to do so.*

*Dear Sirs, this anti-religious, anti-social, love-exterminator, which has devoured this country, has divided us. A regretful thing like this should never have occurred in a country, which is not our own. The immoral path that we have chosen against our brethren will lead to nothing else but increase in animosity and bankruptcy. I can see no ray of hope to terminate our sore feelings. I sincerely wish that we can talk it over and reach to an amicable solution to end this crisis.*

*The earlier efforts alas, have been futile and have instead increased the hostility. The religious leaders do not think of the poor farmers in the villages who bear the brunt of such disputes.*

*If they had any sense, they would have come together and sorted out this problem to reunite the two communities. If they were prompt enough, the affection would not have vanished. However, there is still ample time to retrace our erroneous step and retrieve our lost love for one another. I strongly feel that this is very much possible.*

*My dear friends let me explain how this trouble started. In 1929, the seed of this ill feeling was sown, as we all know. But since there was no ground for the conflict to begin, it lay dormant for a few years. The confrontation blossomed from a tiny bud in La Phondro and engulfed the whole of Surinam within months.*

*I, Munshi Rahman Khan of Dijkveld, no. 4, am witness to the episode that took place at my place during the marriage ceremony of my youngest daughter in 1933. Babu Puroshottam Singh and Kallan Mian were involved in a verbal duel. It was Kallan Mian's fault. After 2 weeks, both the parties came together and Kallan Mian tendered his apology in front of the twenty odd who were present there. Babu Puroshottam Singh forgave him and they shook hands to forget the incident. The problem ended there.*

*Some Hindu brothers however, were not satisfied with the decision. They again demanded an apology from Kallan Mian. Then they resorted to anti-muslim activities and stopped accepting and giving invitations to them. Later on, committee after committee tried to pacify the two parties but failed.*

*After some time, the brahmins formed a group of upper castes and decided to shun the lower caste chamars and the Muslims. But when they realised that their income was falling, because each Baba had 10-30 followers of the low caste, they lifted the boycott off the chamars while the Muslims were left in the cold.*

*My brothers, the Muslims of La Phondro were subjected to harsh treatment, such that if one went to a Janvasha (where the groom and his party rested), which was two or three ketting away from the bride's house, the whole stock and food of the house would be regarded as spoiled. The brahmins of La Phondro refused to eat from it. They, however, ate and drank in the company of Muslims who did not live in La Phondro saying that they were exempted from the ban. Someone has rightfully said: 'look at what kaliyug has shown, brother repulsed and bestowed unknown'.*

*This meant that the Hindus and Muslims living in the same neighbourhood, who shared happiness and sadness and who helped each other, now were prohibited to share the same table lest it be against their religion. Even if a Hindu dined in a Muslim's house out of personal affection, he was ousted from their society and forced to confess that he had committed a crime until which he was not taken back.*

*This caustic attitude of the Hindus had withered away the patience of the Muslims and they now believed that they were no more accepted by the Hindus. It changed their minds and they now contemplated the sacrifice of a cow during the upcoming festival of bakr-id, which was not against their religion. This had never occurred in La Phondro before because the two communities were so close to each other that they cared for one another's feelings sincerely.*

*A similar boycott was attempted earlier also, but since most of the Hindus did not support the movement then, the Muslims did not resort to such a drastic step like this. However, this time the division was more or less complete and the Muslims went on with their sacrifice. It happened only in La Phondro and not anywhere else.*[131] *As a result of this the Hindus replied by killing a pig near the Masjid that very day even though it was no place of their gods or for sacrifice. This was against both religions.*

*I hope this makes you understand how the sequence of these unfortunate events took place and who all were responsible for it and who wanted to set our hearts afire.*

*Dear gentlemen, let us now suppose that the Muslims' sacrifice of a cow was the reason for their boycott. But the Muslims did not isolate the four castes of Hindus who participated in the swine slaughtering! They still invited them on each and every occasion. But due to the intense pressure mounted by the Sanatan religious committee Chairman, Pandit Paltanji, Minister Shivnarayanji* [Seewnarain], *religious preacher Ramnarayanji, Harivansh and other leaders, no Hindu dared to risk his or her expulsion from the society. Even the few exceptions at the time, later on, bowed to these compulsions.*

*It would not have mattered much if this fire of aversion had remained limited to La Phondro only. It could have ceased in 2-4 months by itself. But alas, the above-mentioned gentlemen were not satisfied. They spread the word of animosity by letters or in person and in those places where the unwise were dominant they succeeded in their evil design. (On the other hand, in some areas, the wise rejected them). More than 50 years of bondage between the two communities was shattered to pieces and once friends, they now became bitter enemies.*

*Later on, the Hindus assembled at Pundit Paltanji's house*[132] *for a katha. They invited brahmins from far-off places and organised a Yagya. That day, all brahmins swore an oath to extend this boycott everywhere in Surinam even though the Muslims elsewhere were innocent. It is a mystery as to what the Yagya was meant for – to wash their sins off the cow sacrifice or the swine slaughter, or was it in support of the pig killing?*

*A massive campaign to realize the boycott then started. Hindus of many places stopped inviting and befriending the Muslims. In a few instances, the invited Muslim guests were asked to leave the site of occasion. The Babaji who was present did not heed to any amount of explanation that favoured the innocent Muslims who had not been involved in cow sacrifice. He said: 'no, no, we have passed a resolution under oath to banish this community and if even one single Muslim were present here, no brahmin should carry out the marriage rituals or yagna'.*

*The poor Hindus yielded to this pressure and did as they were ordered. Only the rich could afford to refuse (if one was stubborn), and say: 'alright, if you will not then I shall ask some other brahmin to perform the rites'. In these circumstances the brahmin, not wanting to lose a fat amount of donation would comply and eat alongside the Muslims.*

*Dear Sirs, let me narrate you an incident to prove that this is indeed happening. Listen carefully and realize how our religious leaders are bent upon to violate religion instead of preserving its sanctity. Wake up, sleeping time is over now!*

*Beekhuizen is a place adjacent to La Phondro where Biseshar lived, an ahir and a disciple of Pandit Paltan Maharaj. He was, however, a supporter of innocent Muslims. He said that any Muslim who invited him would be invited in a similar manner whenever any occasion arose.*

*Those who wished to maintain their friendship were welcome. 'I shall refrain from this act of hostility', he said. Therefore, he presented himself among the Muslim fraternity, wherever he was called.*

*When Biseshar refused to heed to the orders of his religious leaders, his neighbour, a chamar, became his enemy either due to his persuasion or due to jealousy. A couple of times he threw stones and bricks at Biseshar's house. This activity stopped after the police was summoned for investigation.*

*A few days later, six chamars attacked and beat up Biseshar at night. On hearing Biseshar's cry for help, a Muslim, Habib who lived in the neighbourhood, came to his rescue but was himself beaten to death. Biseshar sustained multiple fractures of his right upper limb and his head was smashed with sticks, but he managed to survive. He was taken to the hospital where it took several months for him to recover. His right hand, however, has become useless.*

*The six culprits were booked and imprisoned for 8, 5, 4 (two persons), and 3 years respectively. Thus, see, eight families lost their earning members and their children are still living in abject poverty. Who is responsible?*

*When Biseshar was in the hospital, he requested Thakurji to recite the katha and ease his suffering. Later when he was discharged and came home, he asked Pandit Changa Maharaj from Dijkveld: 'Panditji, I wish to listen to the katha but how can I invite the Muslims amidst such friction here?' Panditji replied: 'Wherever I go, both communities are invited and I do not mind'. 'I am of the same opinion' agreed Bishesher, 'kindly fix a date for it'. A date was fixed according to the panchang and Panditji consented to allow Muslims in the gathering. The poor soul did as he was told and invited people of both religions.*

*On the day of the katha, when all the necessary items had been collected for the yagna and katha and preparations for the dinner had begun, Panditji came and said: 'Biseshar, I shall not lead the proceedings, find someone else to do it'. It was afternoon and puris and other foodstuffs were being prepared. Bishesher was stunned! He begged the Pandit not to do so. 'Panditji, he pleaded with folded hands, 'what is my fault? If there is any please forgive me but do not cancel this prayer meet. I am a handicapped man and cannot travel to arrange another pandit in just 2 hours. The preparation for the dinner has already started. If I had 2-3 days to spare, I could have managed it somehow. I did everything after seeking your permission and invited people from both communities'. But Panditji was adamant, 'what can I do? I have been strictly forbidden to carry out this ceremony', he apologized.*

*Poor Bishesher sent for other people requesting them to find another Pandit from elsewhere to carry out the ceremony. But wherever they went, the people turned them down, and said that they could not participate in a yagna where Muslims were also present. Finally when no Sanatani Pandit turned up, Bishesher was very disappointed. He now thought of turning to the Arya Samaj or even accepting Islam or Christianity and distributing all the food brought for the yagna, to the poor.*

*As soon as this news reached the Arya Samaj, Pandit Sukhram from the Arya Diwakar of Surinam came quickly to his rescue at about eight in the evening. He carried out the rituals according to his rules and received the entire family into his society. Chhedi Mahajan and other religious leaders of the Arya Samaj were also present on the occasion.*

*Now tell me, did the Sanatan Dharm Mahamandal do the right thing? Were not the religious leaders responsible for a whole family being forced out of the Sanatan religion? Who is to be blamed for disrupting the yagna, which had this shameful consequence? It is pitiable and pathetic.*

*Dear Sirs, let me not prolong this episode and proceed further. Today, in India there are about 20 crore [200 million] Sanatanis and 9 crore [90 million] Muslims apart from people of other religions. If of these 20 crore Sanatanis, 4 or 5 crore became Muslim, would the Sanatan Dharm break into pieces? Likewise, if of 8 crore Muslims, 2 or 3 crore became Christians, would Islam break apart? Not at all! What I mean to say is, that similarly if 100 or 200 Muslims were converted to the Sanatan Dharm no harm would be done to Islam, but the Sanatan Dharm will not gain anything from it. Yes, the only accomplishment will be the anti-religion path to Hell.*

*From the time God created everything till today, or rather since the invasion of India by the Muslim rulers, millions of Hindus have abandoned the Sanatan religion and have accepted other faith(s) due to various reasons. But still Sanatan persists and waters the roots of other religions. On the other hand, not even a single child has been re-converted to Sanatan faith. The Sanatan Pandit will never let this happen. There is also no provision for this re-conversion in the scriptures. Then how-come the Muslims in Surinam are being 'cleansed' and chastised back to the Sanatan? This only proves that this move that has been instituted here since the last 2-3 months is only to irk the Muslims and to add fuel to the fire or to destroy the Sanatan religion. This means that the so-called protectors [brahmins] turn out to be destroyers of religion.*

*Everyone knows and there is nothing to say against the sanctity and holiness of the Sanatan Dharm. It has no equal. Even if a single drop of water from another community falls on the pitcher of a Sanatani, he discards it saying that it has become contaminated and throws it out from his house never to use it again. If this is the case with an earthen pot why the vedas do not have a mantra to cleanse it? Similarly how can one 'cleanse' a Muslim who is so untouchable that he can adulterate the food store of a barat or a yagna? How can one convert him to a Sanatani? Is that not akin to licking where one spat? And what is the religious principle behind this?*

*Let us see what Pandit Akhlanandji writes in his essay 'Ratanmala' in Sri Venkateshwar [newspaper] of 9 December 1932. He writes that a Muslim cannot be sanitised. 'Who can purify one whose blood is mixed with that of a cow and whose flesh is blended with cow's flesh? For example, just like a sweet is rendered unfit for consumption when it falls in a drain, similarly, a Muslim cannot be undefiled. It is clearly mentioned in the Bhagwat that such a sinner is like a pot of liquor and cannot be purified by any amount of repentance'. Tell me therefore, if there is no mantra to cleanse an earthen pot used for liquor, how can these brahmins here claim to do so? They made, sold and drank liquor. When you yourself are impure, how can you sanitise the Muslims if there is no mantra? My brothers, do you not realise that your leaders have relished contaminated sweets? They will no doubt ask you to do the same. Is this not shameful and disgusting? On top of this: Without using your own brain, you follow what these Babas say whether it is right or wrong or whether it is according to religion or not.*

*Take the story about a disciple who one day asked his guru: 'Baba, tell me whether my cow is pregnant or not'. 'Yes my son, she is', replied the guru without opening his eyes. The follower then asked: 'Baba, is my bull also pregnant?' 'Yes it is', was the reply. The pupil believed him. If such a thing is acceptable to you, then where religion is heading to? These babas, no doubt, will buy land for you in baikunth [heaven] at their own expense and allow you to live there. You know? History provides ample proof of great kings and rulers who gave up everything in the name of religion and have become immortal. None of these ever tried to purify and convert any Muslim to propagate the Sanatan Dharm. There have been several dignified sages and hermits who meditated for many years in the Himalayas and in this way put Sanatan Dharm on the top of the world, above all other religions. But alas, today the very offspring of these great men have plunged this religion into great depths instead of exalting it. It is very sad indeed.*

*During the reign of the Muslim Emperors, millions of Hindu brahmins, rajputs, kayasthas and vaishyas were either forced to convert or gladly accepted Islam out of greed, conviction, or due to circumstances. They could not be re-converted to Hinduism. They were never ever taken back into that fold. It is a well-known fact that Hindus may accept Islam, but it has never happened that a Muslim changed into a Hindu. The Sanatan Dharma leaders have started this tradition in Surinam and one cannot understand how they legitimize it. If there were any provision for this sort of thing in the vedas, why have the great-learned saints not followed it earlier? Why then did they not take back into their fold the millions of Muslims who had left Hinduism and preached about this possibility?*

*Only recently, Harilal[133], the son of world's famous leader and the soul of Bharat (i.e., Mahatma Gandhi) and the son of Lala Harkishun Lal[134] accepted Islam. Why could not the Pandits in Hindustan reconvert them to Hinduism? Why has this tradition been launched here in Surinam when there is already so much bitterness between the Hindus and Muslims? Since the coming of Hindustanis to Surinam this idea had been shelved in order not to disturb peace and communal harmony. Did these extremists not started all this now just to add fuel to the fire? It is disgraceful.*

*Since the last 50-60 years, actually since the arrival of the first Hindustanis here in Surinam, the two communities have been living in social harmony with each other in every aspect. Yet during the last one-and-a-half years, Hindus and Muslims have been antagonized and before the conflict between them could be solved, these reconversion rituals came up to increase tensions between the two communities. Both these two religious traditions are against such reconversions.*

*My dear brothers, tell me then, why this 'cleansing'? An act not described in the vedas, not known to the Sanatan saints, is performed to 'purify' Muslims. You know the people who are responsible for this and you know why they do this. I need not say much about it, because you failed to question the leaders of your community regarding this. Yet I was not able to keep quiet.*

*Whether one invites somebody or not is one's own wish, and Muslims have no business to condemn it. Yet why should I, having some knowledge of religious justice, Hindi, and the rules of the Sanatan Dharm refrain from using my pen against reconversion?*

*Only when I came to know about these reconversions that took place in the month of February, I started writing those two poems that condemned the act. The poems do not criticise any religion, rather protect them. I sent them to the Sanatan pandits in order to get a reply, which you should have provided. I wanted to know, which mantra could purify a Muslim and accordingly inform the elders of both religions where the roots are of these reconversions. The leaders and saints back home in Hindustan should know how staunch the Sanatanis are in Surinam and how they take Muslims back into their religion. If these Sanatanis could explain how their deeds are acceptable, then you were free to reconvert or purify anyone and in this way swell the population of Sanatanis. You could even make brahmins of sudras and sudras of brahmins like the Arya Samajis and no one would even dare to oppose you.*

*Well, this is all that I have to say. Now it is up to you to decide what should be done. Please forgive me if I have offended anyone, my intention was only to solve the problems in an amicable manner.*

*Signed: Munshi Rahman Khan, Dijkveld, Number 4*

When I discovered that on 22 February 1934 Sanatan Dharm *pandits*, in simular fashion as the Arya Samajis, had converted six Muslims to Hinduism by way of 'cleansing', I was astounded. One of the converts was a sex worker named Allarakhi while another was a pimp called Alladin. I then, on 24 February 1934, wrote down these two *chautals* [poetic sermons], which I sent to those Sanatan *pandits* who had been involved in these acts of reconversions everywhere in Surinam and questioned their deeds. I also planned to inform the *Shri Venkateshwar* in India and publish the reply of the *pandits* in this newspaper.

### *Chautal I*

*Which veda do you use to cleanse*
*Oh brahmin lot, you have no face*
*Despicable act shames you not, your religion you disgrace*
*Oh you do cleanse! You do cleanse.*
*In sam-, yajur-, ayur- and rig veda, there is no such sentence*
*It is not there in manusmriti, your false preaching is an offence*
*Oh you do cleanse! You do cleanse.*

*Proclaiming to be a religious preacher, into the air your hands you raise*
*You have not purified yourself but pronounce yourself a sage*
*Oh you do cleanse! You do cleanse.*
*You show yourself to be truly proficient in the vedas*
*Rahman says stop your evil ways: Hell is your end otherwise*
*Oh you do cleanse! You do cleanse.*

*Chautal II*

*You 'cleansed' the sinners, are you not ashamed?*
*By cleansing the sinners what have you gained?*
*Cow's flesh is in their body. How have you refined?*
*Are you not ashamed? Are you not ashamed?*
*To the wrong tradition of the society you have conformed*
*You blame others on top of it, why have you not drowned?*
*Are you not ashamed? Are you not ashamed?*
*By narrating kathas of gods to the polluted, a religious deed is achieved*
*By giving it to the untouchables, the Sanatan religion is being deceived*
*Are you not ashamed? Are you not ashamed?*
*This immoral act does not embarrass you; no goodness is disclosed*
*Rahman says your deed is false; no veda has thus been exposed*
*Are not ashamed? Are you not ashamed?*

## Talks with Pandit Paltanji regarding the 'Cleansing Ceremony'

After my return from Hansu, accompanied by Habibullah and Rahmullah, I once went to visit Karamat Ali who was ill. While returning, we met the Sanatan Mahamandal chairman Pandit Paltanji, Pandit Jadhunath, the Raja of Saramacca and two more *pandits* from either the Kwatta or 'Skopu' plantation [Mattonshoop]. These five important gentlemen were present in the residence of our *Bara Sahab* of the Immigration Department.

We greeted each other. Pandit Paltanji then asked me: '*Munshiji*, did you go to Hansu last week'. I nodded when he asked, 'did you attend a gathering there?' I replied: 'Indeed both Hindus and Muslims had assembled there'. Panditji then inquired, 'did you address them?' I told him that I had read out a religious note in the meeting. He nodded and said: 'Alright, we shall see later'. It now was my turn to question him: 'Panditji, what do you get by converting poor foolish Muslims who never even knew their own religion? You should have accepted a knowledgeable Muslim in your fold so that your fame and religion would increase in status. This is *Bara Sahab's* house and he enjoys more status than we, Hindostanis. Purify my sins here and show everyone which *vedic mantra* you use to achieve this'. The pandit then replied, 'through the conversion of illiterates I receive money and their services as well. What will I benefit from you?' To this I replied: 'Indeed, you get money by purifying the illiterate but if you convert me, I shall teach your children upto middle school and education is far more valuable than money. If you wish, I can recite the *brahmagayatri* or any of the twenty-four *gayatris* or the *gau mantra*, just name it. Cleanse me of my 'Muslimness' and make me a Hindu, or else accept Islam yourself, I can convert you'. To this Panditji said that it was not possible to purify me. I replied: 'Panditji, this is a wrong tradition, which you have initiated. It is against the *vedas* and your religion to do so, but you did not care and have done it only to earn money and to intensify the antagonism between the two communities. In the same way, you have divided the members of Bharat Uday[135] where the Muslims have now lost their rights. It has laid the foundation for an unjust act and has divided us. It is a malicious ploy that harms us'.[136] Saying this I bade them farewell and went home.

Ten days later, the chairman called me to attend a meeting at the Sanatan Mahamandal in 'Pulpangi' plantation [Poelepantje] where leaders and elders of the two warring communities would be present, to devise means to solve the controversies. I accepted the invitation.

## The Constitution of three Committees to resolve the Hindu-Muslim Crisis

The raging fire that had started in 1933 following the cow sacrifice (*kurbani*[137]) in Livorno had engulfed the whole of Surinam by 1934. When the day of Bakr-Id was nearing, the Hindus appealed to the government for a ban on cow sacrifice. Yet the court dismissed the plea saying that the act was admissible according to Islamic law. The Sanatanis were highly dissappointed. Hence, these Hindus had now decided to discuss the issue directly with the Muslims and formed a committee to talk with members of two Muslim Committees[138]. On the prearranged day, I took the letter, which I had read out in Hansu, and went to the meeting.

On Monday 21 March 1934, the letter was read out in the meeting of the Sanatanis. Members of the Anjuman Islam and the Hidayat Islam wanted to unite the two religious communities. There were many learned and wise men present in the gathering but no one gave any reply to my *chautals.* Finally secretary Shiv Narayanji stood up and told me that I would get an answer the following week. I acknowledged him. No leader from the Arya Samaj had attended this meeting and the Muslim chairman Ashgar Ali Sahab therefore asked chairman Pandit Paltanji as to why they had avoided the meeting as: 'How we can come to a solution without their presence?' Chairman Paltanji replied: 'The Arya Samaj is against us hence we did not invite them'. The talks then began between the elders but no satisfactory solution could be ascertained. Each committee had a proposal that was not acceptable to the other. The Muslims wanted the Hindus to withdraw the boycott first and let the two communities befriend each other once more as in that case, 'Your love will ban the slaying of cows'. The Hindus, however, demanded that the sacrifice be stopped first this year (1934), and the boycott would then be lifted the next year. It was 26 March and bakr-id would be celebrated only 5 days later. Neither Hindus nor Muslims were able to enact their declarations regarding the boycott or the sacrifice.

One may recall that the year before, in 1933, it had only be in Livorno that the Sanatanis had pressed for the boycott 9 months before Bakr-Id and the Muslims had answered this demand with a cow sacrifice that was permissible according to their laws. But after this sacrifice, the Sanatan leaders had propelled their agitation leading to a number of cow sacrifices later on as well. In 1934, the same rituals went on in several places as described earlier. However, during this more than 1 ½ year period, the Arya Samaj had taken up no anti-Muslim activities. It had just been the Sanatanis who had been responsible for all the misdeeds. This year however, the Arya Samajis decided to support the Sanatanis' moves.

## The Boycott of 1934

(Or: How the Arya Samajis and Sanatanis dealt with the Muslims)

Someone has rightfully said once:

*A flower, unable to bear its own weight when it gets wet and becomes heavier, asks for help to be planted firmly in the ground.*

Babu Heerasinghji was the chairman of the Arya Diwakar founded by the Arya Samaj in Surinam. When the Sanatanis failed to thwart the cow sacrifice in 1934, they decided to seek support from the Arya Samaj. The society that Pandit Paltanji resorted to on March 28, 1934 received him with open arms. The staunch Sanatanis were transformed into rats and they fell prey to the cat-like Arya Samaj. I regretfully have to state that Pandit Shiv Narayanji who had appealed to all the Hindostanis of Surinam in an article published in the *Sri Venkateshwar* newspaper of 10 November 1933, to be cautious of the Arya Samaj, now took back his words without any shame. Pandit Kaluram Shastri, Pandit Alakhlanandji and poet Ratanji, who had written scores of books on the Sanatan religion and had condemned the Arya Samaj earlier, now also shamelessly sought refuge in the Arya Samaj itself. They had been transformed from a lion to a goat and should have drowned themselves in a handful of water![139] When the two societies met together, they organised a huge convention on 1 April 1934 at the Arya Diwakar and passed an eleven-point resolution against the Muslims. Namely:

1. Stop all business dealings with Muslims.
2. Stop greeting each other.
3. Cease giving and receiving invitations from them.
4. Refrain from sharing water from the same well.
5. Stop talking to them.
6. Hindu women should discontinue help in Muslim delivery cases.
7. Avoid giving alms to Muslim beggars and saints.
8. Make Hindu beggars refuse alms from Muslims.
9. Stop visiting Muslim homes.
10. Prevent Hindus and Muslims from walking in each other's death processions.
11. Do not allow Muslims to partake in the last rites of a Hindu.

These rules were to be strictly followed.

This severe boycott shook the whole nation and created a vast turbulence in the society. The Hindus strictly adhered to the commandments and were harshly punished if they did not.

## The Hindu Bazaar

The Hindu leaders of Surinam had thus decided to oppress the Muslim minority and to share prosperity only among each other. They bought a large plot of land in Paramaribo away from the government shopping mall for 24000 rupees. Without obtaining permission from the government, they then laid the foundation of a market solely meant for Hindus. The bazaar was ready and equipped within one night and early next morning it was opened for everyone except the Muslims. This was another drastic step and showed how united the Hindus were!

But alas, it was not to be. The government took notice of this and sent the police to tackle the situation. The police then began distributing *prasad* [here: beatings] with such a severity that the people at the receiving end would remember them throughout life. The whole bazaar was pulled down in no time. The government refused to admit any appeal from the Hindu leaders and they were thus unable to enforce their eleven-point prohibitions.[140]

There is a saying:

*Land is looted and property is lost. Everything is seized*
*While she cried for her son, the husband died*

Another saying goes:

*Plucking away the hairs will not make the corpse any lighter*

Except for broken hearts and severed ties, the boycott did not affect the Muslims. There were some Hindus however who did not heed to this ban and continued to be close with Muslims.Yet, the overall trust between the two communities, as well as among the members of the same community had vanished. The anti-religious greedy leaders, who made money out of the situation, consumed the sweet fruits of the division during the following 4-5 years. Yet when the golden egg-laying hen was gone, these men became a sorry lot. Cooking in a wooden utensil can only be done once! Afer some time, people stopped donating money to these leaders because they realized they had wasted their hard-earned cash on these leaders who were only involved in merrymaking and were living luxuriously. The public had to bear a heavy loss.

Mehta Jaiminiji had laid the foundation of this great divide in 1929[141]. In 1934, Pandit Ayodhiya Prasadji (B.A.) came to Surinam and fully destroyed the already blemished image of the Sanatanis during the convention held at the Arya Diwakar. During that meeting a stampede had ensued and the Sanatan leaders had been beaten up with sticks. When they had no way to escape, they tried to crawl beneath the wired fence and thus received scratches and bruises, which kept their memories alive. In order to discuss religious matters, the Sanatanis had gone to attend the huge gathering, which had assembled in the Arya Diwakar that evening. Seat- and lighting arrangements had been made to facilitate the proceedings. Yet when Pandit Ayodhiya Prasad turned to address Shrikantji, the lights were dimmed and in darkness, the Arya Samajis did beat up the Sanatanis. This caused a stampede in the premises. The Sanatanis were now enlightened but it took a lot to rectify their acts. Again in 1935, Pandit Satyacharan Shastriji (M.A.) visited Surinam. His deliberations only benefited him and no one else. The people who listened to his lectures became even more divided. In 1936, an Arya Samaj lady named Mahadei Devi, wife of Ramprasad Gosai, personally invited an Arya teacher from *Bharat* to educate the Hindustanis in Surinam. The teacher, Pandit Bhashkaranandji (H.L) was paid 45 pounds for his fare. Yet his tenure here bore no fruit because the divided society of Surinam could not set up a school as required. Finally the poor Pandit had to collect his belongings and flee to British Guyana where he became a successful teacher. The people there were united and within 1 ½ year, a college was built to serve the purpose. It was the result of unity and harmony within the society there. But alas, no Hindi teaching school could flourish in Surinam. Only the religious leaders of Surinam were to blame for this.

After these gentlemen, the representatives of Sanatan Dharm met in Lahore and sent Dr. Pandit Parshuramji Sharma to Trinidad to deliver lectures. His talks had a commendable influence on the people there. Upliftment of religion and motivation for education was achieved in Trinidad. The staunch Sanatan elders then invited Pandit Parshuram to Surinam. Panditji arrived by ship on 9 June 1938. He stayed here for 6 weeks and addressed several gatherings in various places. Everywhere, he laid emphasis on unity, the teaching of Hindi and the correction of religious practices. He asked every-one to denounce a non-vegetarian diet, refrain from alcohol as well as tobacco and give up other harmful habits. A few resolutions were made and the people responded accordingly.

However, it is a well-known fact that a leech cannot hold on to a rock and no sooner had Pandit Parshuram departed, all went back to square one. All his efforts proved futile and his preachings were forgotten. Tulsidas has written in the Ramayan that whatever amount of affection you shower on a crow, he shall not stop eating meat.

The same was the case with these fraud leaders. All the demerits and evil properties of the unholy mentioned in the Hindu scriptures, which were to be displayed in kaliyug had come to the fore. During Pandit Parshuram's visit, a few gentlemen had requested him to initiate a peace talk for the unification of Hindus and Muslims in Surinam. He agreed initially, but when the Muslim leaders approached him for talks, he did not say a word regarding this. Some people had brainwashed him. Those who had tried to resolve the matter were disappointed and the animosity prevailed. The more the medication, the more the disease; O, what a pity!

## Maulvi Sahab's Letter

**(786)**
*Date: 13 September 1934.*
*From: The Jamaat in Livorno*
*To: Janab Mir Maulana Haji Amir Ali Sahab*
*Subject: Invitation to lay the foundation of a Masjid in Beekhuizen*
*By Allah's grandeur, Haji Amir receives a certificate of appreciation*

*Adhar*

*Khalik is the true creator, Rasul, the world's designer*
*Holy Koran, the true scripture, enlightens the true believer*
*True friends are four in this world, the true believer longs for heaven*
*King to commoner, commoner to King, the Lord transforms the men*
*O those who praise Khalik, heaven awaits his dear ones*
*Those who bow before him can withstand the hard times*
*The man who treats Khalik as his own is owned likewise by him*
*A true servant who does service, Khalik gives him freedom*

*Chaupai*

*Nature is all Allah's; man is nothing but water*
*Denounce all sins and contentment will be all over*
*The operator of this world has created the sky*
*Glorify the Lord! The earth lives in agony*
*Nature does not exalt man, but praises the Lord*
*Man is sinful and corrupt, immaculate is God*

*Nabi, Allah's companion, is a true Muslim*
*It would be proper for the Muslims to read and greet him*

## A Request to Janab Mir Maulan Haji Amir Ali

### *Chaupai*

*First accept my greetings, next tell me how you are*
*This is what I have to pen, please try to rid the ire*
*My third sincere request is, to pardon my misconstructing*
*A star rose from Trinidad, and lightened up its surrounding*
*Called Holy Amir Ali, is wiser than the rest*
*The mother be acclaimed, and the birth be blessed*
*Bless the father who taught him, but was allured to a foreign country*
*Thank Khuda my friend, and reap Islam's fruit of divinity*

### *Doha*

*May the Lord bless you everyday, and your stores may he fill*
*May he provide you in abundance, knowledge, courage and skill!*

### *Chaupai*

*Sixty years of leaving India, we never met Wali*[142]
*We waited for so long, and kept our eyes on the street*
*Fortunately today, the Lord's dearest shall we see*
*Our eyes shall be satisfied when through our door you make entry*
*Your presence will be an honour, the birds shall merrily sing*
*Mothers and fathers shall pray, may the heaven God bring*
*We also pray to Khuda, to make you more wise and intelligent*
*May you be blessed with worthy children, God-fearing and obedient!*
*May prosperity be showered upon you, and Khuda show his kindness!*
*I have no tongue to praise, cannot sing to your bounding greatness*

### *Doha*

*Everyday your brightness shines through your brow*
*As nobody keeps red colour of Mehndi in a platter now*
*You are the fountain of knowledge; I have only that one tear*
*To show a lamp to the Sun is no voluntary act*
*You are serene as the Moon; I am like a rough terrain*
*How can I be equal? You are Ali; I am Khan*

*You stand in the Lord's presence, like the number 63*
*Taking me to be just 36, quickly set me free.*[143]

### *Chaupai*

*We brothers greet you with folded hands amass*
*Your stepping here has been so soothing to our eyes*
*You have travelled so far; we are filled with gratitude*
*For the trouble that you have taken, the Lord shall do the good*
*You have indebted us. May Allah bestow Paradise!*
*How well can we honor you, our ability is so small in size*
*We are poor and futile, have nothing to offer*
*Whatever you give us, Rabb will pay you later*
*This is all we wish, to hear how Rabb instructs to walk*
*The darkness of our minds, be enlightened by your talk*

### *Doha*

*We are the poorest of the poor, you the provider of all*
*Our boat is in a whirlpool and in distress and we utter the saviour's call*
*We are lost in a dark well, and have forgotten Islam*
*You are our support and refuge, shine on and enlighten*
*Without knowledge and wisdom, we have been misled*
*In Allah's name do show us, in which way one should tread*

### *Chaupai*

*This is to request you sincerely, to our plea do kindly heed*
*We have been separated from friends and Khuda by our deed*
*Such Muslims do reside here, who have no fear of the Almighty*
*Befriending the enemy, chop their comrades' head aplenty*

*They play foul every moment, and push Islam to the nadir*
*They overlooked Khuda's affection, Rabb has stamped them kafir*
*Cannot tolerate Islam being harmed, think something O wise one*
*Please give some mantra, to end the vain collision*
*Do something effective, for others' and Islam's unison*

### *Doha*

*Enemity, jealousy, and malice prevail among us*
*According to the scriptures, erase these without fail*
*Those who listen to Khalik's sayings with intent*
*Make us understand the message of enlightment*

### *Chaupai*

*Listen all you Muslims, carefully, to what Maulana*[144] *has to say*
*Beware, do not interrupt but remain seated, I pray*
*Then you shall hear God's will, your eyes shall be opened*
*If one wishes to speak, ask Maulana for his permission*
*When you are allowed, say something sensible*
*Futile argument will not work; Koran's word is able*
*Speak nothing falsely to increase the animosity*
*Give an attentive listening to Mir's ministry*
*Accept the Maulana's preaching and imbibe it in your soul*
*With this I end my request, says Rahman to all*

### *Chaupai*

*Not wise, not strong, nor clever a gentleman*
*Not rich, nor virtuous is the writer Rahman*
*I bow and beseech sincerely, to the whole congregation*
*Please pardon my mistakes! I seek our reformation*[145]

## The Responsibilities of the Sanatan Leaders

I request you gentlemen to kindly read and understand how the *brahmins* of Surinam planned to destroy the peace and harmony among the Hindus and Muslims and fuelled the hostility. A poet has truly said:

*Milk is sold mixed with water*
*But their friendships is much shorter*
*They immediately separate at the hour*
*When the milk gets really sour*

Tulsidas has also said:

*Where there is knowledge all goes well*
*Ignorance leads to hell!*

*Date: 24 February 1934*

*Dear Gentlemen,*

*Sukhnandan (whose son Sukhdeo I had taught) informed me on 22 February 1934 that pandits had converted six Muslims to the Sanatan Dharm. Of these six, one was Allahrakhi, a sex worker and another was her pimp, Alladin. Pandit Ramanand of Skropuholo, a leader of the Sanatan Dharm Mahamandal, had carried out the cleansing. What a shameful act! To accept such people in one's community is abominable. The one who does this, not only offends his religion, but also treads on a path which leads to hell and has no way to rid himself of this sin. This is because the brahmin who allows a low caste person to perform rituals like gurumukh, or om, or yagna, himself is transformed into a sudra [low caste], and the sudra becomes a brahmin and is entitled to all the rights of a brahmin. The slokas in vridhparashar and those in atrmadhvacharya confirm this.*

Similar accounts are aplenty and writing about all would be a long and tedious procedure. *A good horse needs only a single whip and a clever man only one clue.*

Many such incidences of reconversion were accomplished by this anti-*veda*, riot-fuelling *pandits* in different places. To correct and teach these *pandits*, I had written to them right in time (February) and asked them to reply to my two *chautals*. No religion was disgraced in these letters. Instead, I had taken care to protect the two religions. My intention was to send their reply to Hindustan so that people back home could learn how the staunch Sanatanis of Surinam have followed their religion; how they have spread their holy religion by these conversions and what their thoughts and deeds are; how they let the Muslims perform *pujas* to their holy deities and heavenly bodies and disgrace them. If someone in our homeland were to prove that there indeed is a *veda-mantra* in the Sanatan Dharm that sanctions this cleansing and convertion, I shall accept it. In that case you can even change a *brahmin* into a *sudra* and vice versa like the Arya Samajis are doing, and spread a foul belief. Nobody would question you in that case. I have said whatever I wanted to and you may do what you think proper. On 24 February 1934, I wrote two *chautals* and sent them to different *pandits* all over Surinam seeking a reply regarding these activities. In these *chautals* I have proven that these acts of conversion are against the spirit of the *vedas*. None of the *vedas* does sanction such so-called purification rites.[146]

## Debate with Priest Ramnarayan Mishra

The following is a talk between Munshi Rahman Khan and the Sanatan Dharm priest Ramnarayan Mishra with regard to the false teachings and misdeeds of the staunch Sanatan *pandits* in Surinam who were not acting according to the *vedshastras*. No *pandit* gave any reply to my *chautals* during the first year. Then, after a year, on 5 March 1935, Mantri Shivnarayanji's younger brother Ramnarayan (a religious preacher) replied and sent the two following *chautals*, which however contain no answer to my queries:

### *Ramnarayan's Chautal I*

*Listen you sardar, this conversion shall continue*
*A preacher's work is to do this harangue*
*A sermon clears the insight and opens the door to truth*
*Conversions are here to continue.*
*Flesh does not purify, I sanitise one's erudition*
*Man is born in this world to spread his own religion*
*Conversions are here to continue.*
*Those who have lost their own religion I retrieve*
*Come to my shelter Mian, pray my saying, believe*
*Conversions are here to continue.*
*Your writing proves your ignorance of the shastras and ved*
*Your intellect has forsaken you. Ramnarayan does feel you degrade*
*Conversions are here to continue.*

### *Ramnarayan's Chautal II*

*You have bit the dust in poetry, O brother of a poet*
*I shall convert brothers of our clan and not evade*
*To tell others to revert back to their original faith*
*O brother of a poet.*
*When this act hurts you, you then began writing*
*Are you not t ashamed? Whom are we offending,*
*O brother of a poet?*
*Who acts in haste, later feels sorry*
*Your misdoings I forgive, this poem thus reveals*
*O brother of a poet.*
*Ramnarayan hereby sends your writings' interest*

*The principal sum will be given when we intersect*
*O brother of a poet.*
*Signed: Ramnarayan Mishra*

## A Sermon for Preacher Ramnarayan Mishra

I immediately wrote down my reply and sent it on 6 March 1935 through Sukhnandan who had brought Ramnarayan's letter with these two *chautals* to me.

### *Chautal I*

*How do you call yourself a vipr [brahmin]? Tell me how you claim?*
*The brahmin is supreme among the four castes, the vedas do proclaim*
*Who is virtuous in this way? You make a living of the sudras who you call low*
*Let me know.*
*Which shastra tells you to impart gita to a donkey?*
*On top of it you call yourself a preacher, fear you have no(ne)?Let me know.*
*Where did you learn to drink liquor and eat meat?*
*Abandoning righteousness each evening, you uselessly conceit*
*Let me know.*
*Where is it written that r a Brahmin should serve an ass each morning?*
*Rahman says your misdeeds have pushed the Shastras to mourning*
*Let me know.*

### *Chautal II*

*You unnessesaryily taint your religion, a brahmin's body you own*
*Sanatan faith is holy, the vedas do acclaim*
*Tampering with the shastras does not cause you shame*
*Brahmin's body you own.*
*Everyday you sell cow milk while singing*
*Selling cows for benefit, which veda does permit?*
*Brahmin's body you own.*
*A brahmin turns into a shudra if he kisses one, says manusmriti*
*How do you transform a shudra into a brahmin's sanskriti?*
*Brahmin's body you own.*
*Despicable acts you daily do, works of a butcher you perform*
*Rahman mocks at your chastity, where has your virtue gone?*

*Brahmin's body you own.*

*I disappointedly state that you are not even competent to hold a pen and have projected yourself as a poet. It is very shameful.*
*Signed: Munshi Rahman Khan, Dijkveld Number 4.*

Eleven days later, Ramnaryan Mishra sent the following four chautals through Sukhnandan. He had deliberated with several Sanatan Pandits and then prepared them. (They were a sorry lot on reading my reply).

Now everyone must be aware that each letter of mine bore a date while Ramnarayanji did neither bother to mention the date, nor did he care to write a word of greeting. Moreover, his chautals contained a number of errors and he claimed himself to be an intellectual.

Ramayan Mishra sent the following four chautals:

### *Chautal 1*

*The shastras explain the meaning of brahmin. Thus listen carefully.*
*Brahmins are superior amongst the four castes, guru and brother of a Muslim*
*I always do the right thing, but will not go to your house willingly*
*Listen carefully.*
*To give and take donations, brother, to learn and to teach*
*Since long I have been performing yags, have prayed and will preach*
*Listen carefully.*
*Where have you seen the gita, being taught to an idiot?*
*If you are a true Muslim, tell me when and prove it*
*Listen carefully.*
*Which day did I drink (alcohol), that you allege to save yourself?*
*Ramnarayana condemns you for fabricating and folly*
*Listen carefully.*

### *Chautal 2*

*You uselessly make hue and cry, a Muslim body you possess.*
*Believe in the Sanatana religion, your salvation lies herein*
*Or else you will waste your entire life, in the dark well of sin*
*A Muslim body you possess.*

*Objectionable writings are there, in the vedas and manushastra brother*
*Which you chanced to see, are you not ashamed to pen it down further?*
*A Muslim body you possess.*
*Where has manu mentioned, that a kiss can turn a brahmin into a shudra?*
*It is shocking and dangerous. Have you not a little wisdom brother?*
*A Muslim body you possess.*
*Ramnarayana does perform, works of a high caste, brother*
*If Rahman accepts shruti, he shall be praised forever*
*A Muslim body you possess.*

*(Warning)*

*With regret I wish to state that you designate yourself as Munshi, but you seem to be more like a moron. I challenge you to prove your statement that I have proclaimed myself to be the brother of a poet in an institution. If you cannot explain this allegation, you must apologise for telling a lie.*

## *Chautal 3*

*Listen O Muslim, Rahman, say that you are sorry*
*Each day I beat Muslims like you to dust*
*How dare you write such letters?*
*To tell me is a must*

*Say that you are sorry.*
*'Munshi' you write in front of your name without shame*
*I think I must have got the meaning wrong or else*
*How you idiot can make such a claim?*
*Say that you are sorry.*
*Where in the Koran is it written, that you can keep donkeys?*
*On top of it you claim to be a maulvi.*
*Take poison or drown into the deep*
*Say that you are sorry.*
*Why did you not complain, when one of your relatives was cleansed?*
*Ramnarayan does condemn you, for writing now unashamed*
*Say that you are sorry.*

*Chautal 4*

*You are at fault and do say so.*
*Where in the Koran is it drafted, that cow's flesh you may eat?*
*In which chapter is it mentioned, truly tell me about it*
*Do say so.*

*(Dangerous Challenge)*

*If you have even a bit of truth in you and are learned, come forward and accept that the shastras do indeed describe the process of cleansing. If you have the guts, call a meeting and clear your doubts.*

*Written by: Ramnarayan Mishra.*

When I received this letter on 17 March 1935 through Sukhnandan, I immediately replied to every word of it and sent it by the same person on 19 March 1935 to preacher Ramnarayan Mishra. The following lines demonstrate my ability to give a striking answer to those idiots who never again dared to write back to me.

## My stunning Reply to Priest Ramnarayan Mishra

*Date: 19 March 1935*

*My greetings to Reverend Ramnarayanji,*

*You may recall that about a year back on 21 March 1934, the Sanatani religious leaders and members of both Muslim factions met at the headquarters of the Sanatan Dharm located at the Koningstraat in Poelepantje. They had gathered there to try and reconcile their differences and become one society once again. That time no Arya Samaji had come to attend the meeting. Our chairman Asghar Ali Sahab asked chairman Paltanji as to why nobody from the Arya Samaj had come. Paltanji had replied that the Arya Samajis were their enemies and therefore had not been called for the meeting.*

*On 26 March 1934, the day of sacrifice (bakr-id), the Hindus and Muslims had e still not reached a compromise. I read out a letter during the meeting in which I gave a detailed explanation of how and why the animosity had been seeded. I asked these Sanatanis to reply to my verses (two chautals) according to the scriptures. I said that I would send their answer regarding the mantras back to Hindustan from where both the religions have emanated. Only after a clarification from there, would I believe that a Muslim could be converted into a Hindu.*

*Many renowned and wise pandits were present on the occasion but none of them said anything. Later, Mantri Shivnarayan Singh told me that he would give me a reply a week later. I had agreed to that. A year has passed since the meeting and his younger brother preacher Ramnarayanji now sends me an absurd reply, which contains no answer to my two chautals. To keep quiet for a year and then rekindle a fire is the work of a fool.*

*The newspaper Sri Venkateshwar of 18 January 1935 contains an article written by Nandkishore of Nickerie. He stated: 'It is a matter of great shame that you have been behaving like an evil spirit and at the same time, trying to be a Sanatani. These men cannot be regarded as religious'. I read out this citation in the midst of all the great religious leaders and got no reply or comment. Why should I again attend a convention of good-for-nothing men and defame myself? I have experienced your righteousness during a whole year. All our papers and letters should be sent to Hindustan to decide and settle right from wrong. It is better to keep silent than to talk to foolish people like you.*

*Doha*

*If fools speak, remain tight-lipped*
*Too much talking will turn you dim-witted*

## Who is a *Brahmin*?

I continued my letter to Ramnarayan Mishra in the following way:

*Sloka*[147]

*Brahmins should desist offerings and sustain their purity.*
*They should forgive others their incivility.*

*You write that I have misinterpreted the books, but I disagree with you. Not me but you have got it all wrong. You have become an ass by serving them for a long time. I am not a poet and am not good enough to be one, but you have designated me as one and have written in the second chautal of your first letter 'Ramnarayan bhai hereby sends your writing interest'.*[148] *Tell me, have you not called (as credit) yourself a brother of a poet? Since payment has not been settled as yet, why are you ashamed of writing so?*

*In the first chautal of your second letter you wrote: 'Guru, brother of a Muslim. What does this mean? Does it mean that your guru is a Muslim's brother? Or, that you are a Muslim's guru? Blessed be you sharp intellect. If your guru is a Muslim's brother, then a Muslim becomes your guru too. You now better keep quiet.*

*In your four chautals you have written: 'Brother to learn and teach', 'brother in the manushastras', 'you know nothing brother', etc. Now let me know how many brothers you made and who they are. It means you use 'brother' only to rhyme a poem and it serves no other purpose. I condemn you for writing such a poem.*

*In my chautal I have said: 'Rahman understands your shruti'. I could comprehend your interpretation of the shruti but now know that you are too ignorant to see the point of my verses. What to do with such a stupid fellow like you! My question was: 'Where has your virtue gone'. This is sarcasm and not a compliment as you think.*

### *Chaupai*

*A frog in a well believes he is all-knowing*
*Does not understand the ocean is never ending*
*You claim to be a brahmin but are ignorant of the meaning of vipr it seems*
*You do not bow and thus do not understand your own language it means*

### *Doha*

*The professional is sure about his aptitudes*
*The amateur is without these attributes*
*If you give nutmeg to a bull*
*He would look at you like a fool*

## Preacher, open your Eyes!

I then wrote in my letter to Ramnarayan Mishra:

### *Chaupai*

*Everybody understands the word munshi*
*Without knowledge nobody can write*
*I therefore will explain the meaning of the word*

*As you all know me, and I have nothing to hide*
*The next seven generations cannot equal the design of the calender I made*
*Even in your next birth*
*You will not create a book like this*
*You cannot match my verses and poems*
*Tell me which defects did you find in them?*
*As long as a camel has not reached the top of the mountain*
*He thinks it is easy to be praised.*[149]
*Your sharp and hurtful tongue reveals your lowly birth*

### Doha

*What will a guru do when his own disciple is imperfect?*
*He plays the flute but does not make music*
*Without the advice of a guru*
*You are like a roaming bull*

*(Now abstain from misdemeanor)*

*As far as the allegation of your drinking is concerned, do not worry. I not only have proof of your drinking but also evidence that you have brewed alcoholic beverages. It will be better therefore that you admit your fault and tender an apology. I have heard you reciting the lessons of the gita and the mantras of the Hanuman chalisa while travelling on an ass-driven cart. I request you to refrain from such activities of contempt for the holy words.*

### Chaupai

*After marriage, the woman belongs to another family*
*The lineage line is through sons and not influenced by daughters*
*You have wrongly stated that there is an adulterous woman in my family*
*And if there would not be a bad Muslim woman in your family*
*Who then would look after you?*
*Such a woman lives in your family*
*Do you not feel ashamed to write about her?*
*As you look after a donkey every day you have got its mind*
*Your intelligence depends on your company*
*Only donkeys can be purified*

*Doha*

*If nobody follows the path, what is its use?*
*You have lost direction and have become a drifter*
*In order to win the battle, you call the name of Ram*
*Roaming around like a bull in human cloths.*[150]

*Note*

*In Livorno, one of my son's sisters-in-law (one of Nirhu's daughters) was characterless and unpopular since her adolescence. Though Nirhu (son's father-in-law) had married her off, she had continued her illicit love affairs and finally ran away with a Hindu boy. This was during the period of the boycott and she got married in the Arya Samaj mandir and was there 'purified'. Nirhu could not be blamed. From that day onwards, Nirhu and the rest of the family debarred her from entering the house and she was treated as dead. Ramnarayan referred to this girl in his chautal when he wrote: 'Why did you not complain, when one of your relatives was cleansed?' In my answer I referred to the fact that during the boycott, a Muslim widow lived in Poelepantje with her disabled son. Ramnarayan's elder brother, Shivnarayan had developed illicit relations with her and had annexed all her property and had put it in his name. He then brought her to his house in Dijkveld where she died and after some time, her son also expired. By referring to her I could beat Ramnarayan with his own weapons.*

## Drown yourself!

I further wrote to Ramnarayan Mishra:

*On 26 March 1934, cows were sacrified in Ayodhyapuri (the town of Shri Ramchandra) [in India] and riots broke out between the Hindus and Muslims there. Many people were injured, some succumbed, some survived. Shops belonging to Muslims were looted and their houses were burnt. Cases were lodged with the government. In a land with 20 crore Sanatanis, the minority Muslim population had won their struggle against them because the Holy Koran of Khuda does allow cow sacrifice. The erring Hindus were fined Rs. 85000, of which 45000 were for investigation and employing justice while the rest was distributed among the poor Muslims who had suffered. This court ruling against the wrongdoers was published in the Sri Venkateshwar on 11 January 1935 in Bombay. Those who are doubtful may consult the newspaper.*

### *Chaupai*

*On Monday 26 March 1934, Muslims assembled in thousands*
*To celebrate a Muslim festival in Ayodhyapuri*
*When kurbani took place in the Masjid and beef was eaten*
*Hindus paid a fine of 85.000 rupees*
*Allah is powerful and brahmins were defeated*
*If the Koran would not have endorsed this*
*We would have been defeated*
*See the greatness of Allah:*
*We proved a little too strong and won*
*Muslims drink liquor. They eat meat and ghee*
*Brahmins drink milk and go to heaven*
*Hindus think: Muslims eat meat and we not*
*This is the cause of jealousy*
*The Koran does not forbid trade*
*Blood is haram*[151] *and meat is halal*[152]
*The Koran sanctions the consumption of beef*
*Without blood there is no production of milk*
*Then why do you all drink milk?*
*Every day you must be reading the newspapers*
*Did you ever see Muslims give way?*
*There is nobody as stupid as you in this wide world*
*You have two eyes but still are blind*
*A useless son like you is born for nothing*
*Without doing any work still want to be praised*
*For that reason I advice you:*
*Convert to Islam and listen to what the Koran has to say*

## Come Preacher purify me

*I am glad that you have offered to cleanse me. I sincerely wish to observe how you purify a Muslim because I have already mentioned in the third stanza of my first chautal that a Muslim cannot be purified as you are yourself unclean since your birth and along with you your whole family is immersed in the ocean of sin. How then can you get rid of the impurities of others?*

*Read what Manu Maharaj (chapter 11, sloka 91, p.394) has said:*

*If brahmins, kshatriyas and vaishas by mistake consume liquor then they can only purify themselves by burning their body using the same liquor. In that case they will be absolved of their sins.*

*God Vrihaspati, Guru of 33 crore of Gods says the same.*

*Again read what is stated in the manusmriti (chapter 11, sloka 98, p.395):*

*If a brahmin consumes liquor, he changes in a sudra. Therefore he should not drink liquor.*

### *Chautal I*

*Oh brother Narainji, you write about purification*
*Though everybody knows about your life history*
*Everybody knows about your religion and to which caste you belong*
*You cannot hide your shortcomings*
*I am from real Hind and have not changed my name*[153]
*How can you call yourself genuine?*
*If the vedas have already discarded you*
*Please recite your twenty-four gayatri mantras*
*And also let me know the gow- mantras*
*You should then tell me the difference*
*My body is slightly deformed*[154]
*This is however my only defect*
*If you can rectify my deformity*
*I will call you my real father and brother*

## Come and embrace Islam Panditji!

### *Chautal II*

*Dear Narayanji, believe my words and accept my religion*
*No saintly people can change the fact that Islam is a world religion*
*Purification ceremonies are not described in the vedas*
*Deeply reflect and accept Islam*
*This will show you a way out of the darkness*
*Stop your idol worshipping*
*If you keep Mohammed in your heart*
*He will forgive all your sins*
*Those Hindus who have converted to Islam*
*Never reverted to Sanatan Dharm*
*Rahman says there still is time*
*To bring order in your life*

*This letter to Ramnarayan Mishra was written by:*
*Munshi Rahman Khan*

All this was written by me, Munshi Rahman Khan on 19 March 1935 and everybody should know that since the day of dispatching the above letter, to Ramnarayanji, no reply has ever come from his end. From that day onwards, those *pandits* kept quiet. I had planned to send this following *chautal* to them if they ever dared to reply.

### *Last Chautal*

*The Muslims are mighty and defeated the brahmins*
*You gossip the whole day*
*Yet when you have to be your own man*
*You swallow your pride*
*All the time you have been doing nothing*
*Except spreading gossips and accusing me*
*With only one letter of mine*
*Your wisdom vanished and your strength broke in pieces*
*After reading the book written by Nathuram*
*You claim to be a pandit*
*But when religion is discussed*
*You have no answers*
*Though you remain silent on matters of religion*
*You do not confess your defeat*
*Rahman says: accept my humility, I will spread your fame*

## End of the Boycott against Muslims

Today, I would like to thank the formless Lord of all forms, the Brahma, on behalf of the Hindus and Muslims for his creations, for the world and its contents, the different races of mankind and the web of *maya* in which we all are entangled. He finally performed his duty of conservation and by his grace the dark and tragic period of Surinam (the boycott which started in Livorno), came to an end on the 5 May 1943. After 10 long and gloomy years, the Hindus and Muslims came together again through several meetings. Government officers were also present during these talks of reconciliation.

However, not all the stains were wiped off, as salt in *daal* does not spread evenly either. I earnestly hope that soon the day will arrive when there shall be no remnants of an unhappy past anymore and when everyone would hoist a flag of peace and love.

### *Doha*

*They tried to boycott us by all means and troubled us a lot*
*Yet no harm was done to Islam.*
*The Almighty protects the one who is true to his religion.*

## Prayer to God

*God is shapeless and acts without using His hand, feet, eyes or ears.*
*He roams all over the world without feet on the ground.*
*The one who does not recognize such a God is blind.*
*God is shapeless so we cannot see Him.*
*We do not have such power to see His qualities.*
*But we bow before Him in due respect.*
*He has created this world, the earth and the sky.*
*The ones who ignore such Being are a depressed lot.*
*He is the conquerer of evil but generous and kind.*
*A true follower of God who feels dejected*
*Can find solace from God and the Koran.*

## Poem written in praise of Maharani Queen Wilhelmina Sahab Bahadur[155]

*You are most loveable, caring and god loving.*
*Your fame is spread the world over.*
*You are great.*
*You are from Holland and symbol of the Goddess.*
*We Hindostanis look upon you for your kindness and blessings.*
*You are a storehouse of knowledge, brains and strength.*
*The light emanating from you is enough to blacken the face of Hitler.*
*You are blessed by the Supreme and have always remained the winner.*
*I pray to God to keep you healthy for many years to come*
*May your possessions remain never-ending!*
*I am not well equipped to praise your fame*
*I bow my head and expect your blessings.*
*Be kind to the people of your Kingdom*
*Let God bless you and your family.*

I present this document to commissioner Hagen Sahab Bahadur on behalf of the people of Livorno and Dijkveld. With thanks to the respected commissaris Hagen Sahab Bahadur and other officials.[156]

Date: 28 September 1945

Signature:
Munshi Rahman
Dijkveld No. 4
Surinam
Dutch Guyana
South America

# Endnotes

1. *Bismillah-hir-Rahman-ir Rahim.* Rahman Khan often starts his writing with these lines or with the numbers 786, which refer to the weight of the above letters in the Arabic script.
2. This is an area near, and now a suburb of, the capital of Surinam, Paramaribo. Rahman Khan's house there does not exist anymore and the new address is: 79 Sir Winston Churchillweg.
3. This was written in the form of a *doha.* Actually, Rahman Khan had kept a diary and this autobiography is a result of his selection of his own writings, some of which were written before 1943 and others a little later. The last writings that he included were written in the year 1945.
4. Rahman Khan mostly uses the words 'Hind' or 'Hindustan' when he refers to what is presently known as India. At times, he uses the word 'Bharat' in similar vein.
5. His five sons were (from the eldest to the youngest): Suleman Khan, Karamat Khan, Dildar Khan, Chotekhan and Faiz Khan.
6. Also written as 'Sura Fatiha',which is the first chapter of the Koran.
7. Songs of praise to the Prophet Mohammed recited in the form of *du'a* (supplication) as well as obligatory prayers (*namaz*).
8. Rahman Khan has included some verses here, which more or less repeat the same message as in the prose but in different form. The first one is a prayer to Allah (God). The second *doha* is a request to the readers. There is also a *chaupai* with apologies to the reader. In another *doha* and *chaupai* he explains why and how he has written his life history. In the last *doha* Rahman thanks his favourite student named Mangruram whose father was called Jungliram and who lived in Livorno. Rahman Khan recognizes the help he has received from Mangal Dev Jungli alias Mangruram, alias Jungli Kaka. One of us interviewed 'Jungli Kaka' (a *pandit* aged 78) on 1 July 2003 in The Hague (the Netherlands) [see photograph]. Jungli was full of praise about Rahman Khan and he could recite many of Rahman's poems. Rahman Khan had gifted him the Ramayana and Jungli said that Rahman never crititized any religion. Jungli Kaka also believed that Mahatma Gandhi used to write letters to Rahman Khan. He narrated that Rahman Khan used

to get books from one Ram Naresh Tripathi of Allahabad. It was through this Tripathi that Gandhiji came to know about Rahman Khan. According to Jungli Kaka, Gandhiji had written to Rahman Khan: 'How is it possible that a man like you got stuck in Surinam?' And Rahman Khan had answered that he had been a bird that had been caged. Gandhiji had also written around the 1930s that he wanted to come over to Surinam.Yet, Rahman Khan had advised him not to come to Surinam, as at that time there were problems between Hindus and Muslims in Surinam. Jungli Kaka had concluded that, 'Gandhiji did not visit Surinam therefore'.

9. Rahman Khan here writes 'Hind'. Later on he also uses 'Hindustan'.
10. Dates, translation and other information that are added by the editors are put in square brackets.
11. This must be a mistake as Ghaznavi died already in 1030. Rahman Khan continuously adds 'A.D.' after the years. Unless we refer to any other calender we have omitted 'A.D.'
12. He was the King of Ghur and his actual name was Muizuddin Mohammad-bin-Sam.
13. These so-called slave-kings ruled from Delhi and were either Turkish or Afghan in origin.
14. Born in 1484 and one of the early Mughal rulers.
15. His full name was, Nur-ud-din Muhammad Jahangir Padshah Ghazi.
16. This might be Trichinopoly.
17. Compare this history with Dalal (2002).
18. Hamirpur was a district in the so-called United Provinces (now Uttar Pradesh) and also encompassed one so-called Princely State. The United Provinces encompassed two regions called Agra and Oudh. Hamirpur was part of the so-called Bundelkhand area, which belonged to the Agra division in British India (Encyclopedia Britanica (1994 –2000) http://www.eb.com/bol/search?type=topic&query=Hamirpur%20 (Uttar%20Pradesh,%20India) & DBase=Articles 3 April 2000).
19. Immigration records provide profiles of the migrants. We have found the immigration certificate of 'Rehman, Mahomed Khan'. Rehman chose on 11 January 1956 for the family name Rahman and the first names: Moenshi Mohamedkhan. Immigration certificates are available online in English at: Historic Database Suriname: Indendured Labour at: http://www.archief.nl/suriname_english/engels/efrm_database.html?hdr_searching

20. Khan (1993) provides a detailed discussion on the *pathans* or *pakhtuns* who lived primarily in Afghanistan but migrated to India in particular during the reign of Mughal emperor Aurangzeb (1658-1707). By the end of the 19th century we find *pathans* all over India but in particular in the so-called North West Frontier, Bihar and the United Provinces and mostly in large cities such as Ahmadabad, Allahabad, Delhi, Karachi, Lahore, Ghazipur, Lucknow and Hyderabad. Eaton (1997:122) convincingly proves that 'the appearance of the millions of Muslim peasant cultivators recorded in the census figures' cannot be explained by the 'immigration theory of Islamization' only. Local conversions must have taken place on big scale. Most of the *pathan* Muslims like Rahman Khan claim however that their ancestors had migrated from Afghanistan. Other *pathans* agree that conversions took place but that they came 'not from the despised low castes, but from the upper orders of Hindu society'.
21. This must be a mistake as Qutb-ud-din Aibak ruled from 1206-1210.
22. Chickrie (2002: 386) writes that 'the Mughals initiated the policy of allotting lands for Afghan settlements' and that 'there was always a strong Afghan presence in Bareilly, Muradabad and Badayun in India. These districts had strong Afghan townships, where over 9000 Afghans settled'.
23. This process must have gone hand in hand with conversions to Islam.
24. On 27 October 2003, one of us interviewed Syed Samsul Hasan (aged 50) of Jalalpur, a farmer. He believes that now 'there is not a single Khan family in Bhattu'.
25. Of course, Surinam is not an island but among the labourers it was known as *tapu*, which literally means 'island'.
26. Compare this with Chickrie (2002: 392) who wrote, 'While the Muslim Indian men wore the Indian shirt and pajama, the Afghan wore the baggy *shalwar* (pants) and *kameez* (shirt). The Afghan prefers loose baggy wear; both males and females wore baggy modest clothing. Indian Muslims wore brighter colour clothing, while Afghan Muslims wore subtle colours'. The *pathans* also wore the *pagri* or the head warp.
27. Tremendous changes took place in this region after Rahman Khan's departure for Surinam. At the turn of the century, the socio-economic position of the Muslim elite in the United Provinces had deteriorated, which was coupled with a loss in status (Brennan 1999: 325).

28. Our informant Syed Samsul Hasan from Jalalpur said about this tomb in Jalalpur in 2003: 'Yes that is a very good tomb and both Muslims as well as Hindus have faith in it. I know that the money of the one who constructs such a tomb should be pure. It should not come from bribes or other malpractices'.
29. It is interesting here to read how Rahman Khan explains the decline of the city, which according to him it is mainly the fault of Muslims themselves, who were in Rahman Khan's opinion lethargic and not religious enough. Brennan (1999: 322-360) feels that the new laws introduced under the new (British) rule had a negative impact on the economic, social, educational and political position of the elite Muslims in the United Provinces. Though Rahman Khan agrees that due to changes introduced by the British, the position of the Muslim elite was weakened in relation to education, government jobs and landholding, Rahman Khan feels that the Muslim response to these changes was not adequate enough.
30. Karim Maudhvi (a *sheikh* aged 64) of Maudaha near Jalalpur was interviewed by one of us on 30 October 2003. He said: '*Pathans* are from Afghanistan and very handsome with good height. But most have inter-married now and lost these qualities. There are only a very few real *pathans* left now and when they speak Hindi they mix some Persian, Arabic and Pakhtun words. Hamirpur became later the district headquarter but first it was Jalalpur. That city was well developed but now almost all the *pathans* have left the place. Actually, the Britishers destroyed Jalalpur city. During the 1857 Mutiny, the *pathans* of Jalalpur city supported Rani Laxmi Bai who was the ruler there. It was because of this that the Britishers started harassing the *pathans* and killed many of them'. Rahman Khan does not explicitly refer to this conflict between *pathans* and the Bristish rulers.
31. Hamirpur was known as 'the gateway of Bundelkhand' (www. hamirpur.nic.in/admin.htm).
32. Hamirpur is a district since 1823 and one of the oldest. Presently it is under the Chitrakoot –Dham division of Uttar Pradesh. It is situated in the south of the state capital Lucknow at a distance of about 150 kms, and 68 kms from Kanpur. On 11th Feb. 1995, Hamirpur was divided and a new district Mahoba was created comprising *tehsil* Mahoba, Charkhari and Kulpahar from Hamirpur district (www. hamirpur.nic.in/admin.htm).
33. One of us interviewed Famun (aged around 80) and her brother Lal Khan (aged also around 80) on 31 October 2003. They are

both *pathans* and reside in the village Mutni near Jalalpur. They are related to Rahman Khan and one Haider Khan. Illiterate and poor farmers, Famun remembered: 'Haider Khan was my father and Wafatan my mother [this might have been a daughter of Rahman Khan's sister]. My grandfather [from father's side?] Bahadur Khan was also a resident of Mutni and had two brothers named Bahadur and Abdul. My mother's maternal grandfather [this must have been Rahman Khan's father] lived in Bharkhari. He worked there for a Marwari. He had come from another place. I think Jalalpur. My mother's maternal uncle [this must have been Rahman Khan] left Bharkhari one day and settled across the *kala pani*. The Britishers had captured him I believe and after that he never returned to Bharkhari. He was the only child of his parents. His father therefore kept on requesting my father to come over to Bharkhari and take over all the property. He never did this however and after my mother's maternal grandfather's death in Bharkhari, Hindus captured all the property'. It is unclear how Famun is exactly related and she might have some memory lapses. Besides, this Haider Khan is not the same Haider Khan as described by Rahman Khan. Yet, we feel that Famun and her brother Lal Khan are indeed children of one of the daughters of one of Rahman Khan's two sisters. Famun and her family give their '*salaam*' to their 'family' in the Netherlands [see also photographs].

34. By this time some members of the family seem to have left the army profession and had become farmers or government employees.

35. One of us interviewed Virendra Dutta Paliwal (aged 77) in Bharkhari on 29 October 2003 who narrated: 'Chetram Marwari had three sons named Hardasilal, Matadin and Dwarka Prasad. Dwarka Prasad was the youngest and had only one son who was my father. Dwarka Prasad was my grandfather. My father had four sons. My father has told me nothing about Khan's family and I only know about him because of the people who came here several times inquiring about him. They showed me Khan's writings. One Choubey came here and through him I came to know that Khan was a servant in my family. I did not even know that Muslims have ever been living here in this village. I also do not know much about Chetram Marwari. Actually my grandfather died when my father (Jagarnath) was three years old only. My own father died in 1948. Choubey came here around 8 years ago and showed me these writings of Khan in Hindi. I think he was a professor of archeology

in the Netherlands. He has a cousin who lives in Lucknow. Later on, one other person came here: Harjeet Singh, who was sent by Rahman Khan's grandson in the Netherlands. I would like to meet his grandson'. It is unclear who this 'Choubey' is, but it might have been Prof. Mohan Gautam who indeed resides in the Netherlands, or one of his students. There are no Muslims in the village anymore. We interviewed Ram Asray (aged 50) a *kuri* labourer in the village who said: 'I think local people have captured the houses of Muslims and their fields here'. On 25 October 2003 one of us also interviewed Mataram (aged 70), a domestic help who works in the Paliwal's family and is also a *pandit*. He remembered that 'Muslims have been living in this village'. He narrated: 'I know that a Muslim was working for the Paliwal family. I think his house was captured by Hindus and now there is no house anymore' [see the photograph included in this book]. Actually, Harjeet Singh from Ranchi has helped making a video film in Bharkhari and at that time people still alleged that the house shown in the video had belonged to Rahman Khan's father. This house was also shown in the documentary on Rahman Khan made in 2003 by Ivette Forster and Sandew Hira of Tapanahoni Productions in the Netherlands (in Dutch). It is possible that the recent great interest in the village and the house has scared the inhabitants who now deny that there ever have been Muslims living in the house. They might fear that the family in Surinam or in the Netherlands have sent these people to reclaim the property. It is clear, however, that Muslims in Bharkhari had already left the place long before communal problems in U.P. initiated flows of Muslims to Pakistan.

36. We could not detect this graveyard during our field trip to the area.
37. Most probably, Rahman means the *pattidar,* the proprietary leaseholder (Pandey 2002: 11-12).
38. This was a Princely State.
39. Often, in this work as well as in letters sent to Rahman Khan in Surinam and written by family members in India (and preserved by Albert Rahman, a grandson of Munshi Rahman Khan in the Netherlands), the years are given according to the Hindu calender, which is 57 years ahead of the Christian calender.
40. It was quite common during that time that the Muslim elite, who held government jobs and owned land, sent their children to school, and participated in the political life of the province (Brennan 1999: 324).
41. Though there is not much difference between the two languages

Hindi and Urdu, apart from using different scripts and the fact that Urdu includes a few more Persian words, language became one of the major issues during communal conflicts when Hindus were normally associated with Hindi and Muslims with Urdu. Things escalated in the United Provinces after the so-called Nagri resolution in 1900 when the devanagari scipt was preferred above the Arabic script that till then had been used for official purposes. Before that, 'Hindustani' was often written in Urdu script. Though there had been communal problems between Hindus and Muslims in cities of the United Provinces, Mushirul Hasan (2002: 348 and 349) writes, however, that, 'By the end of the nineteenth century, there was no sign of the Hindus and the Muslims going their separate ways [...] With the onset of the twentieth-century, there was a tendency towards the use of religious solidarity as a basis of political action. It started with the Nagri resolution of April 1900 which created fissures among the professional classes in UP'. It is important here to remember that Rahman Khan left his 'Hindustan' before the British government translated the principal of divide and rule into formal constitutional arrangements.

42. This is a measure of land: 5/8 of an acre in much of UP.
43. In Umri village, one of us interviewed the farmer Ramzan Khan, on 26 October 2003. He is the only Khan (*pathan*) family left in Umri. Though he knows about Duwarka Prasad and the Paliwal family, he has no memory of Munshi Rahman Khan or his family. He pointed to a *mazar* (tomb) of a Muslim *pir* in Umri situated in a house that belongs to a Hindu family who maintains this tomb [see also photograph in this book]. This points to close Hindu-Muslim relations in this village.
44. See also Mulvi Jalil Ahmed Nizami. 1992. *History of Maudha.* Hamirpur: National Chauraha. (This book is in Hindi).
45. One of us interviewed Haji Jalil Ahmed (a *sheikh* aged 68) on 28 October 2003, who told us: 'Presently, only a few houses here in Maudaha belong to the Afghanis and the rest belong to converted Muslims. The *khans* here are those who stayed back and had been in Md. Gauri's army. At present, around 60 per cent of the population of Maudaha is Muslim and of them 75 per cent is *sheikh* and are converted Hindus. Around 5 per cent is *syed* and another 5 per cent is Moghul *pathan.*
46. Around 1997 in Hamirpur District, the rural Muslim population formed only 6.21 per cent of the total rural population. In urban areas, Muslims constituted around 16.60 per cent of the total urban

population (Hasan 1997: 338).

47. Here we have chosen to omit one *doha* essentially repeating in verse what is described in prosa in this section on the stone idol.
48. Nowhere does Rahman mention the name of his first wife. He also does not provide any other particulars of the girl or his marriage with her. We do not know whether he ever lived with her in one house and whether they had any children. The only fact Rahman provides is that she died 4 years after his departure for Surinam. During our fieldwork in U.P, we have tried to get more information regarding this woman, yet were not successful.
49. Harjeet Singh and A.A.Y Khan of the Support for Sustainable Society (Saptrishi) in Ranchi, India visited this house at Bharkhari and talked with V.D. Paliwal, great grandson of Chetram Marwari and grandson of Dwarka Prasad. Paliwal said all people, including Rahman Khan's family members had left the place and many of them had settled in Maudaha. He also said that Kale Khan, a cousin brother of Rahman Khan, had worked for the Paliwal family. Paliwal also mentioned that his grandfather had lived in Umri, where he and his father also were born. They also talked about the tradition to 'marry a well', described by Rahman Khan. This tradition does not exist any longer. A video film is made of this visit. One of us has also visited Bharkhari, met V.D. Paliwal and talked to some other people in the village [see note 34 and photographs].
50. Rahman Khan's migration certificate indeed mentions this scar on his right cheek.
51. This was his father's second wife.
52. Interestingly, Rahman Khan does not comment on the prediction of the Hakim that he would have five sons and *three* daughters. In fact, in Surinam, Rahman had with his second wife only *two* daughters (besides five sons). This might imply that he had already one daughter from his first wife in India before his departure. During our fieldwork in U.P. we have done some investigations but without conclusive results.
53. We have here chosen to omit one *doha* on Nawab Ali.
54. We have here chosen to omit one *doha*, which praises the power of God and subscribes to the smallness of man.
55. We have here omitted one *doha* that emphasizes that without God (religion, *dharma*) salvation is not possible.
56. Here we have omitted one *doha* that reminds people to remember Lord Ram and ends with a proverd: 'As you sow, so shall you

reap'.

57. Cubical mosque in Mecca and the first mosque to be dedicated to the pure worship of 'One and the Only One God' built by the prophet Abraham. It is a symbol of unity of the *ummah* (Bawany 1978: v).
58. Kanpur is still known for its Ramlila celebrations. At present, there are around twenty-two Ramlila societies in the city, some of which started already 127 years ago. Ramlila is now celebrated during Durga Puja and starts on *nowratri* and ends on *ekadasi*. It lasts for 11 days.
59. We could not trace the old depot in Kanpur.
60. Rather than according to caste background, in Surinam, Hindus are categorized according to this division between the so-called Sanatan Dharm and the Arya Diwakar.
61. One *doha* has been omitted here, which describes the way in which Hindus in the depot gave up the habit of emphasizing caste and religious distinctions among each other.
62. This Head Immigration Officer was in charge of the Immigration Department. Cateau van Rosevelt was the first one and he functioned well from 1873 to 1891. As he was very popular among the immigrants they labeled the function of *Agent Generaal* as *Roshfail* (Rosevelt). Barnet Lyon was the *Agent Generaal* from 1891 till 1902 and also owned plantation Jagtlust (De Klerk 1998 [1953]: 79 and Hira 2003: 358n164 and 359n179).
63. This must have been the *brahmin* Sital Persad Doobay. Mrs. Alice Bhagwandy Sital Persaud (later Alice Bahadur Singh) (1892-1958) was his daughter and wrote an autobiography from which we came to know that Sital Persad, her father, was born in Jyrabad in Uttar Pradesh and had left India by the ship *Ailsa III* in 1882 along with his mother when still a child. On arrival, the two of them started living on the Jagtlust plantation. The owner of this plantation, Barnet Lyon, who later on became the Head of the Immigration Department, adopted Sital Persad. Through his help, Sital Persad had become a head interpreter of Hindi and Urdu (De Klerk 1998 [1953]: 80).
64. We have here omitted one *chaupai* and one *doha*, which are already included in the introduction in their original form (in devanagari), with an English summary of their meaning. These verses describe what is written in Volume I and what will follow in Volume II. We have come across File 48 of 1898, June, Prog. 6, Part B. Arrival at Surinam of the ship Avon with emigrants from Calcutta,

mentioned in the Index to the Proceedings of the Revenue and Agriculture Department (British Emigration) in the National Archives in New Delhi which should provide more details about the *Avon* by which Rahman was shipped to Surinam. Unfortunately this file was not traceable.

65. Though Rahman Khan has put this section at the beginning of his autobiography, we feel that its place here will make it easier for the reader to understand the context. There are quite a few studies that describe the arrival and integration of the 'Hindustanis' in Surinam. Yet, most of these studies are in Dutch. There are a few notable exceptions however: Speckman (1965); Hoefte (1998); Nandoe (2000); Gautam (2003) and several articles in the *Journal of Social Sciences* (University of Suriname, Paramaribo) and in *Caribbean Studies*. See Dew (1996) for a discussion in English on the position of the Hindostanis in Surinam during a later period (after 1942).
66. This refers to Africa-descended Creoles, presently referred to as Afro-Surinamese or Creoles.
67. Compare this with De Klerk (1998 [1953]: 71) who gave a total of 2,541 in 1873 and also stated (1998: 159) that 11,512 returned between 1878 and 1926. It is important to note here that Rahman Khan argues that even after indentured labour was officially abolished, in 1916, ships with workers from India arrived in Surinam till 1938.
68. This section starts with a *doha* that we already quoted in the introduction in its original form (in devanagari) and which describes the content of this second volume.
69. Most likely this was Poodan Sobae from the village Bharatganj near *thana* Mara in Allahabad District (U.P). He came on 14 April 1898 to Surinam and was 25 years old at arrival. He was 1,658 m and a Muslim (Hira 2003: 356n137).
70. Nickerie is situated in the west of Surinam and from the capital Paramaribo it took several days to reach that region. Communication between Bristish Guyana and Nickerie was much easier.
71. Most likely it is 'Horst', yet in our digital version, the name is spelled as 'Hors'.
72. Chandra Sekhar arrived in Surinam on 27-11-1895 and started working on Skerpi. He came from the village Dariapur near the *thana* Kunda in Partabgurh District. He was 17 years old then, and 1,667 m. He left Surinam for Calcutta in 1905 by a ship named

*Rhone* via British Guyana. His migration certificate states that he was a *thakur* [*kshatriya*](Hira 2003: 354n94).

73. Rahman Khan never seemed to have contemplated to bring his own wife along.
74. In our version, Rahman writes 'rupees' (Rs.) and 'annas'. He must have been paid in Surinamese/Dutch guilders (i.e., fl.) and 'cents' however.
75. Again here one should be aware that Rahman uses 'paise' and 'annas' but was paid in *guldens*, *rijksdaalders* (also called: *dollar*) (i.e. 2.50 guilders) and *cents*.
76. Belgar Bhikan came from the village Dumeria near *thana* Utroula in Gondah District and was 18 years old when he arrived. He was a Muslim and 1,614mm tall. His contract ended in 1903 and on 15 May 1909 he took the ship *Mutlah* back to Calcutta. Babo Durbari came from village Merewa near *thana* Payagpore in Bahraich District. He was also a Muslim and 1,645mm. He was 24 years old when he arrived and he married on 18 March 1908 with Bilaree. In March 1911 he left for India with ship *Sutlej* (Hira 2003: 355n108).
77. Albert Rahman, grandson of Munshi Rahman Khan, has preserved some of the letters that were sent to Rahman Khan by his family in India. In the introduction, we have discussed some of these letters. We also interviewed Ramsawroop Patwari on 25 October 2003. Ramsawroop (aged 80), *kayastha*, is the son of Parakshit Patwari, a family friend of the Khan family in Bharkhari. Parakshit Patwari used to write the letters that were dictated by the family members of Rahman Khan and who were illiterate. Ramsawroop narrated: 'I think that my father, as an adolescent, was a friend of Rahman Khan. Here in Bharkhari, we do not have Muslim residents now. They reside in Mutni, Baragaon, Kamheria, Maudaha, and in Umri village. They have very close relations with Hindus and attend Hindu festivals, distribute the Ramayana and respect the Hindu religion. Actually, one of my father's cousins also went away. His name was, I think, Jagernath. My father requested him many times to return to India but he never did so. He had land here, but later we sold it. May be Rahman Khan knew about this person' [see also photograph].
78. We did not find more information about this family member of Rahman Khan.
79. This might refer to the plantation 'Vreeland'.
80. The name of his second wife was Joomenie and according to the

'Historical Database Suriname', Rahman Khan was married to her on 5 April 1911. This might have been the date of the registration of the marriage that had taken place earlier (Hirâ 2003: 355n119).

81. 1 *duim* = 2.65 cm.
82. 50 paise = 8 anna. One rupee= 16 anna.
83. This might have been 'Toolsee' as referred to by De Klerk (1998 [1953]: 80) who also writes that the interpreters were of upmost importance for the functioning of the Head of the Immigration Department. Other important interpreters mentioned by De Klerk were Akrum Meah, Karamat Ali, Balkisoen, Sitalpersad, Dalaya Singh, Ramdas, Sewpersad and M.A. Jabbar.
84. A dyke, also spelled dike, is a thick wall that is built to stop water flooding onto very low-lying land from a river or from the sea. Such dykes are very characteristic for the Surinamese plantation landscape.
85. Rahman Khan actually writes 6 du-annas, which is equivalent to 12 annas.
86. Actually, a *sardar* received a fixed daily salary, whereas labourers received wages according to the amount of work they had carried out.
87. On Skerpi, there were also Javanese labourers who had migrated from the Dutch Indies, now known as the independent nation Indonesia.
88. Marhé (2003: 197) explains the difference between the Sarnami spoken in the district Nickerie and that spoken in other parts of Surinam. While the former uses many loan words from the English spoken in nearby British Guyana, people living in Paramaribo, Commewijne, Saramacca, district Suriname and Wanica, use many loan words taken from the Sranan Tongo. This can be lucidly illustrated by the way different types of fish are named. The word *bachhaun* used by Rahman Khan here actually refers to a fish not available in India and he therefore had to use a new name, which he borrowed from the Sranan Tongo.
89. This is in Sranan Tongo (http://www.dse.nl/~vwgolf3/woordenboek F-J.htm).
90. S.H. de Granada was also Head Immigration Officer (in Dutch: *Agent-Generaal*) between 1921 and 1925 (De Klerk 1998 [1953]: 80).
91. Rahman Khan's family members in the Netherlands have preserved this *lota*.
92. Here we have again omitted a few verses that are already translated

in the introduction. They refer to the contents of the two previous volumes and describe the contents of the next third volume.

93. This, most likely, should be 6 November 1901 (Hira 356 and 357n148).
94. This was a big day in the life of indentured labourers. Almost 80 per cent refused to sign a new contract and of the 20 per cent who did sign for a new period of contract labour, only 4 per cent signed a third time. Actually, the labourer received a bonus of 20 guilders for every year that he would again work under a contract. One third of the migrants returned to India and the government paid for their return passage. Others were offered a piece of land on lease or even for sale and those who gave up the rights to a free passage to India received a bonus of 100 Dutch guilders (De Klerk 1998 [1953]: 150).
95. Rice cultivation started after 1900, and was particularly popular during World War I. During that period, the influx of basic necessities from outside had decreased.
96. Railway construction was started in relation to the upcoming gold mining but construction was stopped when only half had been finished. Employers of plantation labourers also welcomed this railway construction, as they had to pay the labourers their daily wages of 60 cents for men and 40 cents for women even though there was no work for them on the plantations (Hira 2003: 358n160).
97. Hira (2003: 358n162) mentions, however, that Rahman Khan bought the plot from G.F. Ziel in 1903 and sold it in 1909.
98. De Klerk (1998 [1953]: 72) mentions that this ship arrived on 18 January 1887 in Paramaribo. Compare this with Hira (2003: 358n165) who states that the ship arrived on 3 January 1889 carrying 360 passengers.
99. The sluice and the graveyard are still there.
100. These are followers of the *bhakti* poet Kabir of India who established the Kabir Panthi Sanstha in 1952 (De Klerk 1998 [1953]: 196n55).
101. Rahman Khan uses the word *kafir* in different ways. He at times talks about Surinam as 'the land of *kafirs*', thus including the white colonial rulers and all others, though there were Muslims in Surinam too (from the Dutch Indies). Generally, he refers to *kafirs* however when referring to the Afro-Surinamese non-Muslim population in Surinam. They were often Christians.
102. Meant is the military hospital now called 'Land's hospitaal' located

in Paramaribo at the Gravenstraat (Hira 2003: 359n176).

103. This means: 'Be generous towards others, in spite of them hurting you.'
104. Here we left out one *doha* of which the meaning is: 'With God's blessings, no harm will befall you.'
105. This means: 'be careful boy. I will take revenge!'
106. This refers to a child of mixed marriage (between a white and a black).
107. This is now part of Paramaribo.
108. The United Fruit Company decided to produce congobacoven for export (Hira 2003: 360n212).
109. This is a dance ritual to please the snake goddess.
110. This was a product imported from America.
111. Here we have removed one *doha* with the meaning: 'We all suffer at times. Those who have inner strength can bear sufferings without pain. Those who cry are foolish. We remember God in adverse situations only but we should always remember Him'.
112. See: www.wordgumbo.com/pc/sra/ersraeng.htm
113. Here Rahman Khan quotes a verse from the Ramayana, which warns men to be careful if they are in love with a woman as 'love blinds'.
114. The *Shri Venkateshwar Press* was established in Bombay in 1871 and still functions.
115. According to the Encyclopaedia Britannica Swami Dayanand Saraswati was born in a *brahmin* family in 1824 in the village Tankara in Morvi State in Kathiawar (present day Rajkot District in Gujarat). See: www.britannica.com/ebc/article?eu=387657
116. The original version of Rahman Khan's autobiography, which one of us has had a chance to consult, contains a copy of this detailed horoscope of Swami Dayanand Saraswati.
117. See Pandey (2002) for an analysis of these communal riots in Uttar Pradesh between 1920 and 1940.
118. This means 'The Light of Truth' and was the title of a book written by Maharishi (Swami) Dayanand Saraswati and published in 1875. It contains a summary and interpretation of the *vedas*. This book is also known as the 'Bible' of the Arya Samaj. Note that Rahman Khan gave his own autobiography the title *Jeevan Prakash* (i.e., Light of Life).
119. This might have been Pandit Mathura Persad Dube (De Klerk 1998 [1953]: 195).
120. Bihari Lal (1595-1664) from India wrote the *Satsai*, a book of poems

of love and wisom. His verses resembled those of other Indian poets such as Kabir and Rahim (Bahadur 1991 and Ram 1986).

121. Organisations had their sub-committees consisting of five members (*panch*).
122. Often, these meetings were organised in cinema halls such as Luxor at the Zwartenhovenbrugstraat and Bellevue at the Domineestraat (Hira 2003: 366n250).
123. The members of this organisation were the same as those of the organisation called the *'Surinaamsche Immigrant Vereeniging'* (established in 1910), which changed its name into the *Bharat Uday* in 1922 (Klerk 1998 [1953]: 192).
124. Rahman Khan might here refer to Gosain Rampersad Sukul who had been a very influential 'othodox' (i.e., Sanatan Dharm) *pandit* but in 1929 became a prominent member of the Arya Samaj. In 1930, the Arya Diwaker was founded. Rampersad [Sukul] was also the chairman of the Bharat Uday.
125. This means: 'The bad man makes the good dance to his tune.'
126. Nowhere in his biography does Rahman Khan mention the name of his youngest daughter yet according to Albert Rahman, his grandson, her name was Nasiban who married Hanief Joemmanbaks.
127. The Report of the District Commissioner Simons (No.33 dated 20-3-1933, Immigratie en Kolonisatie Dep. F, Landsarchief Suriname, Paramaribo) provides more details of these altercations between Hindus and Muslims in Livirno. See also the Report on these problems between Hindus and Muslims in Livorno as perceived by the Assistant-Inspector A. van Trikt (No.305 dated 11-04-1933, Immigratie en Kolonisatie, Landsarchief Suriname, Paramaribo).
128. Rahman Khan writes: *Apna sa muh lekar rah jana* (Being uable to provide a rejoinder). .
129. What is meant is *shuddhi*, a movement for the purification and reclamation of Hindus. This also took place in the U.P at the time (Pandey 2002: 96).
130. Rahman Khan here refers to the Sanatan Dharm organisation that was established in 1929. Since the arrival in 1912 of the so-called non-orthodox or reform Hindus who established the Arya Samaj in Surinam, other Hindus started calling themselves orthodox Sanatis. The Sanatan Dharm was linked to the Bharata Dharma Mahamandala in India. The first founding members of the Sanatan Dharm were Paltan Pandit, Jadoenath Pandit, Samundar Sardar, Ramharakh Oepadhia, Rampertap Pandit, H. Seewnarain, B.

Tewari, Bhawni Bhikh, Raghubar Sing, Tribhwandath and R. Parsaram (De Klerk 1998 [1953]: 194).

131. De Klerk (1998: [1953]: 197) writes however that there had been similar problems about the killing of cows by Muslims, in among others the Corantijnpolder in the Nickerie district in 1929-1930. De Klerk adds that after this year the killing of cows had been outlawed in all districts where Hindostanis (Muslims and Hindus) lived.
132. Pandit Paltan was a member of the Sanatan Dharm and also of the Bharat Uday (De Klerk 1998 [1953]: 173 and 194).
133. Parikh (2001) describes how and why Harilal, Gandhiji's 'lost jewel', converted to Islam.
134. Ghosh (1999) writes the following about Lala Harkishun Lal, 'It all happened in London in 1889. That year, the Muslim students of London started the Anjuman Islamia, which used to meet every Sunday at the residence of its members. Although its members were all Muslims, its debates were open to the participation of non-Muslims as well. Some of its members, in later life rose to distinguished positions in India's public life. Thus we had men like: Sir Ali Imam, Hasan Imam, Mozharul Huq, all barristers of Bihar, Sir Abdur Rahim of Bengal, Sir Muhammad Shafi of Punjab, all studying Law at the Middle Temple. There were only two Hindu members of the Anjuman: M.K. Gandhi and Harkishan Lal of Lahore, who later founded the Punjab National Bank. The Muslim members belonged to the school of thought that gradually developed into the Muslim League. Jinnah arrived after Gandhi had left in 1891 and then Jinnah took over the newly named Muslim League. Until then, it was M.K. Gandhi who had been the number one member of the Muslim League alias Anjuman Islamia. But this fact has been kept under the lid for so many years. Only now, many such facts are coming out in driblets' (Sword of Truth Web Magazine Issue 1999.17, April 20th. http: www//ryerson.ca/~jbhathal/sikh_article1.html).
135. A report of a meeting of the Bharat Uday (in Dutch spelled as 'Oeday'), held in Thalia on 24 June 1934, and reproduced in 'Onze Stem' as well as another one about the same meeting that appeared in the newspaper named 'De West' (Nieuwsblad uit en voor Suriname) (10 July 1934), clearly illustrates that there were divisions within the two communities as well and that the divide between Muslims and Hindus was only part of the problems within the community of Hindostanis. Most of the members who attended

the meeting (around 400 Hindostanis) were members of the Arya Samaj. The report both mentions the tensions between Arya Samajis and Sanatanis, and between Hindu and Muslim Hindostanis. The chairman of the meeting, Ragoebar Sing regrets the tense relation between the Hindus and Muslims and explains that its roots lie in 1927, 'owing to the slaughtering of cows'. He asks: 'Since 1872, British Indians are in this country and we have always lived as brothers, so how can we explain these changes?' He himself answers: 'The Muslims should not slaughter cows. We should work together if we want to get somewhere, still one party should not try to destroy the other. The action will diminish'. [This is translated from the Dutch].

136. B.R.A. Sovan in his comment on this report of the Bharat Uday meeting, initially published in the newspaper named 'Onze Stem' and reproduced in the newspaper 'De West' (6 July 1934), provides a different explanation for the tension between Hindu and Muslim Hindostanis. We quote: 'in section five of the report, the president regrets the tense relations between the Muslims and Hindus. He continues that the British Indians have lived in peace from 1872 to 1927 and that the unbalanced relations among them date from 1927. So for 55 years they have lived in harmony. Why is this harmony now disturbed? Actually, during that year the sect of Aryans has come into existence in Surinam. Its main goal is to turn everyone into a "Sudhi", a follower of the Aryan faith, and since the Muslims are not easily persuaded, the Aryans have started their campaign of "Kudjat", the outcasting of Muslims. They preach amongst the conservative Hindus and against the Muslims. Because of their tolerant attitude, the Sanatanis have accepted much. What did the Muslims do? They did not care about all this and started their own organisation, to facilitate contacts amongst themselves. Then the president continues about cooperation instead of opposition. Where does opposition come from? This comes neither from the Sanatanis, nor from the Christian Hindostanis, or from the Muslims. The antagonism comes in fact from the Aryans who are Board members of the Bharat Oeday'. Sovan further narrates that two members of Bharat Uday's Board (Kalikhan and Katwaroe) had prepared a list of sixty-five names of men, all Muslims, who wanted to become member. As the Board rejected the majority of these names, a severe conflict erupted during the meeting and Sovan concludes that, 'it was clearly noticeable that all who were present were not pleased with the composition of

the board of the Bharat Oeday. Only the Aryans consented. The police had to interfere repeatedly to maintain order.'[This is translated from the Dutch].

137. Note that here Rahman Khan uses the word *kurbani*, which refers to the killing of cows for religious purpose; it is different from 'slaughtering' and its equivalents in Hindi.
138. Muslims had established the '*Surinaamsche Islamietische Vereeniging*' (Surinamese Islamic Association, SIV) in 1929 and more purely religious organisations were the Khilafat Anjuman and the Hidajat Islam Ahle Sunnat Wal Jamaat (Klerk 1998 [1953]: 196).
139. This refers to a Hindi proverb: '*Chullu bhar paani mei doob marna.*' (They should be ashamed of themselves!)
140. The newspaper 'The West' (18 June 1934) mentions that the building, which was bought during the boycott and was supposed to function as a 'Hindu market', would now (i.e. 1934) function as a common place for Muslim and Hindu Hindostanis for the sale of agriculture produce. A power conflict developed, however, between the Arya Samaj and the Sanatan Dharm over the supremacy of the building.
141. Mehta Jaiminiji wrote a book entitled *Dakshin Amerika ki yatra* (Agra: n.d) in which he narrates his visits to Surinam and British Guyana.
142. This refers to Allah.
143. This refers to the arrival of Moulvi Ameer Ali of Trinidad in Surinam. Hindostani Muslims in Surinam broke up in several organisations and are divided over many mosques. Fragmentation and institutionalisation began soon after the contract labourers settled as free immigrants in Surinam. The first and most profound division among Muslims is between Sunnis and Ahmadis. This separation goes back to the early 20th century when Surinamese Muslim leaders were looking for scholars from (British) India to teach them about Islam. The Surinamese Islamic Association (SIV) approached Himayal Ill Islam in India for assistance and he encouraged them to contact Moulvi Ameer Ali of Trinidad. Ameer Ali then visited Surinam and preached the ideology of Ahmadiyyaism. Here, like in Trinidad, the introduction of the new ideology caused a schism among the Muslims. Soon, the SIV came to be dominated by the Ahmadiyya doctrine causing many Sunni Muslims to leave and form several orthodox groups (Kassim 1999: 176-77). It seems Rahman Khan had sympathy for the ideas propagated by Moulvi Ameer Ali.

144. Rahman Khan refers to Ameer Ali, the Ahmaddiyya reformer who spent 7 years at a theological college, named the Anjuman Ishaat-I-Islam in Lahore (now part of Pakistan). Ameer Ali also spent almost a year in Egypt and Syria and had performed *hajj* before returning to Trinidad. Ameer Ali preached reform. He propagated gender equality for instance. Actually, the SIV in Surinam approached Moulvi Ameer Ali for assistance (Kassim 1999: 176).
145. Speckman (1965: 50) concludes that the introduction of the *Ahmaddiyya* ideology led to, 'A reappraisal by the Moslems [sic] of their own religion and culture [...]. The commotion round the Ahmaddiya offered ample scope for satisfaction of the craving for prestige, whether in discussions or in organizational sectarianism'. It should be emphasized that this process should not be isolated from the processes that took place among the Hindu Hindostanis described by Rahman Khan. These clearly also affected the ideology and identities of Muslim Hindostanis in Surinam.
146. Rahman Khan cites the full text of these two *chautals* in his autobiography.
147. Rahman Khan first quotes the Sanskrit *sloka* from the *manusmriti* and subsequently provides the Hindi translation of it.
148. Rahman Khan means that he still expects an answer to his question, which *vedas* sanction conversions and purification ceremonies. Though he is addressed as 'brother' (i.e., his payment as 'interest'), he feels that unless he is provided with an answer (i.e., his full payment), Ramnarayan still owes him.
149. This is quite similar to the Hindi proverb: '*Ab aya unth pahar ke niche*'. (Do not halloo before you are out of the wood).
150. Here Rahman Khan means to say that this strategy will not work. Once you have lost your religion you will have to face defeat. One can say: 'Make yourself all honey and the flies will devour you'.
151. This means that which is forbidden by the Koran
152. This means that which is sanctioned by the Koran
153. Contract labourers, generally, just used their first name and contract number. At times they added their father's name after their first names. In 1916, all *freemen* (i.e., all contract labourers who had stopped working on a contract as well as their descendants) were allowed to choose their own title and first name, and thereupon many changed their titles (De Klerk 1998 [1953]: 182-184).
154. This refers to the circumcision that Muslim boys undergo.
155. The Dutch Queen made Rahman Khan a 'Companion of the Order of Orange-Nassau'. Actually, the royal family in Netherlands

knew Hindostanis in Surinam for their loyality. De Klerk (1998 [1953]: 208) mentions, for instance, their slogan in 1947, when India and Pakistan gained independence, which was: '*Iswar ki kripa se Maharani ka des sada svatantr rahe*' (may God help to keep the Queen's country fully independent!).

156. Here Rahman Khan most likely refers to the District-Commissioner of Paramaribo (J. Hagen) known for his defamatory words against Creole politicians in 1943 (Dew 1996: 51 and 51n18). Three *dohas* and one *chaupai* in praise of commissioner Hagen Sahab Bahadur and his officers follow Rahman Khan's thanksgiving.

Remains of Munshi Rahman Khan school in Umri village (Hamirpur, India)

Munshi Rahman Khan's school (madarsa) situated in Maudaha (Hamirpur, India)

Remains of Munshi Rahman Khan's school in Bharkhari (U.P., India)

Rajkunwari's well in village Bharkhari (Hamirpur, India)

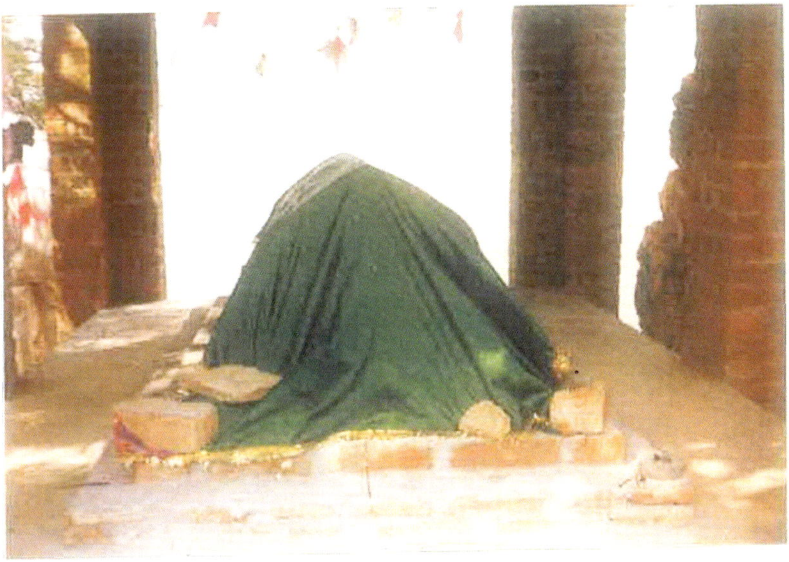

Tomb of Jalal Khan Wali in Jalalpur city (U.P., India)

Tomb of landowner Chetram Marwari in Bharkhari (U.P., India)

Relatives of Munshi Rahman Khan in their one-room house in Mutni (Hamirpur District, India) interviewed on 31 October 2003

Sitting: Munshi Rahman Khan and his wife Joomenie.
Standing: Their five sons and two daughters.
(From left to right: Faiz Khan, Chote Khan, Dildar Khan, Karamat Khan, Suleman Khan, Mariyam and Nasiban)

Munshi Rahman Khan, his five sons and daughter Mariyam in front of the shop owned by his second youngest son Chote Khan in Surinam (Rahman Khan has been added later on)

Burial of Munshi Rahman Khan in 1972

Albert Rahman, grandson of Munshi Rahman Khan (son of Chote Khan) and his mother late Hadja Hafidjan Rahman-Bakridi (wife of Chote Khan) in The Netherlands

Pt. Mangal Deo ('Jungli kaka') in The Netherlands (close friend of Munshi Rahman Khan mentioned in his autobiography)

Remains of house of Plantation-owner in Surinam

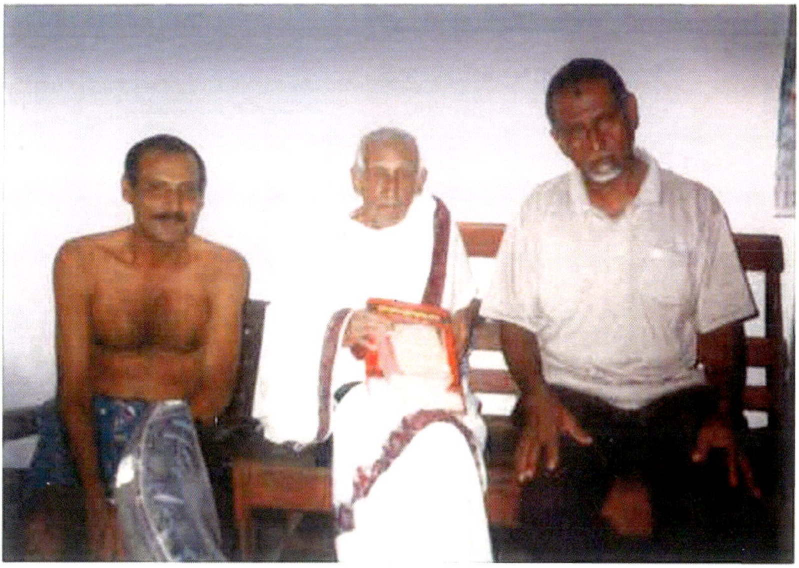

In the middle: Pt. Durga Mishr in Surinam
(94 years old student of Munshi Rahman Khan)

A typical sluice in Surinam

# References

## Introduction

Anthias, Floya, 1998, Evaluating 'diaspora'. Beyond ethnicity? *Sociology,* 32, 3: 557-580.

Bahadur, K.P. (trans.), 1991, *The Satsai,* New Delhi: Penguin.

Bal, E. and Sinha-Kerkhoff, 2004, Een Hindostaanse diaspora. India en de Moslim Hindostanen in Nederland en Suriname. *OSO. Tijdschrift voor Surinaamse taalkunde, letterkunde, cultuur en geschiedenis,* no. 2, November 236-256 (in Dutch)

Bandhyopadhyay, S., 2003, Community formation and communal conflict. Namasudra-Muslim riot in Jessore-Khulna. *In* Bidyut Chakrabarty (ed.), *Communal identity in India. Its construction and articulation in the twentieth century.* New Delhi, Oxford University Press: 214-231.

Bawany, E.A., 1978, *Islam. The first & final religion.* Karachi, Begum Aisha Bawany Waqf.

Bhagwanbali, Radjinder, 1996, *Contracten voor Suriname. Arbeidsmigratie vanuit Brits-Indië onder het indentured-labourstelsel 1873-1916,* Den Haag, Amrit

Bijlert, V. Van., 2002, Hindus and Muslims in Bengal. Is religious experience a unifying factor? *In* Jerald D. Gort, Henry Jansen, Hendrik M. Vroom, eds., *Religion, conflict and reconciliation. Multi-faith ideals and realities,* Amsterdam and New York, Rodopi: 37-51.

Biswamitre, C.R., 1973, Hindostaans leven. *In* Albert Helman (ed)., *Cultureel mozaiek van Suriname.* Zutphen, De Walburg Pers, 205-26.

Brennan, Lance, 1999 [1993], The illusion of security. The background to Muslim separatism in the United Provinces. *In* Mushirul Hasan, (ed)., *India's partition. Process, strategy and mobilization.* New Delhi, O.U.P: 322-360.

Brennan, Timothy, 2001, The cuts of language. The East/West of North/ South. *Public culture,* 13, 1 (Winter), 39-64.

Chandra, Bipan, 1984 *Communalism in modern India,* New Delhi, Vani Educational Books.

Chatterji J. 1995, *Bengal divided. Hindu communalism and partition, 1932-1947,* Cambridge, Cambridge University Press.

Chatterji, J. 1999, The fashioning of a frontier. The Radcliffe line and Bengal's border landscape, 1947-1952, *Modern Asian Studies* 33, 1: 185-242.

Chickrie, R., 2002, The Afghan Muslims of Guyana and Suriname, *Journal of Muslim minority affairs*, 22, 2: 381-399.

Choenni, C.E.S., 2003, Migratie naar en vestiging in Nederland, *In* Choenni, Chan E.S. ed., *Hindostanen. Van Brits-Indische emigranten via Suriname tot burgers van Nederland*, Den Haag, Sampreshan, 54-70.

Dalal, R., 2002, *The puffin history of India for children 3000 BC-AD 1947*, New Delhi, Puffin.

Damsteegt, T., 1990, Hindi and Sarnami as literary languages of the East Indians in Suriname, *In* M. Offrrendi. (ed)., *Language versus dialect. Linguistic and literary essays on Hindi, Tamil and Sarnami*, New Delhi, Manohar.

De Klerk, C.J.M., 1998, (First published in 1953). *De immigratie der hindostanen in Suriname*. Den Haag, Amrit.

Dew, E., 1996, *The difficult flowering of Suriname. Ethnicity and politics in a plural society*, Paramaribo, Vaco.

Eaton, Richard M., 1997, *The rise of Islam and the Bengal frontier, 1204-1760*. Delhi, Oxford University Press.

Gautam, Mohan, K., 1995, Munshi Rahman Khan (1874-1972), An institution of the Indian diaspora in Surinam', Unpublished paper presented at the *ISER-NCIC conference on challenge and change. The Indian diaspora in its historical and contemporary contexts*. The University of West Indies, St. Augustine and the National Council of Indian Culture, St. Augustine, Trinidad And Tobago, 11-18 August.

Gautam, Mohan, K., 2002, The construction of the Indian image in Surinam: Deconstructing colonial derogatory notions and reconstructing of the Indian identity, *In* M. Gosine and D. Narine, (eds.), *Sojourners to settlers. The Indian migrants in the Caribbean and the Americas* (http//www.saxakali.com/indocarib/sojourner7.htm).

Gautam, Mohan, K., 2003, Ethnic identity of the East Indians in Surinam, *In* R. Sharma and E. Annamalai. (eds.), *Indian diaspora. In search of identity,* Mysore: Central Institute of Indian Languages, 200-217.

Ghafoerkhan, K., 2003, Urdu a cultural heritage of India. Paper presented during the 7th World Hindi Conference in Paramaribo (5-9 June).

Gobardhan-Rambocus, L., 2001, *Onderwijs als sleutel tot maatschappelijke vooruitgang. Een taal- en onderwijsgeschiedenis van Suriname, 1651-1975*. Zutphen, Walburg.

Gottschalk, P., 2000, *Beyond Hindu & Muslim. Multiple identity in narratives from village India*, New York, Oxford University Press.

Grierson, G.A., 1883, *Report on colonial emigration from the Bengal Presidency*. Appendix to File 15-20/21, Calcutta, Calcutta State Archives.

Hasan, M., 1997, *Legacy of a divided nation. India's Muslims since independence*. London, Hurst & Company.

Hasan, M., 2002, *Islam in the subcontinent. Muslims in a plural society*. New Delhi, Manohar.

Hasan, M., (ed.), 1999 [1993], *India's Partition. Process, Strategy And Mobilization*, New Delhi, Oxford University Press.

Hira, Sandew, (ed.), 2003, *Het dagboek van Munshi Rahman Khan*, Den Haag/Paramaribo, Amrit/NSHI.

Hoefte, R., 1998, *In place of slavery. A social history of British Indian and Javanese laborers in Suriname*. Florida, University Press of Florida.

Jain, Ravindra K. 1993. *Indian Communities Abroad. Themes And Literature*, New Delhi, Manohar.

Jalal, A., 1985, *The Sole Spokesman: Jinnah, The Muslim League, And The Demand For Pakistan,* Cambridge, Cambridge University Press.

Jayaram, N., (ed.), 2004, *The Indian diaspora. Dynamics of migration*, New Delhi, Sage.

Jayawardena, C., 1968, Migration and social change. A survey of Indian communities overseas, *The American geographical society,* 58: 426-449.

Kassim, Halima Sa'adia, 1999, Schisms in Caribbean Islam. Ideological conflict in the Trinidadian Muslim community, 1920-1950, *Journal of social sciences,* 11, 1&2: 156-185.

Khan, I., 1993, *Warrior race. A journey through the land of the tribal pathans*, New York, Random House.

Khan, M.R., 1954, *Gyan prakash arthath shikshaprad dohe kundaliyan*, Delhi, Dehati Pustak Bhandar.

Khan, M.R., 1953, *Doha shikshawali*, Delhi, Dehati Pustak Bhandar.

Kishwar, M., 1989, The daughters of Aryavarta, *In* J. Krishnamurty, (ed.), *Women in colonial India. Essays on survival, work and the state,* Delhi, Oxford University Press: 78-114.

Krishna, G., 1982, Indian Muslims in the nation-formation process. *In* Gopal Krishna (ed.), *Contributions to South Asian studies 2.* Delhi, Oxford University Press, 110-146.

Landman, Nico., 1992, *Van mat tot minaret. De institutionalisering van de Islam in Nederland.* Amsterdam: VU Uitgeverij.

Malkki, L., 1992, National Geographic, The Rooting of Peoples and the Territorialization of National Identity Among Scholars and Refugees, *Cultural Anthropology,* 7,1: 24-44.

Marhé, R.M., 2003, Sarnami: Erfenis van de kantraki's in verdrukking, *In* Choenni, Chan E.S. ed., *Hindostanen. Van Brits-Indische emigranten via Suriname tot burgers van Nederland*, Den Haag, Sampreshan: 190-204.

McNeill, J., 1915, *Report to the Government of India on the Conditions of Indian Immigrants in Four British Colonies and Surinam.* Part II: Surinam, Jamaica, Fiji, and general remarks, London, His Majesty's Stationery's Office.

Mohapatra, P.P., 1995, Longing and belonging. Dilemma of return among Indian immigrants in the West Indies, 1880-1940 (Mimeo). Unpublished paper presented at the *ISER-NCIC conference on challenge and change.*

*The Indian diaspora in its historical and contemporary contexts,* The University Of West Indies, St. Augustine And The National Council Of Indian Culture, St. Augustine, Trinidad And Tobago, 11-18 August.

Mustapha, N., 2004, The influence of Indian Islam on fundamentalist trends in Trinidad and Tobago, *In*: N. Jayaram, (ed.), *The Indian diaspora. Dynamics of migration*, New Delhi, Sage, 127-147.

Nag, S., 2001, Nationhood and displacement in the Indian subcontinent, *Economic And Political Weekly,* 36, 5: 4753- 4760.

Nandoe, K., 2002, Suriname, *In*: S. Kumar, (ed.) *Pioneers of prosperity*. New Delhi, Antar- Rashriya Sahayog Parishad Bharat, 235-244.

Pandey, Gyan., 1983, Rallying round the cow. Sectarian strife in the Bhojpuri region, c. 1888-1917, *In* Ranajit Guha, (ed.), *Subaltern studies II. Writings on South Asian history and society*, New Delhi, Oxford University Press: 60-130.

Pandey, Gyan., 1992 (Orig. 1989), The colonial construction of 'communalism'. British writings on Banares in the nineteenth century, *In* Ranajit Guha (ed.), *Subaltern studies VI. Writings on South Asian history and society,* Delhi, Oxford University Press, 132-169.

Pandey, Gyanendra, 2001, *Remembering partition. Violence, nationalism and history in India,* Cambridge, Cambridge University Press.

Pandey, Gyanendra, 2002, *The ascendancy of the congress in Uttar Pradesh. Class, community and nation in northern India, 1920-1940,* London, Anthem Press.

Pandey, P.N., (ed.) 1965, *A Book of India*, Collins, London and Glasgow.

Parikh, N., 2001, Gandhiji's lost jewel, Harilal Gandhi. New Delhi, National Gandhi Museum.

Pillai, S.K., 2003, Emergence of Hindu identity in Caribbean countries, *In* S.K. Pillai, (ed.), *Indentured Indians. Jahaji bhai seminar presentation*, New Delhi, Siewdass Sadhu Cultural Center, 34-80.

Prins, J., 1961-1962, De Islam in Suriname: Een orientatie. *Nieuwe West-Indische Gids* 41: 14-37.

Puniyani, R., 2003, *Communal politics. Facts versus myths*, New Delhi, Sage.

Ram, K.S., 1986. (trans.), *Dohavali. Short poems of Kabir, Bihari Lal and Rahim*, Calcutta, Writer's Workshop.

Ramdin, R., 2000, *Arising from bondage. A history of the Indo-Caribbean people*, London, I.B. Tauris and Co.

Ramsoedh, H. and Bloemberg, L., 2001, The institutionalization of Hinduism in Surinam and Guyana, *In T.S.* Rukmani, (ed.), *Hindu diaspora. Global perspectives*, 123-165.

Reeves, P.D., 1991, *Landlords and governments in Uttar Pradesh. A study of their relations until zamindari abolition,* Bombay, O.U.P.

Report of the VII GOPIO International Convention, 2004, *Empowering PIOs for socio-economic development. A task under the second phase of GOPIO,* Kuala Lumpur, GOPIO.

Robinson, F., 1993, *Separatism among Indian Muslims. The politics of the United Provinces Muslims, 1860-1923*, Cambridge, O.U.P.

Safran, William., 1991, Diasporas in modern societies. Myths of homeland and return, *Diaspora*, 1, 1. (Spring): 83-99.

Sewradj-Debipersad, R., 2001, *Emancipatie van Hindoestaanse vrouwen. Een beschrijving van veranderingen in het leven van Hindoestaanse vrouwen in Suriname vanaf 1873.*Paramaribo, CERDES.

Singh, Prabhakar P., 2002, The press and communal consciousness in Bihar, *In* Ratneshwar Mishra, (ed.), *Region in history. Perspectivising Bihar.* Patna and New Delhi, Janaki Prakashan.

Sinha-Kerkhoff, K. and Bal, E., 2003, Eternal call of the Ganga. Reconnecting with people of Indian origin in Surinam, *Economic and political weekly,* 38, 38 (September 20-26), 4009-4021.

Speckmann, J.D., 1965, *Marriage, kinship among the Indians in Surinam,* Assen: Van Gorcum

Taj, A., 1997, *Urdu through Hindi. Nastaliq with the help of devanagari,* New Delhi, Rangmahal Press.

Vertovec, Steven., 2000, *The Hindu diaspora. Comparative patterns,* London and New York, Routledge.

Whitcombe, E., 1971, *Agrarian conditions in Northern India, vol.I. The United Provinces under British rule, 1860-1900.* Berkeley and Los Angeles, UCAL.

Zachariah, K.C., 1965, *A historical study of internal migration in the Indian sub-continent 1901-1931*, London, Asia.

# Glossary*

| | |
|---|---|
| *Aarti* | Hindu prayer. |
| *Adhar* | Verse recited (mostly by Muslims) with a needle between the teeth. |
| *Agent Generaal** | Protector of Emigrants (also called: *Bara* (Grant) *Sahab*). Head Officer of the Immigration Department in Paramaribo (Surinam). |
| *Ahir* | Caste of cattle holders and milkmen. |
| *Ahmadiy(y)a* | Messianic movement founded by Mirza Ghulam Ahmad (d.1908), in Qadian, a village in Punjab. |
| *Allah* | The primary name for the One God of Islamic faith. |
| *Anjuman* | An association |
| *Ana* | 1 *ana* = 1/16 of a rupee. |
| *Aryas* | Members of the Arya Samaj (in Surinam known as more progressive Hinduism). |
| *Babu* | Properly a term of respect attached to a name. |
| *Bacoven** | Bananas. |
| *Badshah* | Ruler. |
| *Bakkeljauw** | Kind of salted fish. |
| *Bakr Id* | The feast of sacrifice. Muslim festival associated with pilgrimage to Mecca (Haj). |
| *Bakra** | White person (a European). Also: *firangi*. |
| *Baniya* | Trader caste among Hindus. |
| *Barelwis* | Followers of Maulana Ahmad Riza Khan (1856-1921), resident of Bareilly in Uttar Pradesh. |

* Dutch and Sranan Tongo (Surinamese) words.

| | |
|---|---|
| *Basia** | Friend. |
| *Bhai(ya)* | Brother. |
| *Bhakti* | Devotion. |
| *Bharat(varsha)(vasiyon)* | India and inhabitants of India. |
| *Bhatije* | Nephews. |
| *Bigah* | Just over half an acre. |
| *Bhunja* | Roasted grains. |
| *Bijlander** | Bilander (vessel). |
| *Brahma* | Principal God among Hindus |
| *Brahmin* | One of the four categories of the Hindu *varna* system, traditionally considered priests. |
| *Chalisa* | Forty verses of prayer. |
| *Chaliswan* | Religious performance 40 days after someone's demise. |
| *Chamar* | A Hindu caste associated with leatherwork; considered among the most ritually impure of Hindus in India. |
| *Charpoi* | Cot; a bed. |
| *Chaupai* | Verse (four verses style). |
| *Chautal* | Song/verse. |
| *Chhuchundar* | Kind of rodent. |
| *Chowk* | Open place in the middle of a city/ town. Also: market. |
| *Chowkidar* | Caretaker or watchman (during nights). |
| *Chura* | Flattened rice. |
| *Commissaris** | Commissioner or Chief if related to police. |
| *Creole** | Ethnic Africans in Surinam. |
| *Crore* | Ten million, written 10,00,00, 00. |
| *Daal* | Pulses/lentils. |
| *Damad* | Son-in-law |
| *Dargah* | Muslim shrine or tomb of a holy person (saint or Sufi). |
| *Daroga* | Governor, also official or Head of Police. |
| *Deewan (Diwan)* | Revenue collector or Minister |
| *Dharm* | Religion. |

| | |
|---|---|
| *Dheki* | Rice mill. |
| *Dhoti* | Piece of white cloth for men to wrap around their hips and cover their legs. |
| *Dhuss* | Scarf. |
| *Doha* | Songs written mostly by Hindi poets (two verses style). |
| *Doli* | Palanquin. |
| *Dom* | A name of a very low caste, sometimes called untouchable in India (often funerary workers). |
| *Du'a* | A form of personal prayer derived from Islamic traditions. |
| *Duim** | 1 *duim* = 2.65 cm. |
| *Darbar* | A formal, public audience held by a ruler. |
| *Eigenaar** | Owner |
| *Fakir* | Poor, needy; |
| *Freeman** | Those labourers who had finished their contract labour period. |
| *Garamsara* | Owner. |
| *Gaurakshini Sabha* | Organization for the protection of the cow. |
| *Gayatri* | Sacrifice to attain true knowledge |
| *Ghat* | Landing place on the bank of a river. |
| *Girmit* | Labour contract (from agreement), |
| *Gulguley* | Sweet dish. |
| *Gumbaz* | Round shaped top of mosque. |
| *Guru* | Teacher |
| *Gurumukh* | The ritual through which a student is assigned to his teacher. |
| *Habsis* | Ethnic Africans |
| *Haj* | Pilgrimage to Mecca and Medina; an incumbent religious duty. |
| *Hakim* | Healer; a doctor. |
| *Halwai* | Sweet maker. |
| *Haraam* | Prohibited; That which is unlawful. |
| *Haring** | Kind of salted fish. |
| *Hawan* | The vessel in which a brahmanical fire sacrifice is performed. |

| | |
|---|---|
| *Holika dahan* | Fire one day before *Holi* (spring festival of Hindus). |
| *Hukm-nama* | Order or fiat. |
| *Id* | Muslim festival at the end of the month of fasting; Id-al Fitr as opposed to Id-al Zuha or *Bakr Id.* |
| *Idgah* | A large courtyard set aside specifically for *Id* prayers. |
| *Imambara* | Place where *tazias* are kept to be carried in procession. |
| *Jahazia bhai* | Ship brotherhood. |
| *Jalebis* | Kind of sweet |
| *Jamaat* | Assembly; organization. |
| *Jamadar* | Security officer. |
| *Janamaaz* | Cloth on which Muslims sit for prayer? |
| *Janau* | Holy thread worn by Brahmins. |
| *Jetha Tazia* | Main (most important) *Tazia* |
| *Jizya* | A tax levied by Muslim rulers upon non-Muslim rulers. |
| *Julaha* | A Muslim caste of lower social status than *pathans* and associated with weaving. |
| *Kafan* | White cloth to cover the dead body. |
| *Kafir* | Non-Muslim without a revealed book. |
| *Karahi* | Cooking vessel. |
| *Karbala* | The site in Iraq where Imam Husain was assassinated. |
| *Karinda* | Assistant. |
| *Katar* | Sharp weapon. |
| *Katha* | Recitation of religious stories. |
| *Kayasta* | Caste of scribes; in between the *brahmins* and the *vaishyas.* |
| *Kazis* | Chief registrars. |
| *Keelaks (or Bebani kalam)* | Kind of pencil. |
| *Ketting** | 1 *ketting* = 20 meter. |
| *Kharif* | Monsoon crop. |
| *Khoti* | House. |
| *Khuda* | Allah (God). |

| | |
|---|---|
| *Koelie* | Appellation for the Hindostani migrants in Surinam (has negative connotation). |
| *Kofimamabomen** | Trees that are planted to provide shadow for cacao and coffee plants. |
| *Koker** | Shaft. |
| *Kshatriyas* | The warrior-king division or *varna* of the classical Indian social model. |
| *Kundli* | Horoscope. |
| *Kurbani* | Sacrifice. |
| *Kurta* | Long shirt. |
| *Laddus* | Kind of sweet. |
| *Lagan* | Tax. |
| *Lakh* | Unit of one hundred thousand, written 10,00,00. |
| *Lota* | Bronze or clay jar. |
| *Lukuman** | Exorcist. |
| *Madarsas* | Colleges especially those connected with a mosque. |
| *Mahajan* | Elite/rich people. |
| *Makbara* | Mausoleum. |
| *Maktab* | School for teaching children the elements of reading, writing and Koranic recitation. |
| *Mandir* | Hindu temple. |
| *Manjha** | Manager (also translated at times as Director). |
| *Mantra* | Religious verse; incantation |
| *Marwaris* | Business community from Rajasthan. |
| *Masjid* | Mosque. A place of worship. |
| *Mauja* | Village. |
| *Maulud* | The celebration on the Prophet's birthday. |
| *Maulvi* | A religious leader or learned person. |
| *Mela* | Fair or big gathering. |
| *Memsahab* | Madam. |
| *Meneer** | Mister (Mr); Sir. |
| *Mevrouw** | Mrs; Madam. |
| *Minar* | Tower. |

| | |
|---|---|
| *Mohalla* | Quarter of a city or neighbourhood. |
| *Moharram* | First month of the Muslim lunar calender, the month in which Husain was assassinated. |
| *Mug(h)al* | Muslims who claim descent from the formerly ruling Mughal dynasty in India. |
| *Mulazmi* | (Government) service. |
| *Mulat(tin)** | Offspring from mixed parentage (African-European in Surinam). |
| *Mundan* | A ritual during which the hair of a small boy is shaved. |
| *Munshi* | Teacher. Also: clerk. |
| *Mussalmans* | Muslims. |
| *Namaaz* | The prescribed ritualised Muslim prayers performed five times daily. |
| *Naya* | New. |
| *Negre** | Local Language. |
| *Negro** | Surinamese African. |
| *Pagri* | Head-gear. |
| *Panch* | A five member committee. |
| *Pandas* | Head-gear. |
| *Pandit* | Priest. |
| *Pathans* | A Muslim caste associated with the tribes of Afghanistan and the Hindu Kush. |
| *Pattidar* | Proprietary leaseholder. |
| *Pir* | A Sufi master on the mystical path. |
| *Prasaad* | A gift empowered through proximity with a superhuman agent. |
| *Pudina* | Mint leaves. |
| *Puja* | Hindu religious worship. |
| *Pulao* | Dish of fried or boiled rice and meat with spices. |
| *Purana* | Old. |
| *Rabbul* | One of the names of Allah. |
| *Rajputs* | Landowning caste, traditionally considered (according to the four *varna* system of ranking) a *Kshatriya* caste. |

| | |
|---|---|
| *Ram* | One of the avatars of Vishnu celebrated as a human king in the Sanskrit Ramayana and the Hindi Ramcaritmanas. |
| *Rotis* | Round and thin breads made out of flower. |
| *Roza* | Fast from dawn to sunset during the ninth month of the Islamic calender. |
| *Sabelman** | Digger. |
| *Sadhu* | A Hindu renunciant who lives an ascetic life in pursuit of release from the cycle of birth. |
| *Sahab* | Mr. (polite), Sir. |
| *Samadhi* | Father-in-law of one's son or daughter. |
| *Sanatanis* | Members of the Sanatan Dharm (in Surinam known as more orthodox Hindus). |
| *Sarai* | Inn. |
| *Sardar* | Headman or Supervisor. |
| *Shaman** | One acting as a medium between the visible and spirit worlds and practices sorcery for healing or divination. |
| *Sheikh* | Muslim caste group (*biradari*). |
| *Shirini* | Sweets. |
| *Shuddhi* | Purification, a set of rituals introduced by the Arya Samaj to reconvert Hindus lost to other religions; also to raise untouchables to caste status. |
| *Sindur* | Vermilion. |
| *Skreeman** | Assistant Manager or clerk. |
| *Slokas* | Verses from the *Vedas*. |
| *Smriti* | Codes of Hindu law (literally 'remembered'). |
| *Sranan Tongo** | Local Language (*Nengre*). |
| *Subedar* | Governor of a Province. |
| *Sudras* | *The lowest ranked among the four divisions or varnas in the classical social model.* |

| | |
|---|---|
| *Sunnat* | Circumcision of boys as required by Islamic law. |
| *Surahis* | Water pots; a jugs. |
| *Tabeez* | Usually comprising some Arabic phrases inscribed on some article, presumably verses from the Koran, and worn as an armlet for warding off evil spirits. |
| *Tazia* | Wood and paper models of the tombs of Imam Husain (grandson of the Prophet) and his family. |
| *Tazim or Tanzeem* | Organization. |
| *Terahvi* | 13th day after the death of a peron. |
| *Thana* | Police station; Police headquarters. |
| *Thanedar* | Station house officer at a police station. |
| *Thesil* | Subdivision of a district. |
| *Tilak* | Red/orange dot on forehead. |
| *Timmerman** | Carpenter. |
| *Tobbe** | Tub. |
| *Tola* | A neighbourhood in a city, town or village. |
| *Tolk* | Translator. |
| *Umma* | Term occurs sixty-four times in the Koran and is used to express the essential unity of Muslims in diverse cultural settings. |
| *Ustad* | Master. |
| *Vaishyas* | Traders and artisans; third caste in the Hindu social hierarchy. |
| *Vazu* | Islamic ablution procedure (washing oneself) before prayer. |
| *Vedas* | Earliest books of Hindu religious scripture in Sanskrit (about 1000 B.C.). |
| *Vipr* | Brahmin |
| **Voodoo* | Black magic. |
| *Wali* | Protector, guardian. |
| *Yag(na)* | Fire sacrifice to attain the highest good (through true action, i.e., good deeds). |
| *Zamindar* | Landholder or Landlord. |